SHOP DRAWINGS
For Blacksmiths

SHOP DRAWINGS
For Blacksmiths

written and illustrated by
Jerry Hoffmann

Hoffmann Publications, Inc.
Washington, Missouri
Publisher of the *Blacksmith's Journal*

Copyright © 2005 by Jerry Hoffmann

All rights reserved. No part of this publication may be reproduced or transmitted in any form or by any means, electronic or mechanical, including photocopy, recording, or any other storage and retrieval system, without written permission of the publisher.

Published by
Hoffmann Publications, Inc., Washington, MO
www.blacksmithsjournal.com

Library of Congress Control Number: 2005927889

ISBN 0-9769479-0-0

Printed in the United States of America

First Edition June, 2005
8 7 5 4 3 2

Hoffmann Publications Inc. and its staff does not warrant, guarantee, or endorse any of the tools, materials, designs or products contained in *Shop Drawings for Blacksmiths*. Hoffmann Publications Inc. disclaims any responsibility or liability for damages or injuries as a result of any construction, design, use, manufacture or other activity undertaken as a result of the use or application of information contained in *Shop Drawings for Blacksmiths*.

All artwork and many of the ideas presented in *Shop Drawings for Blacksmiths* were designed and developed by Hoffmann Publications, Inc. unless otherwise noted. We encourage the application and reproduction of this information by individuals for their own use, however, the manufacture, sale and distribution of this material for purposes other than individual use is prohibited without express permission from Hoffmann Publications, Inc.

Table of Contents

Introduction ix

1. Blacksmithing Tools & Equipment 1
    Air Gate 2
    Anvil Stand 4
    Bick Iron 6
    Chamfer Tool 7
    Coal Forge 8
    Filing Vise 11
    Flatter 12
    Gas Forge 13
    Hold Down 15
    Hot Cut Chisel 16
    Portable Forge 17
    Portable Forge Stand 18
    Post Vise 19
    Post Vise Stand 21
    Punch Tongs 22
    Rail Anvils 23
    Scroll Tongs 25
    Skillet Form 26
    Slot Press 27
    Smithin' Magician II 28
    Smithin' Magician III 30
    Smithin' Magician Pedestal 31
    Spacing Punch 33
    Spring Tool 34
    Spring Vise 35
    Square Corner Swage 36
    Traveler 37
    Treadle Hammer 38
    Twisting Machine 40
    Work Table Vise 41

2. Other Tools and Equipment 43
    Bar Clamp 44
    Double Calipers 45
    Drill Press Stand 46
    Garden Fork 48
    Grinder Guard 49
    Hack Saw #1 51
    Hack Saw #2 52
    Hand Wheel 53
    Nail Puller 54
    Pliers 56
    Railing Protractor 57
    Roller Stand 58
    Rope Pulley 59

Slate Roofing Hammer	60
Spatula	61
Stone Chisel	62
Wood Gouge	63

3. Hardware   65

Barrel Hinge	66
Cabinet Handle	67
Cabinet Hinges	68
Door Catch	69
Door Chime	70
Door Knob	72
Door Knocker	73
Door Latch	74
Draw Latch	75
Gate Pull	76
Gutter Bracket	77
Latch Plate and Handle	78
Sliding Door Hanger	80
Shutter Dog	82
Strap Hinges	83
Traditional Door Latch	84

4. Interior Ironwork   87

Candle Holder #1	88
Candle Holder# 2	89
Chandelier	90
Coat Rack	92
Curio Shelves	94
Floor Lamp 1	95
Floor Lamp 2	96
Floor Register	97
Grill 1	99
Grill 2	101
Hand Rail Bracket	102
Headboard 1	103
Headboard 2	104
Headboard 3	105
Keepsake Box	106
Lamp Base	107
Lamp Shade	108
Mahogany Pod	109
Pedestal	110
Pot Rack	111
Privacy Screen	112
Scale	113
Spiral Stairs	114
Table and Stools	115
Tissue Stand	116
Vessel	117

Wine Rack	119

5 Fireplace Accessories — 121

Andiron	122
Fireback/Grate	123
Fireplace Crane	125
Fireplace Doors #1	126
Fireplace Doors #2	128
Fireplace Screen #1	129
Fireplace Screen #2	130
Fireplace Tools #1	132
Fireplace Tools #2	134
Wood Rack	135

6 Exterior Ironwork — 137

Patio Bench	138
Boot Scraper	139
Bracket #1	141
Bracket #2	142
Cresset	143
Flag Holder	144
Flat Bar Floral Elements	145
Historic Marker	147
House Number Sign	148
Lamp and Bracket	150
Clam Shell Wall Sconce	151
Mailbox	152
Ornamental Bell #1	154
Ornamental Bell #2	156
Flower Pot Bracket	157
Sign Frame	158
Sign Bracket	160
Sundials	161
Weathervane	162
Window Grill	164

7 Gates and Railings — 165

Back Bar Hinge	166
Cane Bolt	167
Post and Handrail	168
Post and Railing #1	169
Post and Railing #2	170
Post and Railing #3	172
Railing Panel #1	173
Railing Panel #2	174
Spring Latch	175
Trellis Gate	176
Walkway Gate	177

Introduction

Starting in the 1960's, blacksmithing experienced a period of rediscovery that changed the focus from classic forms to more self-expressed forms. As a result, organizations such as the Artist Blacksmith's Association of North America and the British Blacksmiths Association came into existence to help spread this new brand of blacksmithing. The Blacksmith's Journal, the first periodical published outside of these organizations, came along in 1990. It became a resource for those interested in the art to find how-to information about technique and design. The Blacksmith's Journal's subtitle "A Journal of Illustrated Techniques" aptly describes its purpose.

Since its beginning, the Journal has offered ideas that not only reflect, but expand today's style of blacksmithing. Many of these ideas include new tools that help blacksmiths, often working alone, perform the tasks once carried out by two or more workers. Among these is the "Smithin' Magician", (pages 28-32), a tool that not only dispenses with the need for a striker, but is more accurate than traditional top and bottom tools. What really makes the Journal stand out however, is the quality of the drawings. These include the vector drawings in this book, as well as thousands of pencil drawings that clearly illustrate the blacksmithing process. This style and unique way of exposing key features within the work make it easy to grasp concepts and understand techniques.

The drawings in this collection were originally published between 1990 and 2005. They are distilled from more than two thousand pages of information, and represent nearly all the shop drawings published to date. The topics have been categorized, alphabetized and put into chapters. It is fitting that the first two chapters cover tool designs, because they are the foundation upon which blacksmiths work. In this printing, the drawings become a quick reference guide for project ideas and techniques that can be used by blacksmiths, fabricators, architects, designers or those simply interested in the art of blacksmithing.

All of the designs printed herein were originally created for the Blacksmith's Journal. The material is reproduced in its original format, so the drawing style, call-out's, arrows, etc. vary slightly from drawing to drawing. At the end of each drawing description are numbers (e.g. **39|481**) that indicate the issue and page number from which the drawing came.

This is the first in a series of books that puts the vast amount of Blacksmith's Journal information into perspective. It is a visual index for the projects, theme variations and how-to information that will follow in subsequent volumes. Its purpose is to help the reader better understand the possibilities abundant in this craft and to inspire one's own work and appreciation for blacksmithing.

x

1 Blacksmithing Tools & Equipment

Air Gate – ¾ scale

Air gates control the amount of air (draft) supplied by a blower in a coal forge. This one mounts between the blower and firepot, and is designed to allow control from both sides of the hearth through a common linkage. The hinged gate lever provides smoother operation than conventional in-line air gates. **65|802**

#8 RND. HD. MACH. SCREW

1/4" RIVET

10 3/16"

7 3/8"

DRILL & CTR. SINK 4 HOLES FOR #8 FLAT HEAD SCREW

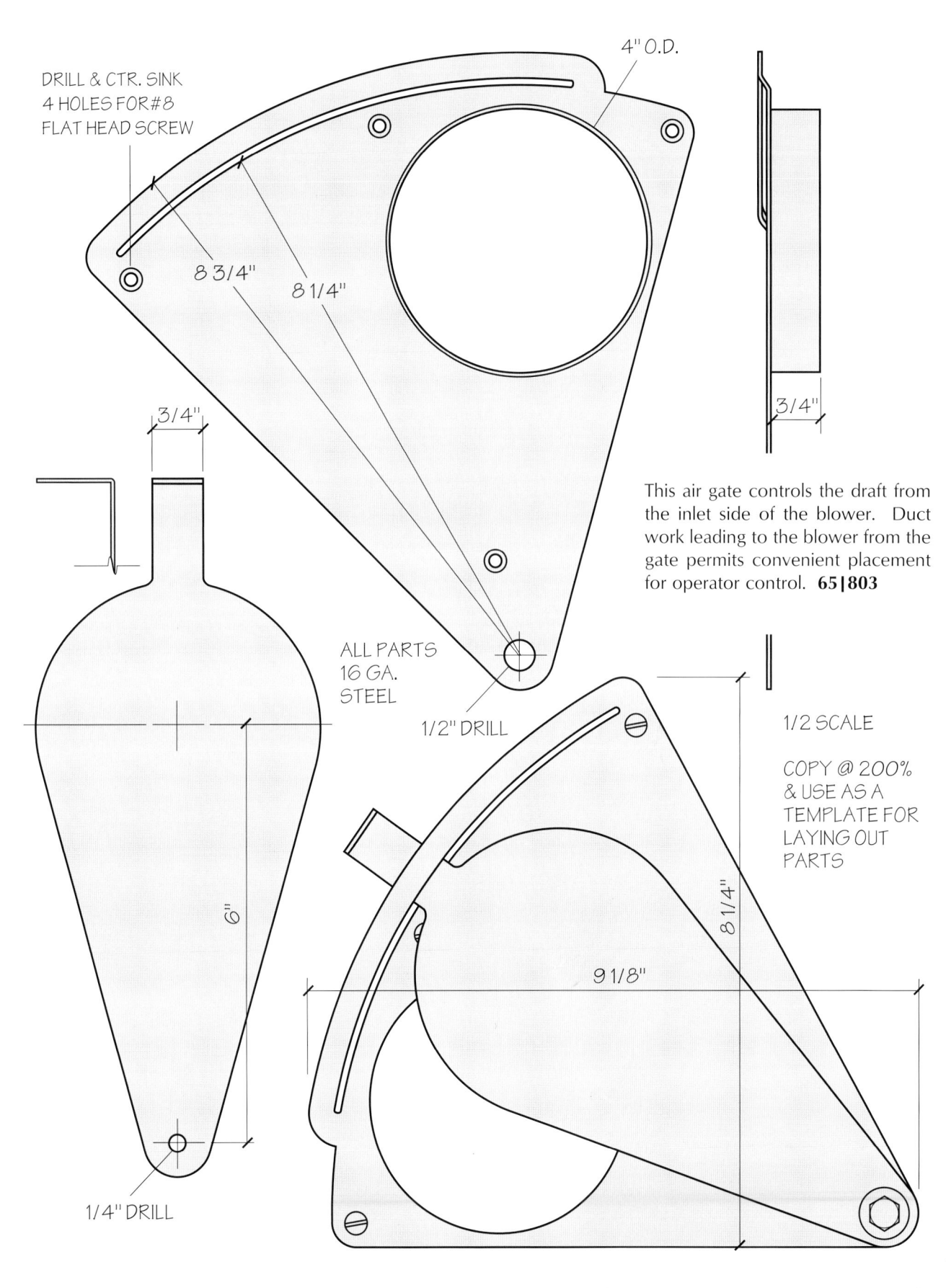

4" O.D.

8 3/4"

8 1/4"

3/4"

3/4"

ALL PARTS 16 GA. STEEL

1/2" DRILL

6"

1/4" DRILL

This air gate controls the draft from the inlet side of the blower. Duct work leading to the blower from the gate permits convenient placement for operator control. **65|803**

1/2 SCALE

COPY @ 200% & USE AS A TEMPLATE FOR LAYING OUT PARTS

8 1/4"

9 1/8"

3

Anvil Stand -not to scale

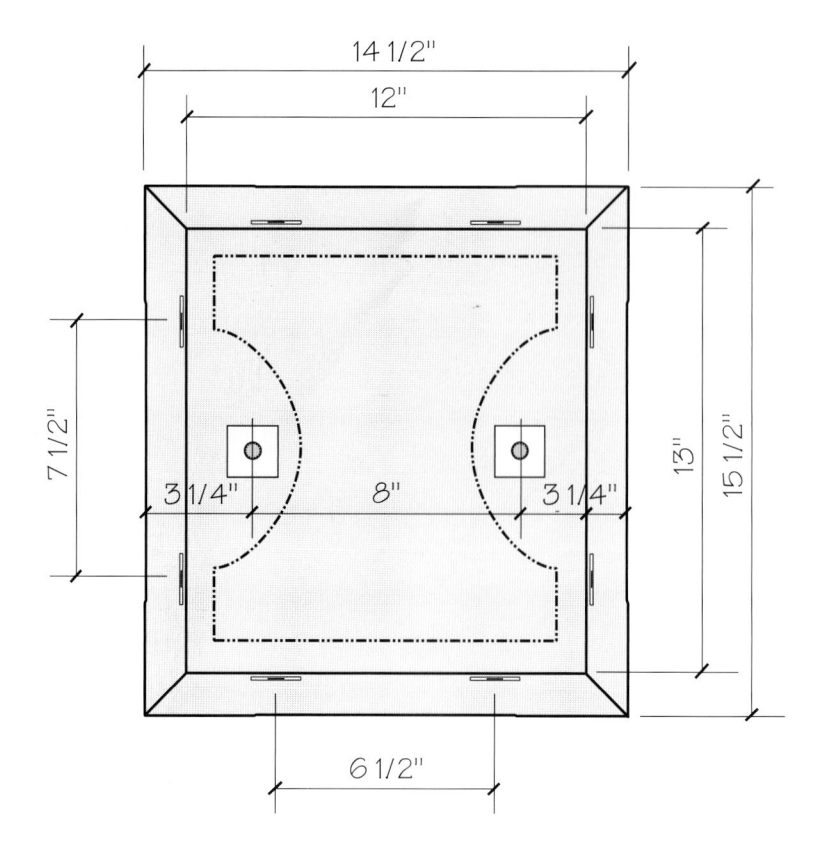

Concrete is perhaps the best material for an anvil stand. This stand features drilled and tapped mounting lugs imbedded in the concrete. It is very stable and won't "walk" like wooden stands. It also helps dampen the ring of the anvil and gives it an extremely solid feel. Dimensions shown are for use with a 200 lb. Hey Budden anvil; the height will vary between users. **68|840**

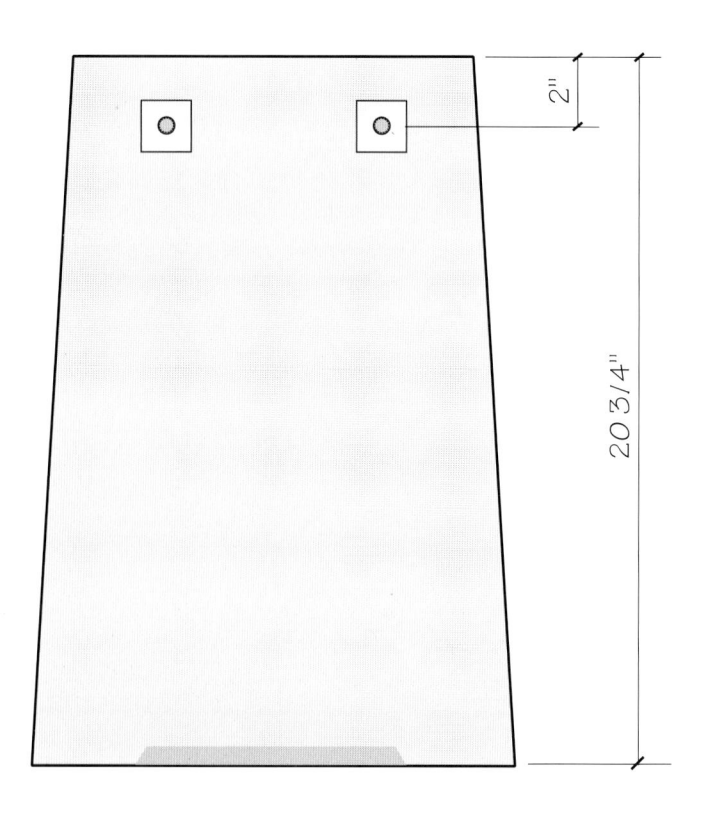

Concrete Form

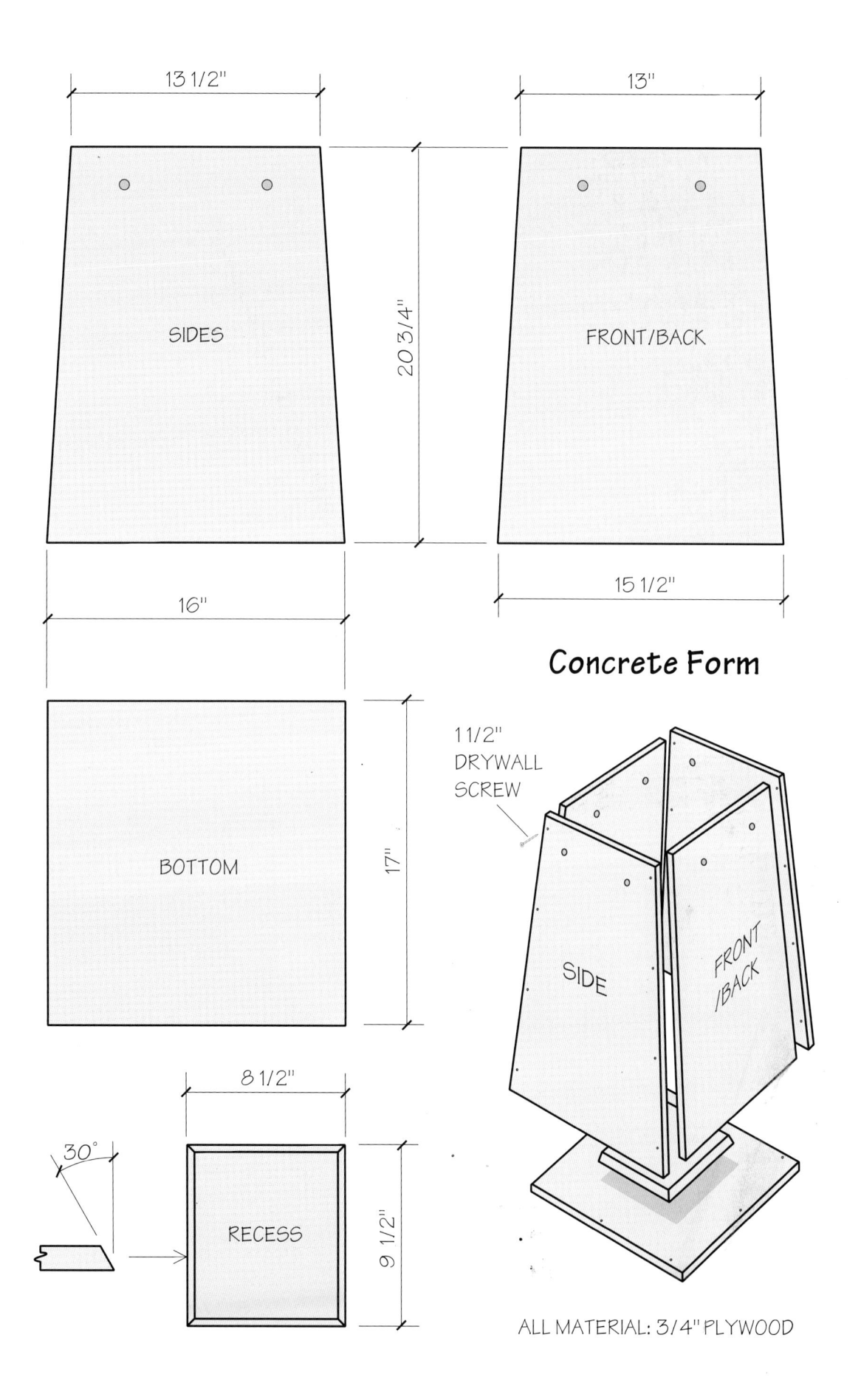

SIDES
- 13 1/2" (top)
- 20 3/4" (height)
- 16" (bottom)

FRONT/BACK
- 13" (top)
- 15 1/2" (bottom)

BOTTOM
- 17" × (width)

RECESS
- 8 1/2" × 9 1/2"
- 30°

1 1/2" DRYWALL SCREW

SIDE

FRONT/BACK

ALL MATERIAL: 3/4" PLYWOOD

Bick Iron -not to scale

Bick irons are similar to anvils, but they are generally smaller and are commonly driven into a wood block or tapered stake holder. The one shown here is secured in the hardy hole of an anvil. **114|1404**

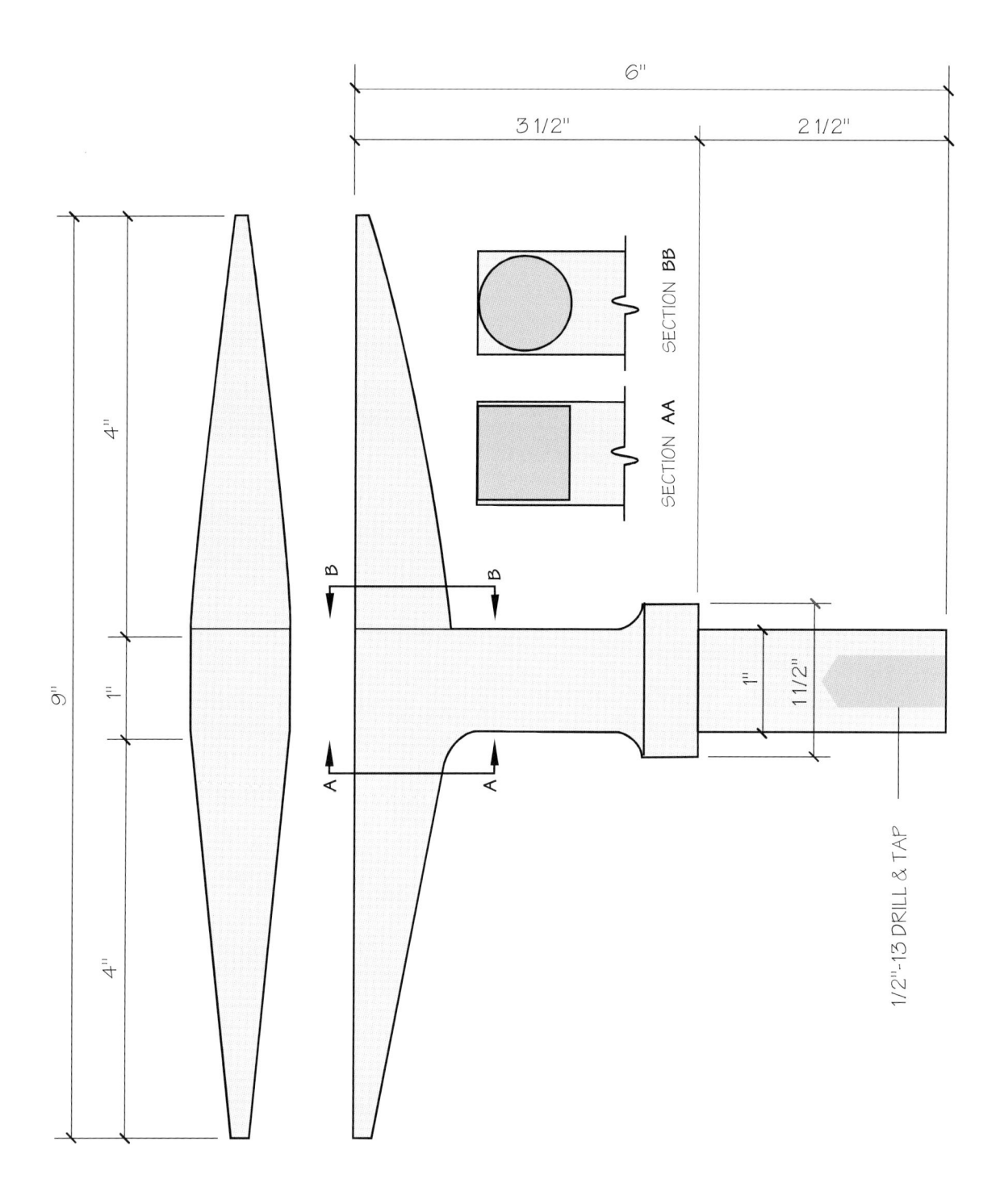

Chamfer Tool -full scale

Unlike square stock, making a 45° chamfer on flat stock can be tough because there is no way to adequately back up the work. One solution is this hardy tool made from ½" x 1½" stock. It cradles the work facilitating solid 45° hammer blows. The tool stock is shouldered and bent to form both the square hardy stem and flat work surface. This version is for an 1⅛" hardy hole. Size the stem to fit your anvil.
162|2035

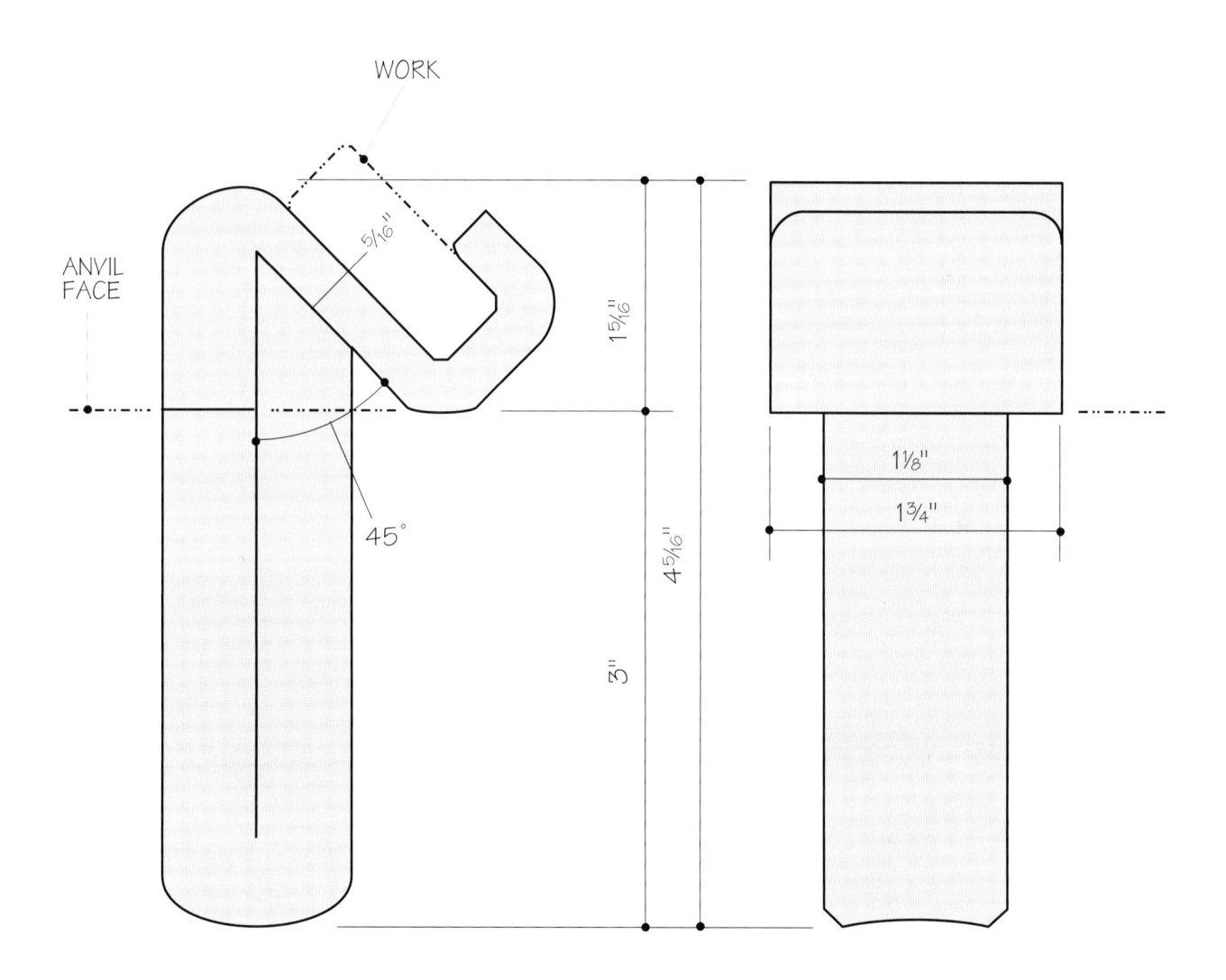

Coal Forge - 1/12 scale

Coal forges fall into two basic categories: stationary and portable. Portable forges usually have a cast iron hearth supported by removable legs, hood and blower. Stationary coal forges are commonly made of masonry construction with a hood or side draft chimney vented to the outside. The coal forge shown here is a stationary forge, but unlike masonry forges, it can be moved to another site if necessary. Both types share approximately the same inside dimensions. **25|302**

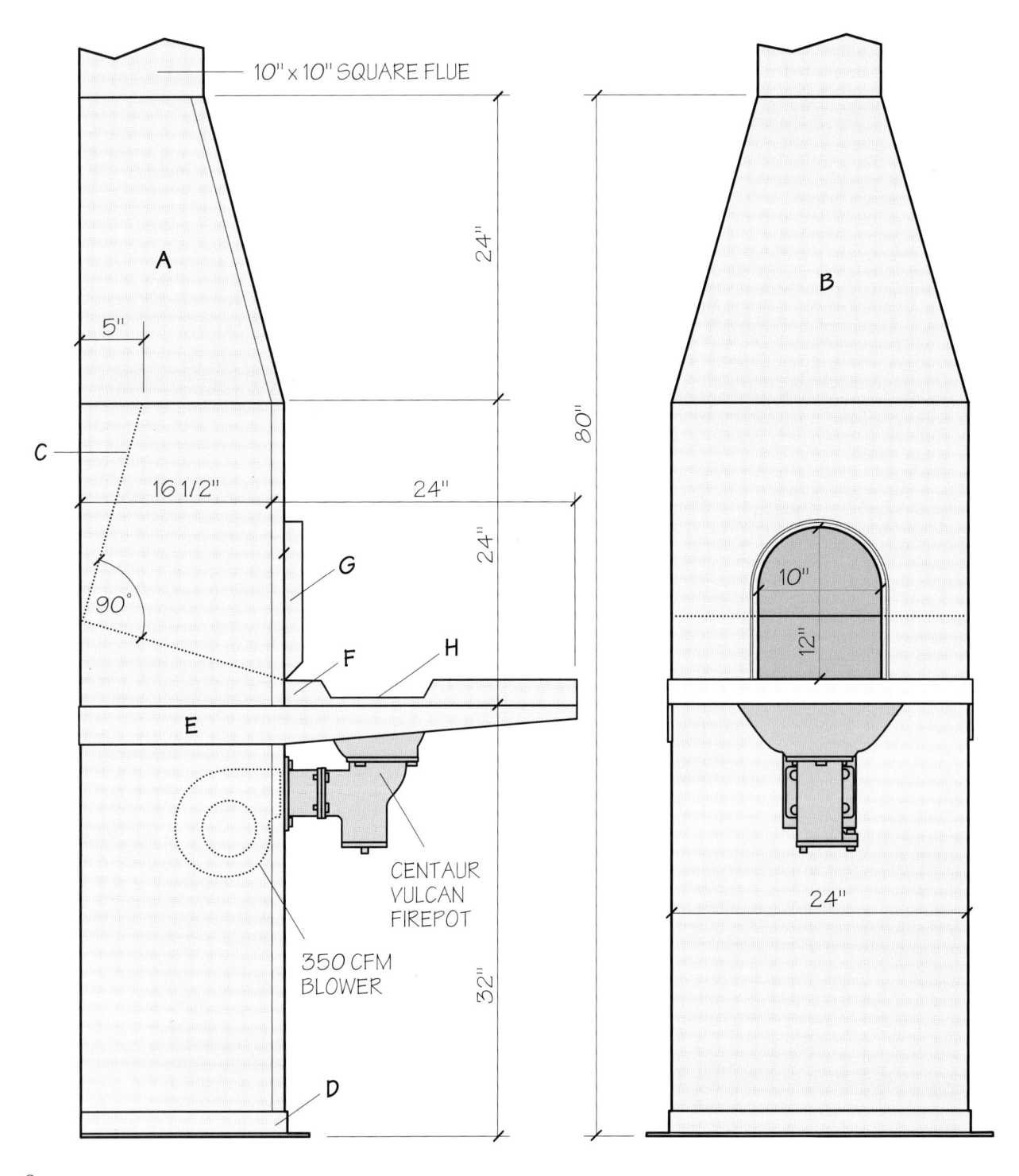

HOOD ASSEMBLY DETAIL

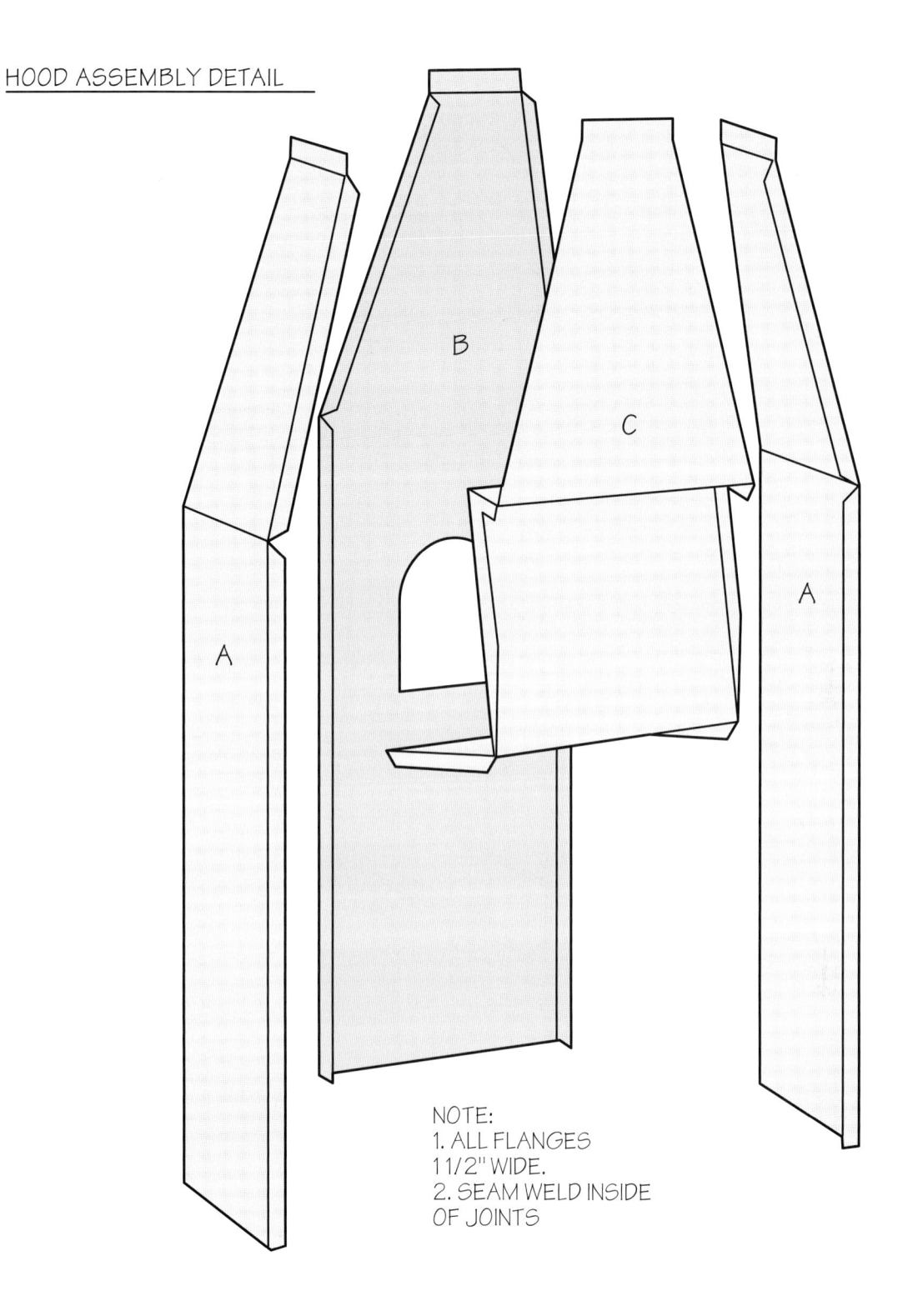

NOTE:
1. ALL FLANGES 1 1/2" WIDE.
2. SEAM WELD INSIDE OF JOINTS

MATERIALS	
A 14 GA. SHEET	E 1/4" X 3" FLAT
B 14 GA. SHEET	F 2" x 2" x 3/16" ANGLE
C 14 GA. SHEET	G 1/8" x 1 1/2" FLAT
D 2" X 2" x 3/16" ANGLE	H 3/16" PLATE

CENTAUR OR
BUFFALO VULCAN
FIREPOT

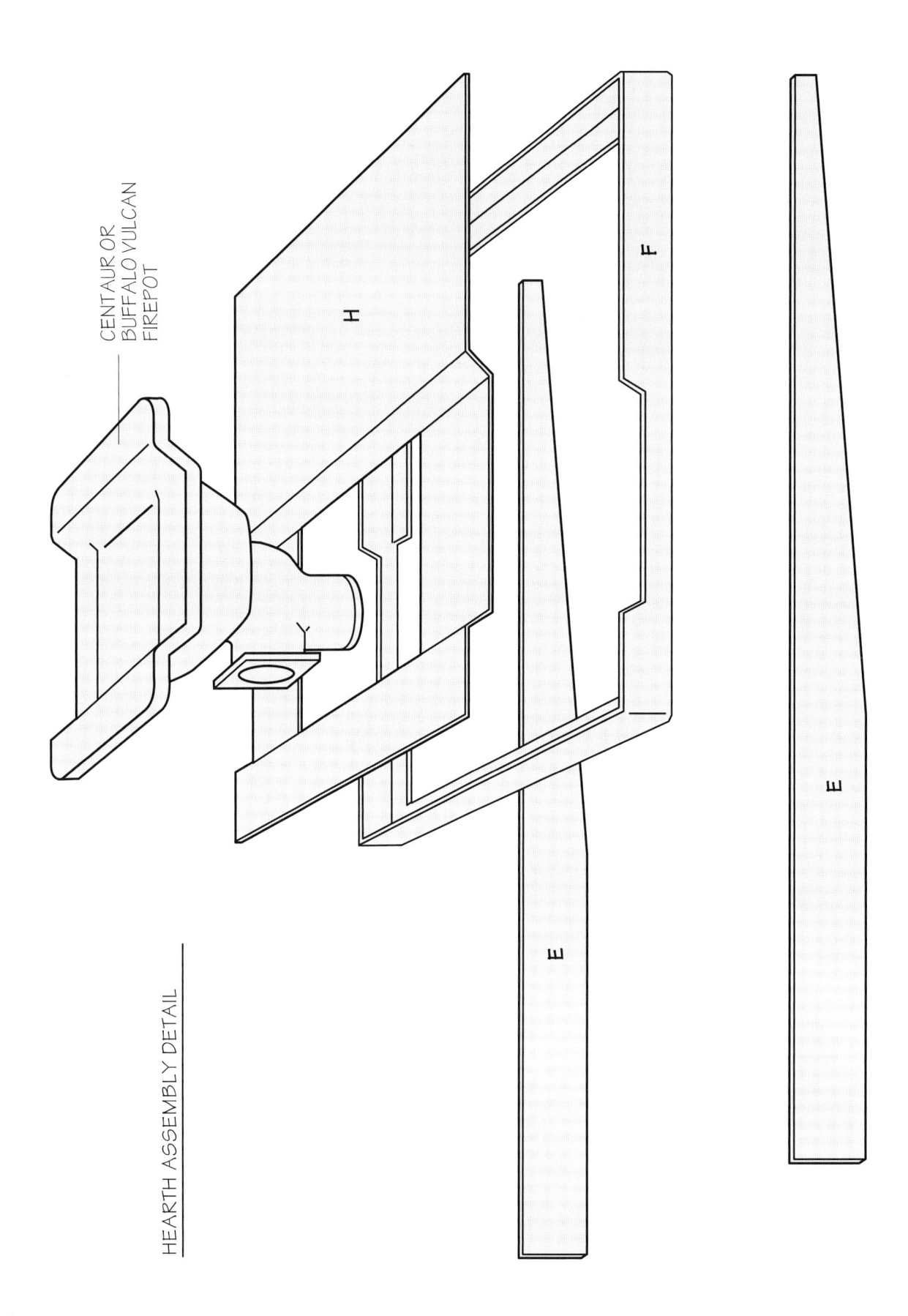

H

F

E

E

HEARTH ASSEMBLY DETAIL

Filing Vise - ½ scale

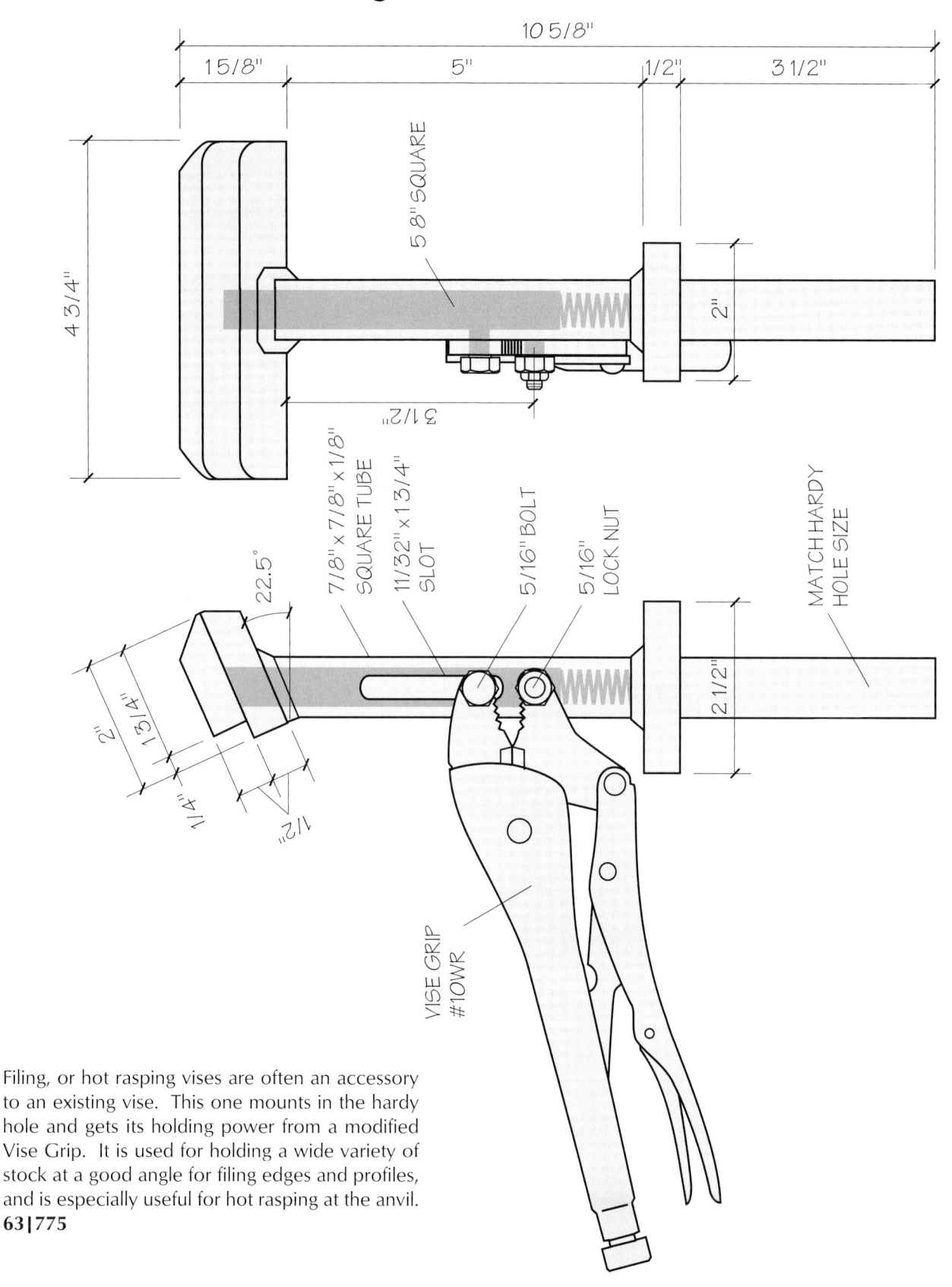

- 10 5/8"
- 1 5/8"
- 5"
- 1/2"
- 3 1/2"
- 4 3/4"
- 5/8" SQUARE
- 2"
- 3 1/2"
- 22.5°
- 2"
- 1 3/4"
- 1/4"
- 1/2"
- 7/8" x 7/8" x 1/8" SQUARE TUBE
- 11/32" x 1 3/4" SLOT
- 5/16" BOLT
- 5/16" LOCK NUT
- 2 1/2"
- MATCH HARDY HOLE SIZE
- VISE GRIP #10WR

Filing, or hot rasping vises are often an accessory to an existing vise. This one mounts in the hardy hole and gets its holding power from a modified Vise Grip. It is used for holding a wide variety of stock at a good angle for filing edges and profiles, and is especially useful for hot rasping at the anvil.
63|775

Flatter -full scale

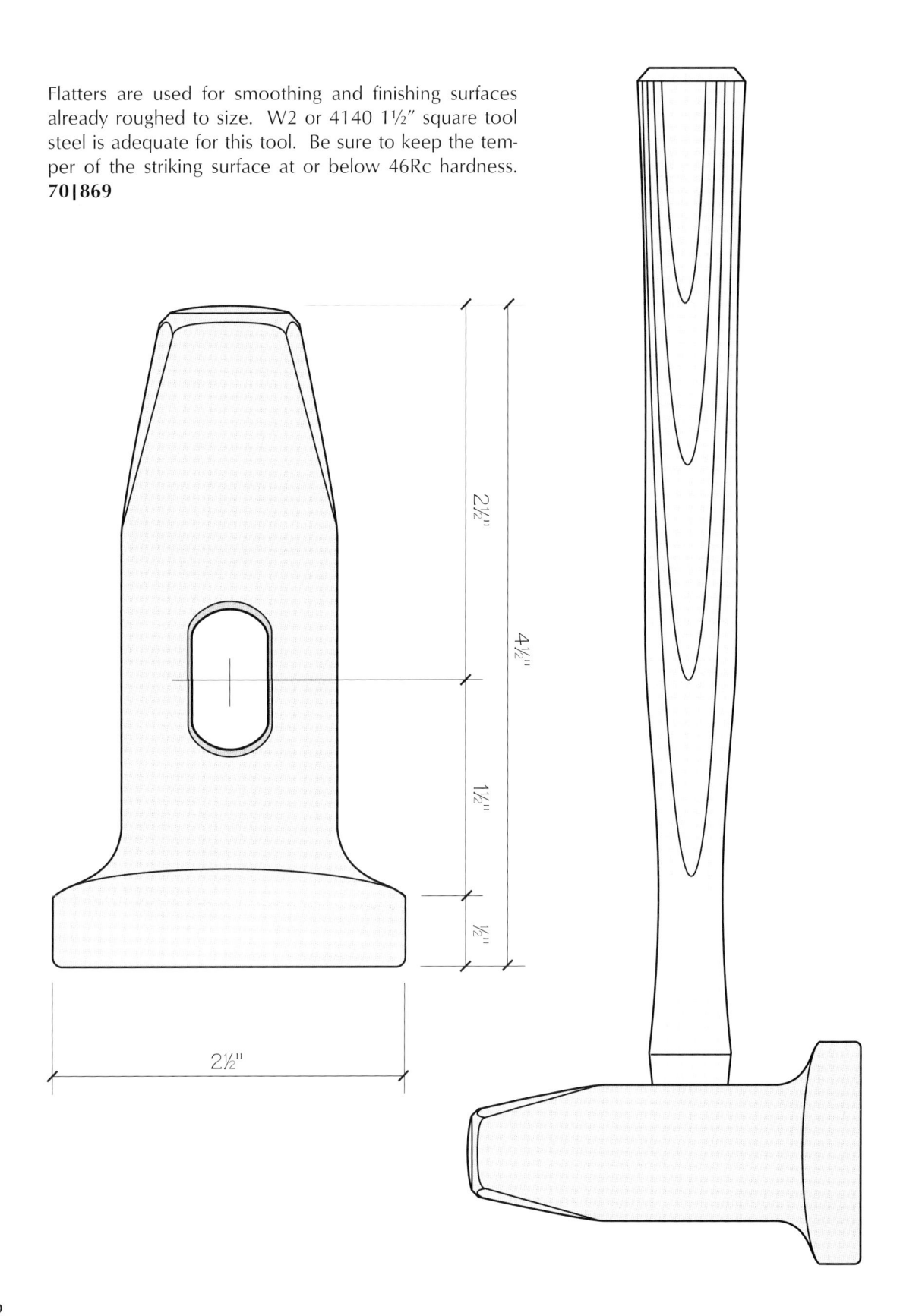

Flatters are used for smoothing and finishing surfaces already roughed to size. W2 or 4140 1½" square tool steel is adequate for this tool. Be sure to keep the temper of the striking surface at or below 46Rc hardness.
70|869

2½"

4½"

1½"

½"

2½"

Gas Forge -not to scale

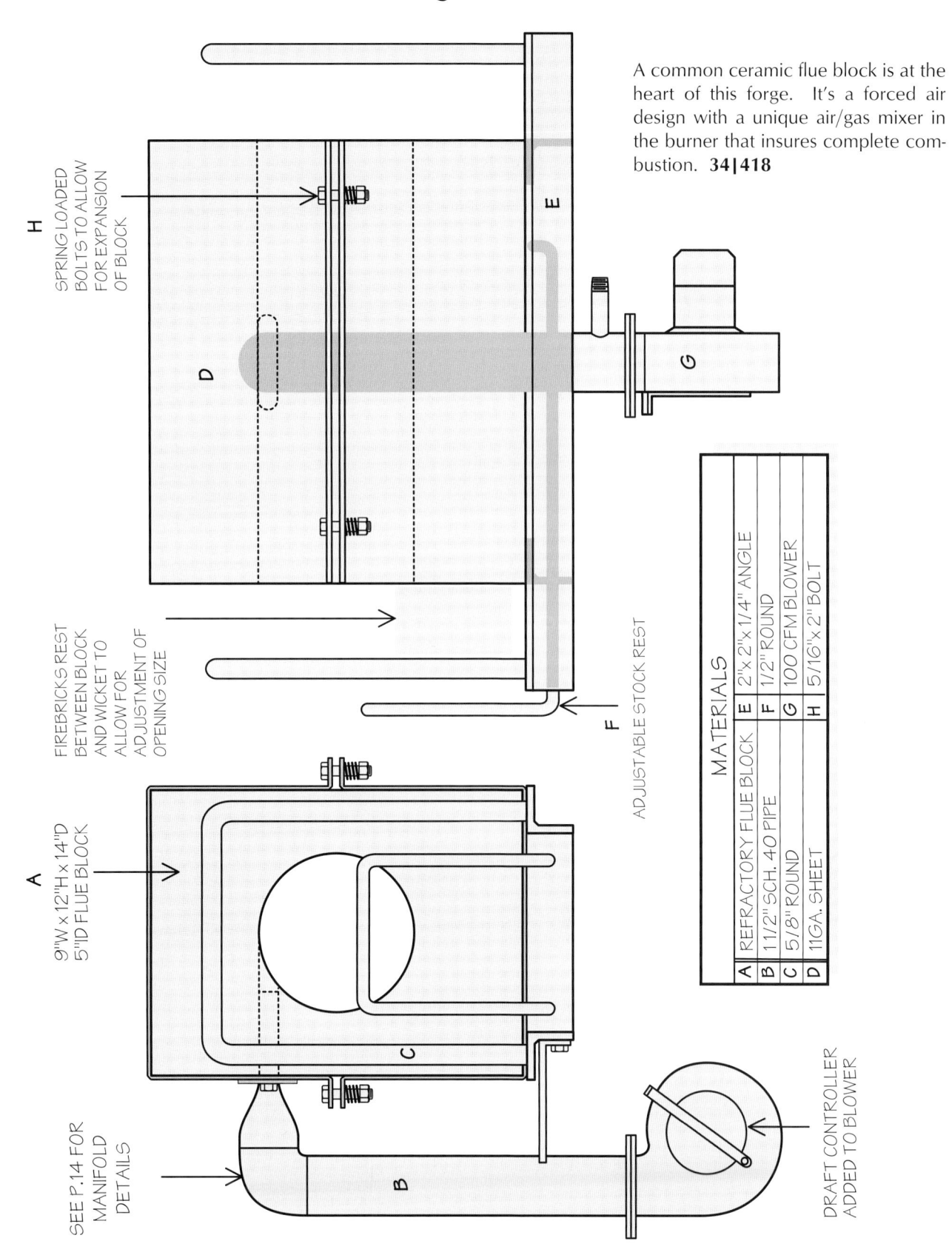

A common ceramic flue block is at the heart of this forge. It's a forced air design with a unique air/gas mixer in the burner that insures complete combustion. **34|418**

Labels

- **H** — SPRING LOADED BOLTS TO ALLOW FOR EXPANSION OF BLOCK
- **F** — FIREBRICKS REST BETWEEN BLOCK AND WICKET TO ALLOW FOR ADJUSTMENT OF OPENING SIZE
- **F** — ADJUSTABLE STOCK REST
- **A** — 9"W x 12"H x 14"D 5"ID FLUE BLOCK
- SEE P.14 FOR MANIFOLD DETAILS
- DRAFT CONTROLLER ADDED TO BLOWER

Materials

A	REFRACTORY FLUE BLOCK	E	2"x 2"x 1/4" ANGLE
B	1 1/2" SCH. 40 PIPE	F	1/2" ROUND
C	5/8" ROUND	G	100 CFM BLOWER
D	11 GA. SHEET	H	5/16"x 2" BOLT

13

Gas Forge, cont.

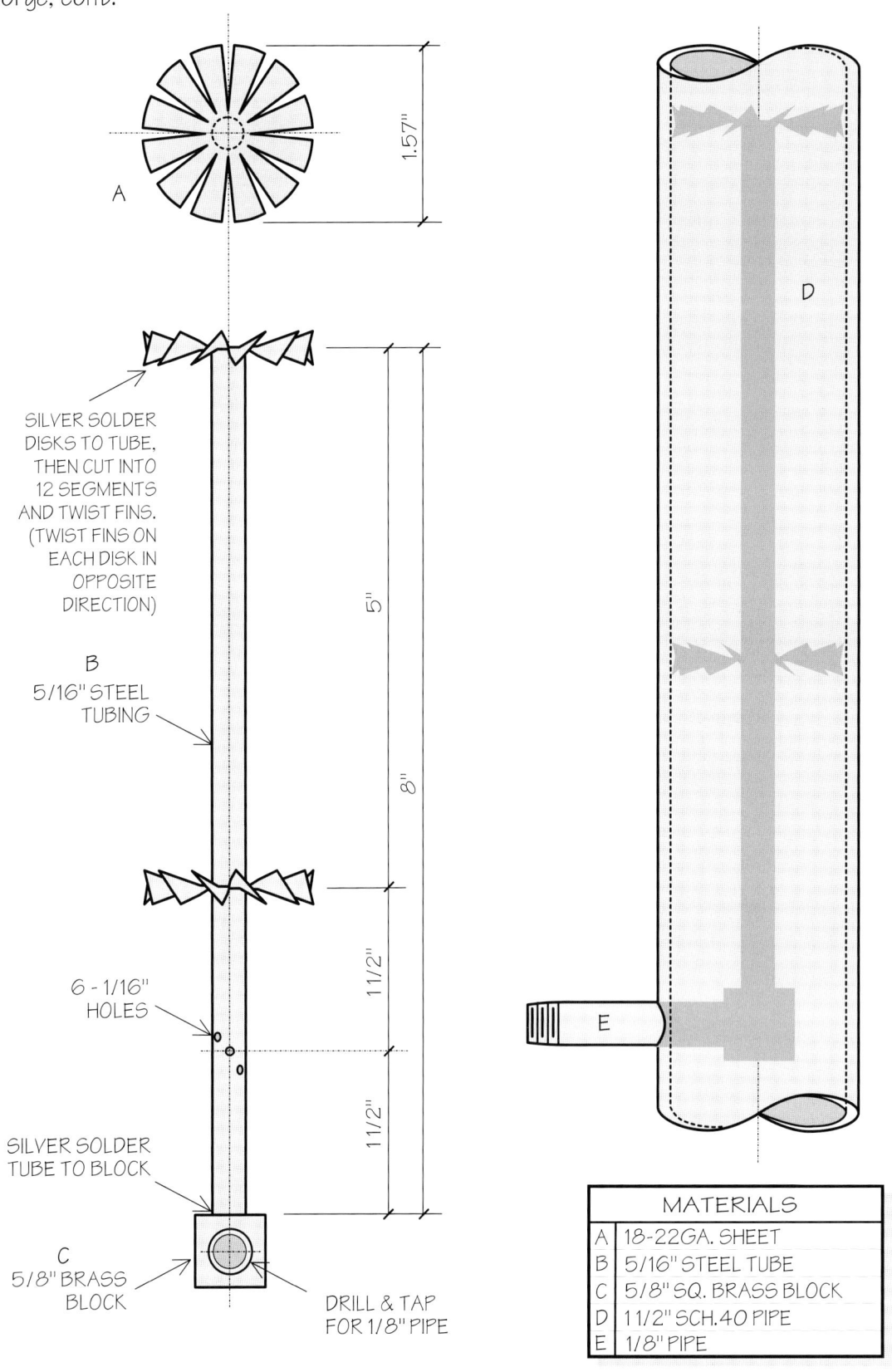

A

1.57"

SILVER SOLDER DISKS TO TUBE, THEN CUT INTO 12 SEGMENTS AND TWIST FINS. (TWIST FINS ON EACH DISK IN OPPOSITE DIRECTION)

B
5/16" STEEL TUBING

5"

8"

1 1/2"

6 - 1/16" HOLES

1 1/2"

SILVER SOLDER TUBE TO BLOCK

C
5/8" BRASS BLOCK

DRILL & TAP FOR 1/8" PIPE

D

E

	MATERIALS
A	18-22 GA. SHEET
B	5/16" STEEL TUBE
C	5/8" SQ. BRASS BLOCK
D	1 1/2" SCH. 40 PIPE
E	1/8" PIPE

MIXER AND BURNER TUBE

14

Hold Down – not to scale

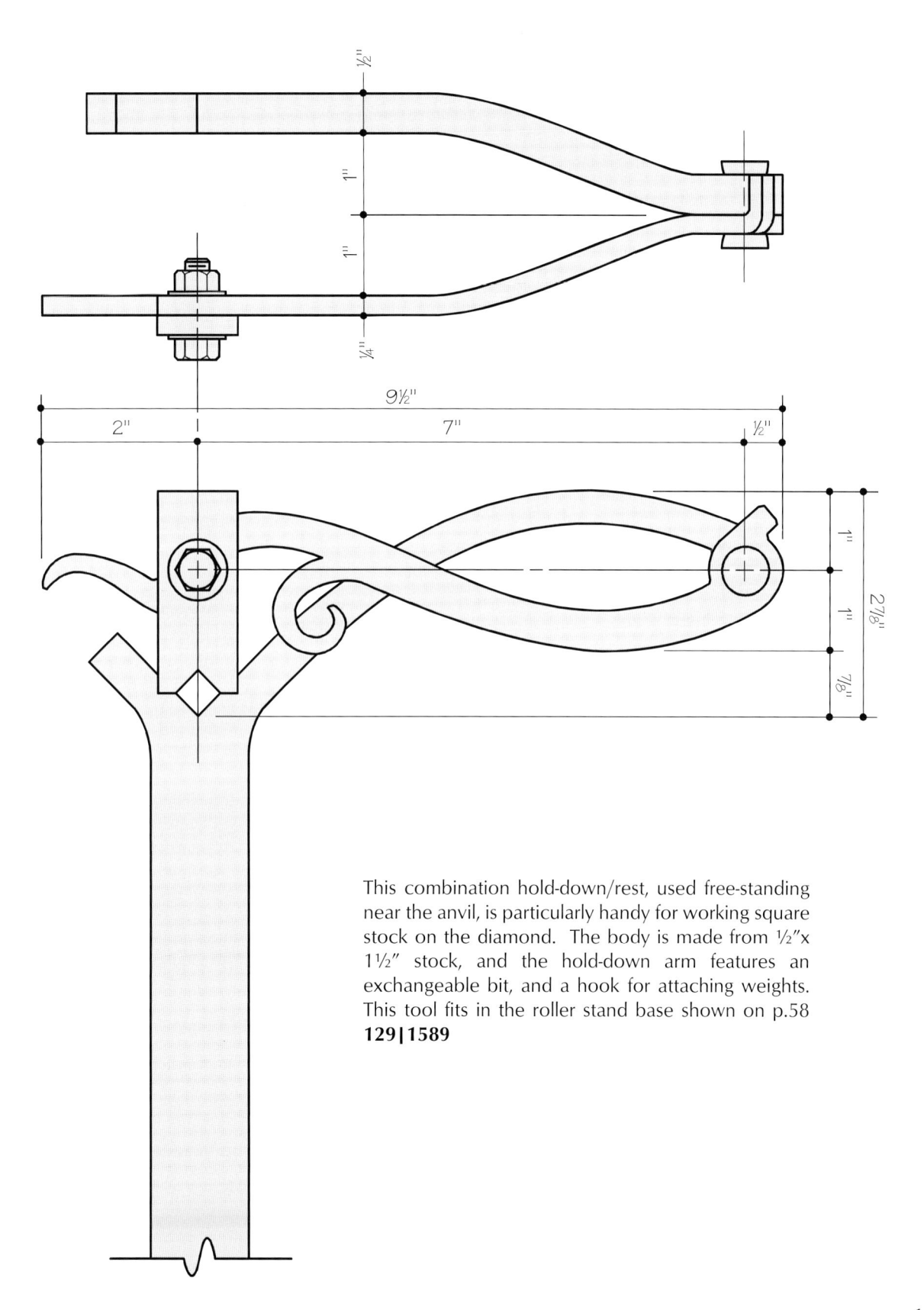

This combination hold-down/rest, used free-standing near the anvil, is particularly handy for working square stock on the diamond. The body is made from ½"x 1½" stock, and the hold-down arm features an exchangeable bit, and a hook for attaching weights. This tool fits in the roller stand base shown on p.58
129|1589

Hot Cut Chisel -full scale

Hot-cut chisels can be sharpened for slitting, or for cut-off applications. 1¼" W2 or 4140 square tool steel is adequate for this tool, but S7 is the best choice. Be sure to keep the temper of the striking surface at or below 46Rc hardness. **25|316**

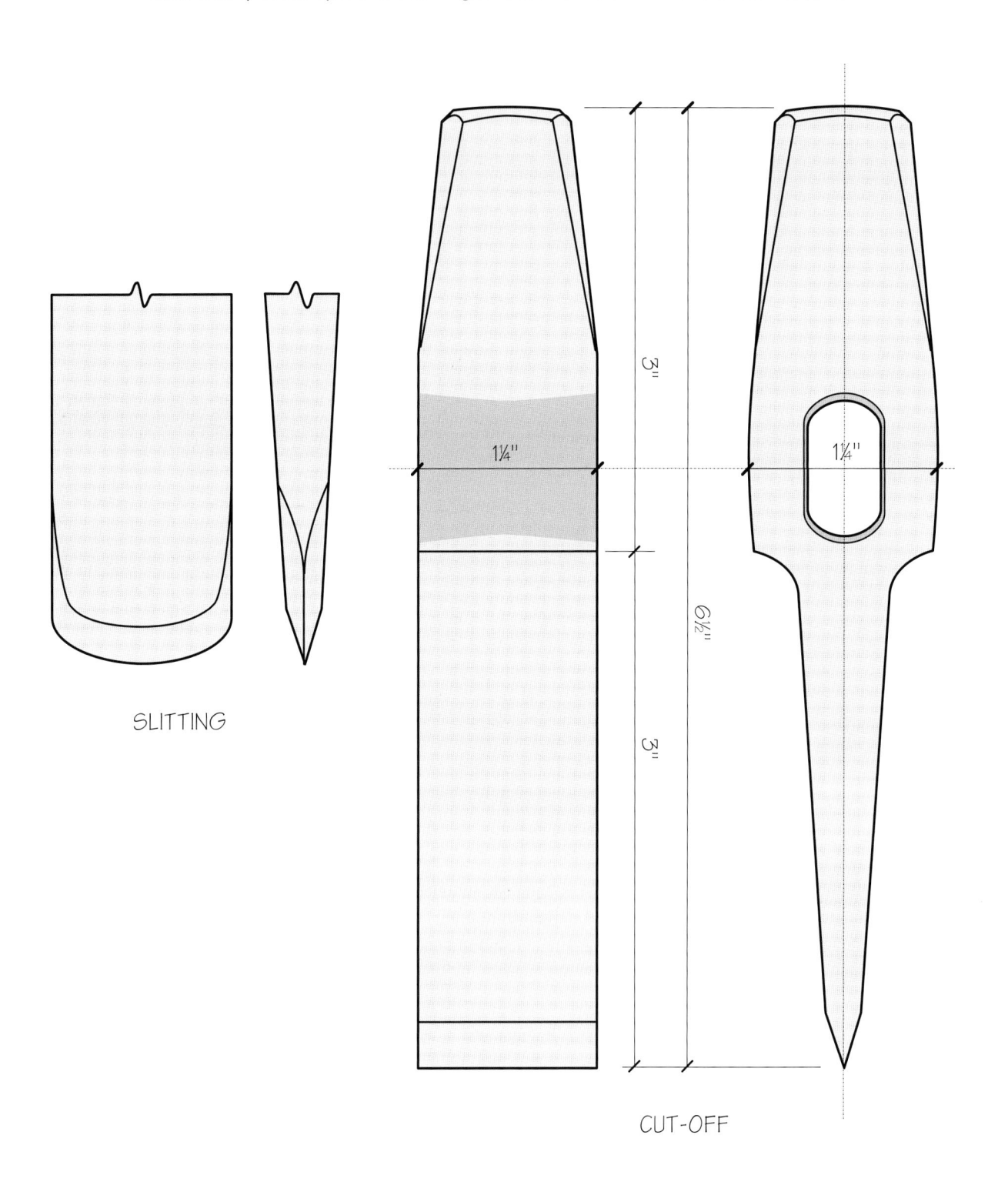

SLITTING

CUT-OFF

Portable Forge -¼ scale

The main body of this forge consists of a 14ga. fabricated steel case lined with wool or castable refractory (check local suppliers, and obtain refractory with at least a 2700° rating). The face plates are 11ga. steel with lugs for hanging a variety of interchangeable doors. It works with a ¾" pipe burner. **149|1862**

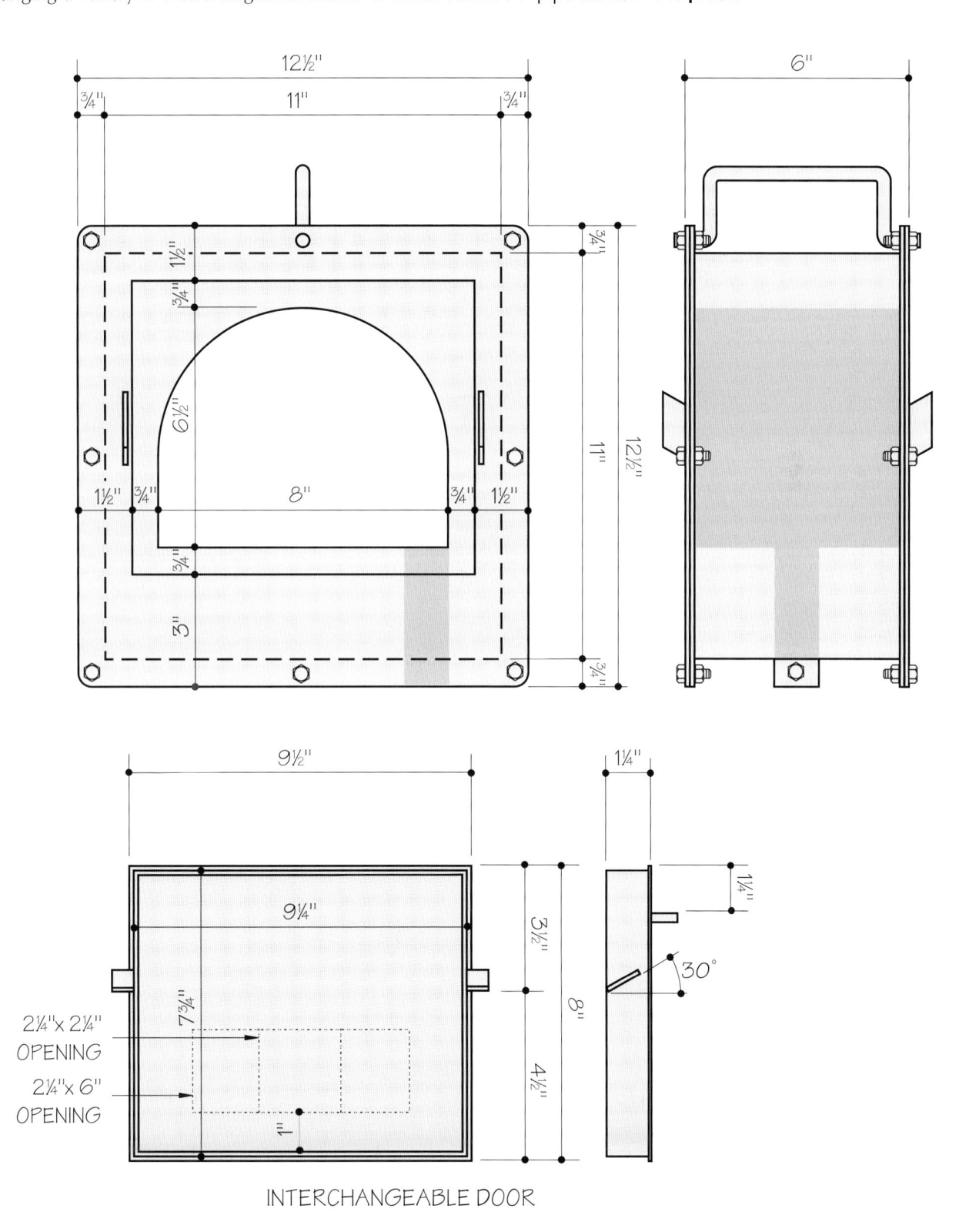

INTERCHANGEABLE DOOR

Portable Forge Stand -not to scale

This fixed forging station features a sliding stock rest and storage for up to four doors. Remember to keep LP tanks well away from the forge, preferably outside. **149|1885**

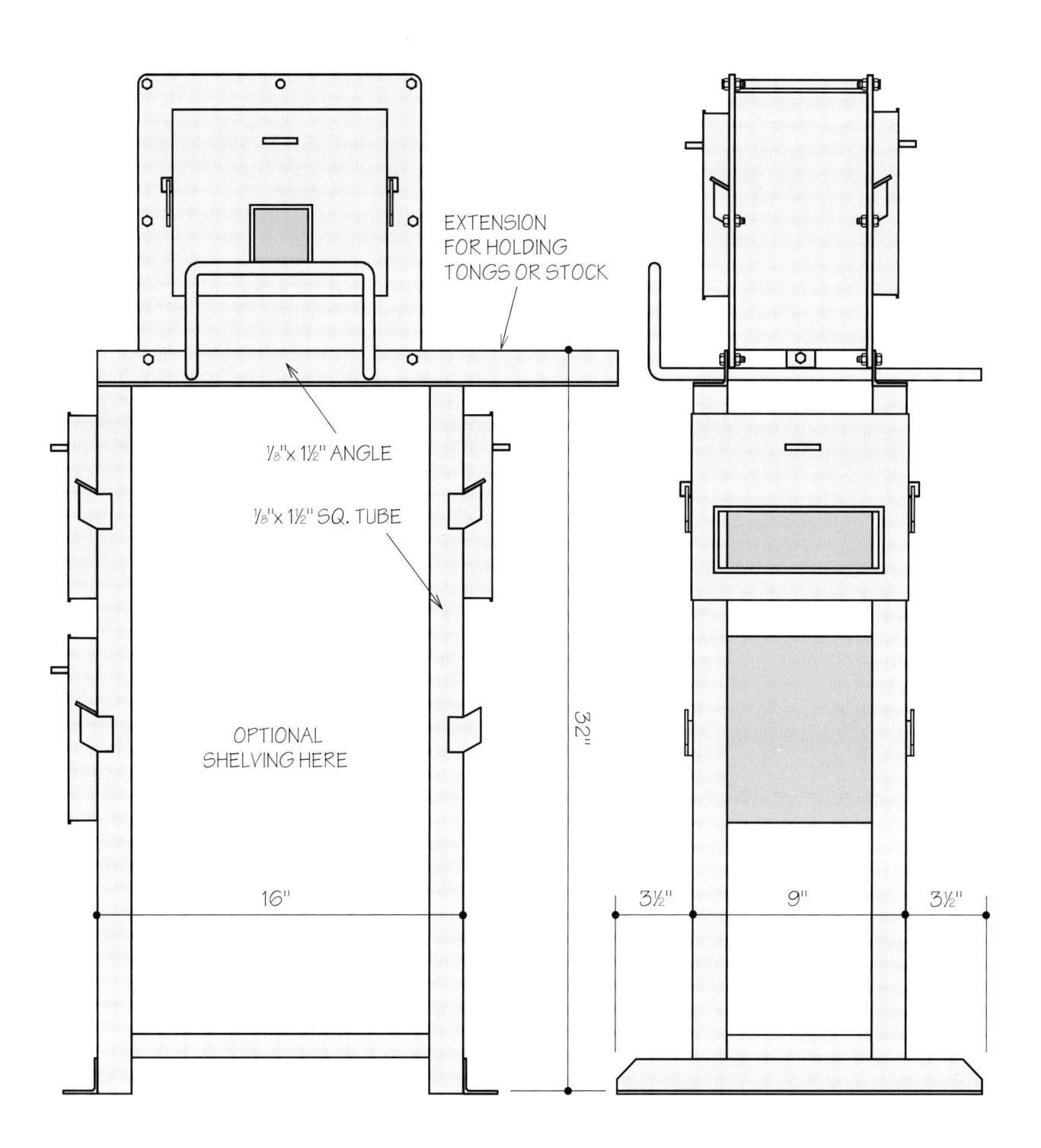

EXTENSION FOR HOLDING TONGS OR STOCK

1/8" x 1½" ANGLE

1/8" x 1½" SQ. TUBE

OPTIONAL SHELVING HERE

32"

16"

3½" 9" 3½"

18

Post Vise – not to scale

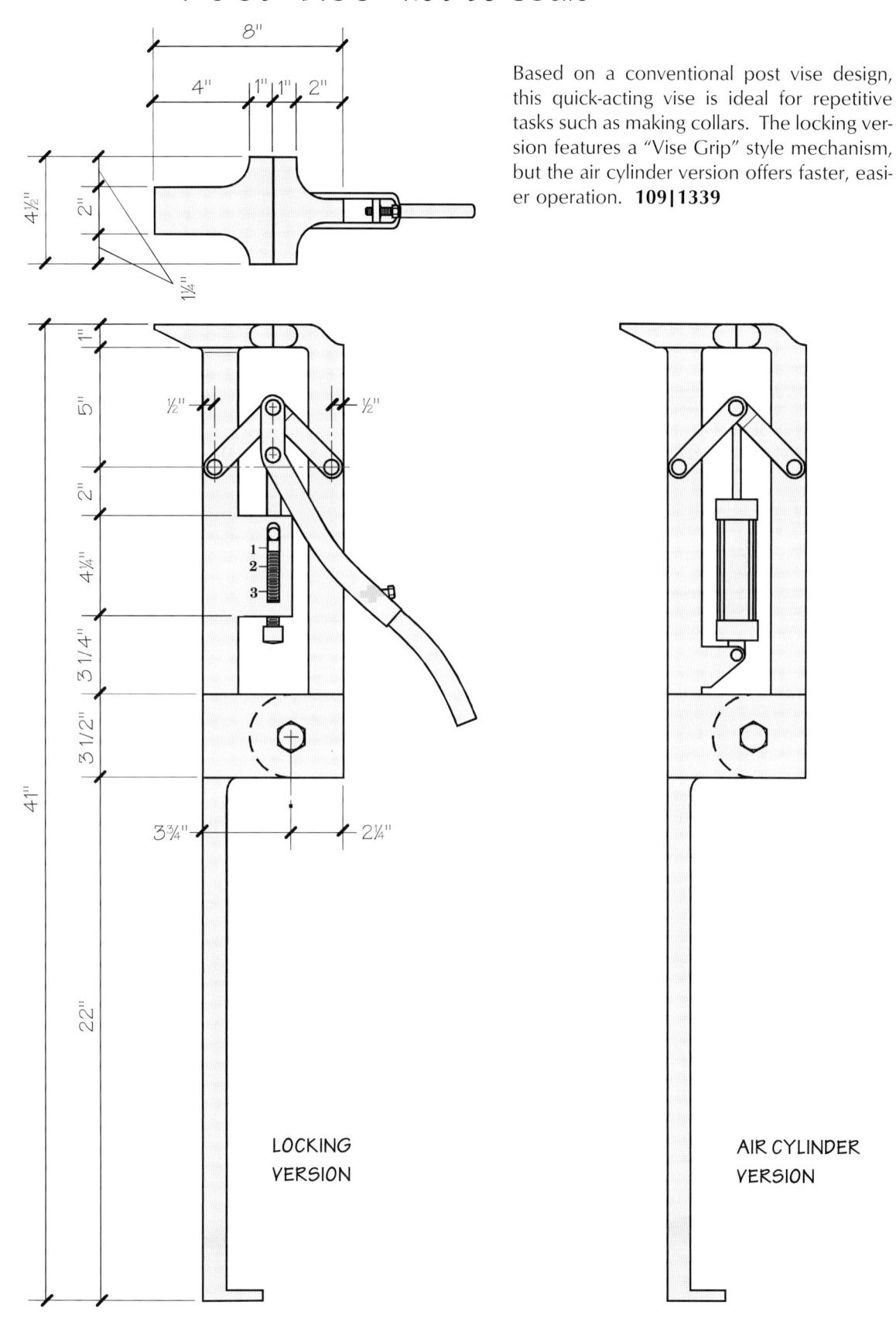

Based on a conventional post vise design, this quick-acting vise is ideal for repetitive tasks such as making collars. The locking version features a "Vise Grip" style mechanism, but the air cylinder version offers faster, easier operation. **109|1339**

LOCKING VERSION

AIR CYLINDER VERSION

Post Vise, cont.

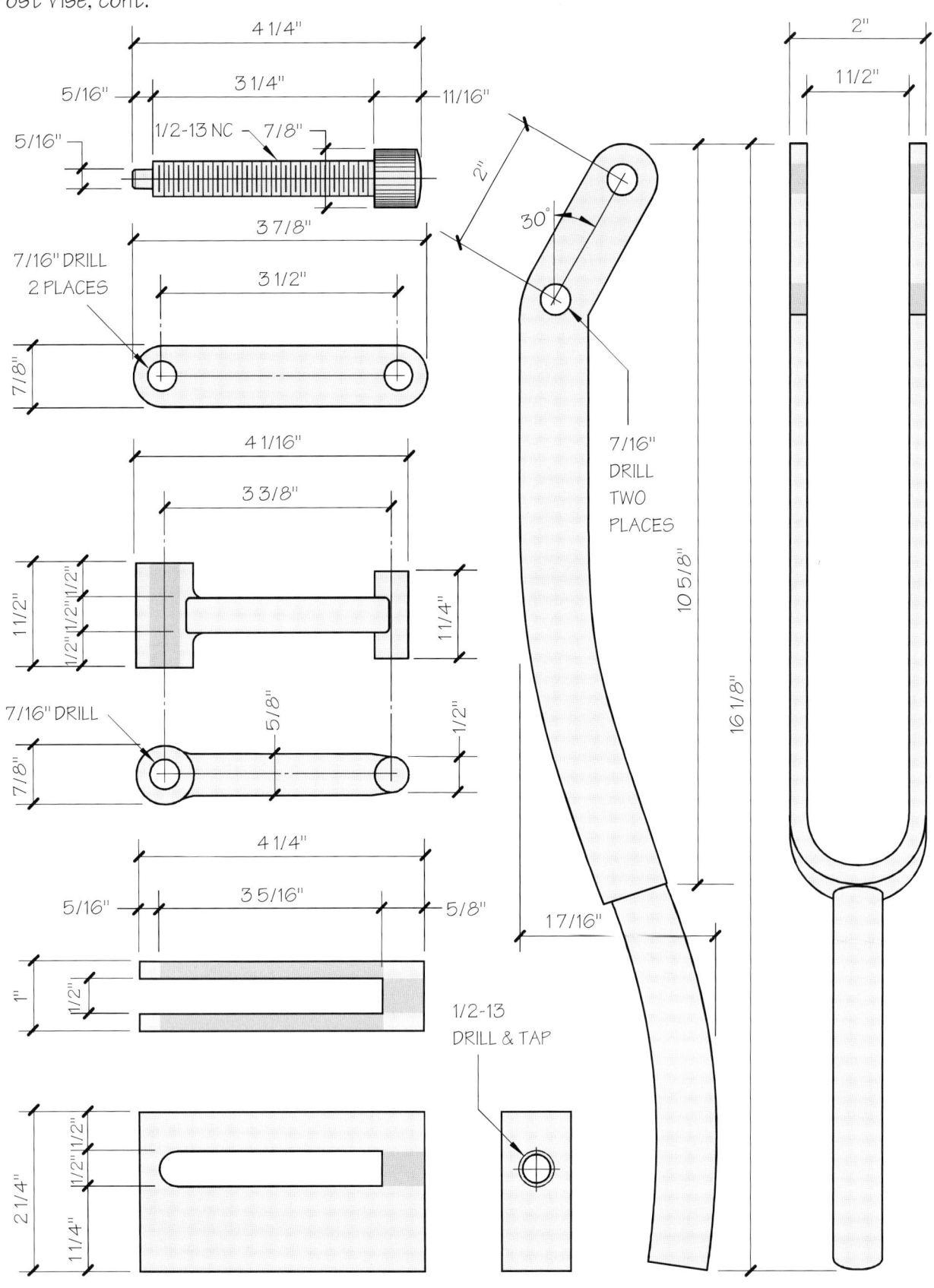

Post Vise Stand – ⅛ scale

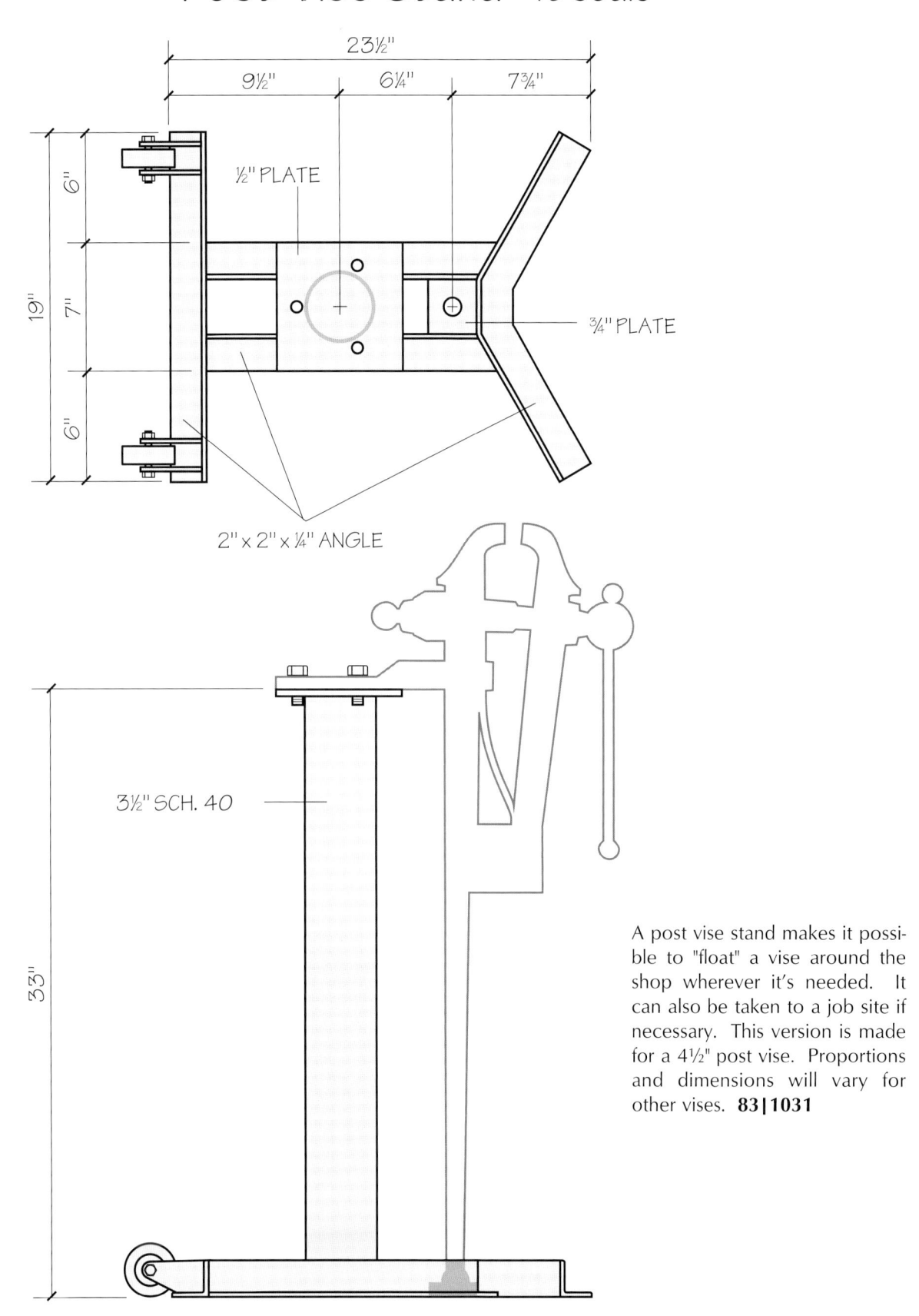

23½"
9½" 6¼" 7¾"

6"
19" 7"
6"

½" PLATE
¾" PLATE
2" x 2" x ¼" ANGLE

3½" SCH. 40

33"

A post vise stand makes it possible to "float" a vise around the shop wherever it's needed. It can also be taken to a job site if necessary. This version is made for a 4½" post vise. Proportions and dimensions will vary for other vises. **83|1031**

Punch Tongs - not to scale

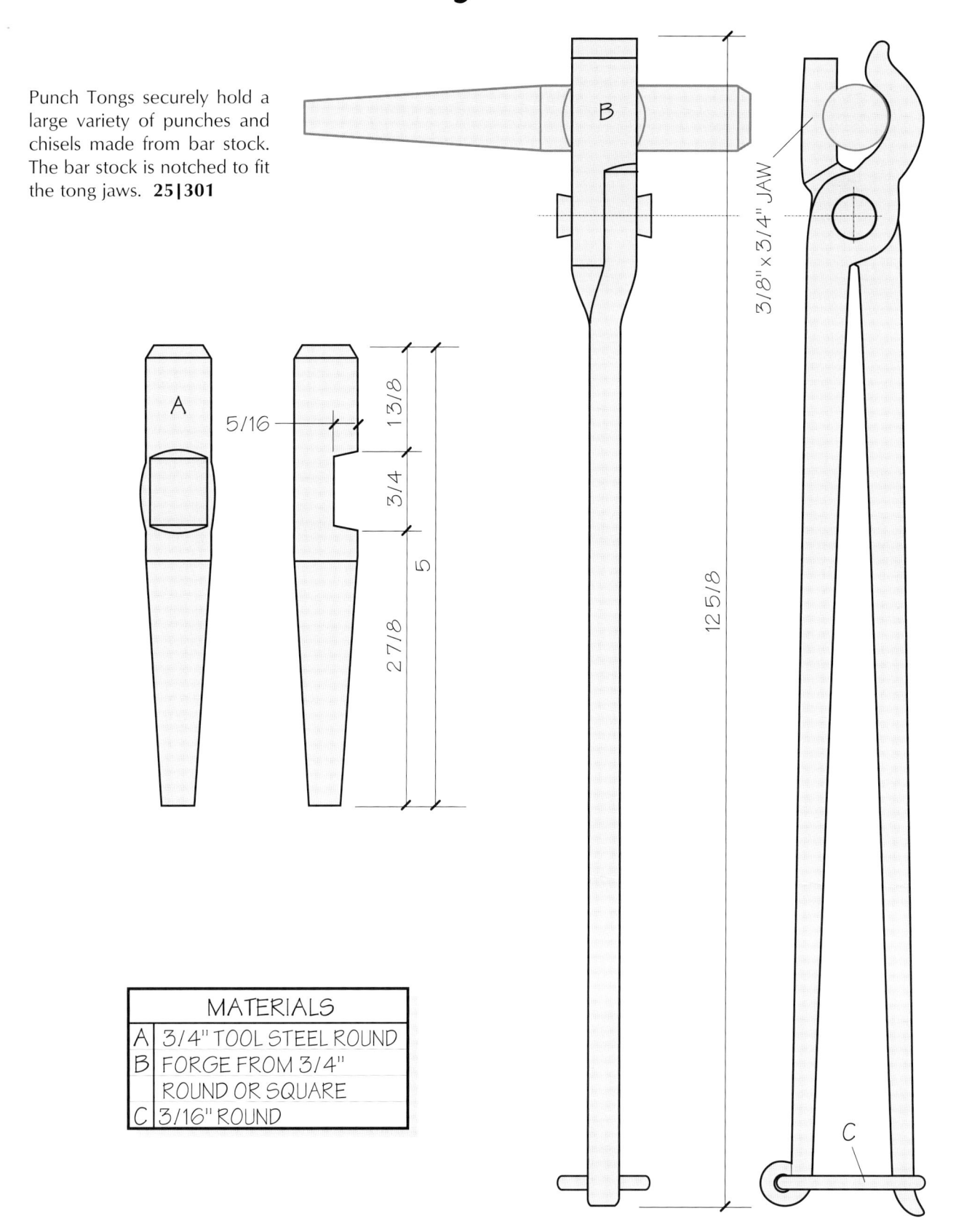

Punch Tongs securely hold a large variety of punches and chisels made from bar stock. The bar stock is notched to fit the tong jaws. **25|301**

3/8" x 3/4" JAW

5/16
1 3/8
3/4
5
2 7/8

12 5/8

MATERIALS	
A	3/4" TOOL STEEL ROUND
B	FORGE FROM 3/4" ROUND OR SQUARE
C	3/16" ROUND

22

Rail Anvils - 1/3 scale

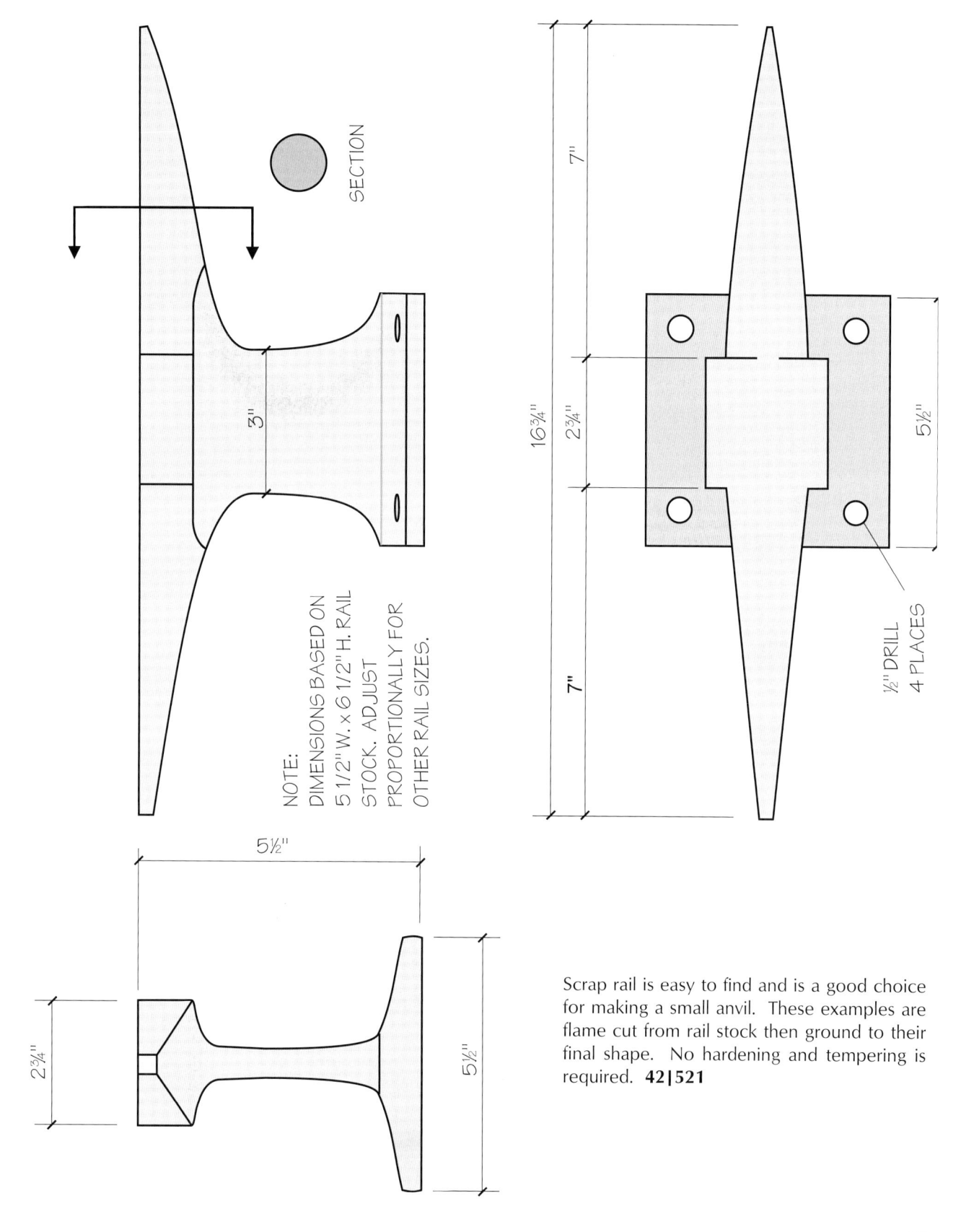

SECTION

3"

16¾"
7"
2¾"
7"

5½"

½" DRILL
4 PLACES

NOTE: DIMENSIONS BASED ON 5½"W. x 6½"H. RAIL STOCK. ADJUST PROPORTIONALLY FOR OTHER RAIL SIZES.

5½"
2¾"
5½"

Scrap rail is easy to find and is a good choice for making a small anvil. These examples are flame cut from rail stock then ground to their final shape. No hardening and tempering is required. **42|521**

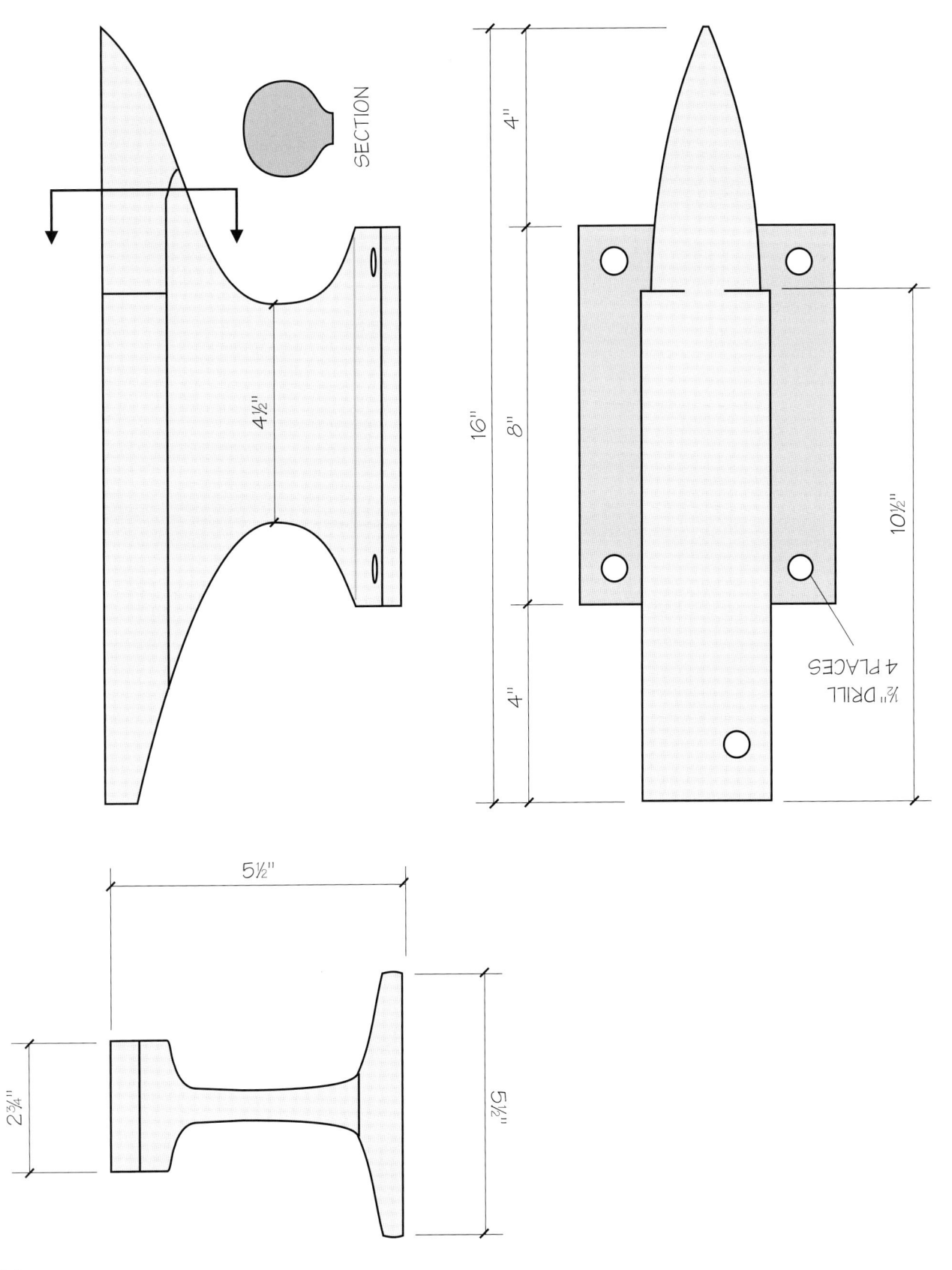

Rail Anvils, cont.

Scroll Tongs -not to scale

Scroll tongs are useful for making tight bends, or small scrolls and loops in just about any situation where bending small parts is required. **162|2039**

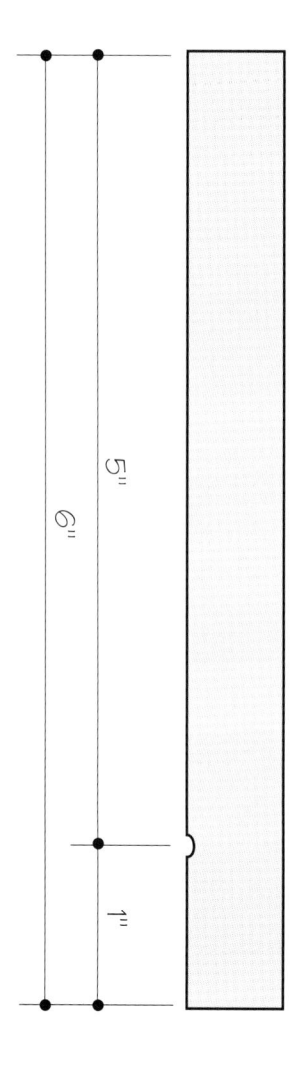

5/8" SQUARE STOCK LAYOUT FOR EACH JAW

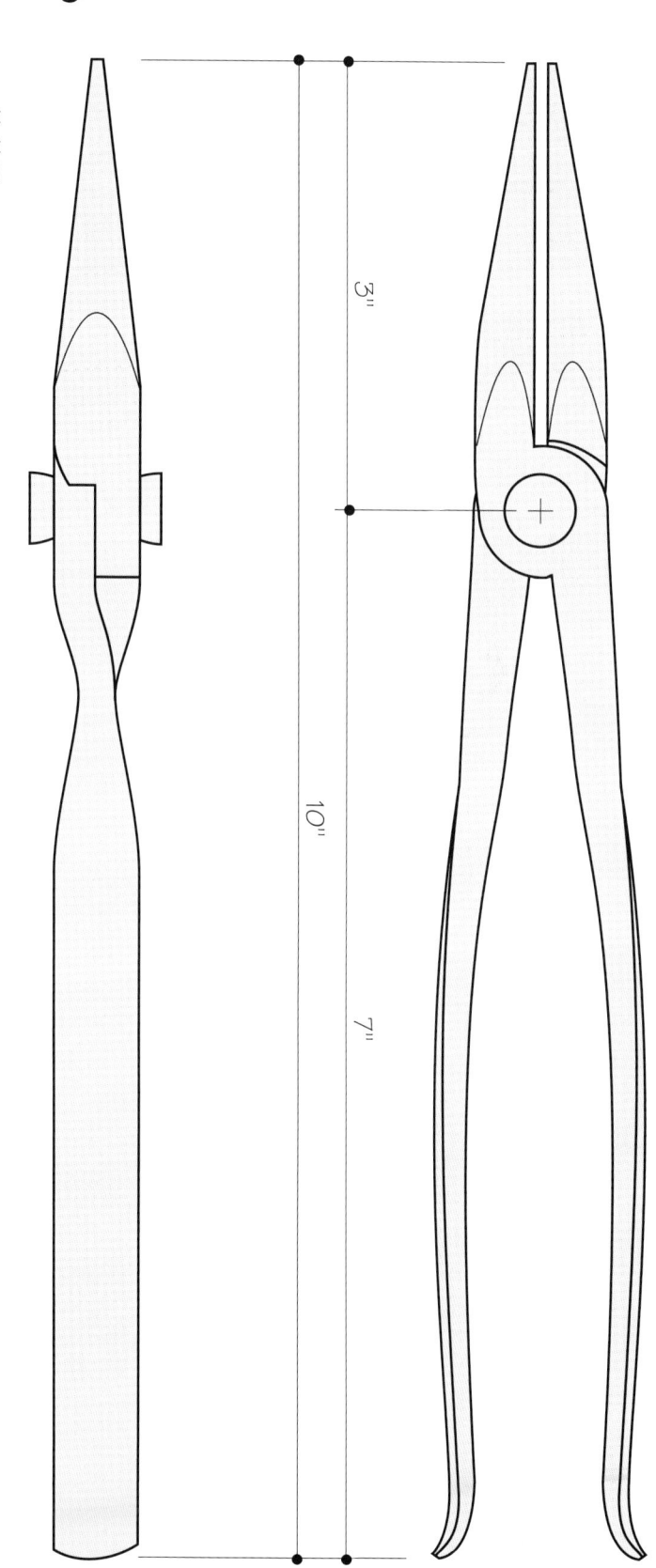

25

Skillet Form - ¼ scale

Developed by Doug Hendrickson, Lesterville, MO., this tool is used for forging skillets and pans from up to 3/16" thick stock. Clamp a blank disk to the form, then heat with a torch and draw over the edge with a hand hammer. Trim the edge and rivet on a forged handle to finish. **21|253**

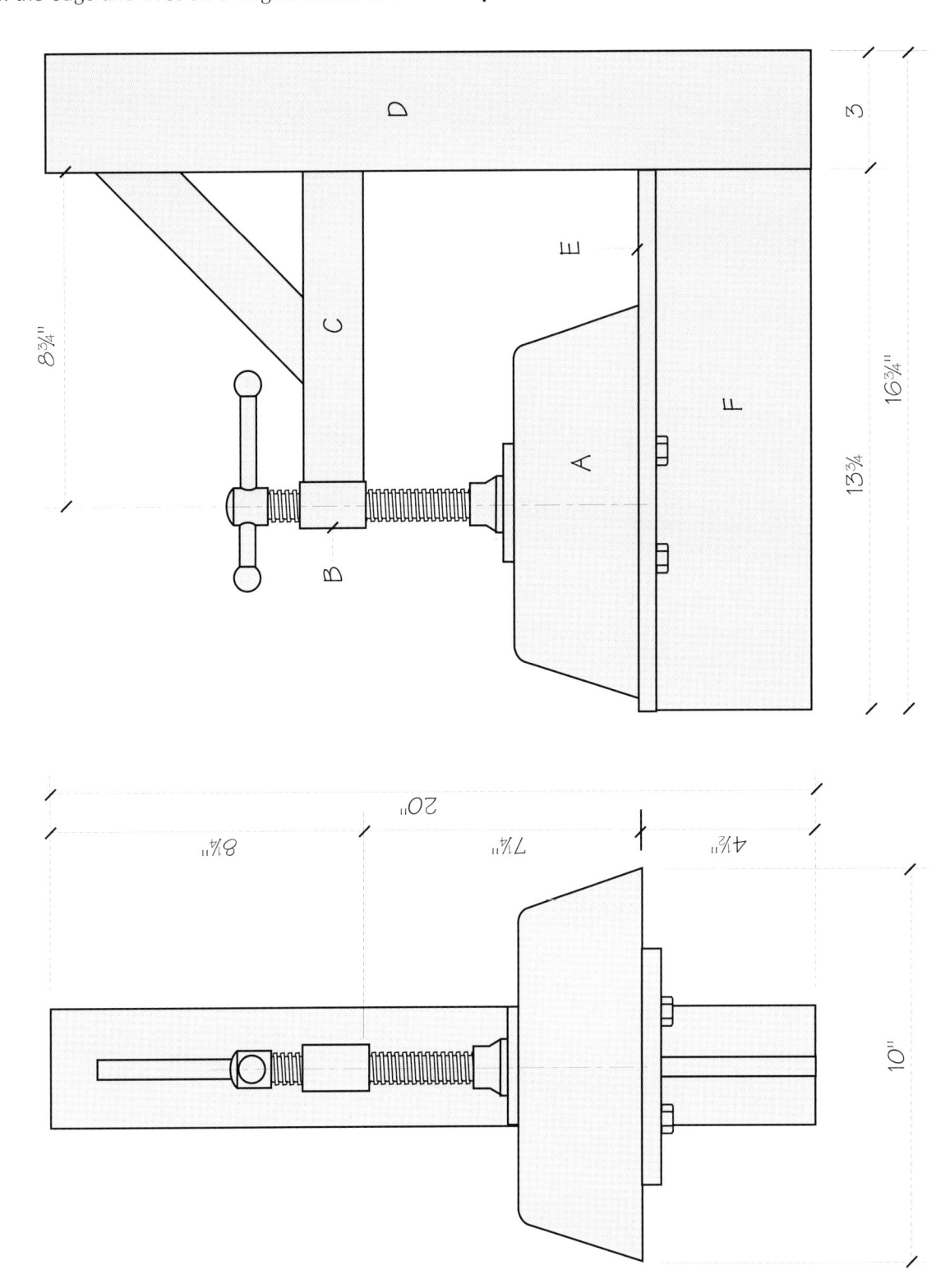

Slot Press -not to scale

If you've ever struggled with keeping the bar aligned when opening up a slot, or have a lot of slots to open, this press is for you. It consists of a stop and two guides that slide on heavy gauge tubing. Power comes from a bottle jack at the base of the press. To use, adjust the stop to match the length of the bar, then adjust the guides so that they are positioned above and below the slot. Place the bar in the press, heat around the slot with a torch, and use the jack to open it up. **161|2021**

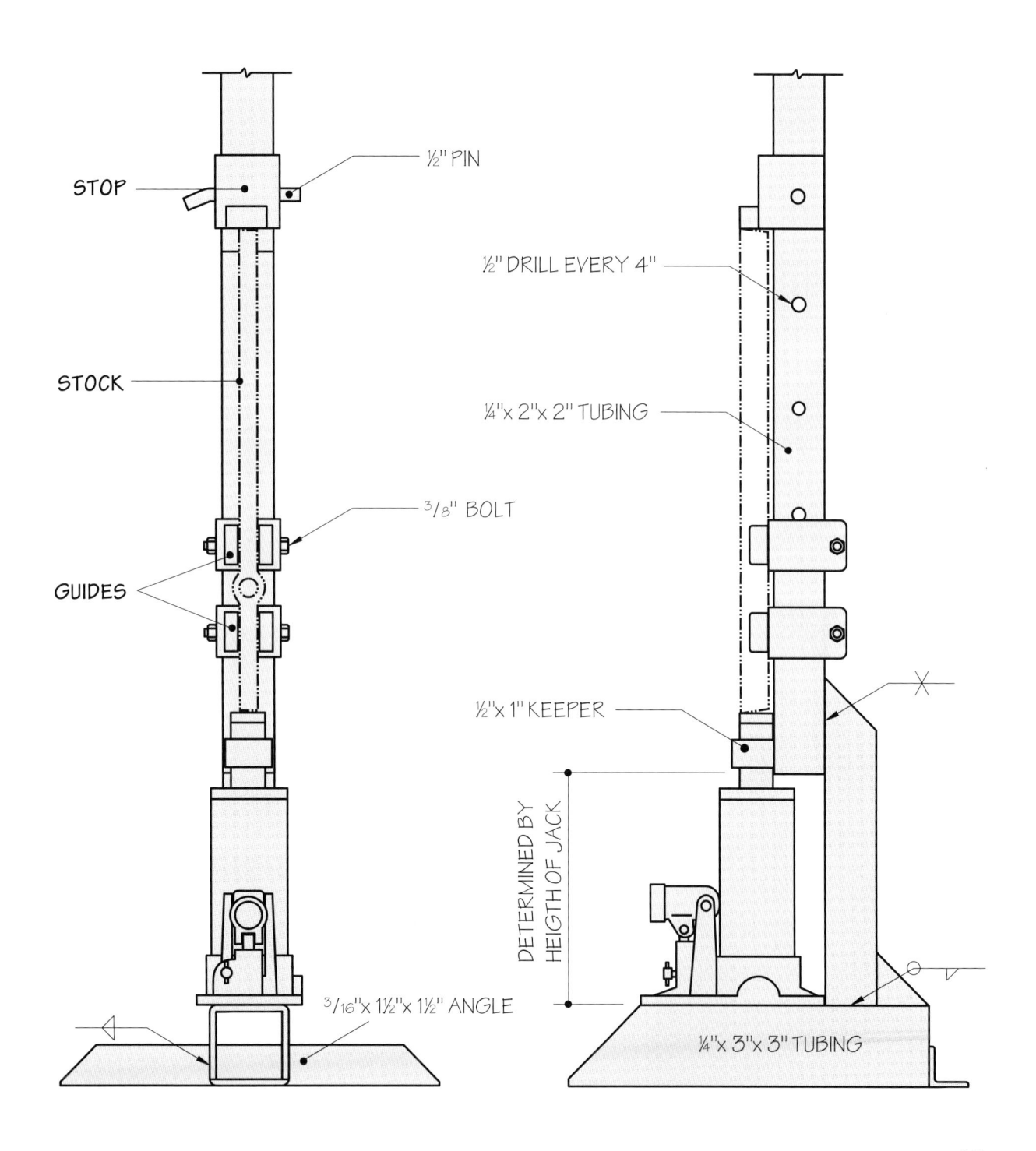

- STOP — ½" PIN
- STOCK — ½" DRILL EVERY 4"
- ¼" x 2" x 2" TUBING
- GUIDES — ⅜" BOLT
- ½" x 1" KEEPER
- DETERMINED BY HEIGHT OF JACK
- 3/16" x 1½" x 1½" ANGLE
- ¼" x 3" x 3" TUBING

27

Smithin' Magician II -½ scale

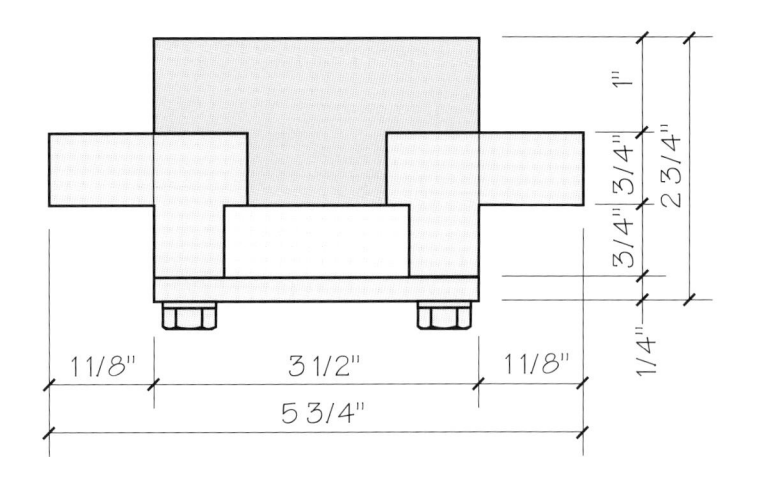

The generic name for this tool is "guillotine tool". It works like traditional top and bottom tools for swaging stock. The interchangeable ¾"× 2" dies are offset from the main body for working stock perpendicular to them. **39|481**

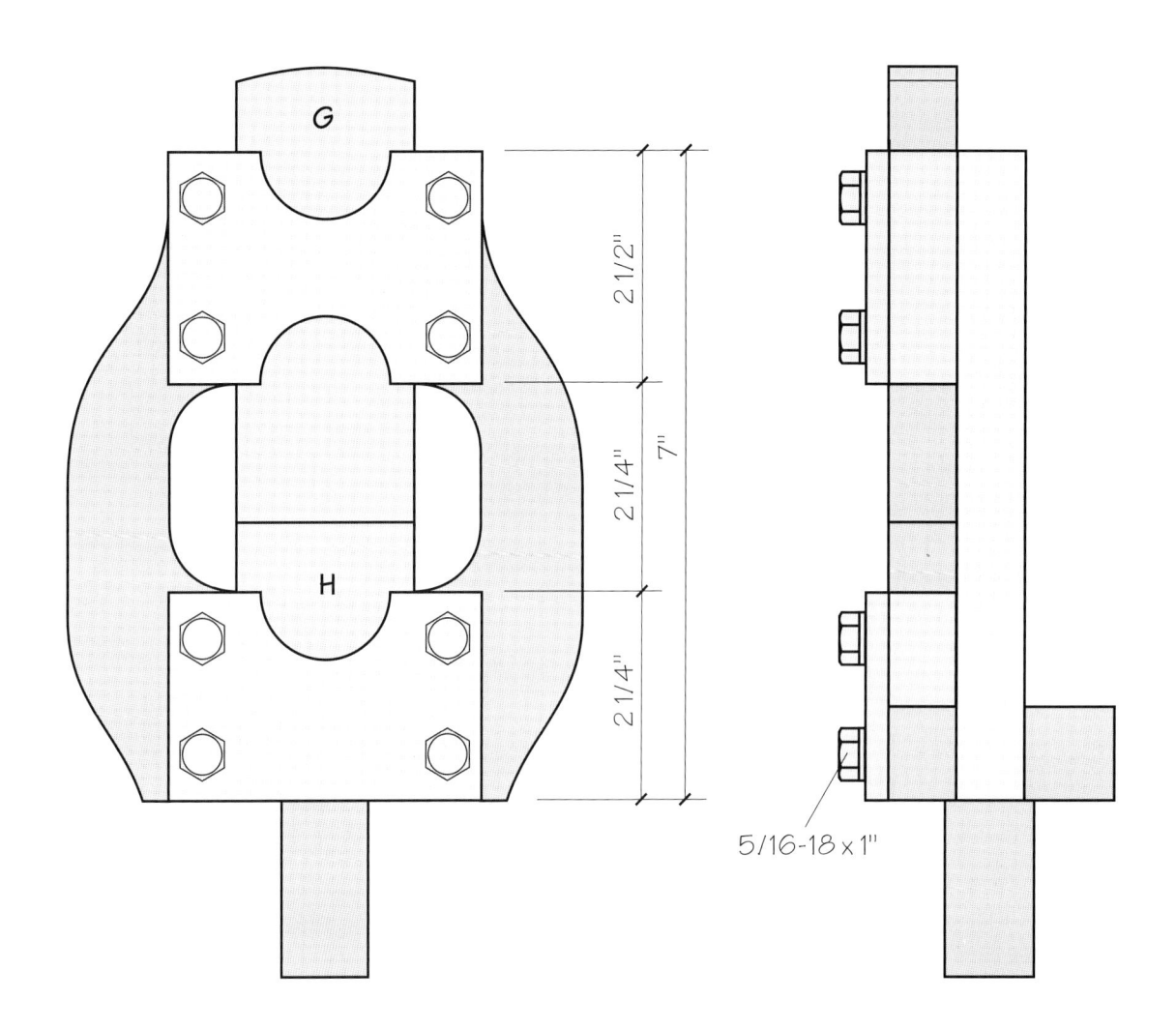

5/16-18 x 1"

MATERIALS

A	1" PLATE
B	3/4" PLATE
C	1/4" x 2 1/2" FLAT
D	1/4" x 2 1/4" FLAT
E	1" SQUARE
F	3/4" SQUARE
G	3/4" x 2" x 5" DIE STOCK
H	3/4" x 2" x 2" DIE STOCK

FULL-SIZE TEMPLATE
FOR PART B

Smithin' Magician IIIA - ½ scale

This simplified version of the Smithing Magician can be made using only a drill press and oxy-acetylene equipment. Its key feature is the guide bar/hardy stem for use on the anvil. The pin at the base of the stem is for securing the tool with a wedge under the heel of the anvil. **104|1284**

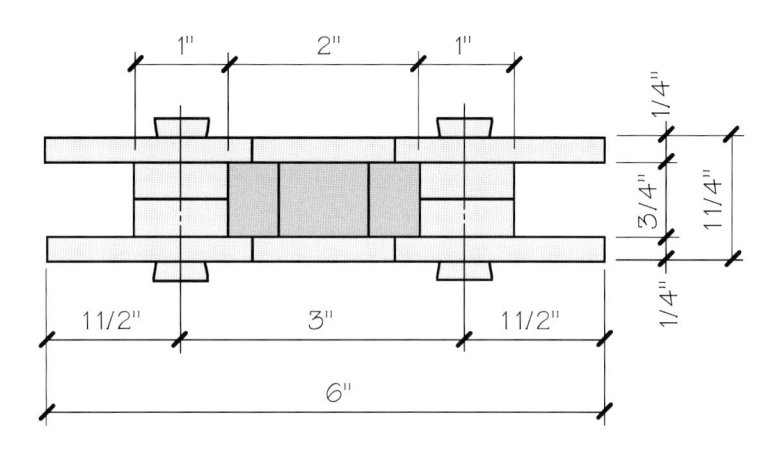

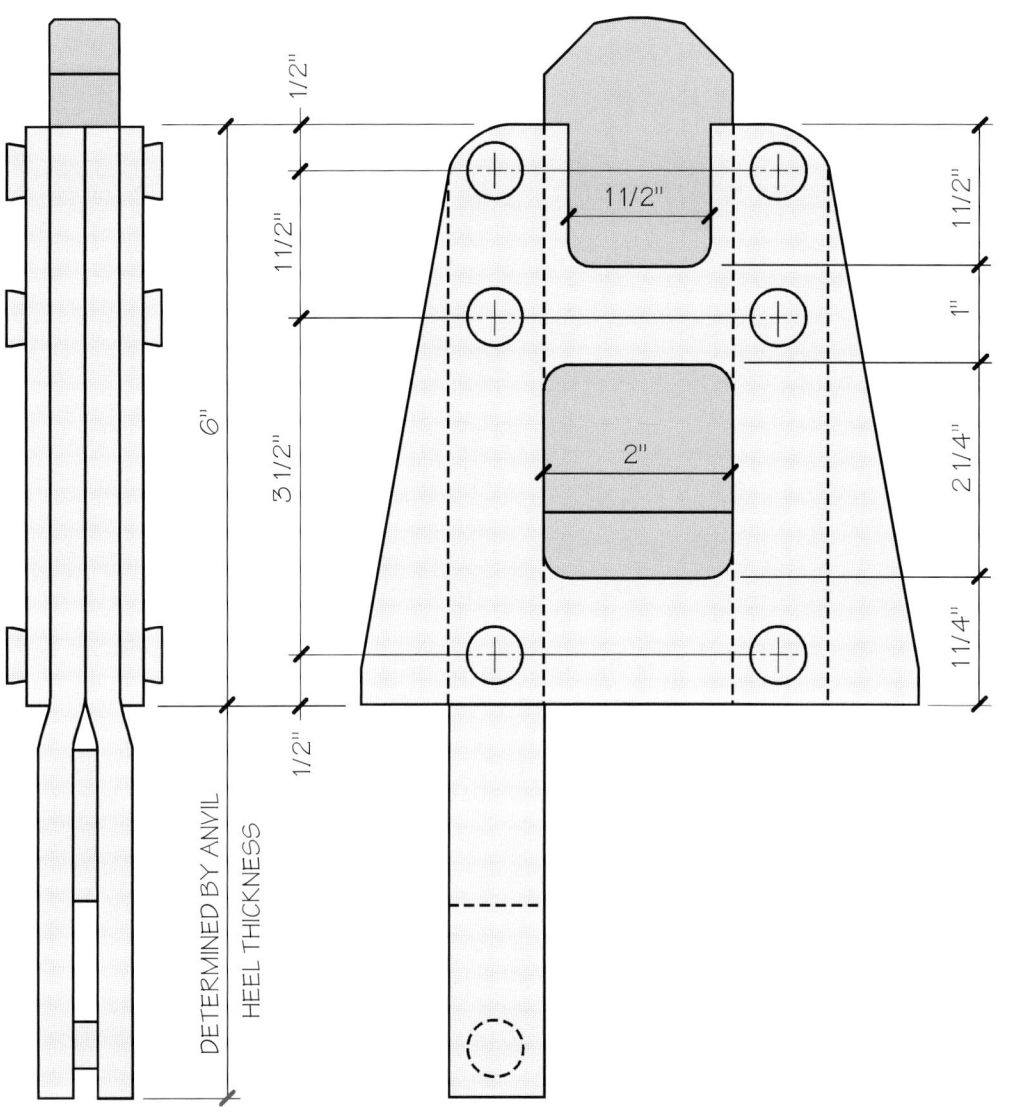

Smithin' Magician Pedestal –not to scale

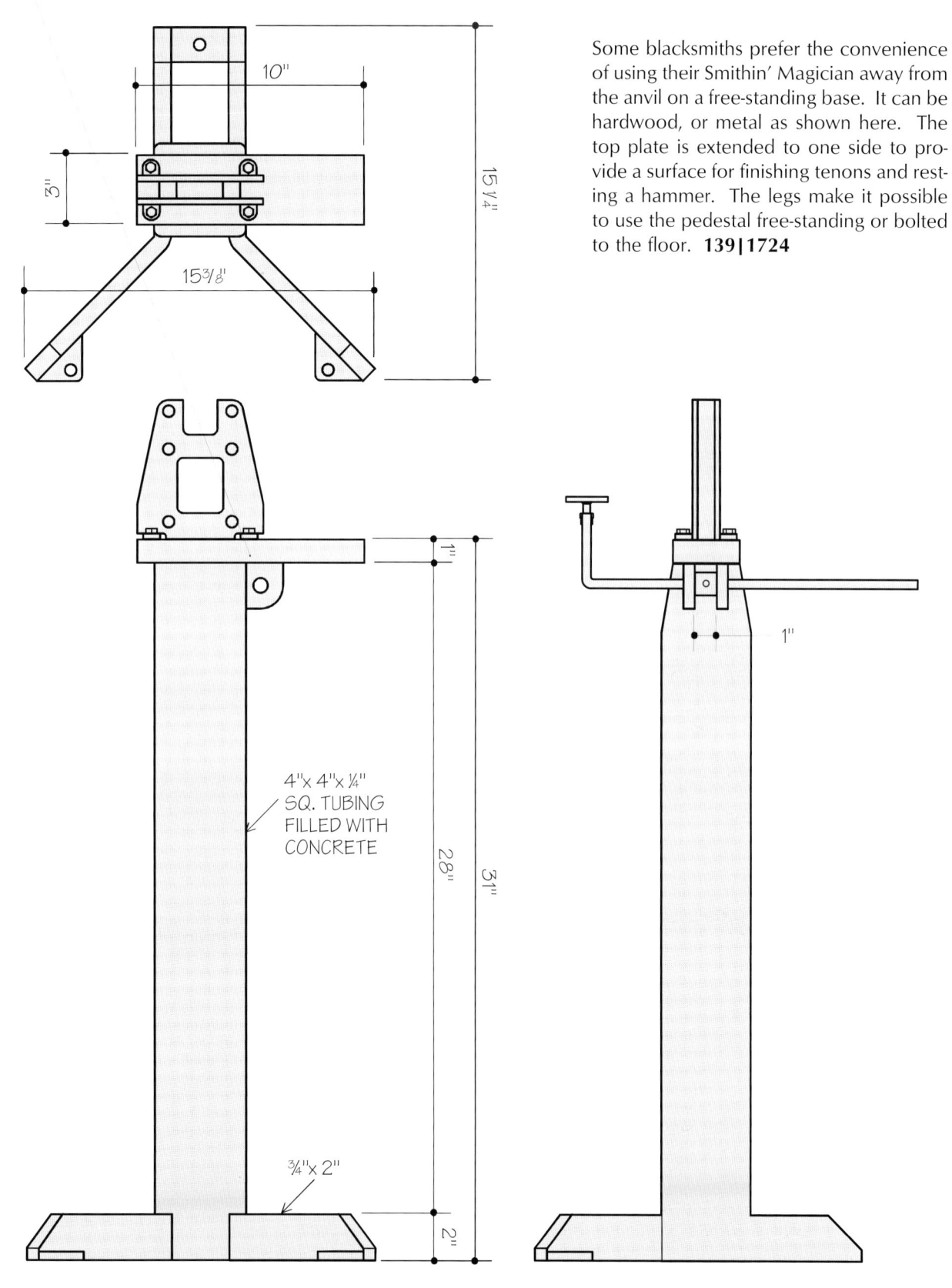

Some blacksmiths prefer the convenience of using their Smithin' Magician away from the anvil on a free-standing base. It can be hardwood, or metal as shown here. The top plate is extended to one side to provide a surface for finishing tenons and resting a hammer. The legs make it possible to use the pedestal free-standing or bolted to the floor. **139|1724**

4"x 4"x ¼" SQ. TUBING FILLED WITH CONCRETE

¾"x 2"

Smithin' Magician Pedestal, cont.

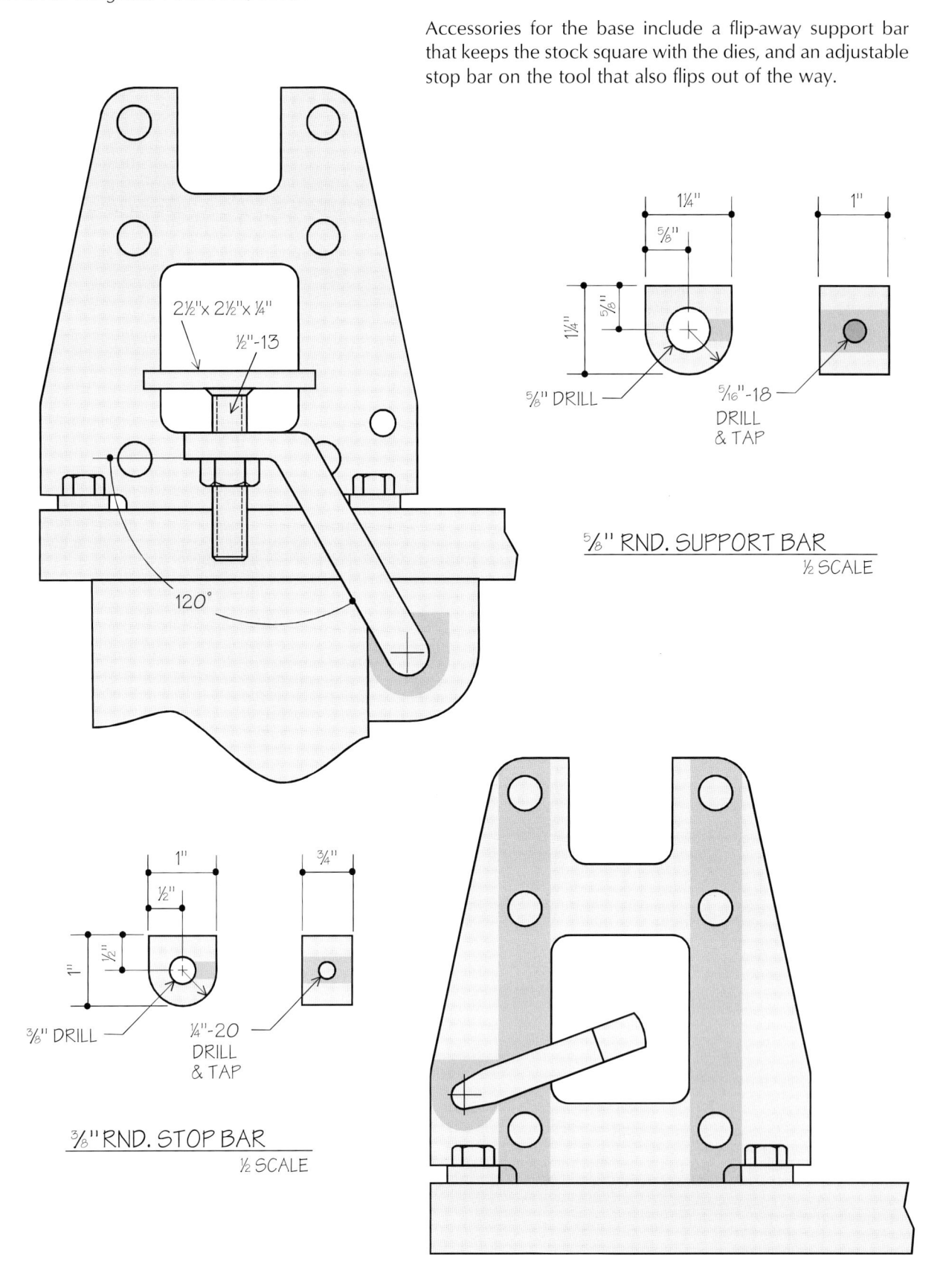

Accessories for the base include a flip-away support bar that keeps the stock square with the dies, and an adjustable stop bar on the tool that also flips out of the way.

2½" x 2½" x ¼"
½"-13
120°

1¼"
⅝"
1¼"
⅝"
⅝" DRILL
1"
⁵⁄₁₆"-18 DRILL & TAP

⅝" RND. SUPPORT BAR
½ SCALE

1"
½"
1"
½"
⅜" DRILL
¾"
¼"-20 DRILL & TAP

⅜" RND. STOP BAR
½ SCALE

32

Spacing Punch -not to scale

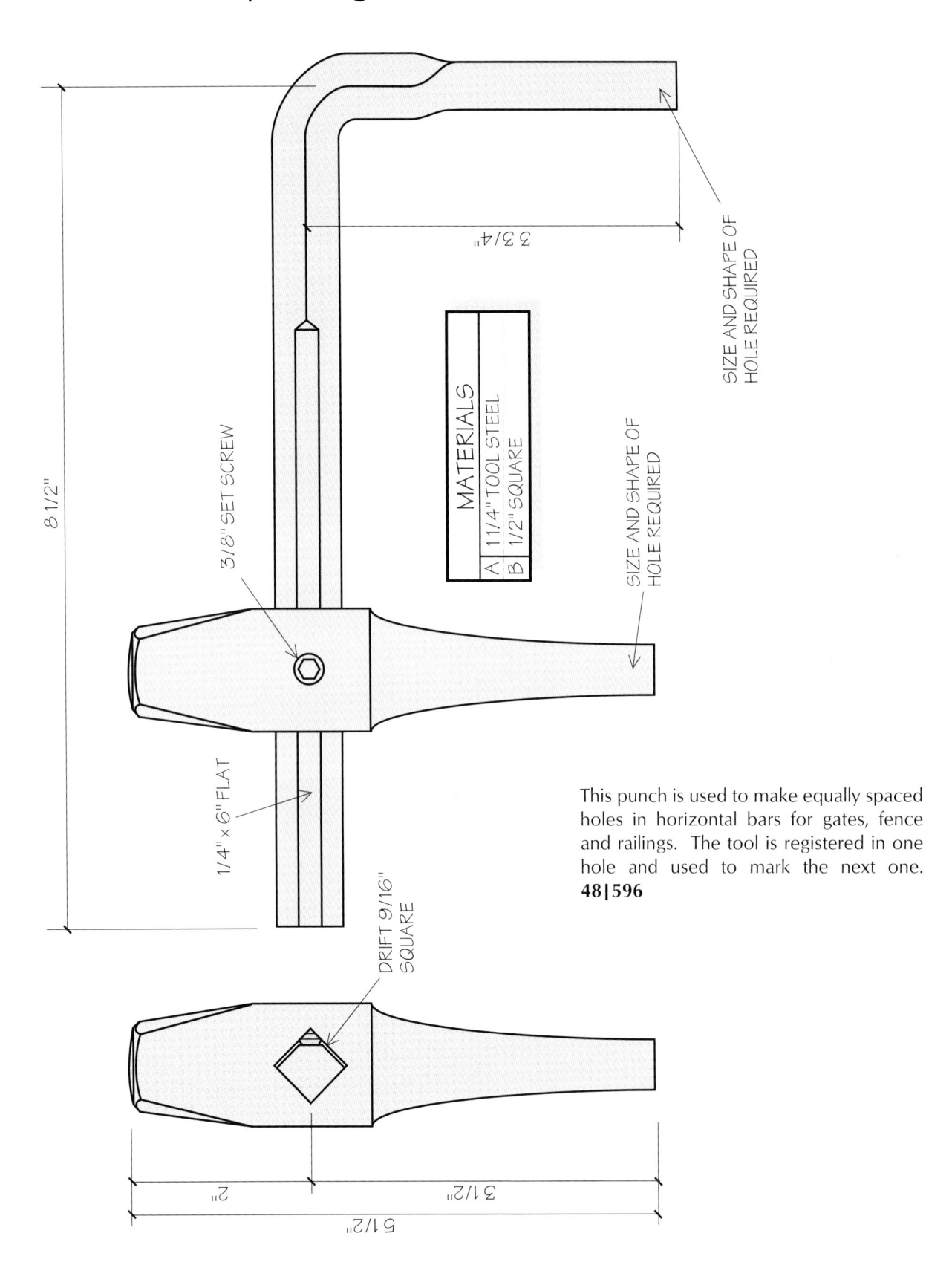

MATERIALS		
A	1 1/4" TOOL STEEL	
B	1/2" SQUARE	

- 3 3/4"
- SIZE AND SHAPE OF HOLE REQUIRED
- 8 1/2"
- 3/8" SET SCREW
- SIZE AND SHAPE OF HOLE REQUIRED
- 1/4" x 6" FLAT
- DRIFT 9/16" SQUARE
- 2"
- 3 1/2"
- 5 1/2"

This punch is used to make equally spaced holes in horizontal bars for gates, fence and railings. The tool is registered in one hole and used to mark the next one.
48|596

Spring Tool -½ scale

This spring tool features interchangeable dies and a hardy stem for use at the anvil or treadle hammer. The dies are each punched with a rectangular hole, and have a set screw for holding them in place. **85|1054**

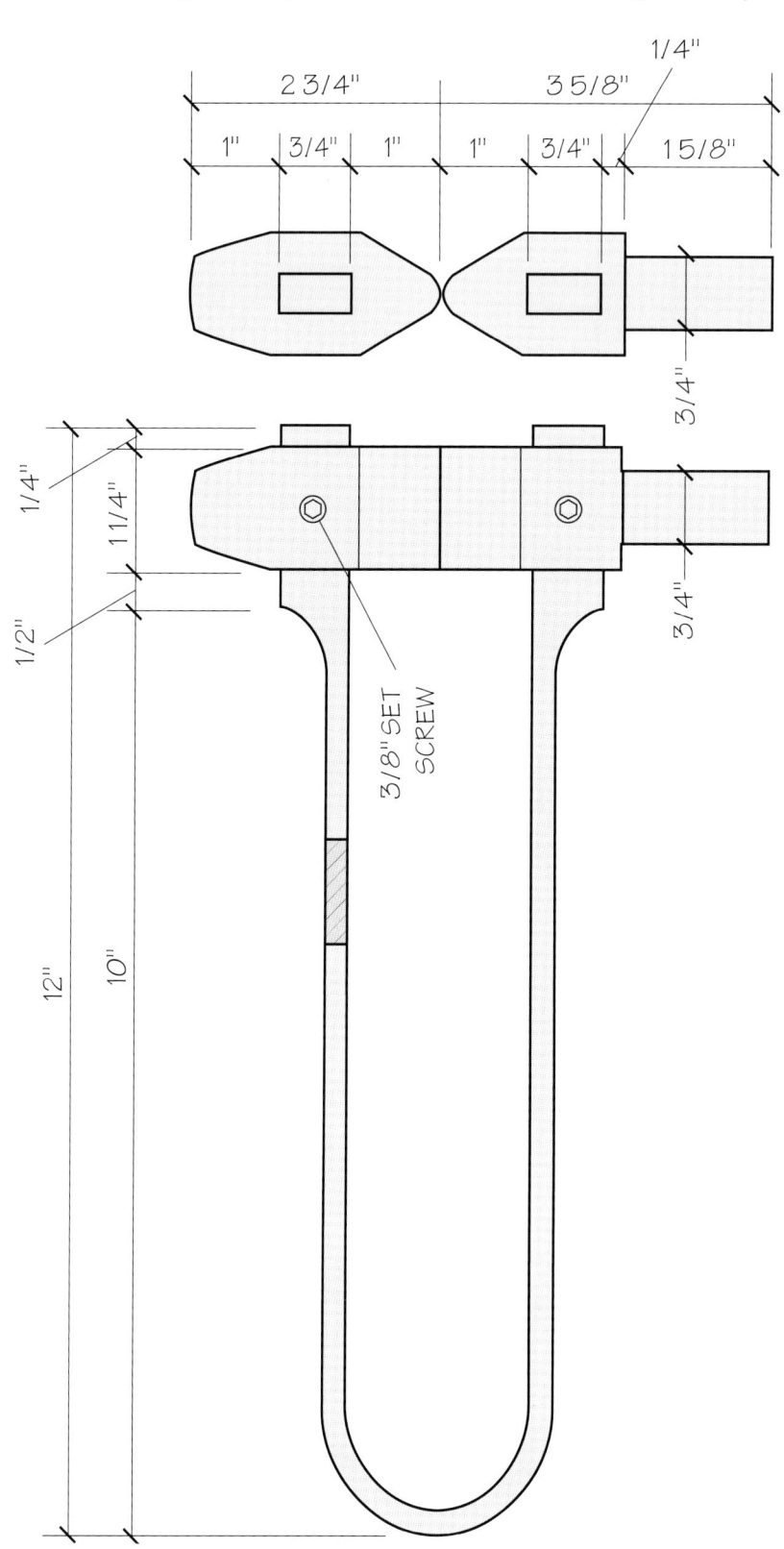

Spring Vise -not to scale

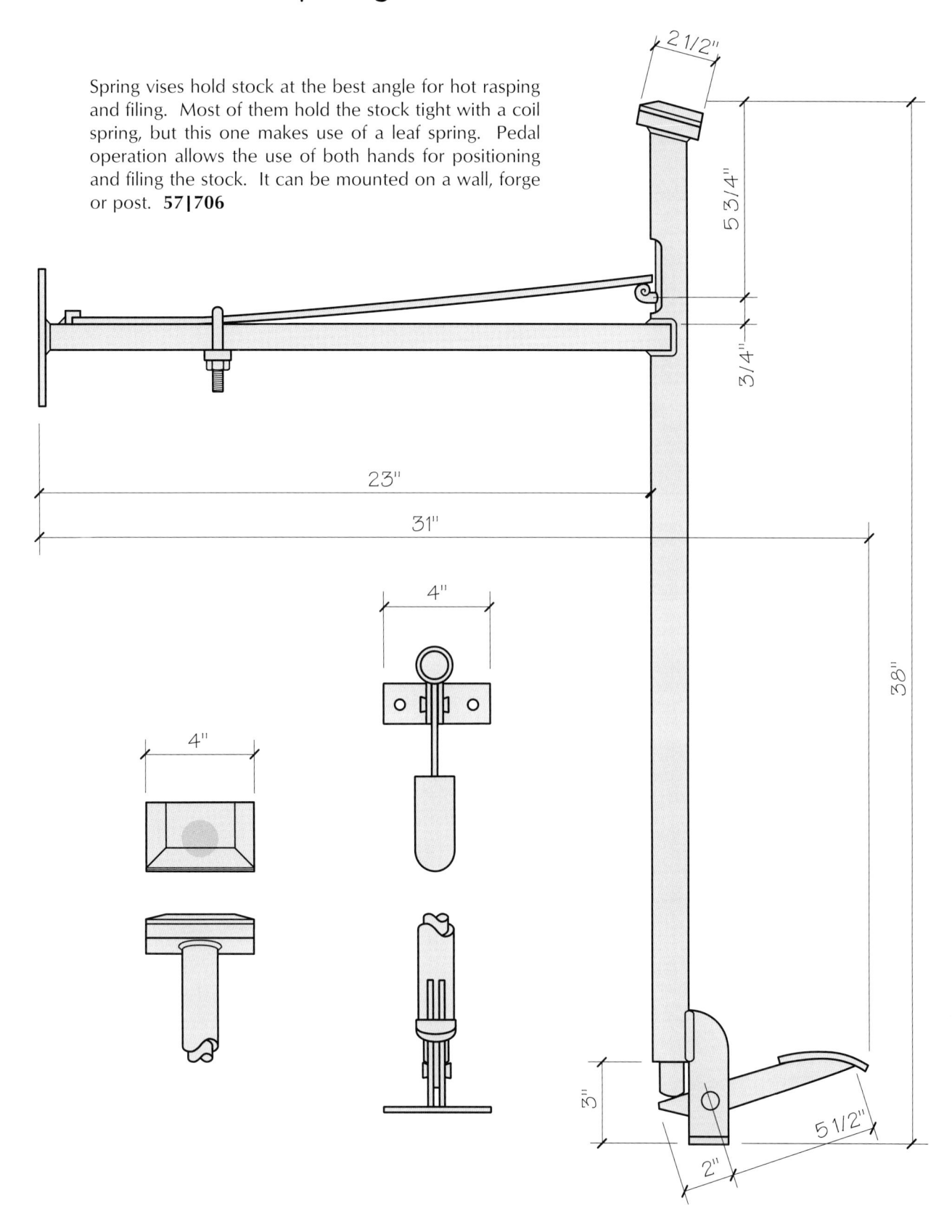

Spring vises hold stock at the best angle for hot rasping and filing. Most of them hold the stock tight with a coil spring, but this one makes use of a leaf spring. Pedal operation allows the use of both hands for positioning and filing the stock. It can be mounted on a wall, forge or post. **57|706**

Square Corner Swage -full scale

When working on the diamond, it is not possible to strike the edge of the stock with a hammer without damaging it. This spring swage permits backing up ½" square stock on the diamond so a top swage can be used for upsetting a square corner. **147|1833**

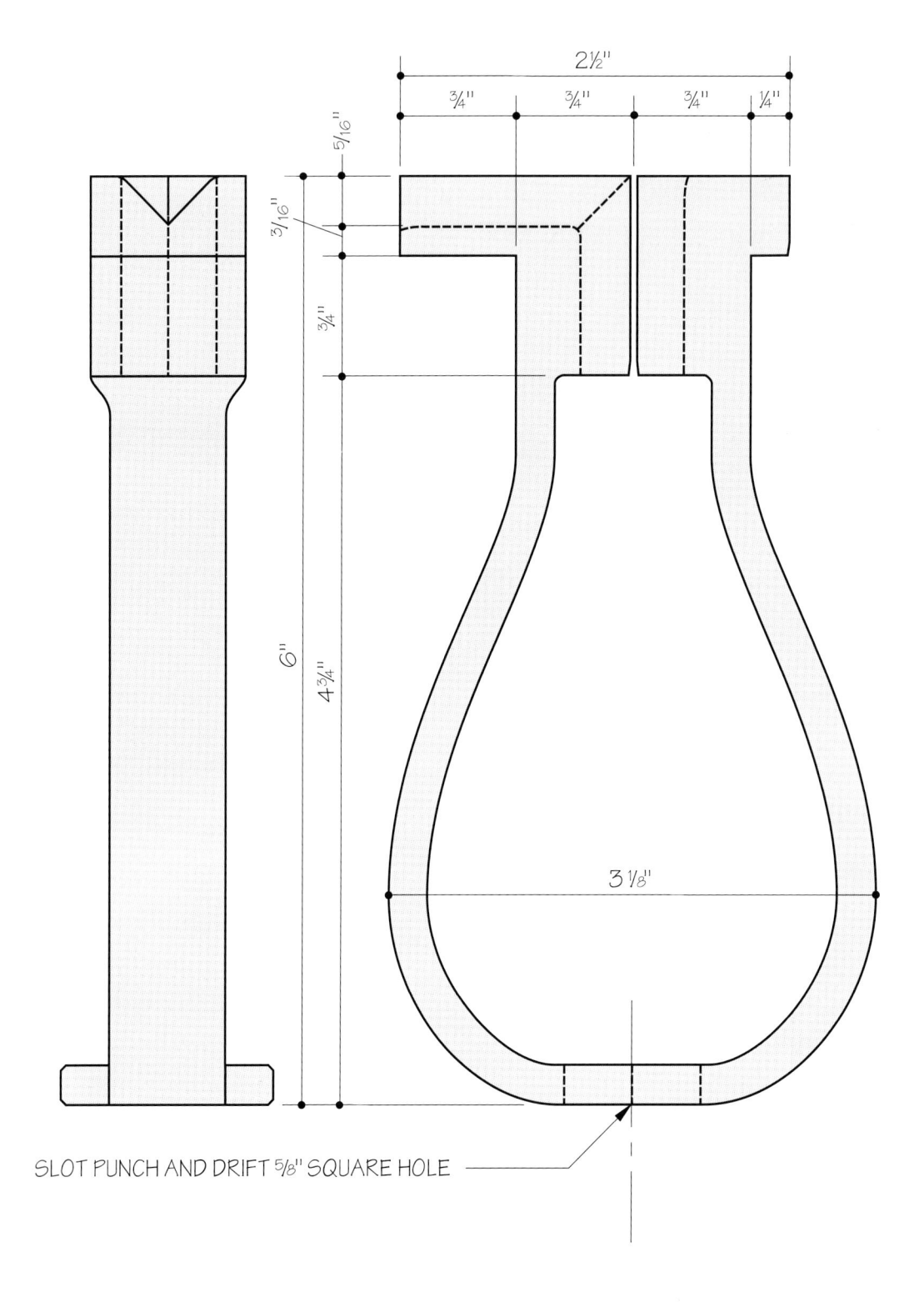

SLOT PUNCH AND DRIFT ⅝" SQUARE HOLE

Traveler -full scale

A traveler is used for measuring lengths and is particularly handy for measuring odd shapes and curves. This one is made to measure feet and inches. The circumference of the wheel is 12". **112|1375**

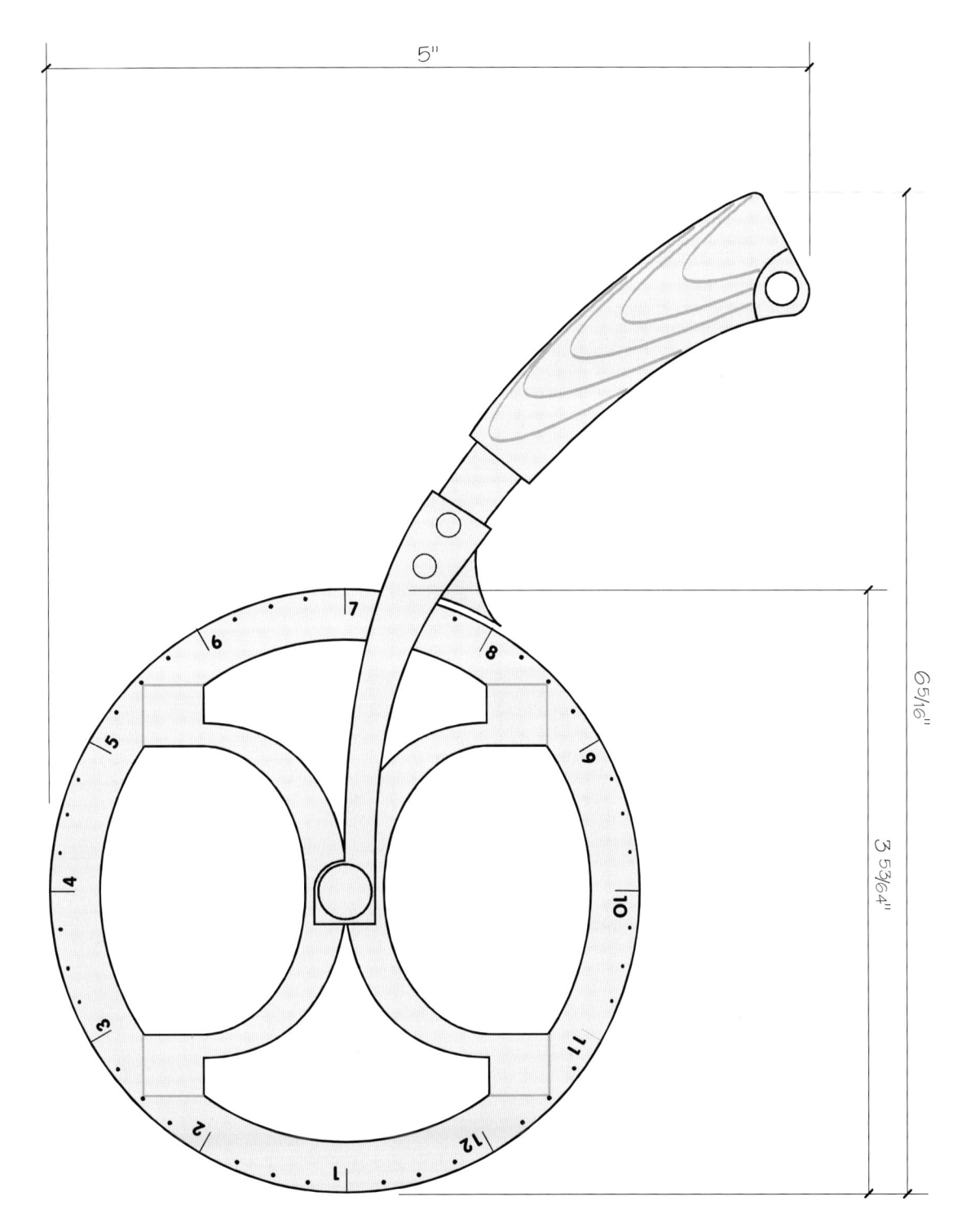

37

Treadle Hammer –not to scale

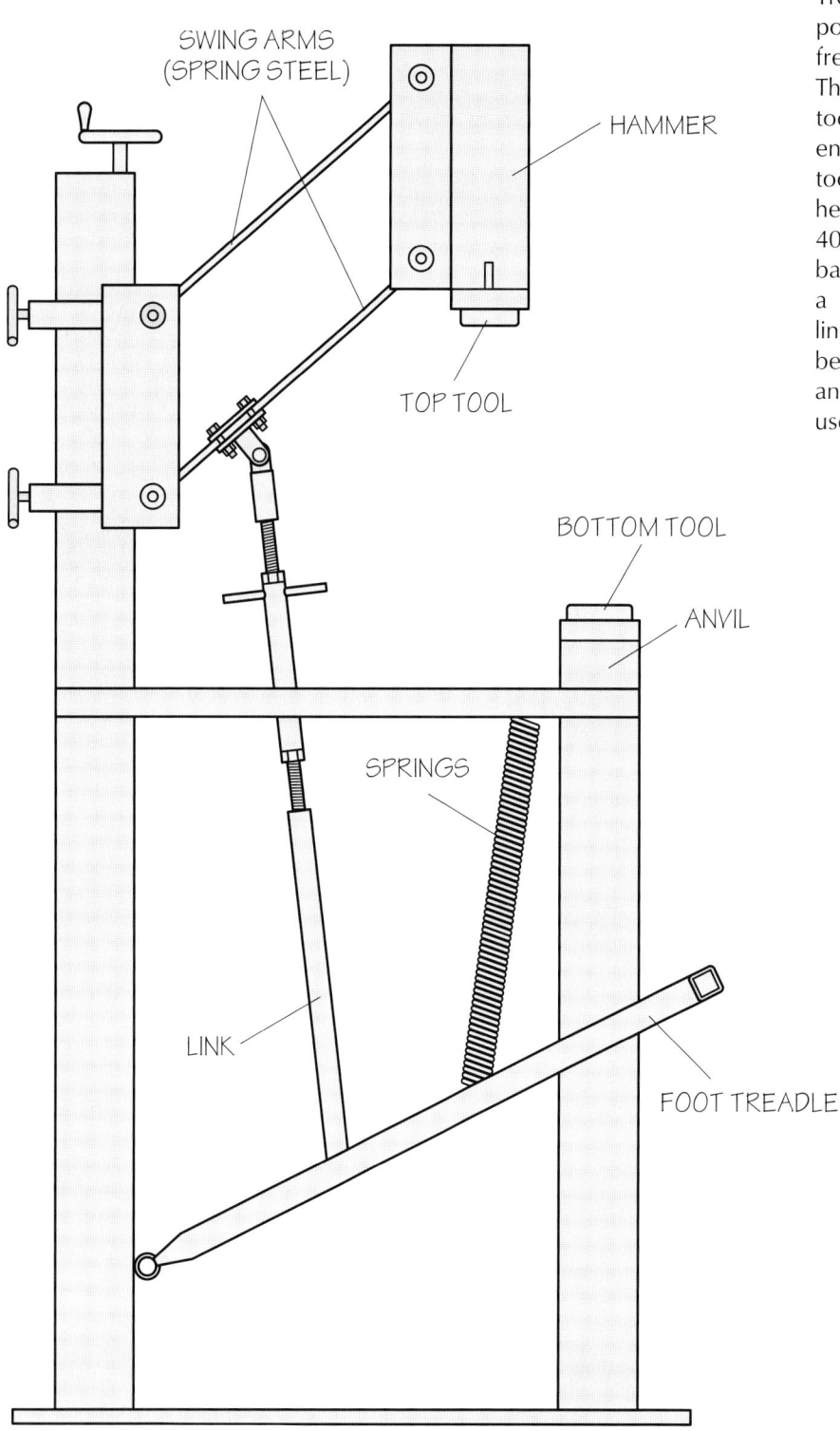

Treadle hammers permit more power, greater accuracy and the freedom to use both hands. They are the ideal "in between" tool when hammer and anvil isn't enough and a power hammer is too much for the job. Hammer heads typically weigh between 40 and 60 lbs. and are counterbalanced by springs that activate a foot treadle and connecting link. Top and bottom tools can be mounted to the hammer and anvil, hand tools can also be used. **59|729**

Sliding the swing arm/hammer assembly up or down adjusts a treadle hammer for different size stock or tools. The swing arm adjuster, shown here in section, accomplishes this with an acme screw. Tightening screws on the back of the assembly hold it in place after being adjusted.

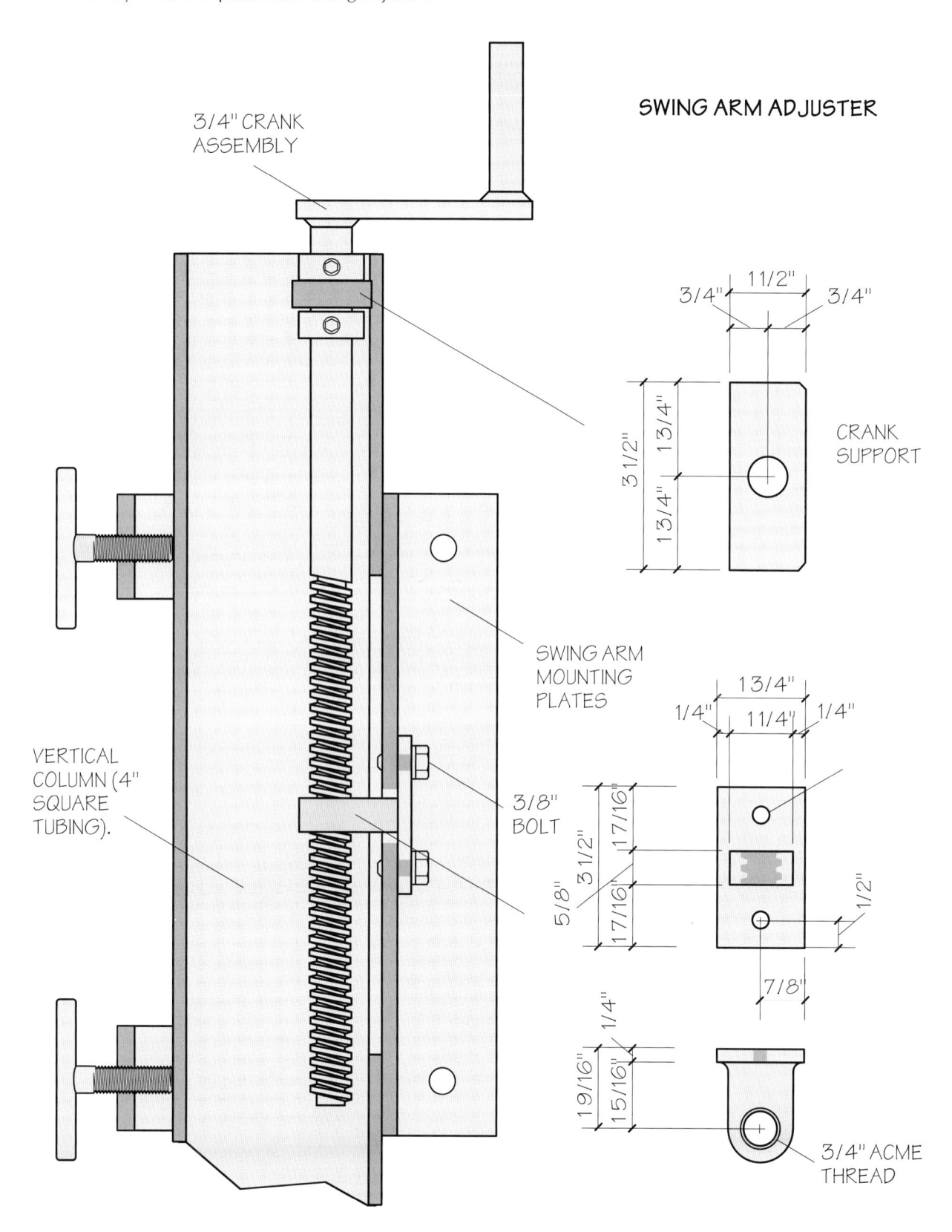

SWING ARM ADJUSTER

- 3/4" CRANK ASSEMBLY
- CRANK SUPPORT
- SWING ARM MOUNTING PLATES
- 3/8" BOLT
- VERTICAL COLUMN (4" SQUARE TUBING).
- 3/4" ACME THREAD

39

Twisting Machine – 3/8 scale

Using this fixed base manually operated twister helps keep stock straight while it is being twisted. It consists of a bed (typically 3' -6' long), sliding tail stock and fixed head stock with interchangeable bar size heads made from pipe cap. **47|583**

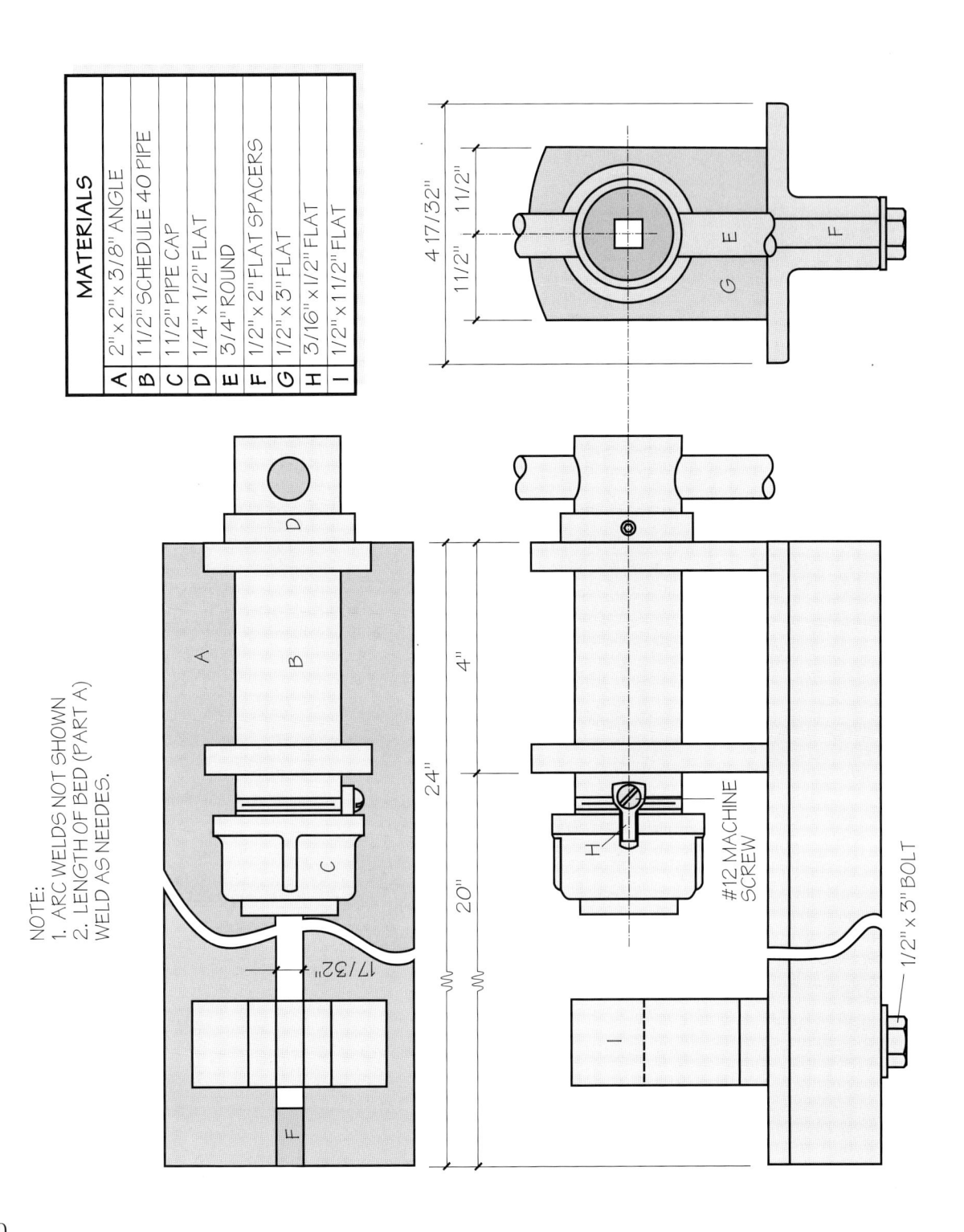

	MATERIALS
A	2" x 2" x 3/8" ANGLE
B	1 1/2" SCHEDULE 40 PIPE
C	1 1/2" PIPE CAP
D	1/4" x 1/2" FLAT
E	3/4" ROUND
F	1/2" x 2" FLAT SPACERS
G	1/2" x 3" FLAT
H	3/16" x 1/2" FLAT
I	1/2" x 1 1/2" FLAT

NOTE:
1. ARC WELDS NOT SHOWN
2. LENGTH OF BED (PART A) WELD AS NEEDED.

#12 MACHINE SCREW

1/2" x 3" BOLT

40

Work Table Vise -not to scale

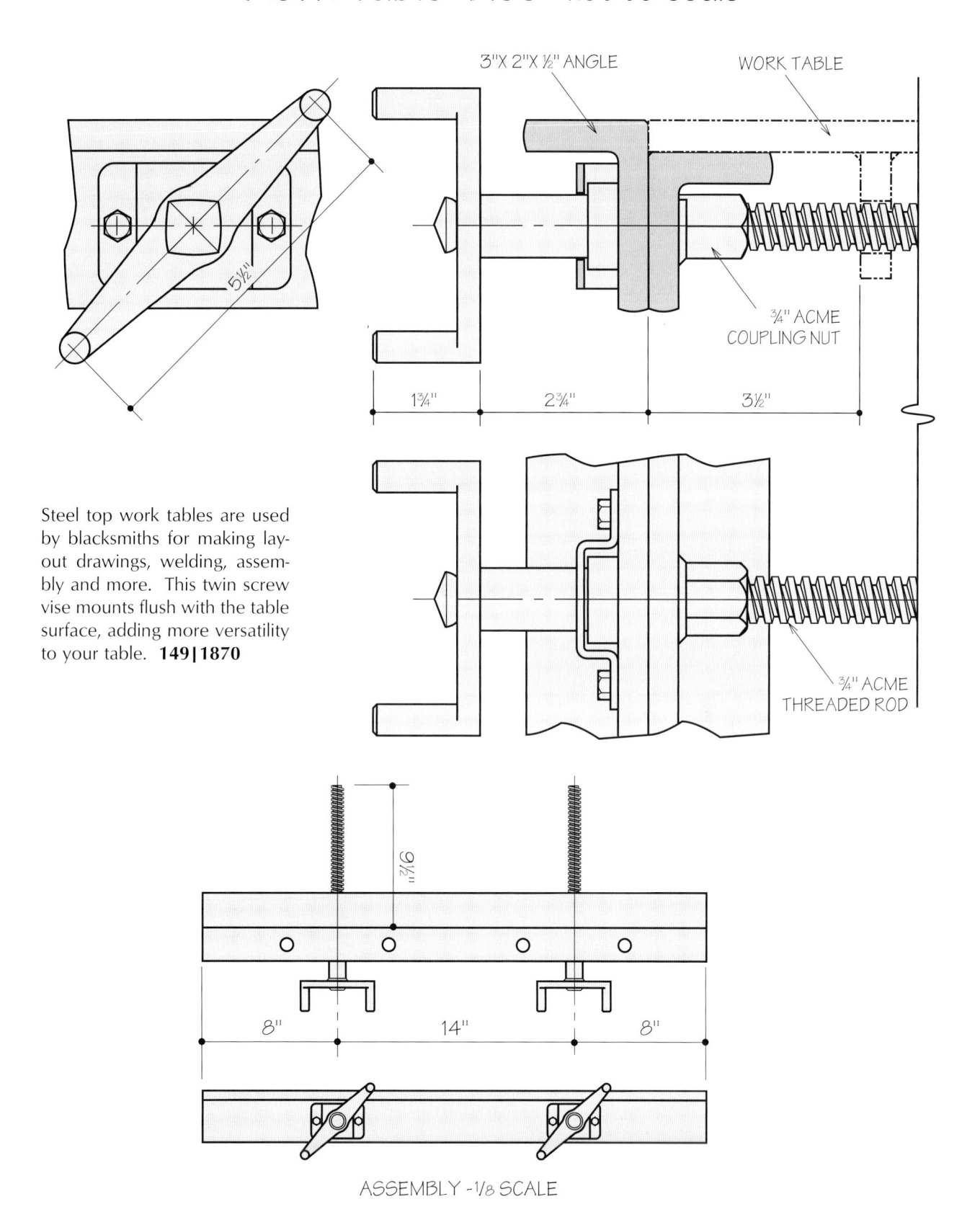

3"X 2"X ½" ANGLE

WORK TABLE

5½"

¾" ACME COUPLING NUT

1¾"   2¾"   3½"

Steel top work tables are used by blacksmiths for making layout drawings, welding, assembly and more. This twin screw vise mounts flush with the table surface, adding more versatility to your table. **149|1870**

¾" ACME THREADED ROD

9½"

8"   14"   8"

ASSEMBLY -1/8 SCALE

41

2 Other Tools & Equipment

Bar Clamp -½ scale

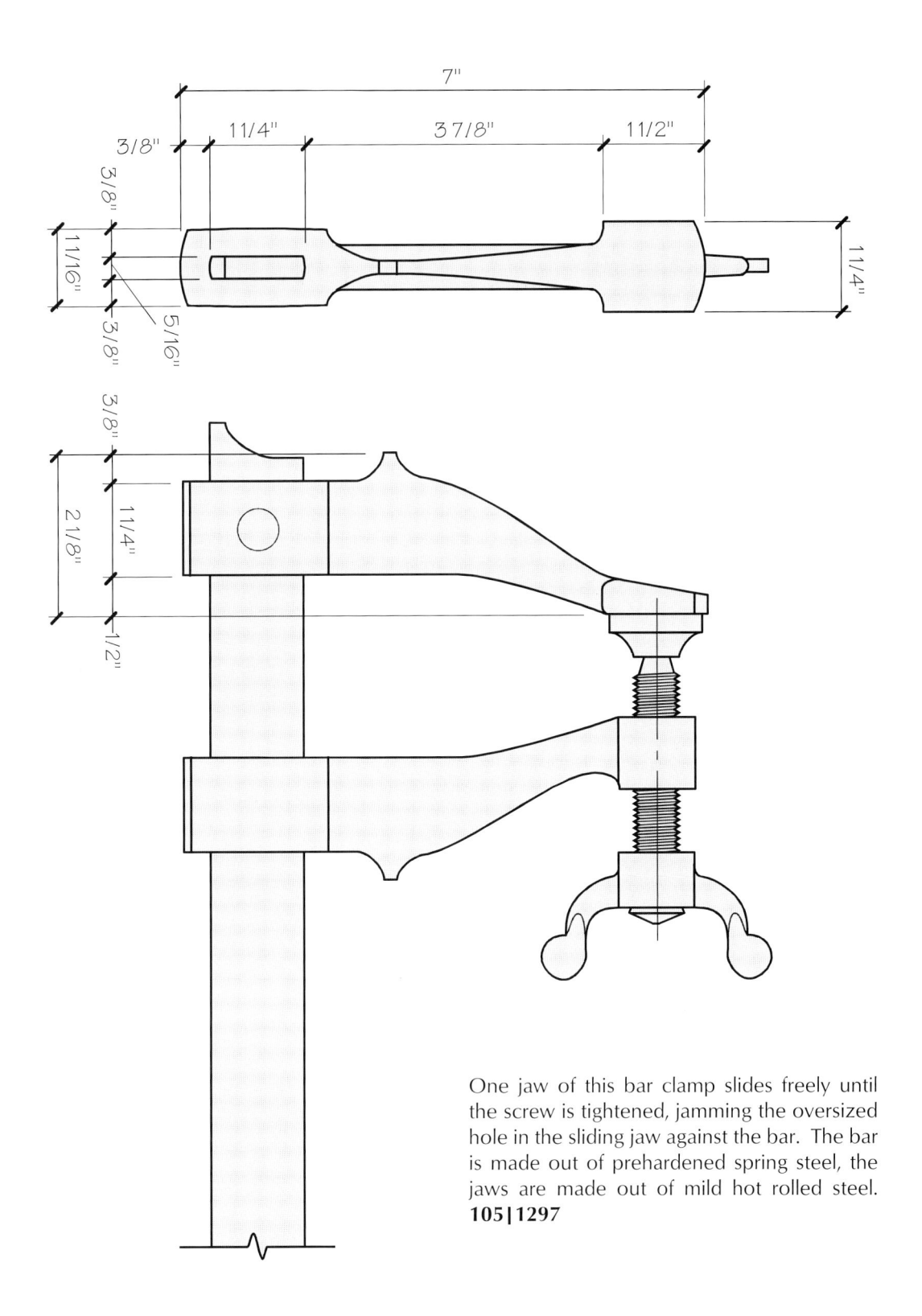

One jaw of this bar clamp slides freely until the screw is tightened, jamming the oversized hole in the sliding jaw against the bar. The bar is made out of prehardened spring steel, the jaws are made out of mild hot rolled steel.
105|1297

Double Calipers -full scale

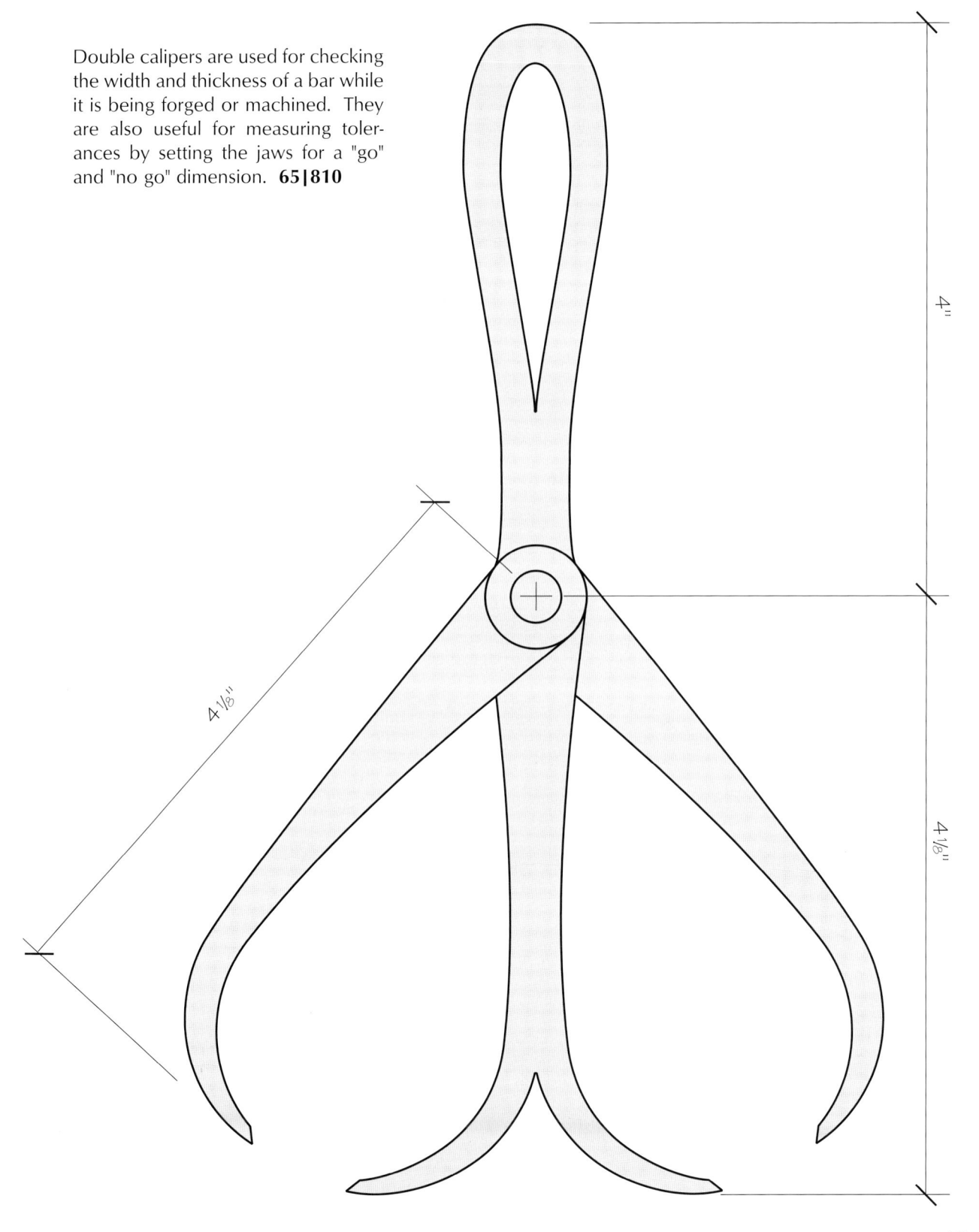

Double calipers are used for checking the width and thickness of a bar while it is being forged or machined. They are also useful for measuring tolerances by setting the jaws for a "go" and "no go" dimension. **65|810**

45

Drill Press Stand – ⅛ scale

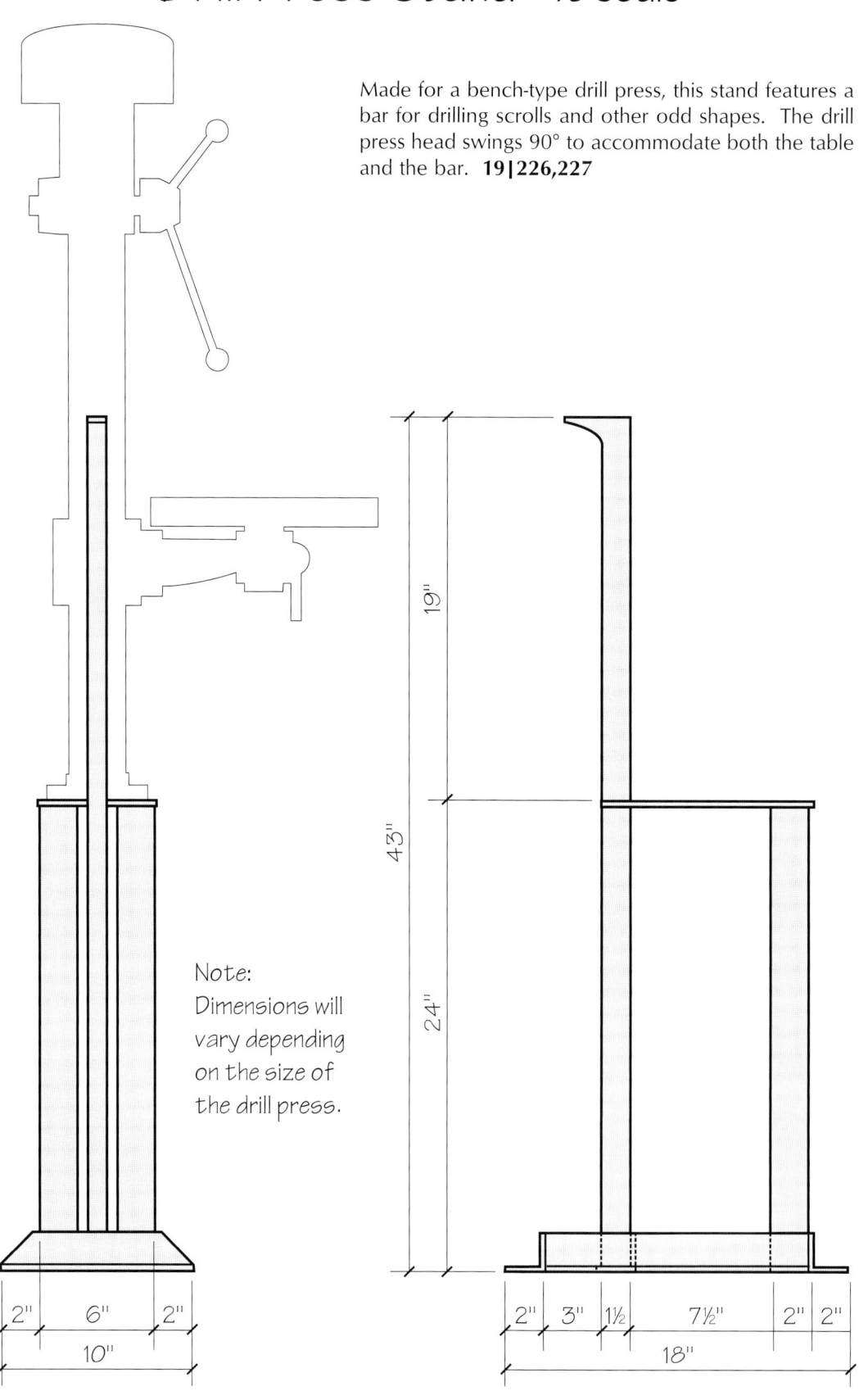

Made for a bench-type drill press, this stand features a bar for drilling scrolls and other odd shapes. The drill press head swings 90° to accommodate both the table and the bar. **19|226,227**

Note: Dimensions will vary depending on the size of the drill press.

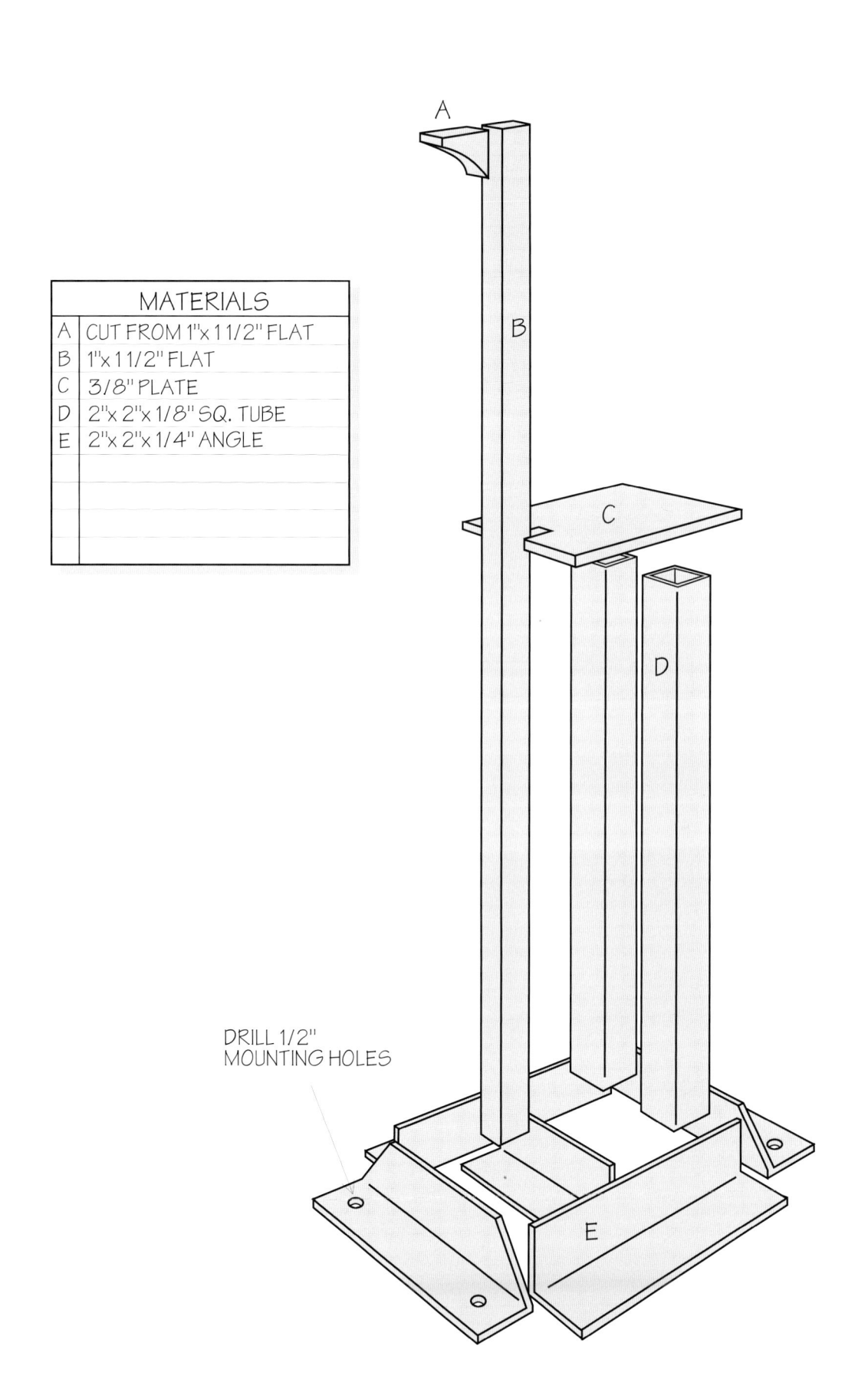

	MATERIALS
A	CUT FROM 1" x 1 1/2" FLAT
B	1" x 1 1/2" FLAT
C	3/8" PLATE
D	2" x 2" x 1/8" SQ. TUBE
E	2" x 2" x 1/4" ANGLE

DRILL 1/2" MOUNTING HOLES

Garden Fork -½ scale

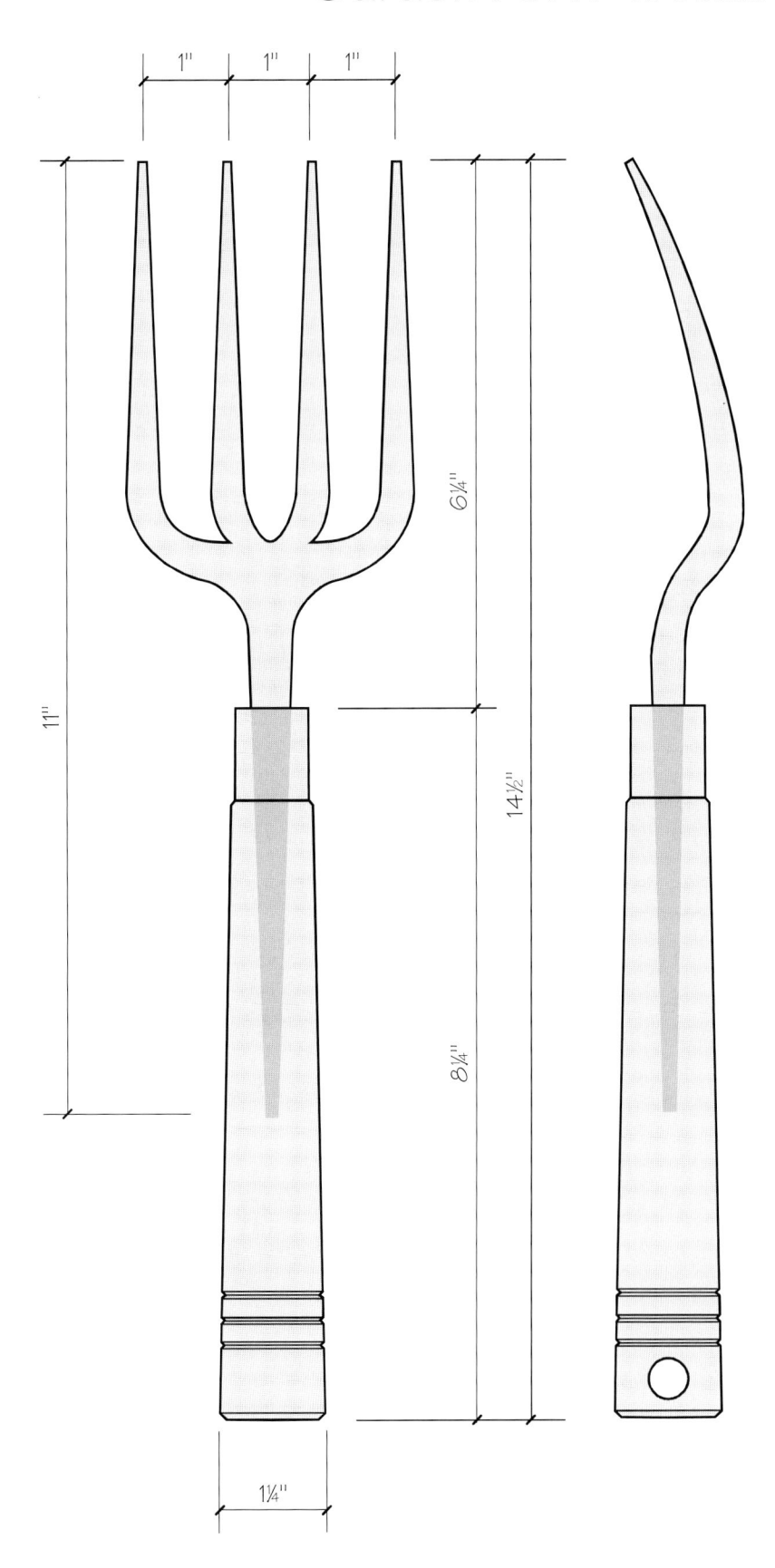

Old automotive leaf springs are useful for making tools that require toughness and wear resistance. In this case, a piece of $3/8"$ x $1 1/2"$ truck spring is used for making a garden tool. The tang is fit into the predrilled wooden handle while hot, making a perfect fit. **111|1369**

Grinder Guard -not to scale

The guard here and on page 50 are for a grinder converted to use abrasive cut-off blades. This one is for making cuts straight into the blade, the other is for ripping all the way through the top of the blade. A 1 h.p. or greater grinder is recommended. **33|406**

MATERIALS			
A	1/2"x 1 1/2"x 1/8" CHANNEL	E	3/4" SCH. 40 PIPE
B	1/8" PLATE	F	5/8" ROUND
C	1/2"x 1"x 1/8" CHANNEL	G	3/16" FLAT OR PLATE
D	1/4"x 5/8" FLAT	H	18 GA. SHEET

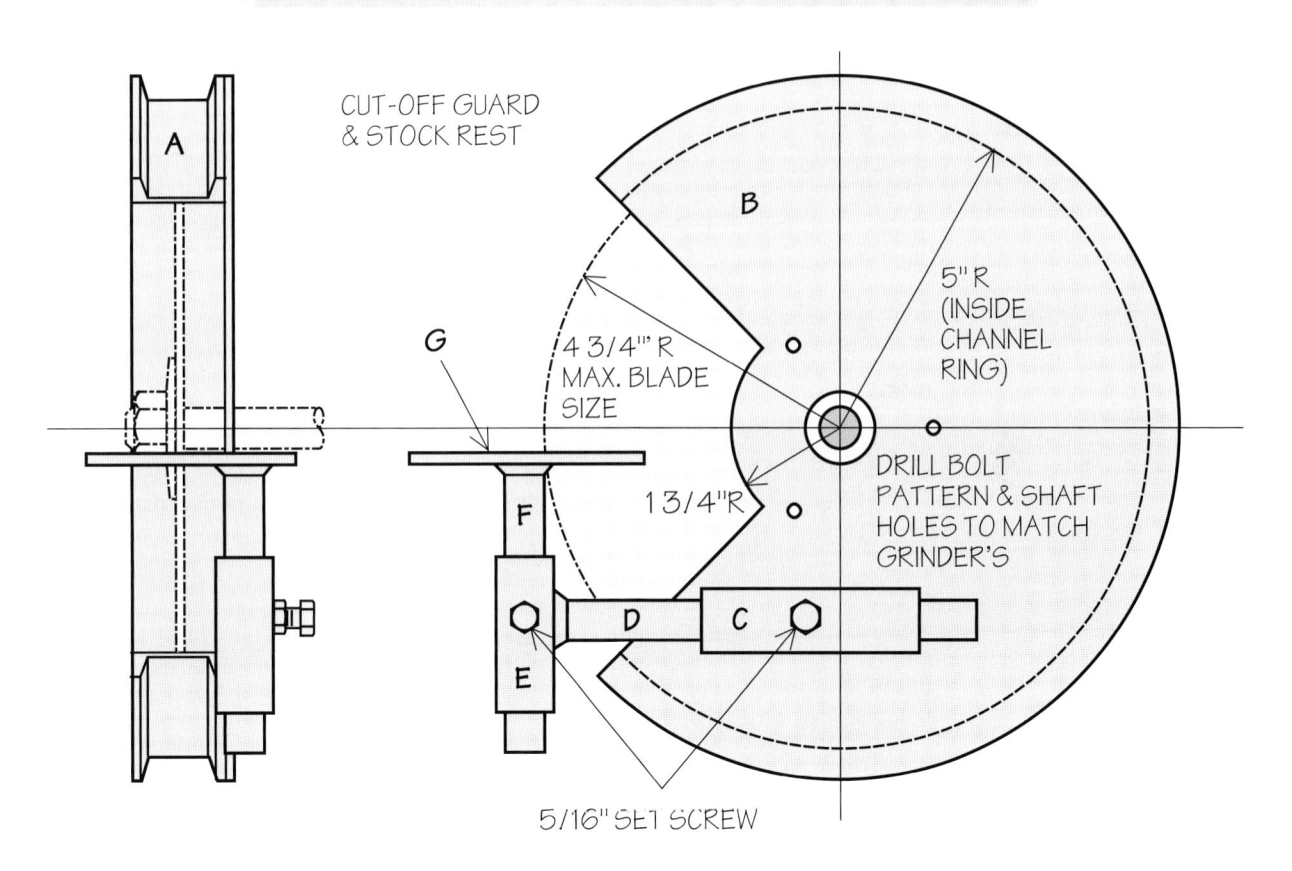

CUT-OFF GUARD & STOCK REST

5" R (INSIDE CHANNEL RING)

4 3/4" R MAX. BLADE SIZE

1 3/4" R

DRILL BOLT PATTERN & SHAFT HOLES TO MATCH GRINDER'S

5/16" SET SCREW

Grinder Guard, cont.

RIP GUARD & TABLE

DRILL & TAP FOR A 1/4-20 C.S. SCREW

4"
1 1/2"
2 1/2"
G
7 3/4"
11 1/2"

WELD GUARD TO TABLE
H
1 3/8"R
5 1/2"R
45°

GUARD

DRILL FOR #10 SCREW

1"
11 1/2"
1" 9 1/2" 1"

B
DRILL BOLT PATTERN & SHAFT HOLES TO MATCH GRINDER'S
22°
1 3/4"R
5 1/2"R
45°

MOUNTING PLATE

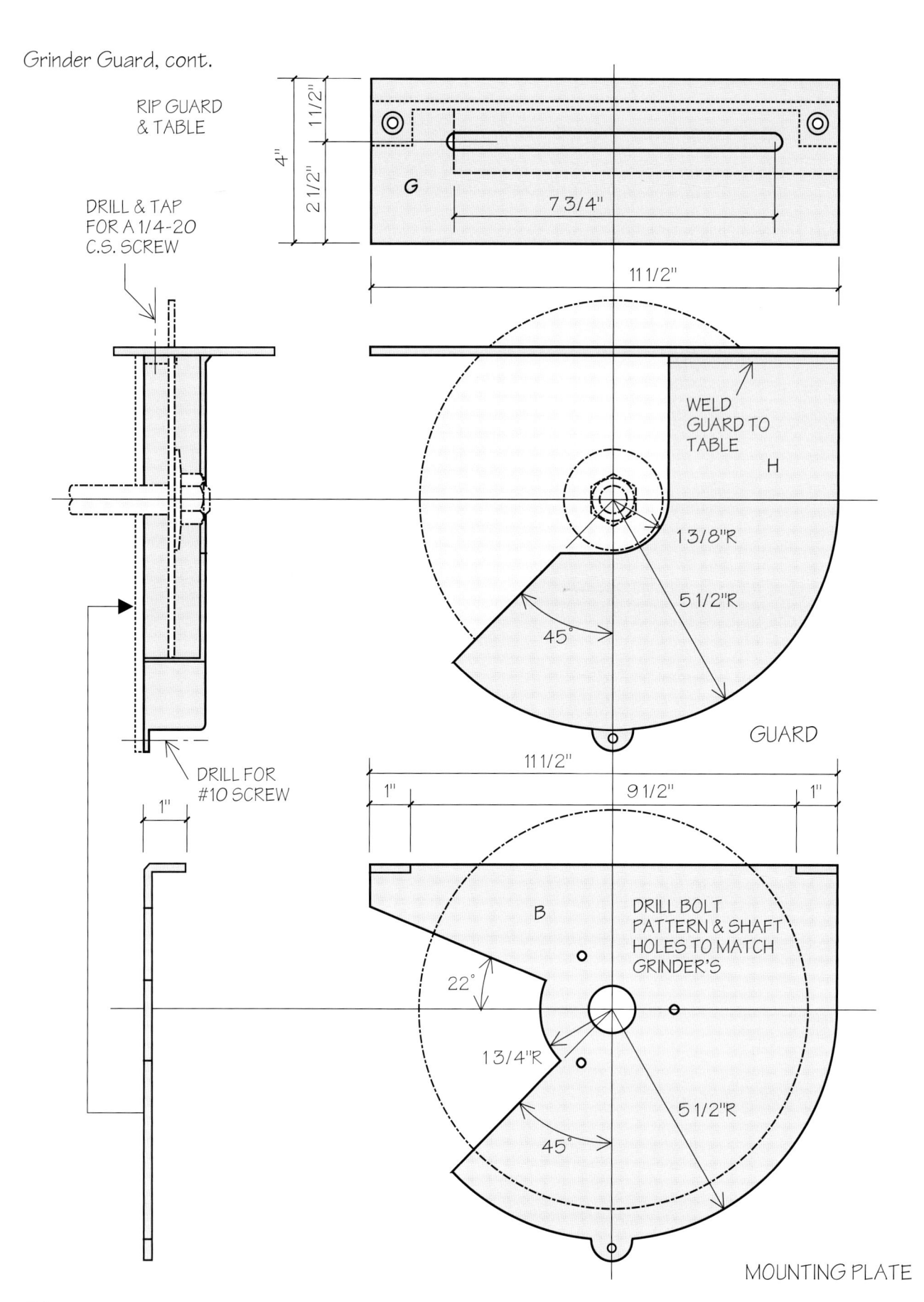

50

Hack Saw #1 -½ scale

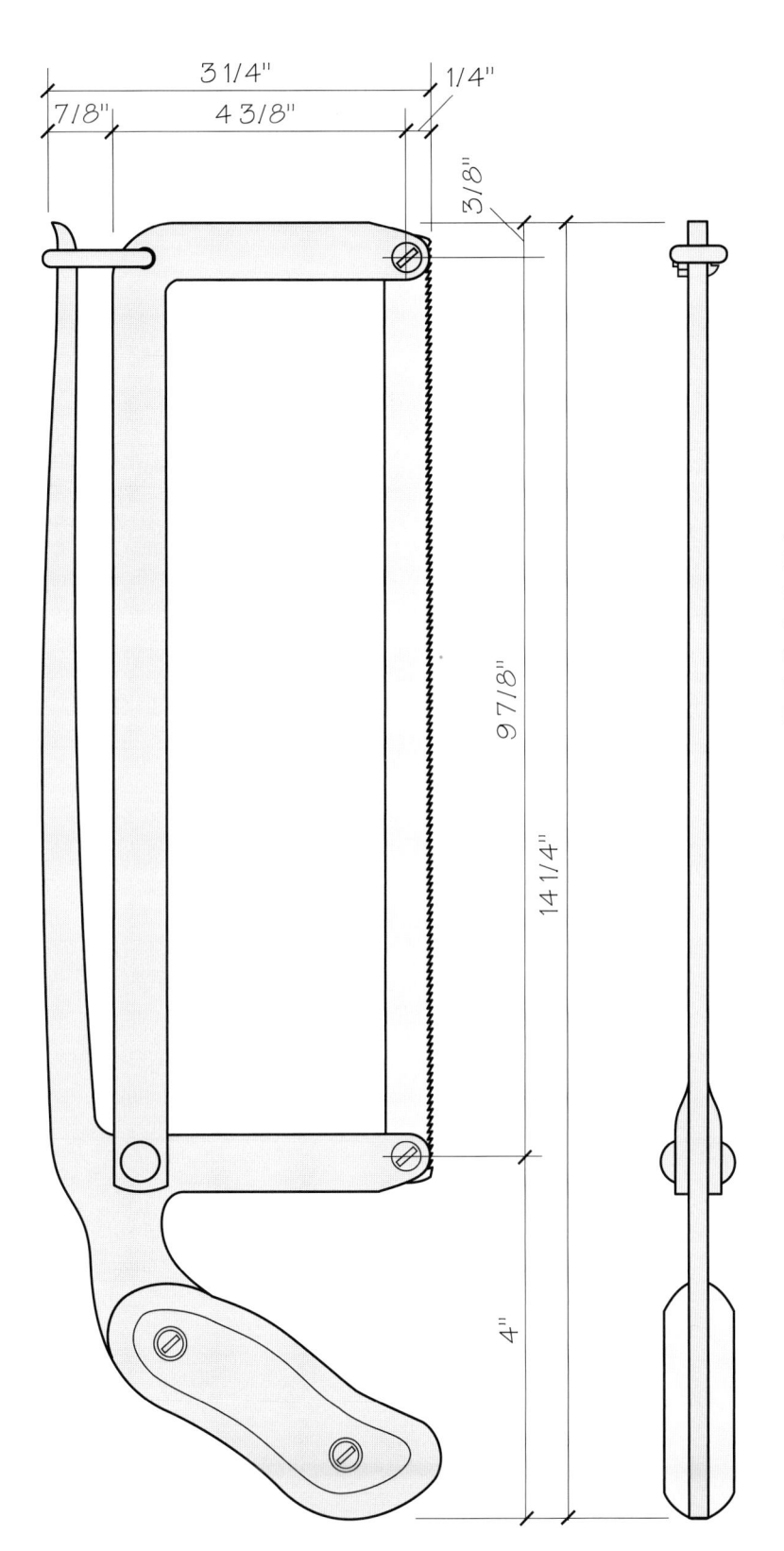

Most commercially available hack saws feature sloppy screw-type blade tighteners and flimsy construction. This saw has a spring loaded frame that keeps the blade tight and rigid for accurate cutting. **73|907**

Hack Saw #2 -½ scale

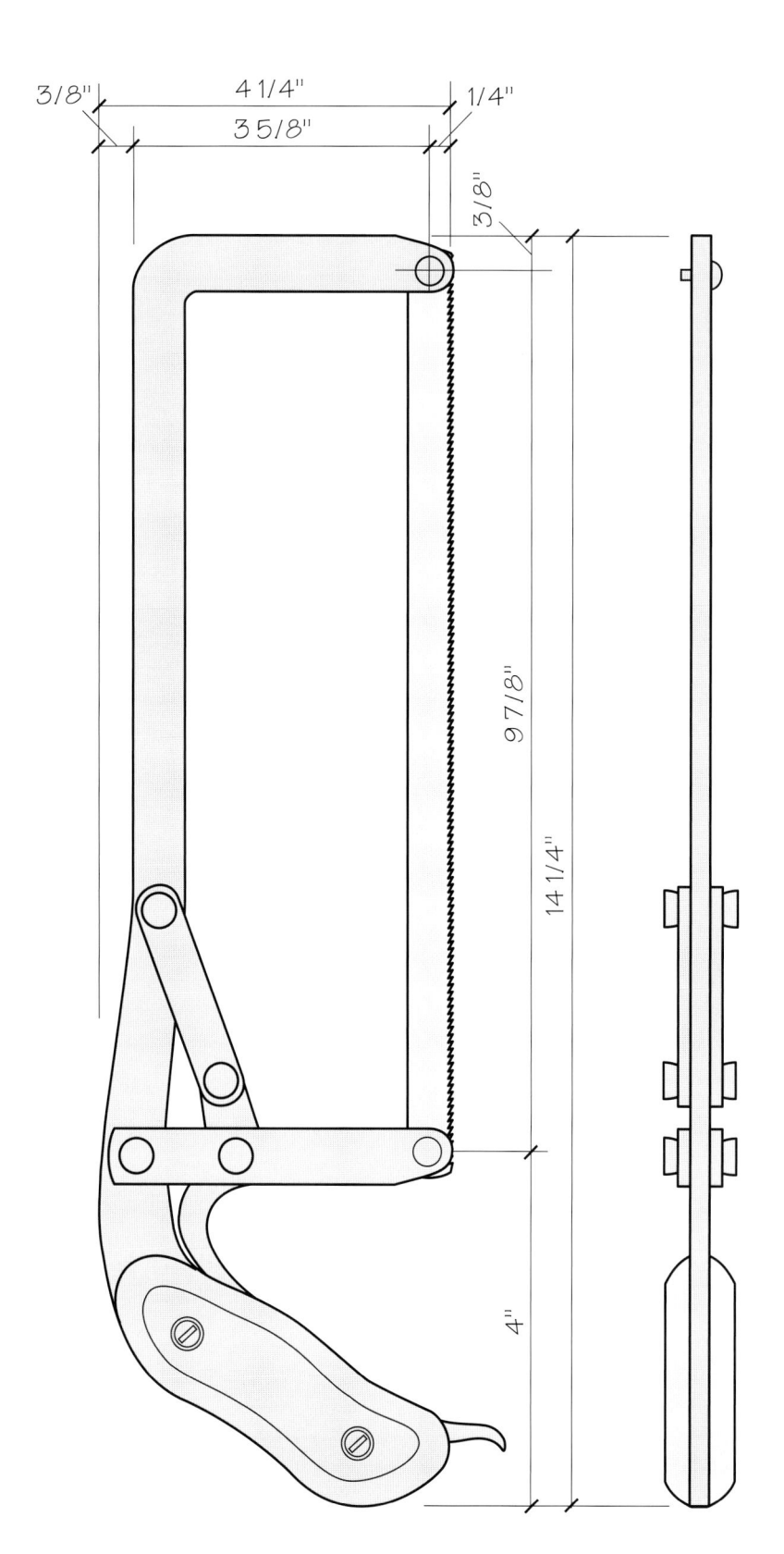

The central feature of this saw is the "vise grip" mechanism featuring a locking lever that fits within the handle when in the locked position. Like the saw on the previous page, a rigid frame combined with strong blade tensioning make for more accurate cuts.
74|911

Hand Wheel -full scale

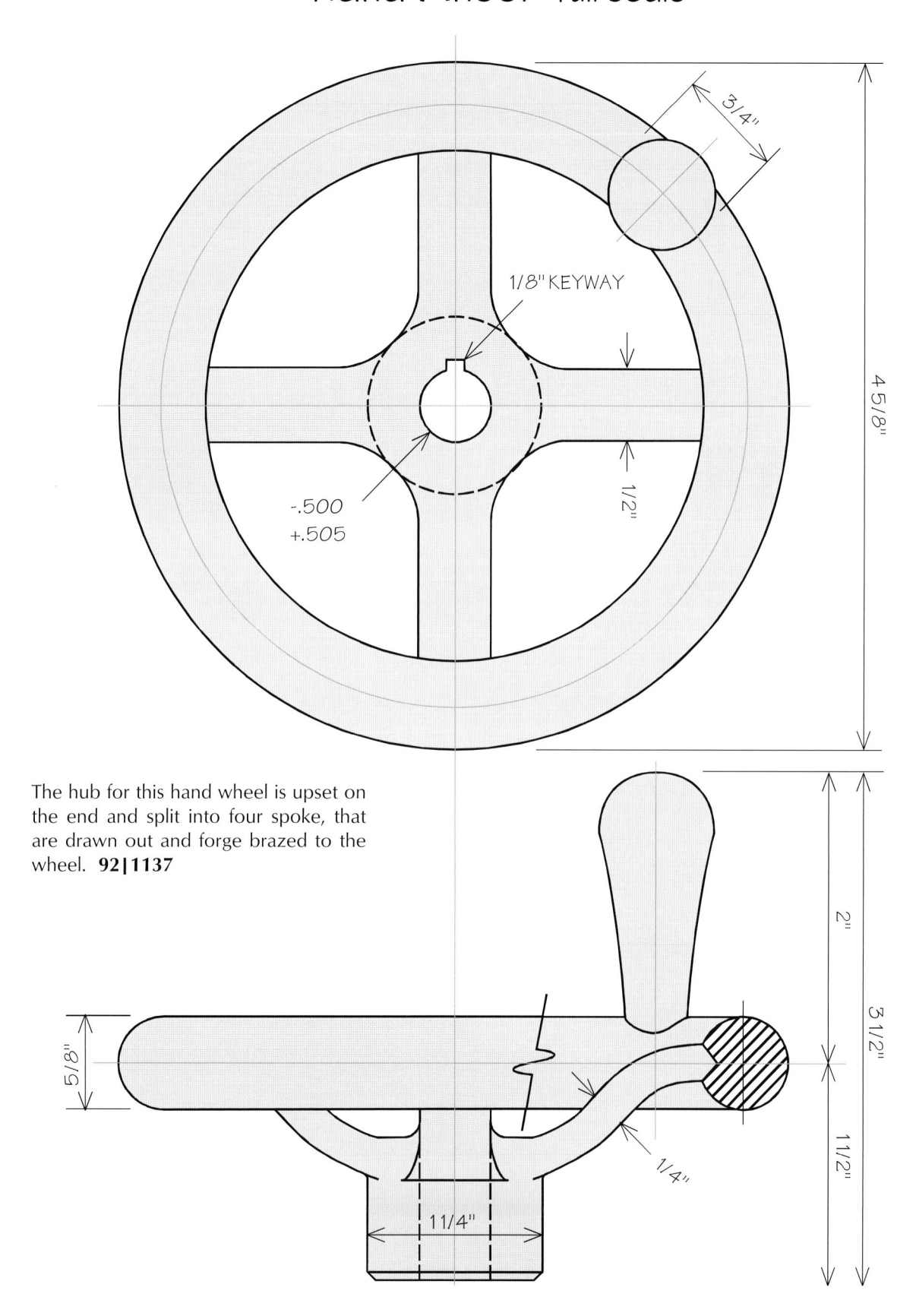

The hub for this hand wheel is upset on the end and split into four spoke, that are drawn out and forge brazed to the wheel. **92|1137**

Dimensions:
- 3/4"
- 1/8" KEYWAY
- -.500 / +.505
- 1/2"
- 4 5/8"
- 5/8"
- 2"
- 3 1/2"
- 1 1/2"
- 1/4"
- 1 1/4"

Nail Puller -¾ scale

If you've ever had to dig out a nail that's been hammered flush, you'll appreciate this tool. It is designed to be used in conjunction with a cheater bar for digging out large nails. The handle is made from ¾" octagon W1 tool steel; the jaw is ¼" x 1½" W1. **122|1495**

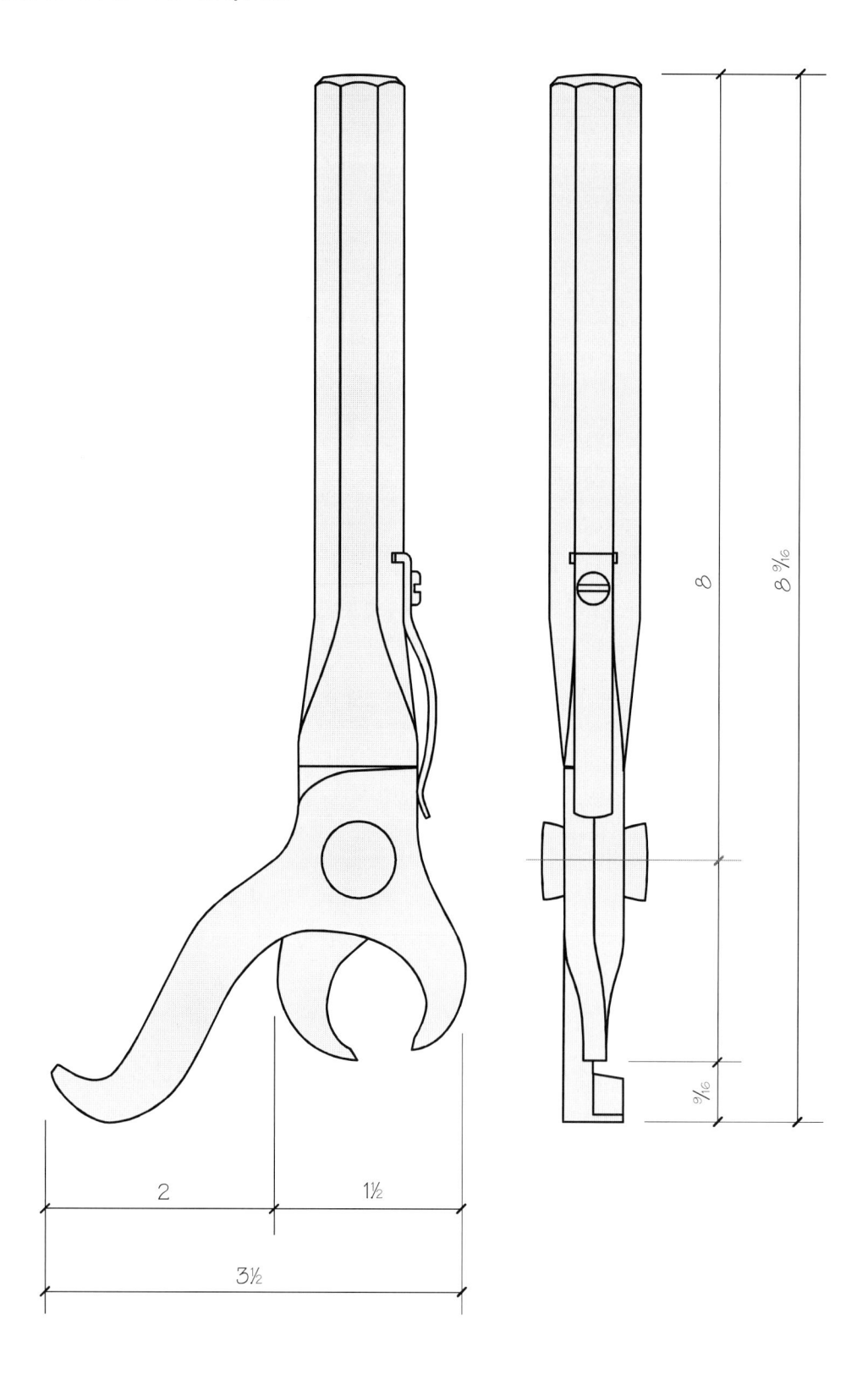

FULL-SIZE PARTS

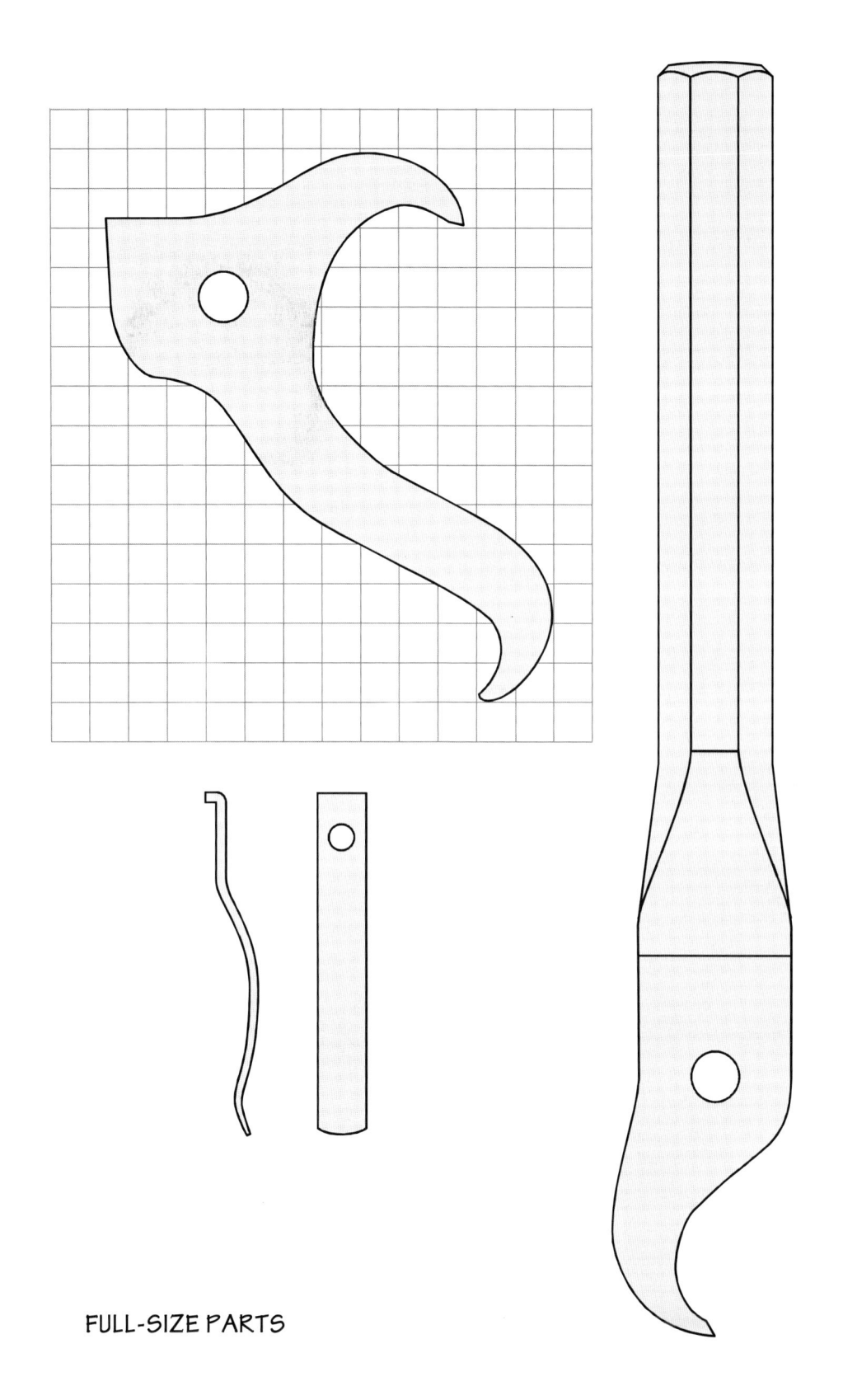

Pliers -full scale

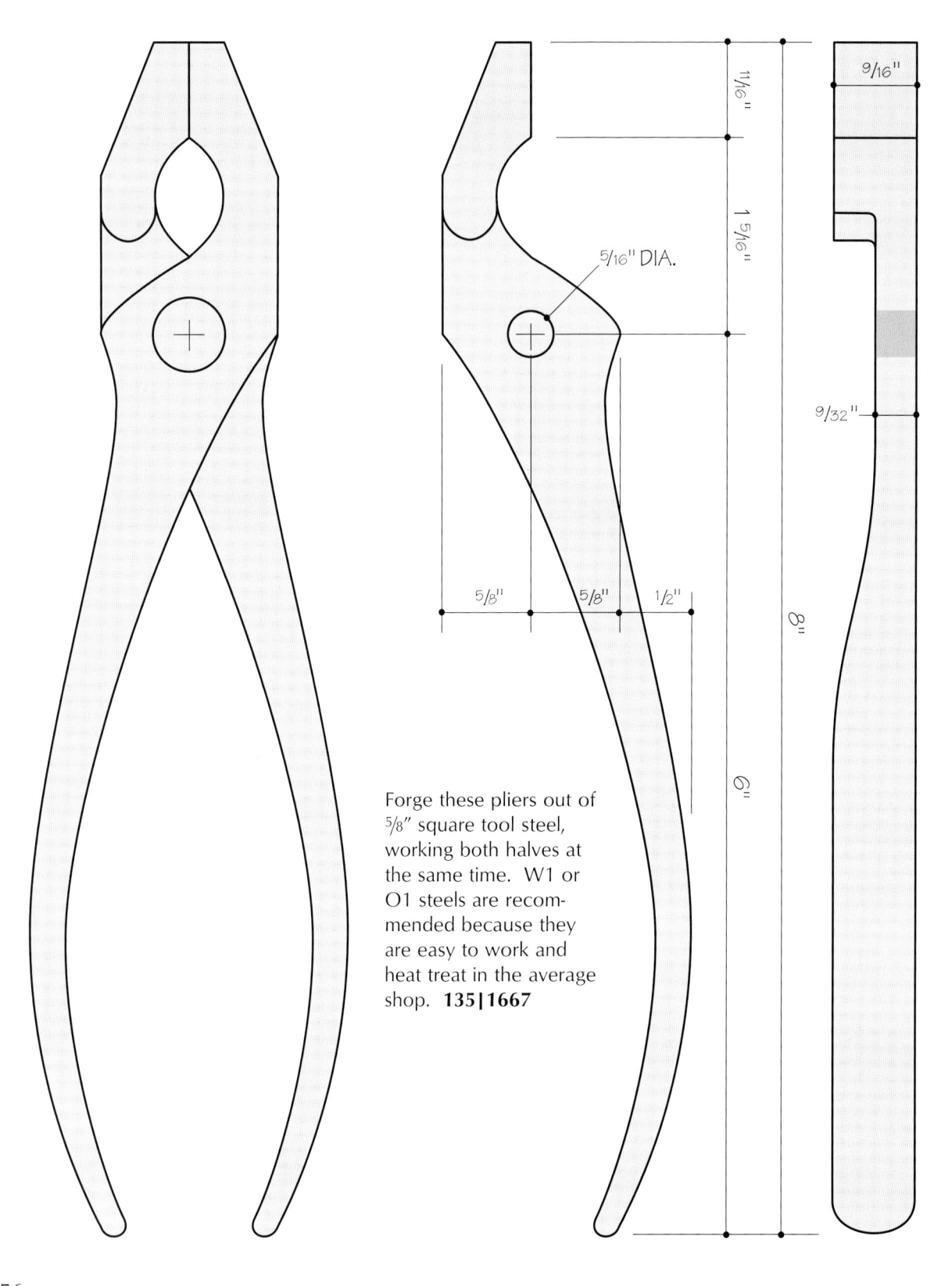

Forge these pliers out of ⁵⁄₈" square tool steel, working both halves at the same time. W1 or O1 steels are recommended because they are easy to work and heat treat in the average shop. **135|1667**

Railing Protractor -not to scale

Stair railings require careful field measurements to insure an accurate fit. This protractor is used in conjunction with a level to obtain accurate stair angles necessary for layout and fabrication in the shop.
54|663

Roller Stand - ⅛ Scale

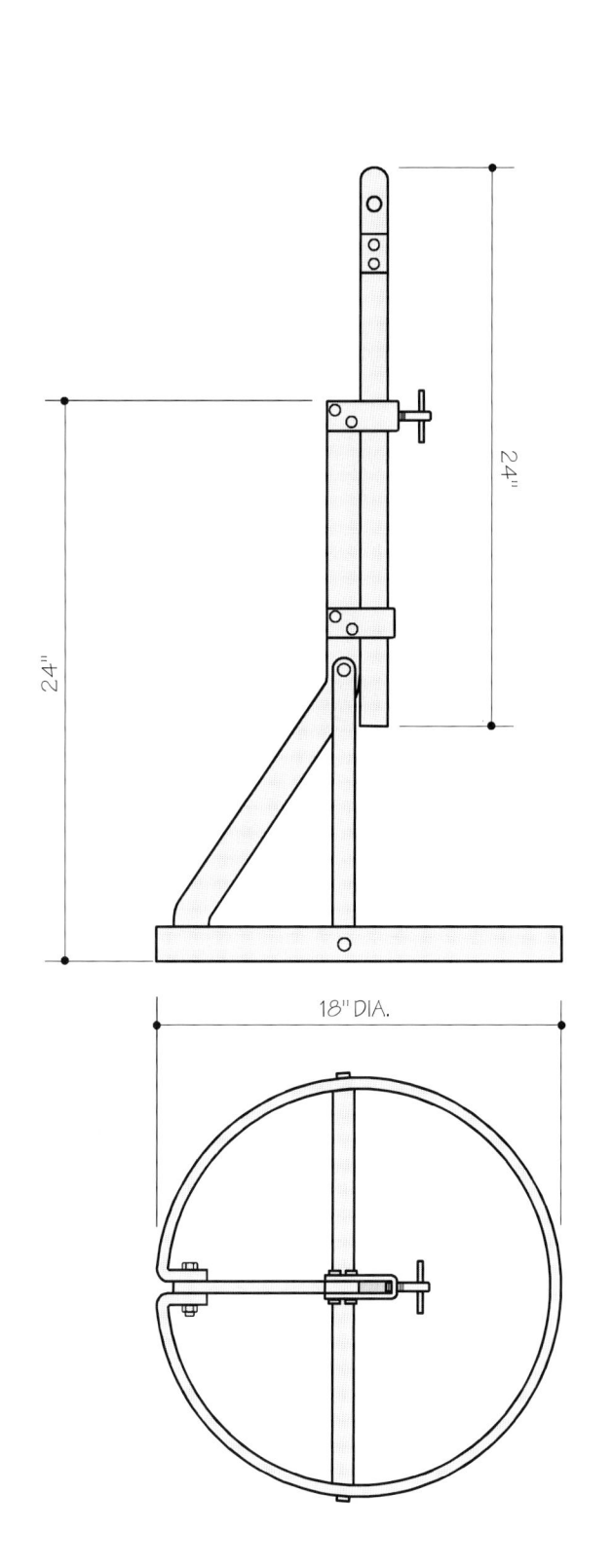

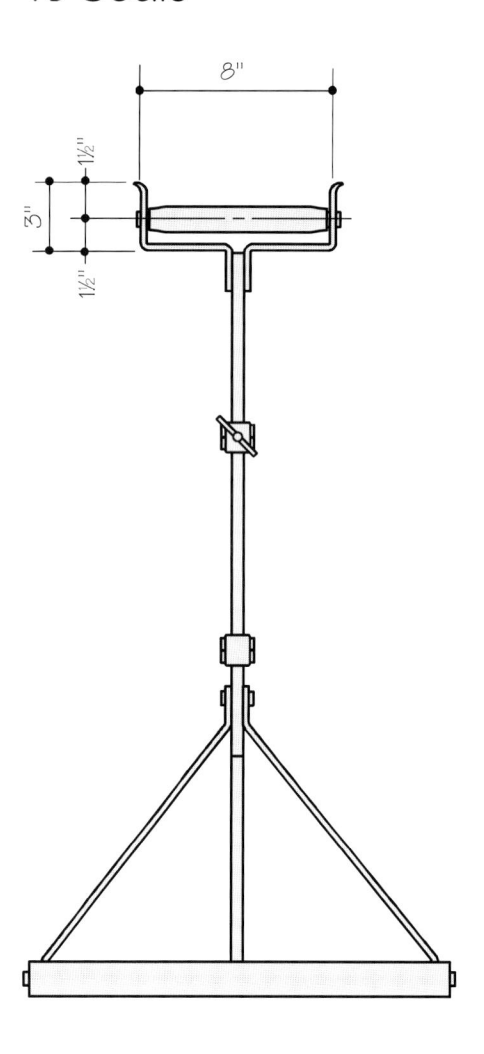

This shop-made roller stand looks right at home in a blacksmith shop. The same stand can be made by fabricating all the components, but the one shown here requires some forge work and riveted joinery. The base is made round so it can be tilted and rolled from place to place. **29|1583**

Rope Pulley -full scale

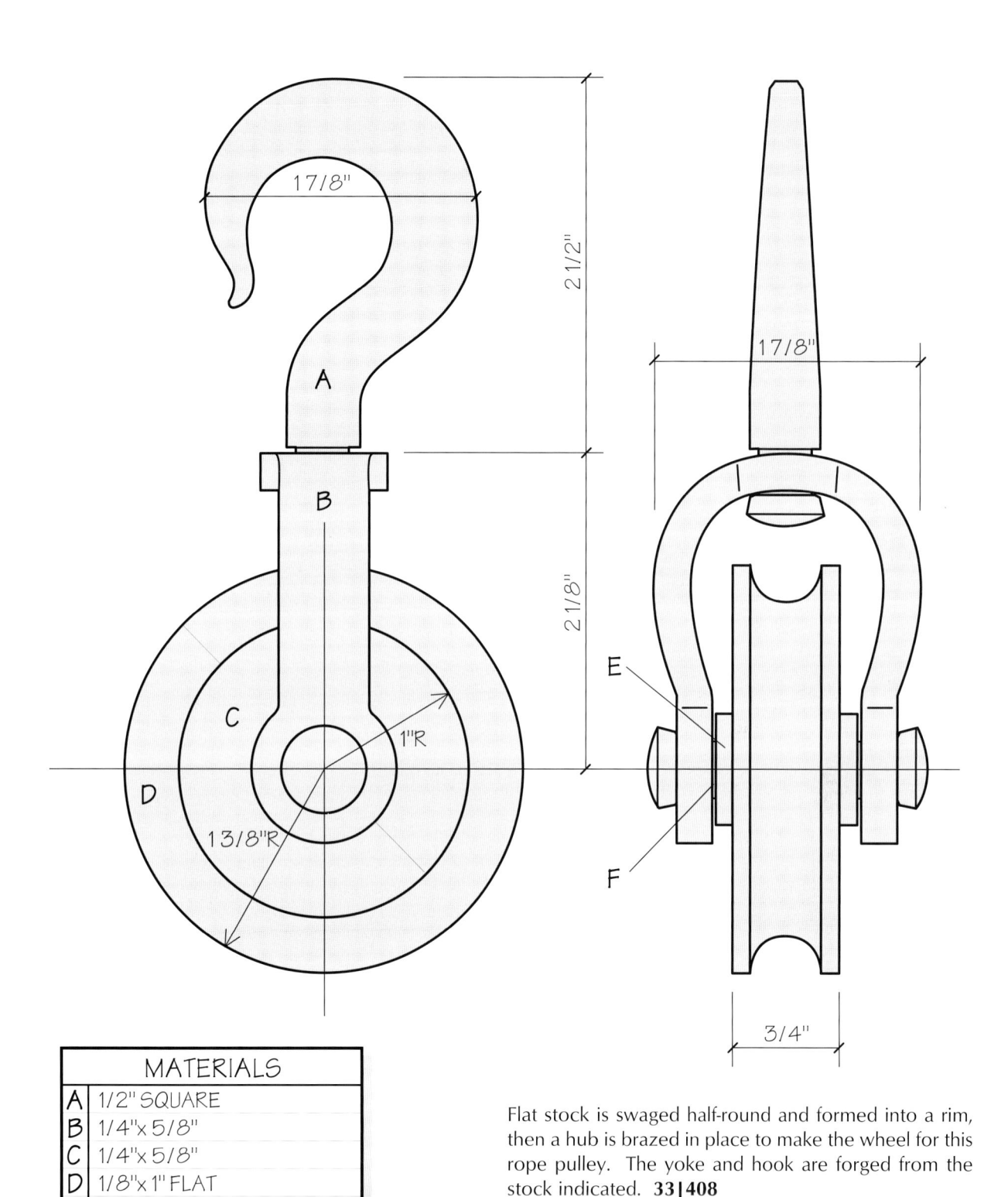

MATERIALS	
A	1/2" SQUARE
B	1/4"x 5/8"
C	1/4"x 5/8"
D	1/8"x 1" FLAT
E	3/4" ROUND
F	3/8" ROUND

Flat stock is swaged half-round and formed into a rim, then a hub is brazed in place to make the wheel for this rope pulley. The yoke and hook are forged from the stock indicated. **33|408**

Slate Roofing Hammer – ½ scale

Good slate roofing hammers are rare, and a hand forged one is a prized possession. These hammers can drive and pull nails, punch nail holes, and rip slate shingles. They are traditionally made out of straight high carbon steel, but an alloy like S-7 is best. **36|445**

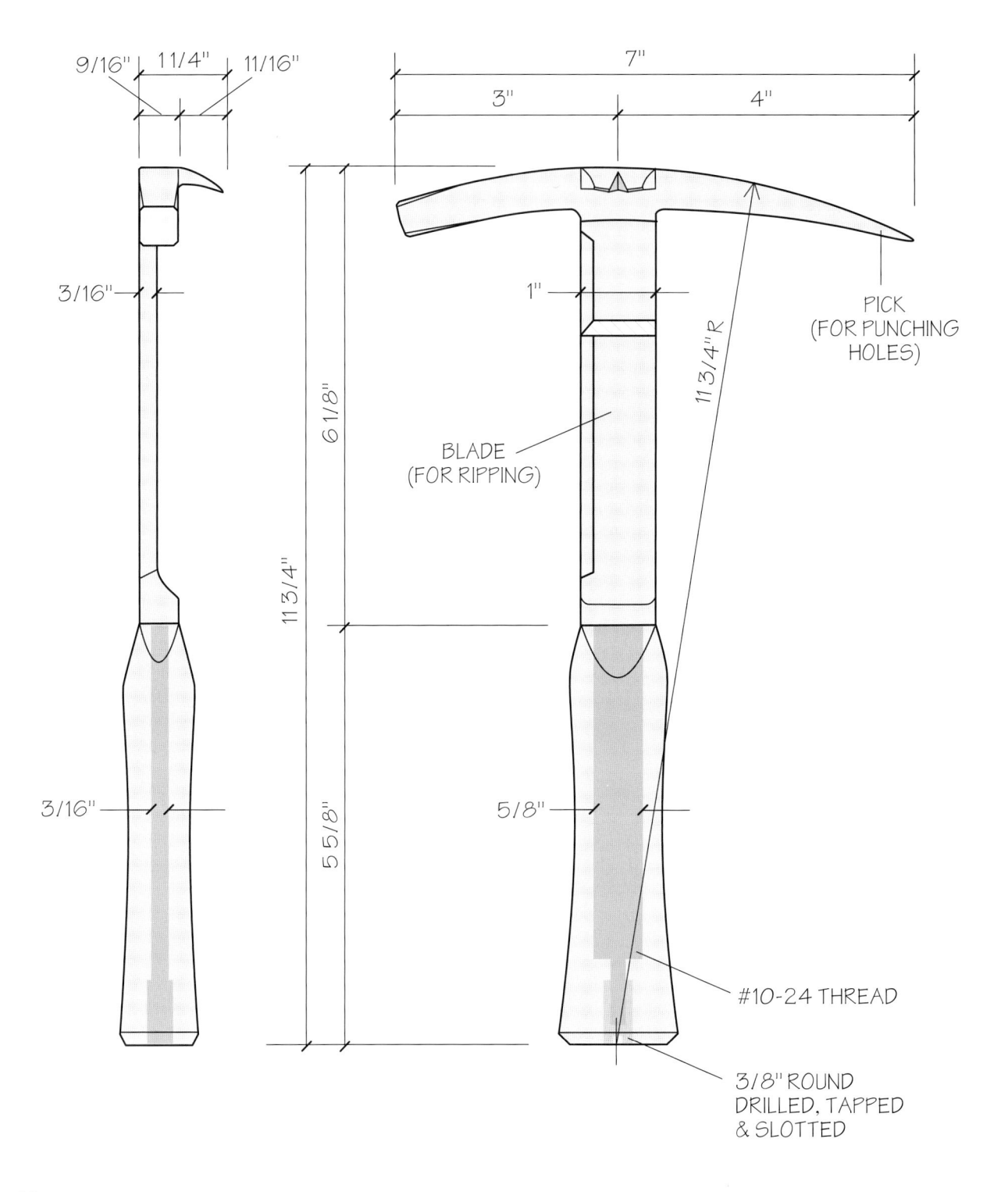

PICK (FOR PUNCHING HOLES)

BLADE (FOR RIPPING)

#10-24 THREAD

3/8" ROUND DRILLED, TAPPED & SLOTTED

Spatula -½ scale

A stainless steel blade and forged steel handle team up to make this attractive spatula. Use a square punch to create the zig-zag pattern on the the edge of flat stock. The blade is sandwiched in a slot at the end of the handle and secured with rivets.
163|2050

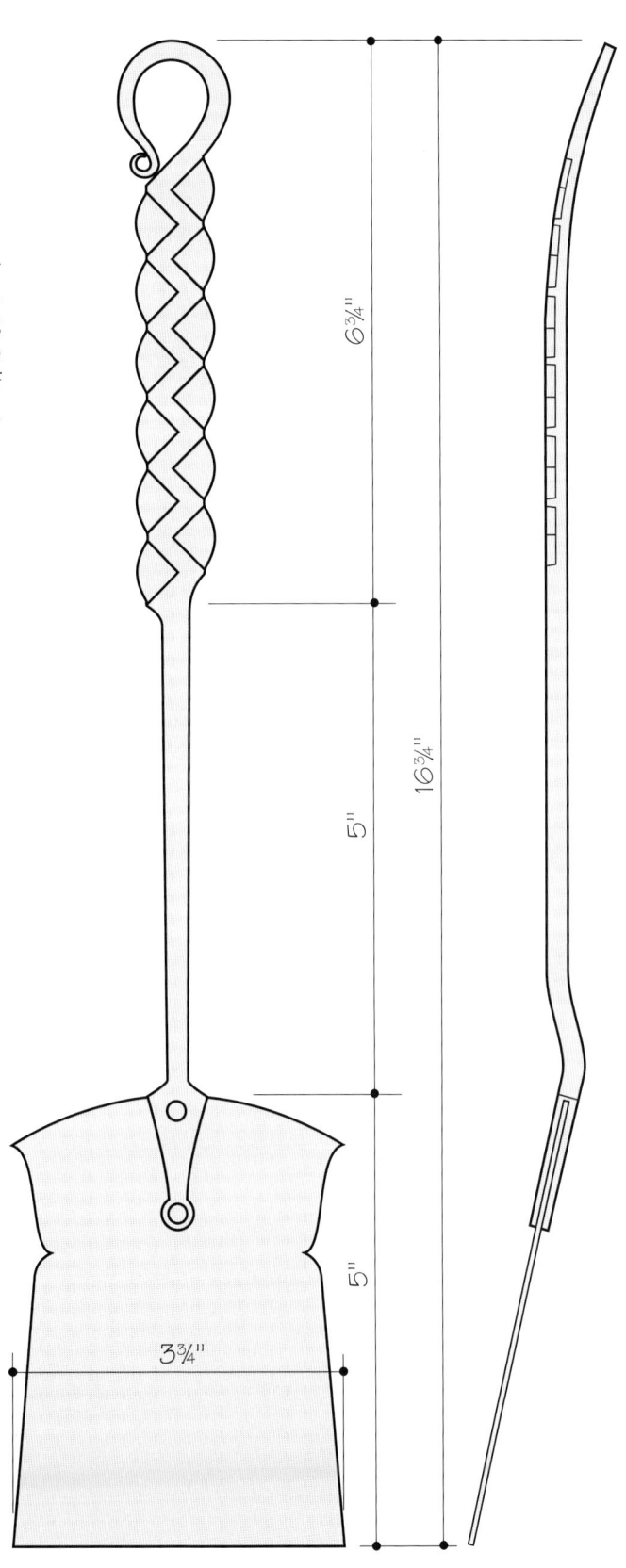

Stone Chisel -¾ scale

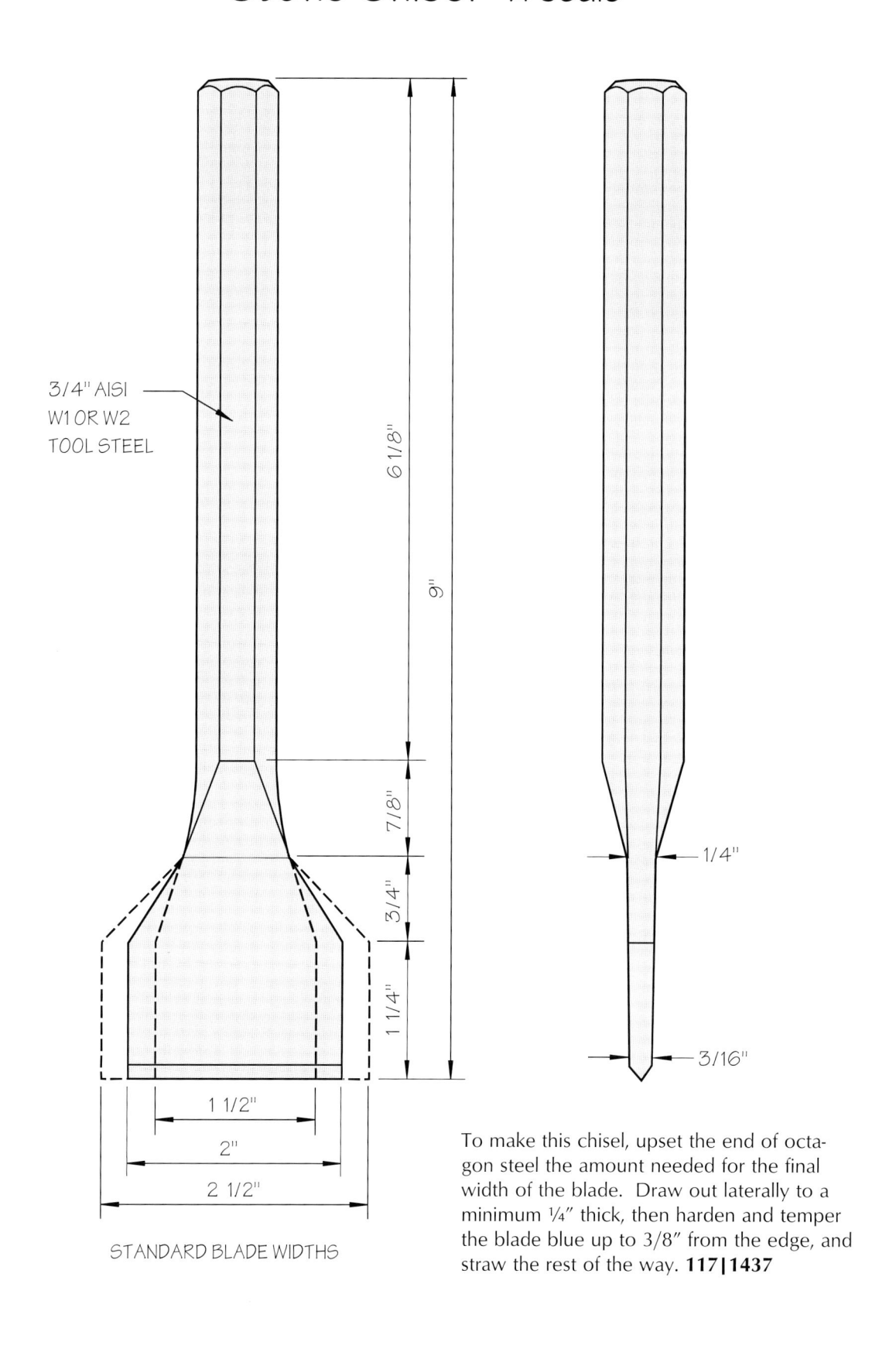

3/4" AISI W1 OR W2 TOOL STEEL

6 1/8"

9"

7/8"

3/4"

1 1/4"

1 1/2"
2"
2 1/2"

STANDARD BLADE WIDTHS

1/4"

3/16"

To make this chisel, upset the end of octagon steel the amount needed for the final width of the blade. Draw out laterally to a minimum ¼" thick, then harden and temper the blade blue up to 3/8" from the edge, and straw the rest of the way. **117|1437**

Wood Gouge - ¾ scale

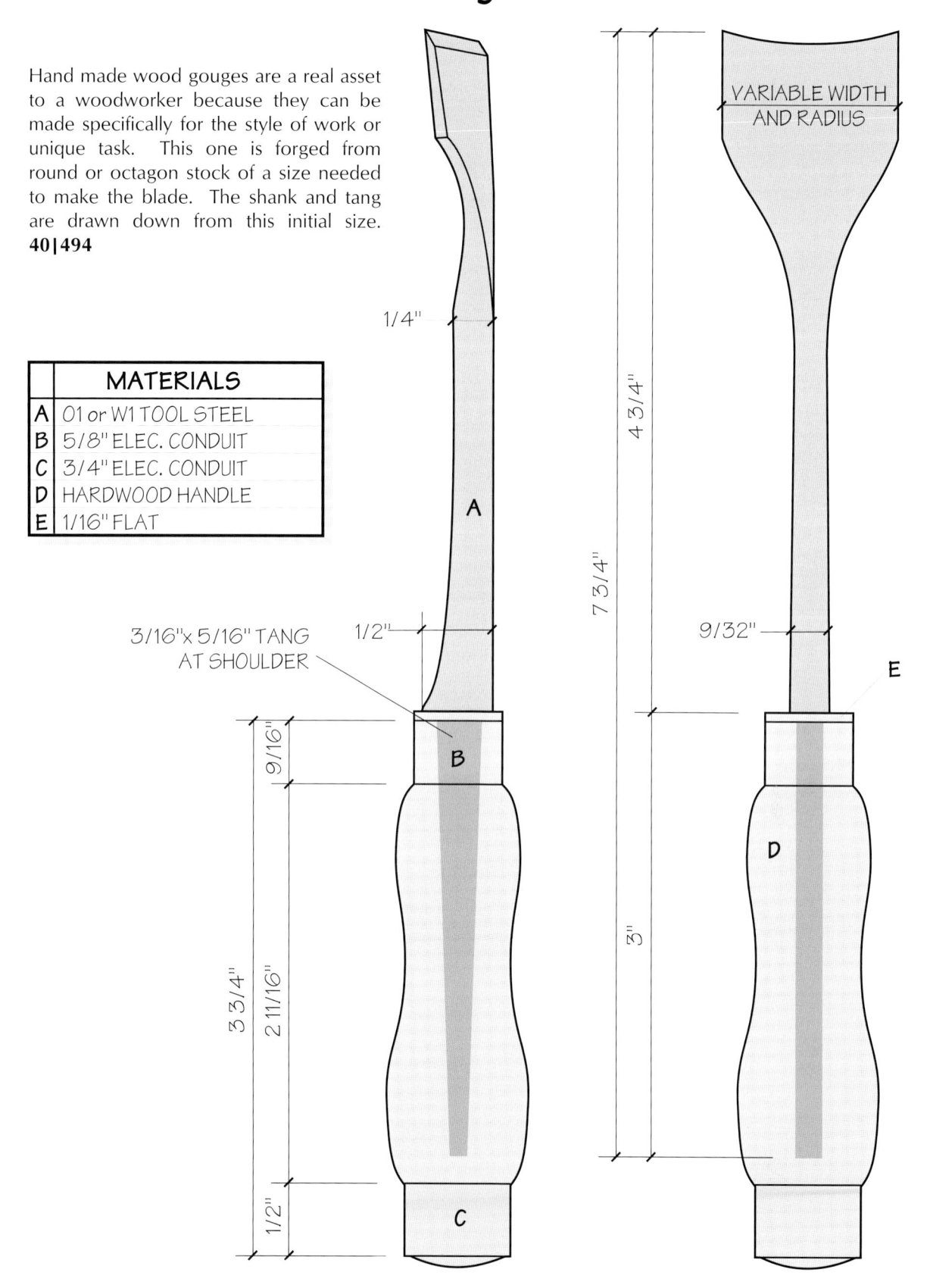

Hand made wood gouges are a real asset to a woodworker because they can be made specifically for the style of work or unique task. This one is forged from round or octagon stock of a size needed to make the blade. The shank and tang are drawn down from this initial size.
40|494

	MATERIALS
A	O1 or W1 TOOL STEEL
B	5/8" ELEC. CONDUIT
C	3/4" ELEC. CONDUIT
D	HARDWOOD HANDLE
E	1/16" FLAT

3/16" x 5/16" TANG AT SHOULDER

VARIABLE WIDTH AND RADIUS

63

3 Hardware

Barrel Hinge -full scale

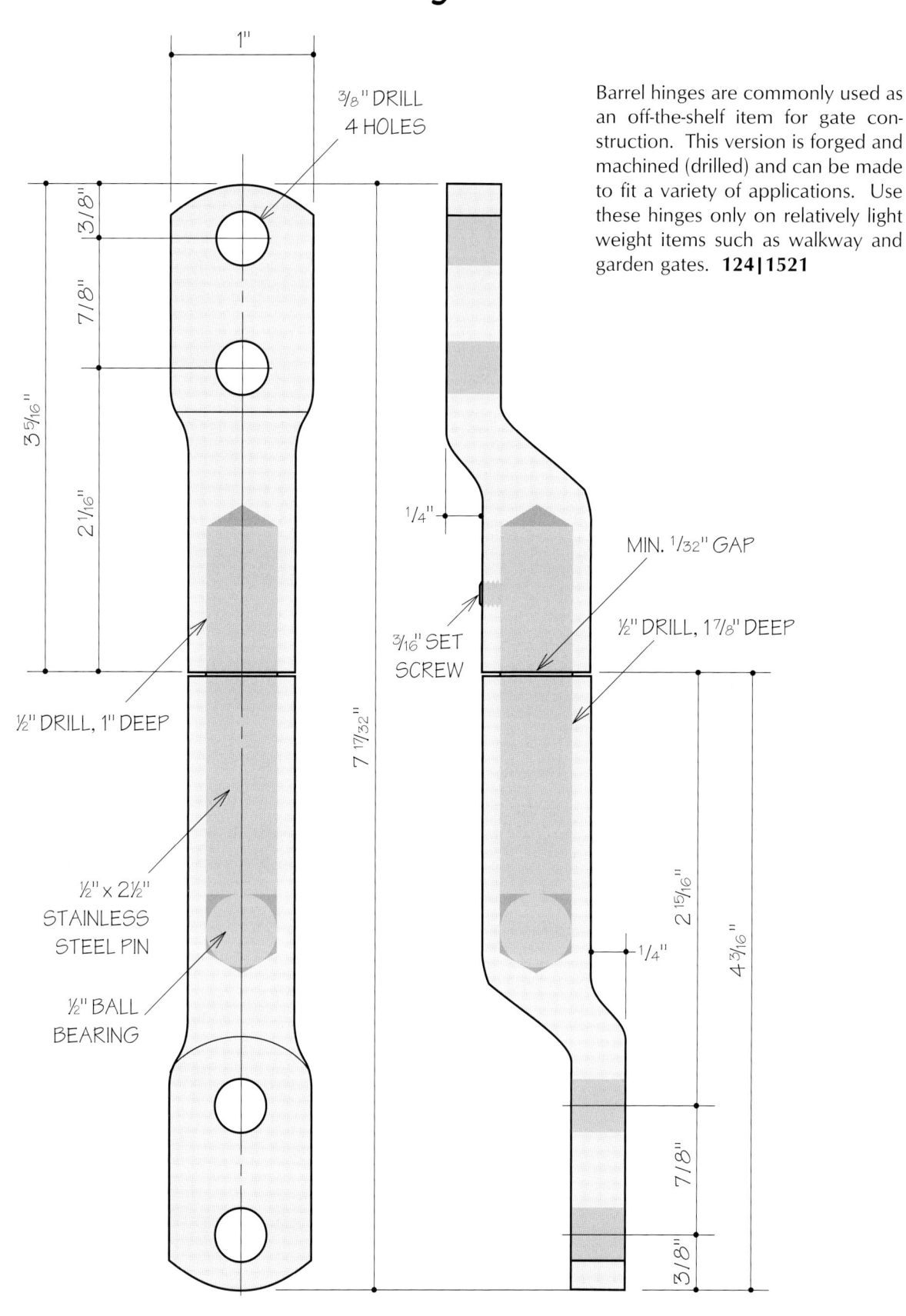

Barrel hinges are commonly used as an off-the-shelf item for gate construction. This version is forged and machined (drilled) and can be made to fit a variety of applications. Use these hinges only on relatively light weight items such as walkway and garden gates. **124|1521**

- 1"
- 3/8" DRILL 4 HOLES
- 3/8"
- 7/8"
- 3 5/16"
- 2 1/16"
- 1/2" DRILL, 1" DEEP
- 1/2" x 2 1/2" STAINLESS STEEL PIN
- 1/2" BALL BEARING
- 1/4"
- 3/16" SET SCREW
- MIN. 1/32" GAP
- 1/2" DRILL, 1 7/8" DEEP
- 7 17/32"
- 2 15/16"
- 4 3/16"
- 1/4"
- 7/8"
- 3/8"

Cabinet Handle -full scale

All it takes to make this simple but elegant door handle is a piece of ½" square stock. Spreading the legs of the split stock on opposing surfaces gives the handle added dimension and style. **121|1488**

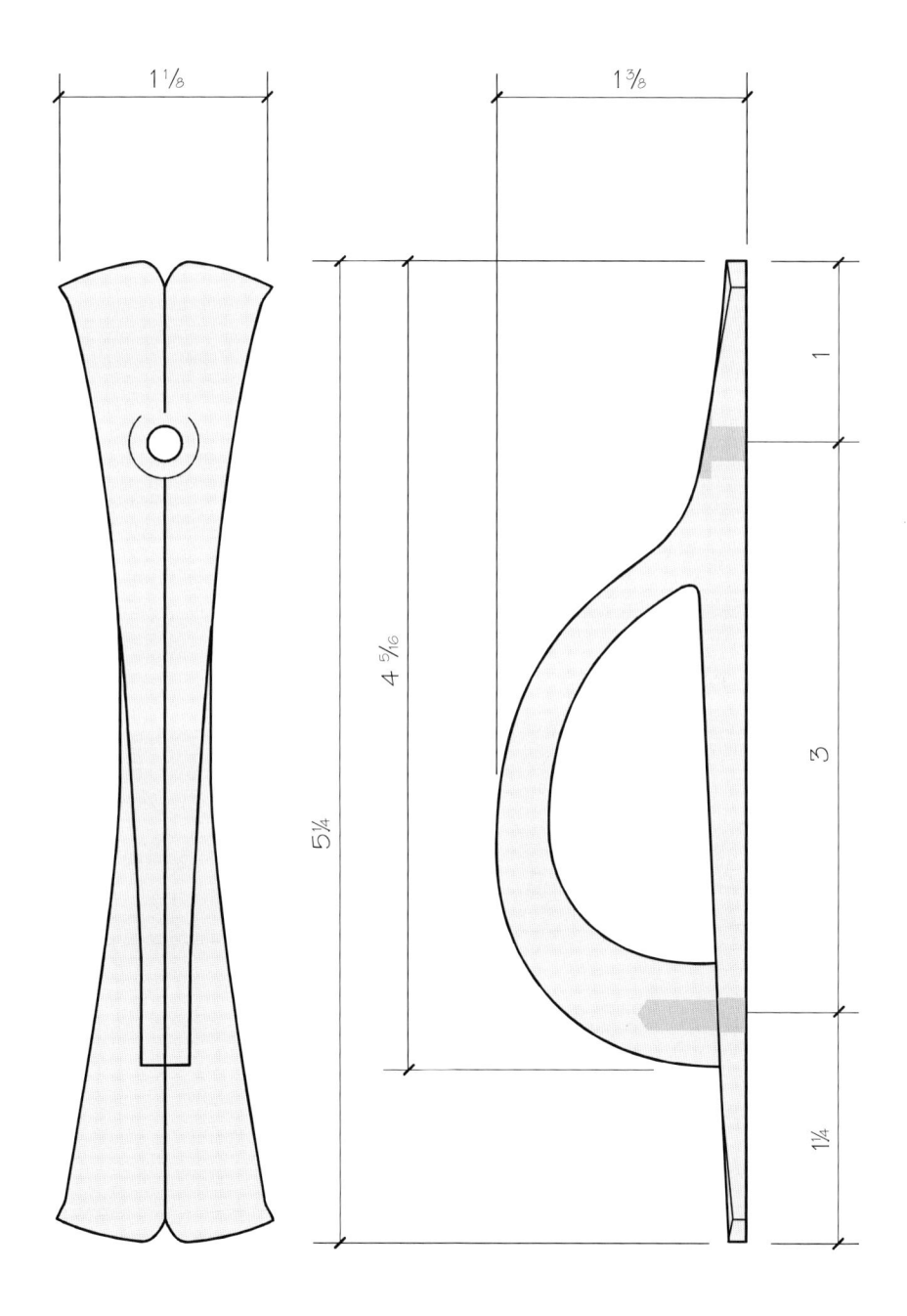

Cabinet Hinges -full scale

These cabinet hinges are unique because the barrels are folded over and drilled instead of rolled. Once in place, the mounting screws keep the barrels from opening up. The fold also facilitates many two-layer designs, four of which are shown here. **135|1671**

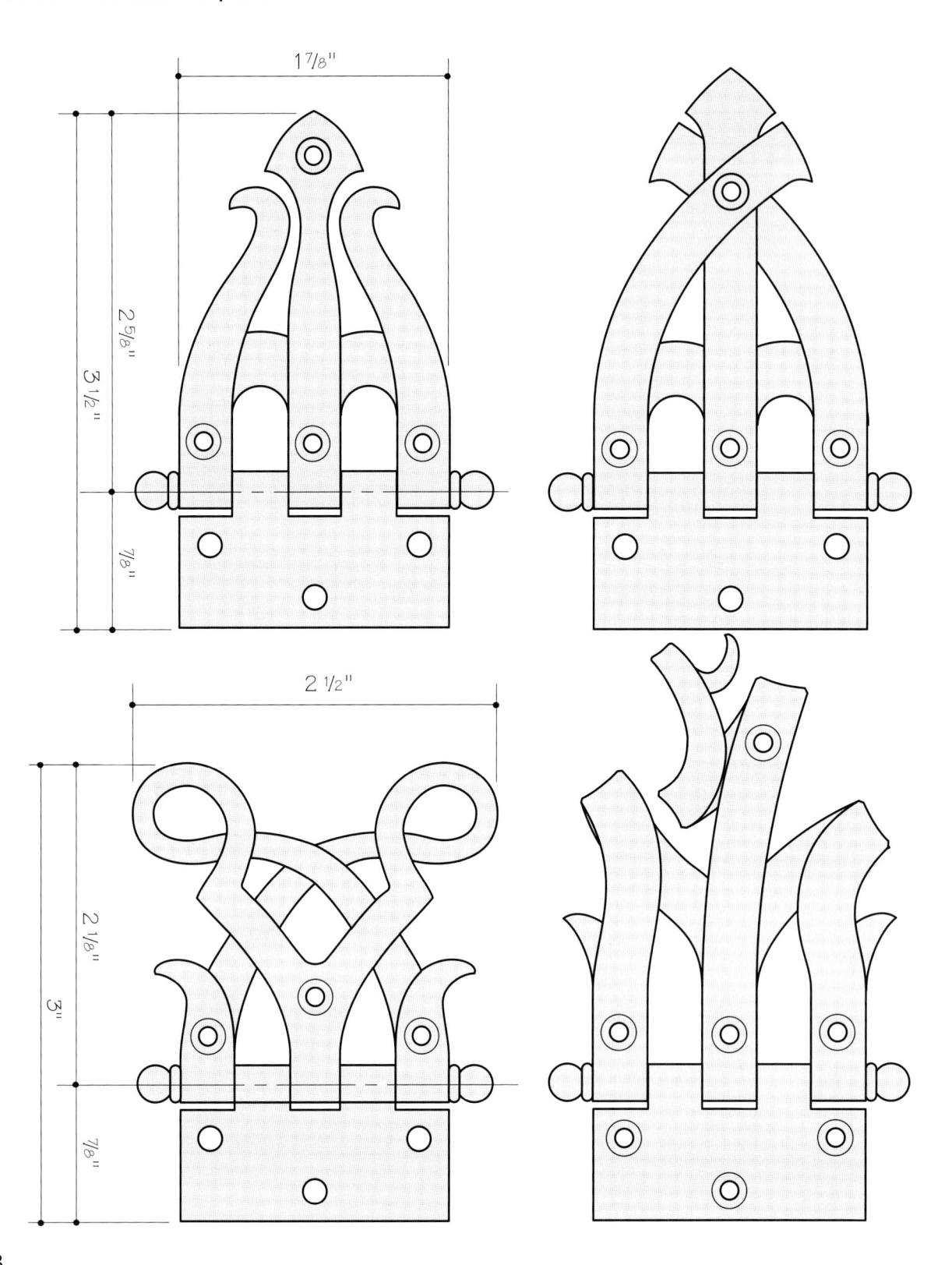

68

Door Catch - full scale

Intended for interior doors, this door stop automatically catches the door when opened all the way. The door is released by stepping on the lever. **73|901**

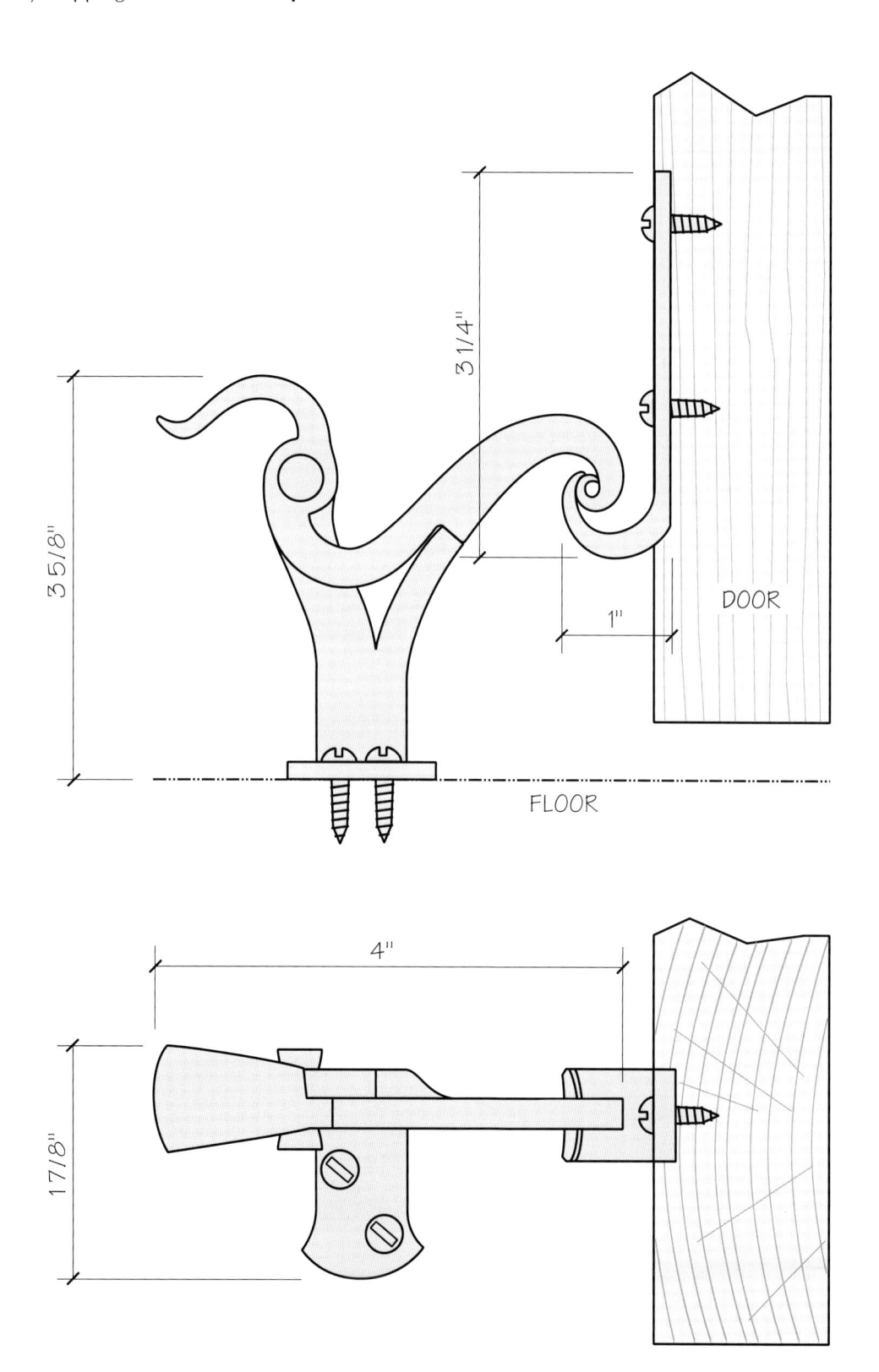

Door Chime -3/4 scale

When you rotate the cam on this door chime it cocks and releases a hammer that strikes coiled spring steel, much like a grandfather clock. Mounting it to a wooden door amplifies and deepens the sound. **72|887**

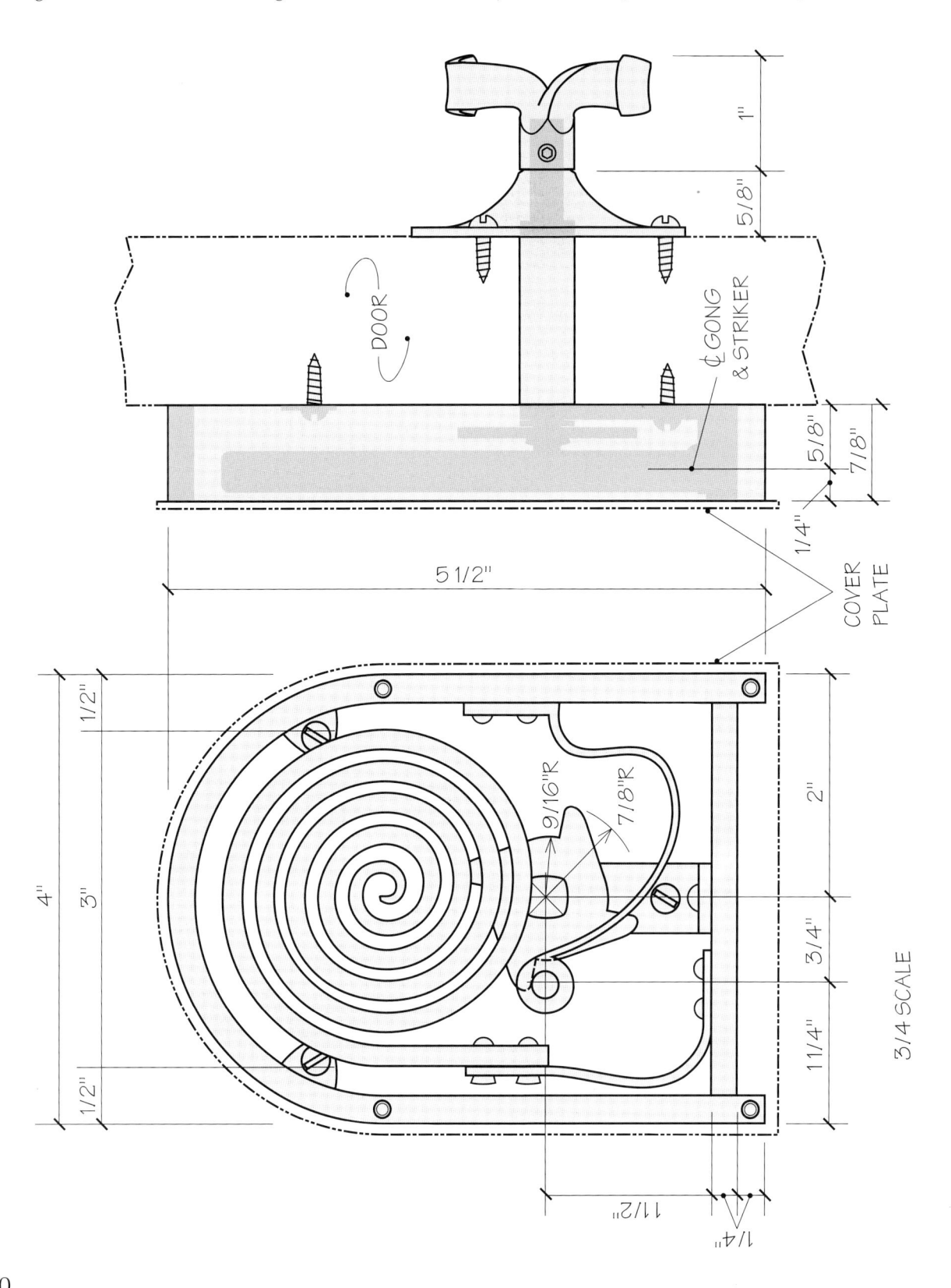

ASSEMBLY

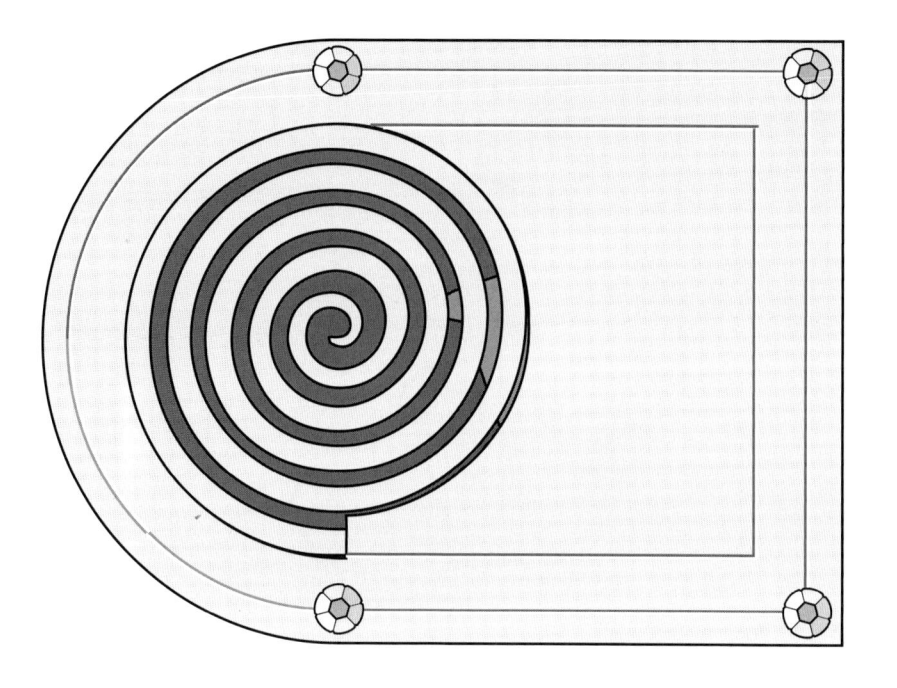

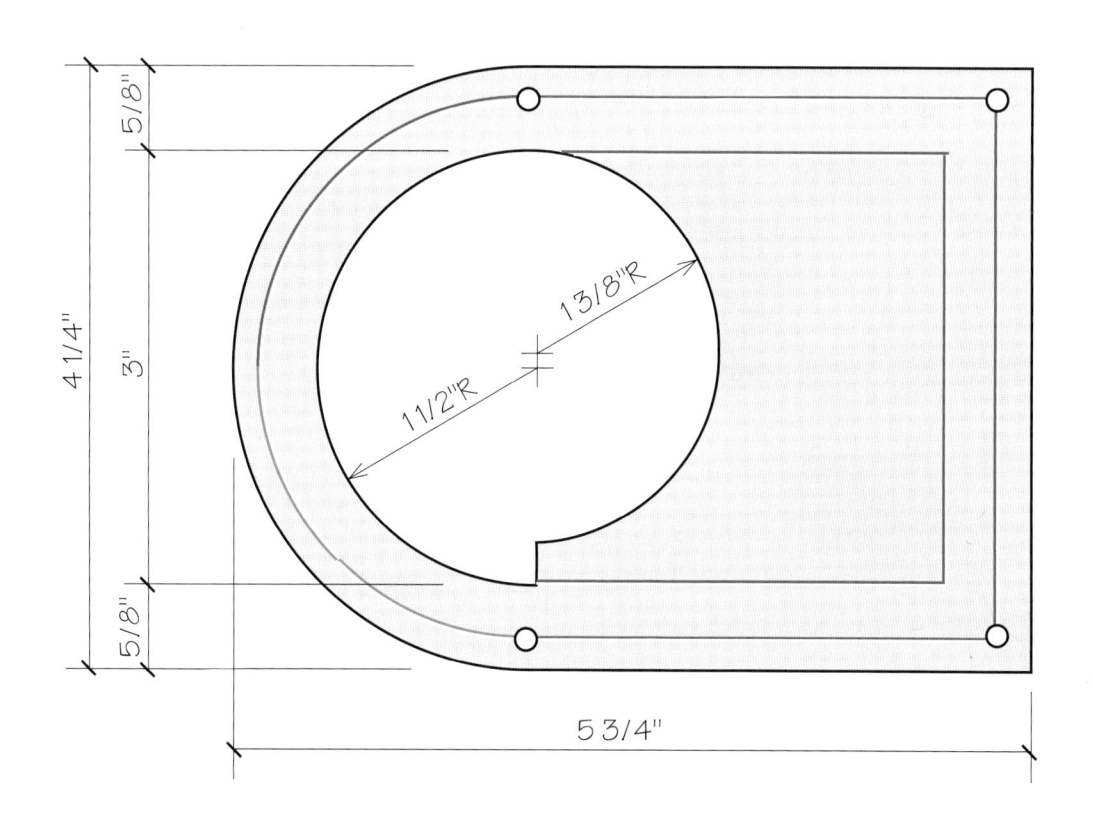

COVER PLATE

5/8"
4 1/4"
3"
5/8"
1 1/2"R
1 3/8"R
5 3/4"

Door Knob - full scale

The pattern for this door knob can be cut out by hand or laser cut "starters" can be made, ready for grooving and forming. Draw the shaft down to fit a variety of lock sets. **43|572**

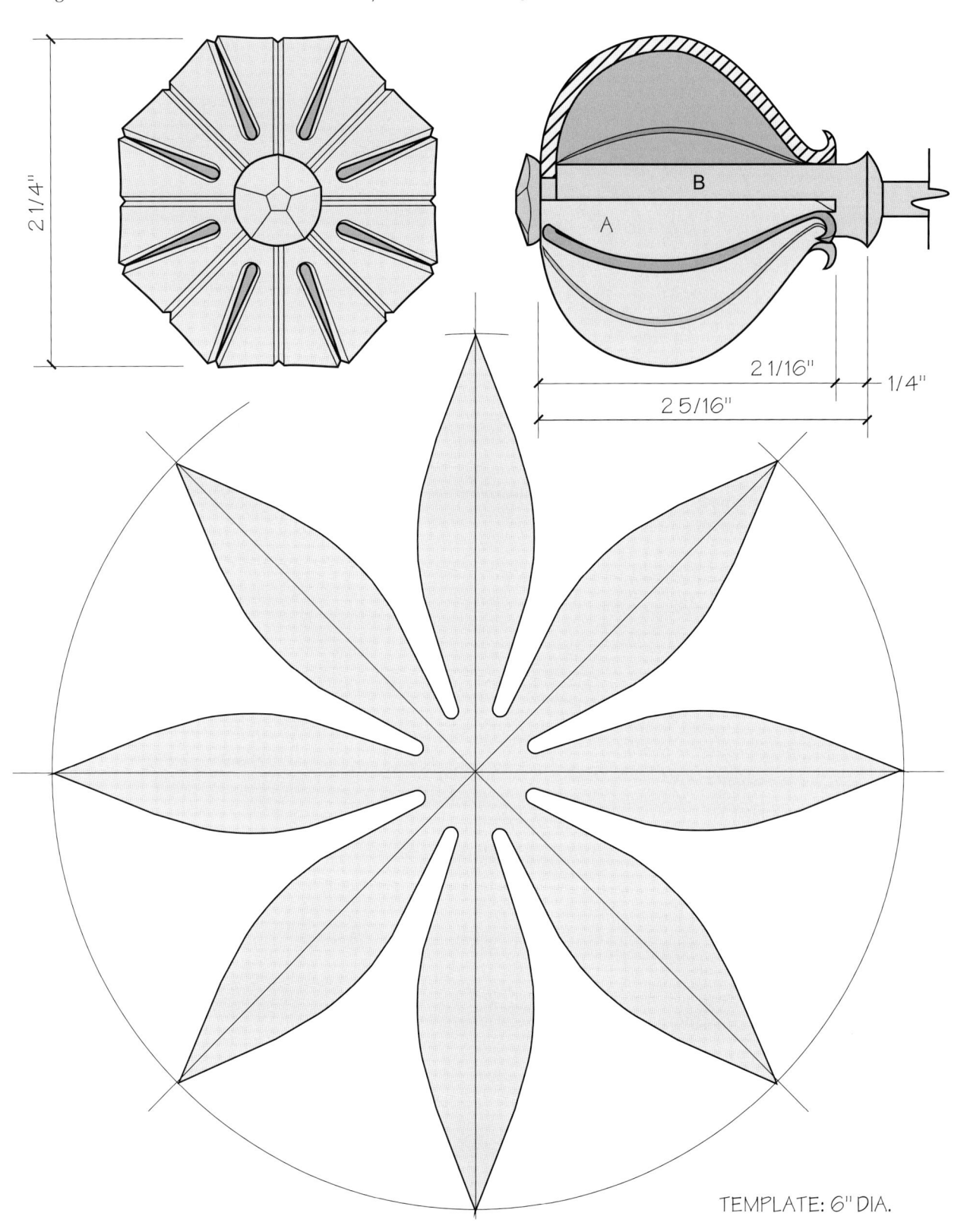

2 1/4"

2 1/16"

1/4"

2 5/16"

A

B

TEMPLATE: 6" DIA.

72

Door Knocker - full scale

The simplicity of this door knocker makes it both elegant and easy to make. It's forged from two pieces of 1" square, drawn and finished on the hinge end and left square on the other end. **92|1145**

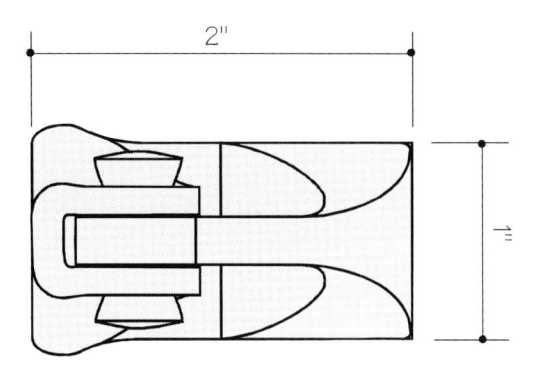

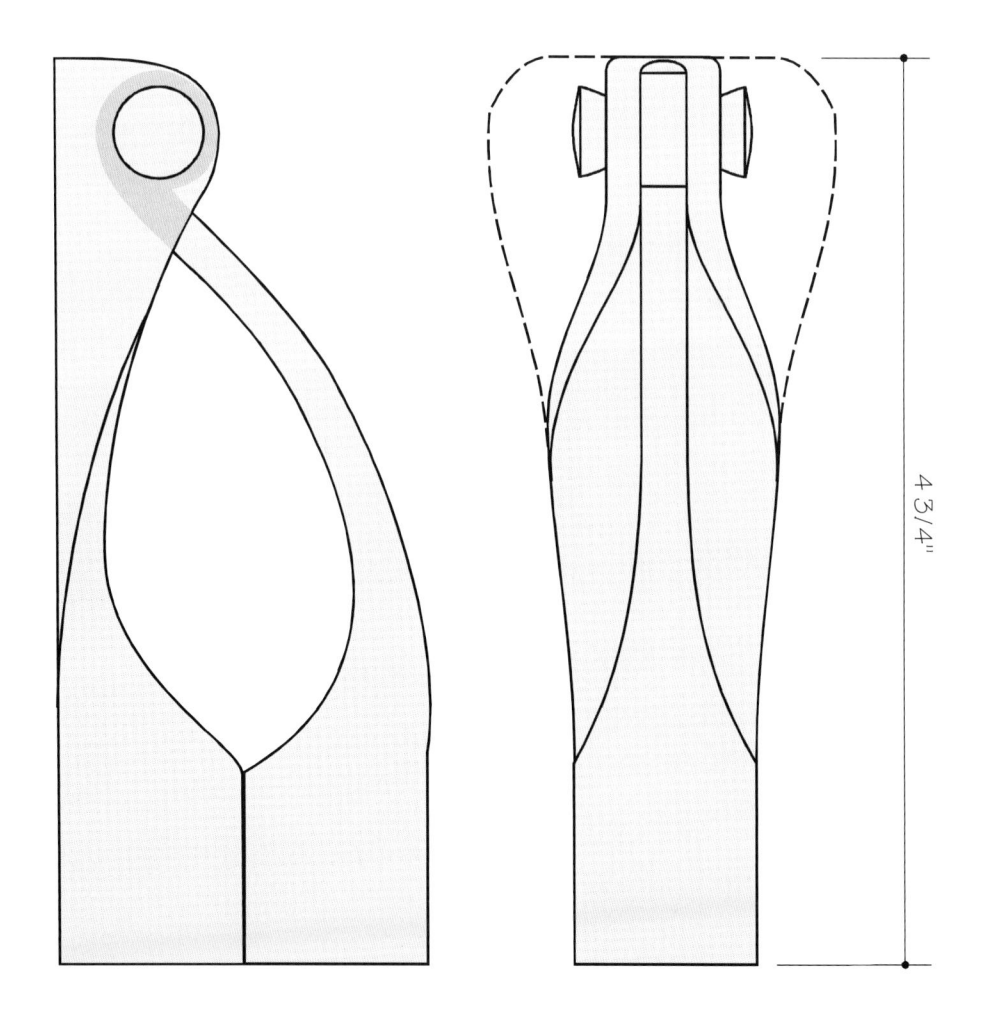

Door Latch - not to scale

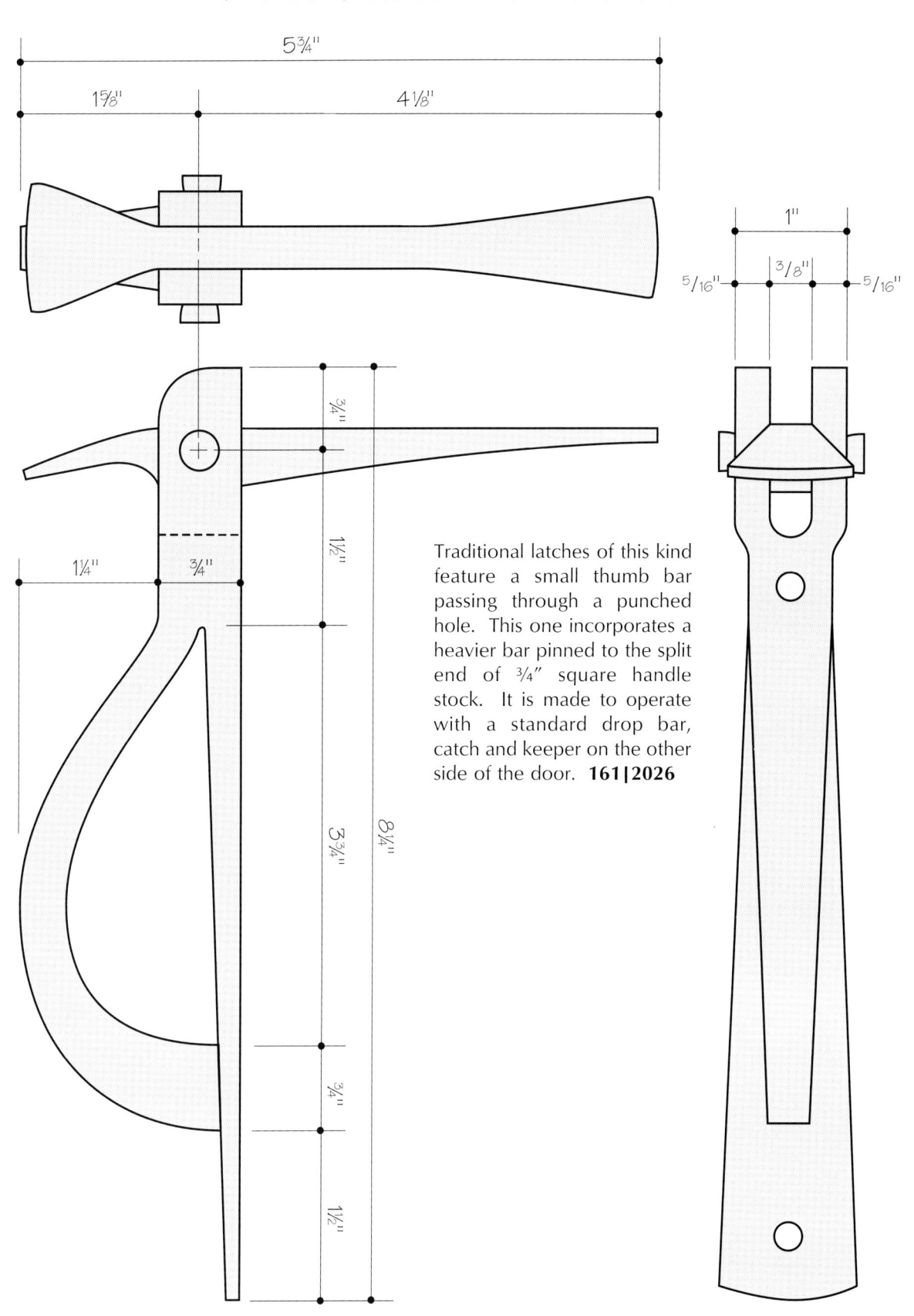

Traditional latches of this kind feature a small thumb bar passing through a punched hole. This one incorporates a heavier bar pinned to the split end of ¾" square handle stock. It is made to operate with a standard drop bar, catch and keeper on the other side of the door. **161|2026**

Draw Latch - full scale

Most commercial draw latches are made of stamped steel; this solid forged version is much more substantial. The size of the latch can be modified to work with a specific application by changing the parent stock sizes while keeping the same proportions. **116|1423**

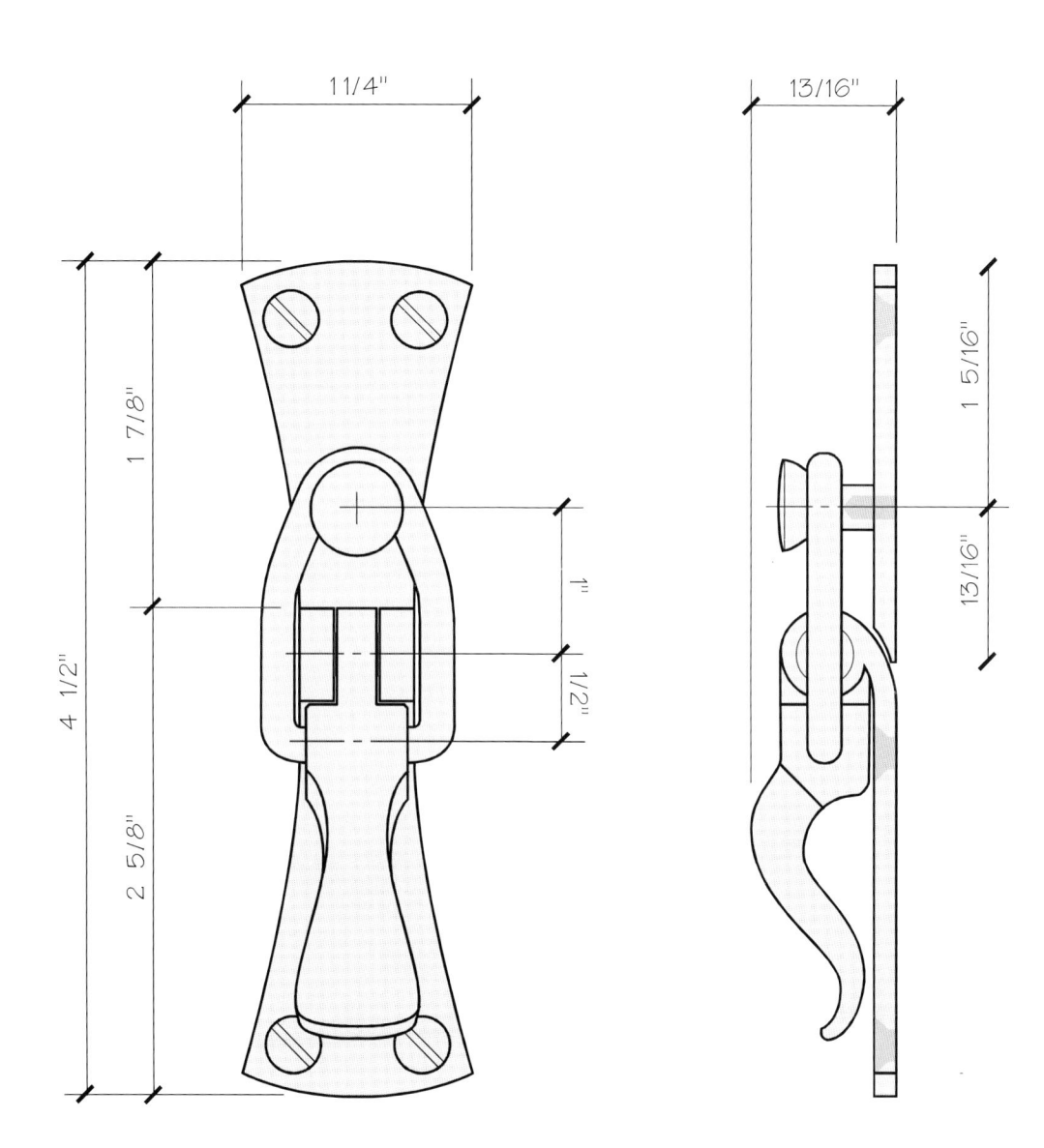

Gate Pull - not to scale

First forge a horse head blank out of 1"x 1½" stock, then add details by filing and using special tools (working hot) for the nose mouth and eyes. Forge weld the scroll stock to the horse head stock, and add the ring. **25|317**

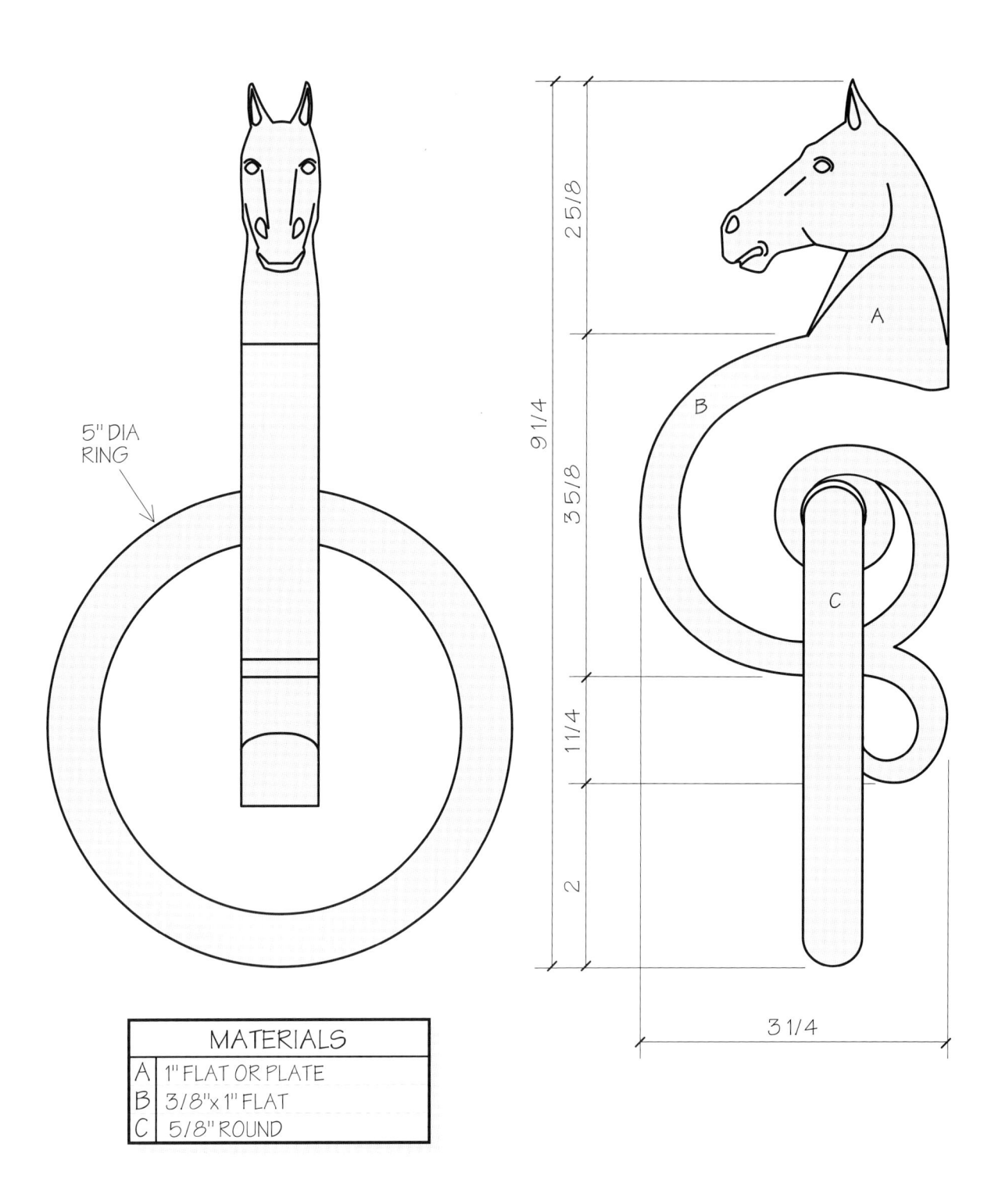

5" DIA RING

MATERIALS	
A	1" FLAT OR PLATE
B	3/8"x 1" FLAT
C	5/8" ROUND

Gutter Bracket - not to scale

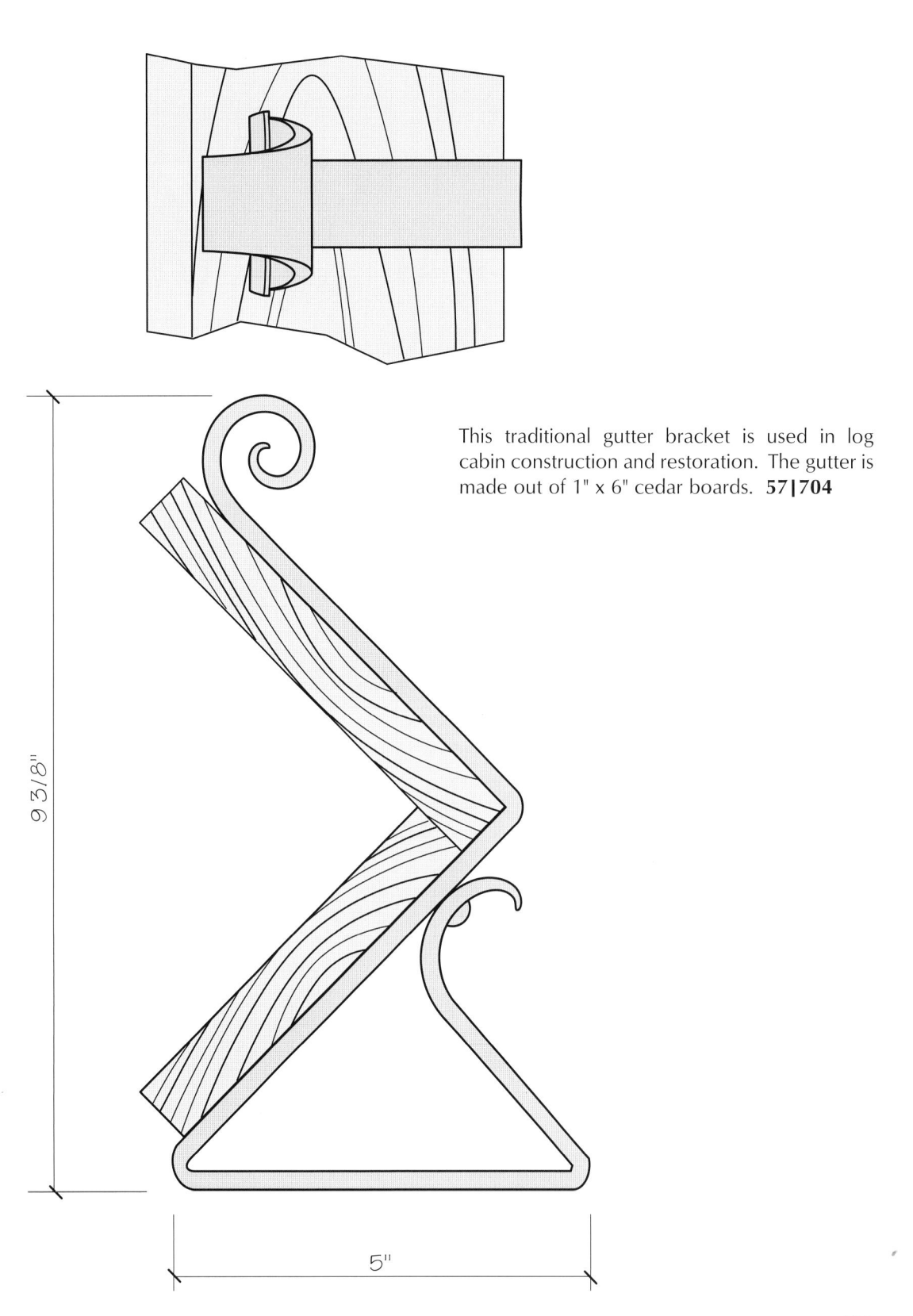

This traditional gutter bracket is used in log cabin construction and restoration. The gutter is made out of 1" x 6" cedar boards. **57|704**

9 3/8"

5"

Latch Plate and Handle - full scale

The scroll shape for the handle is mirrored on this two-piece latch plate. A key cylinder opening can also be added to the plate if necessary. **41|508**

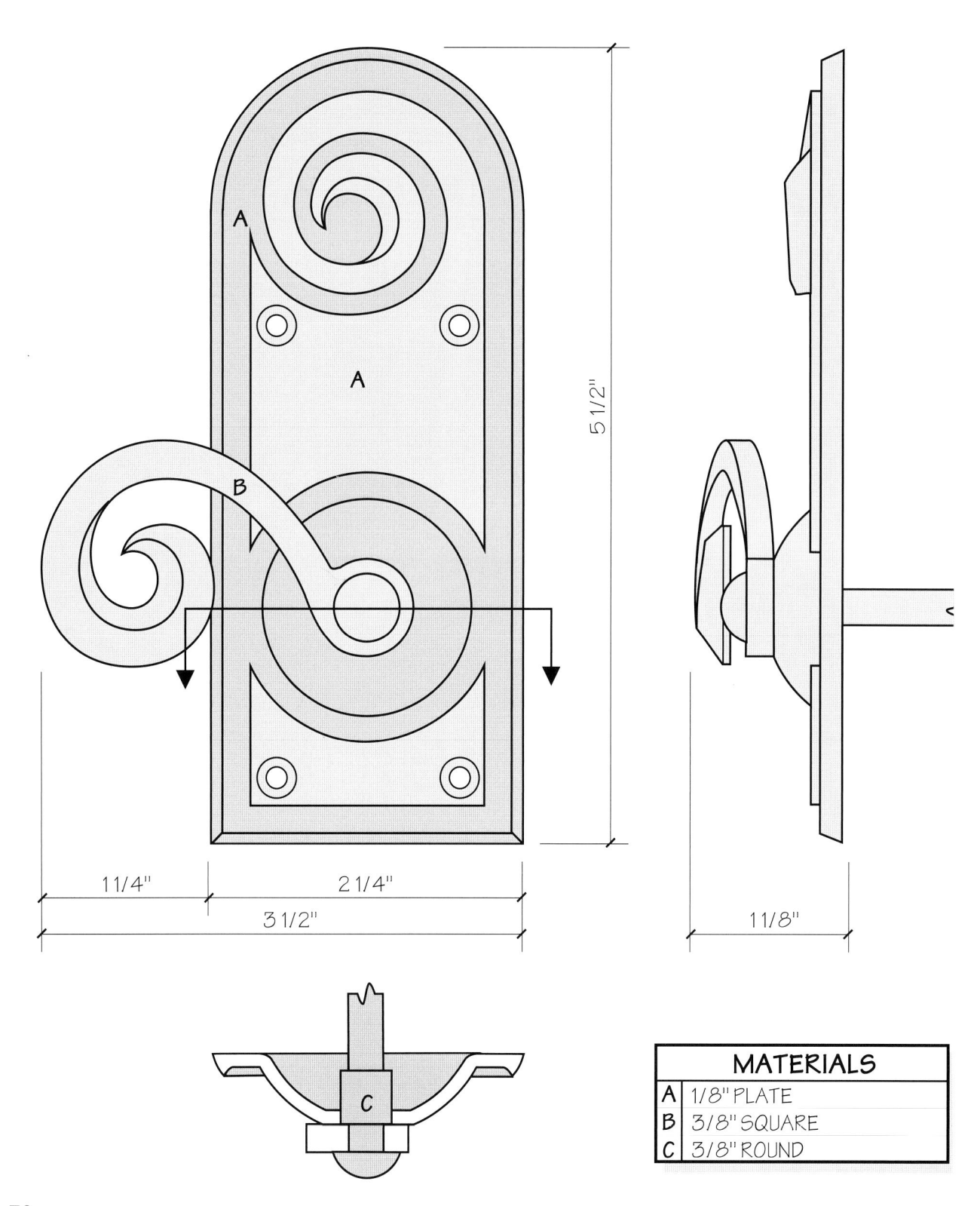

MATERIALS	
A	1/8" PLATE
B	3/8" SQUARE
C	3/8" ROUND

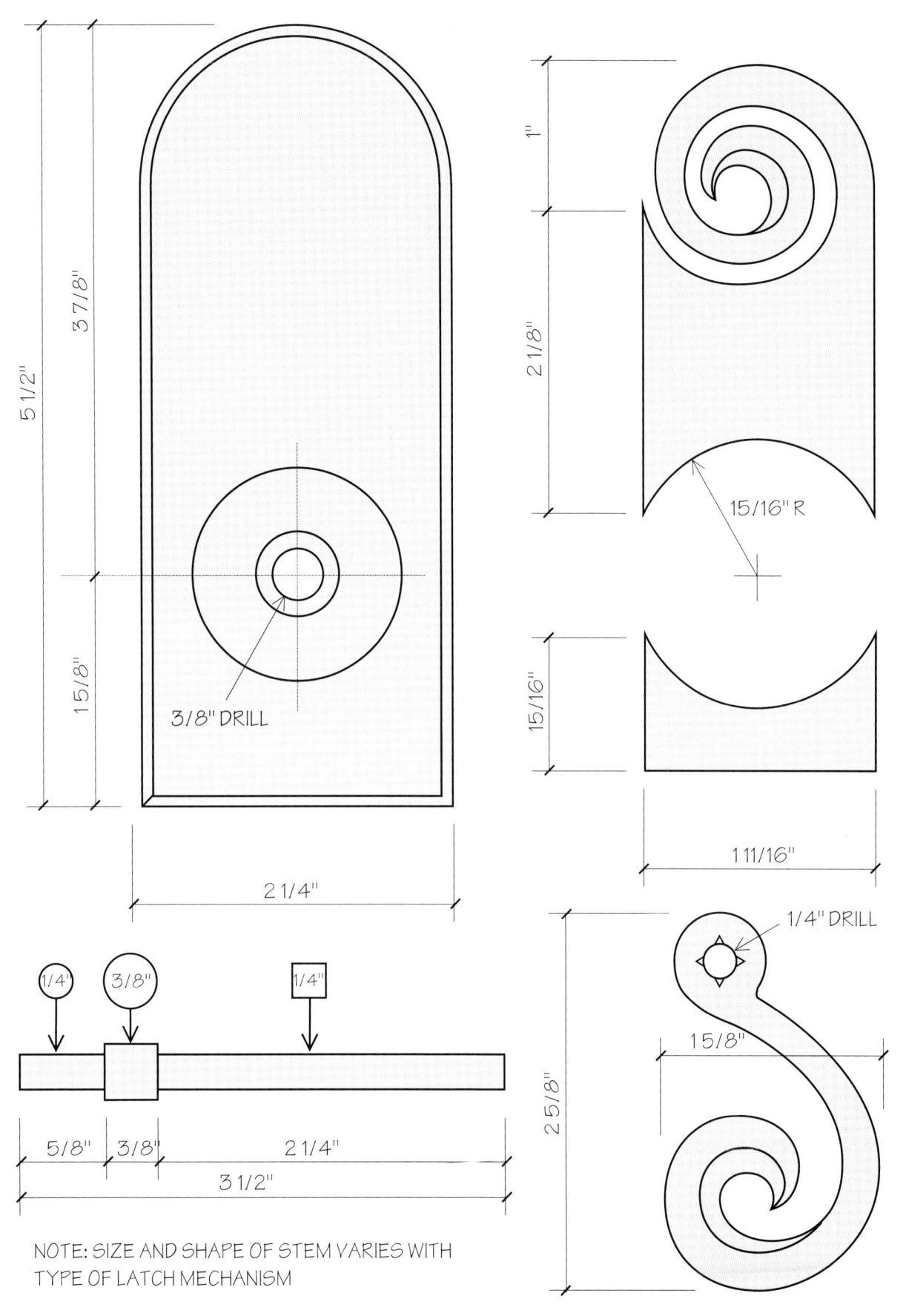

NOTE: SIZE AND SHAPE OF STEM VARIES WITH TYPE OF LATCH MECHANISM

Sliding Door Hanger – ½ scale

This hardware is designed for heavy sliding doors, and it mounts on the wall above the door opening. The track is 1" square stock and the V-groove cast iron wheels are a common off-the-shelf item.
144|1793

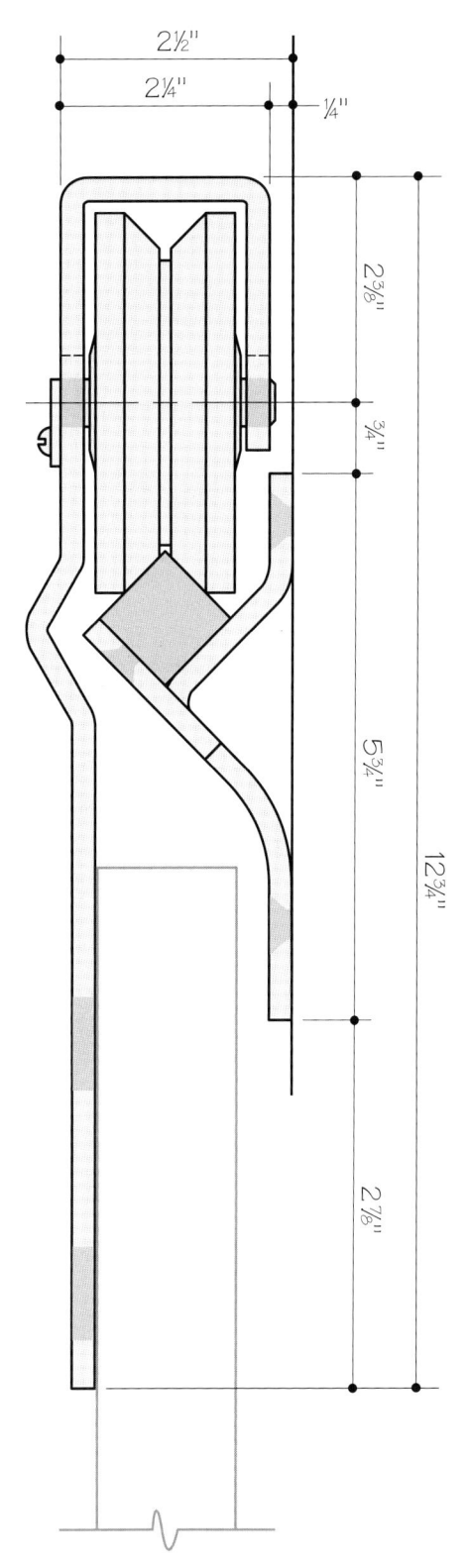

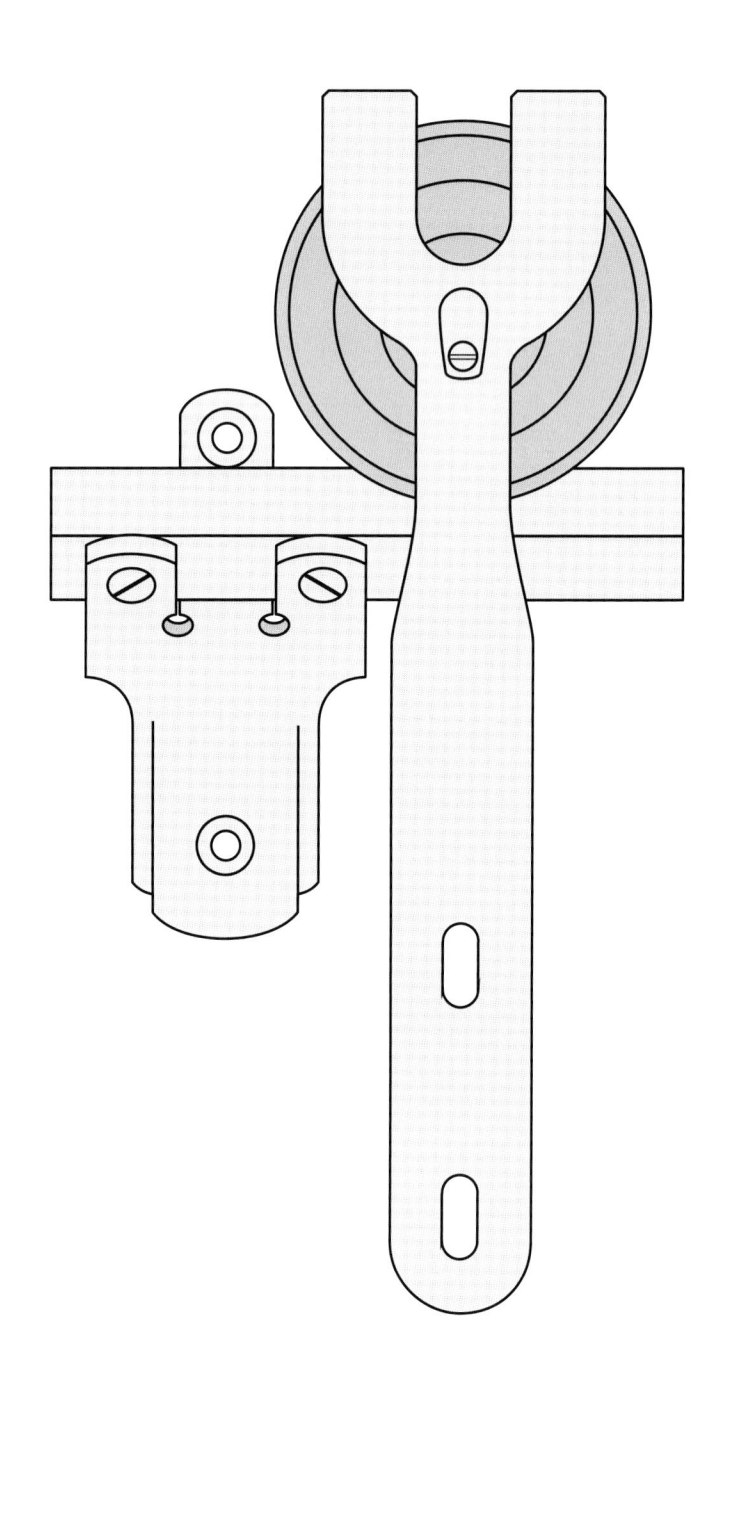

81

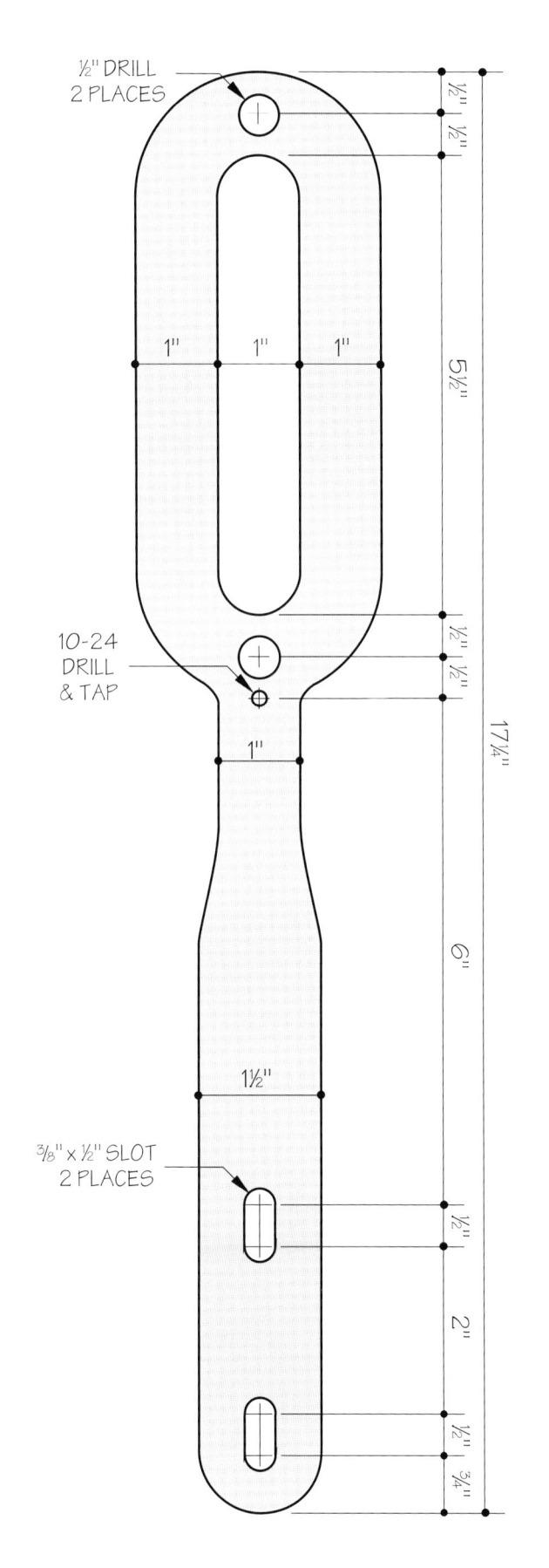

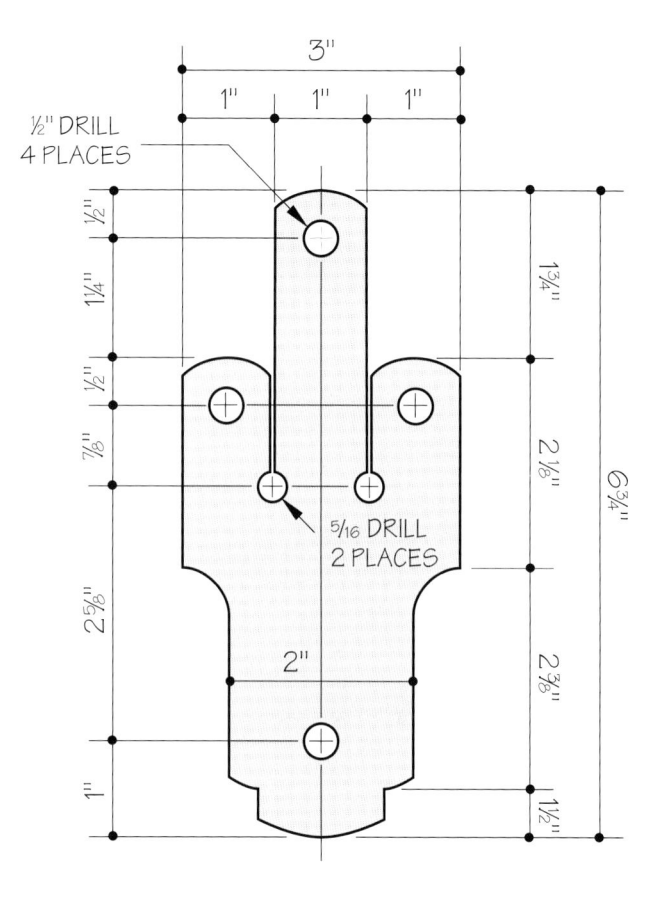

Shutter Dog - not to scale

Shutter dogs hold window shutters in an open position. This one can be installed in masonry by using an expansion shield, or by screwing into wood siding and studs. **57|701**

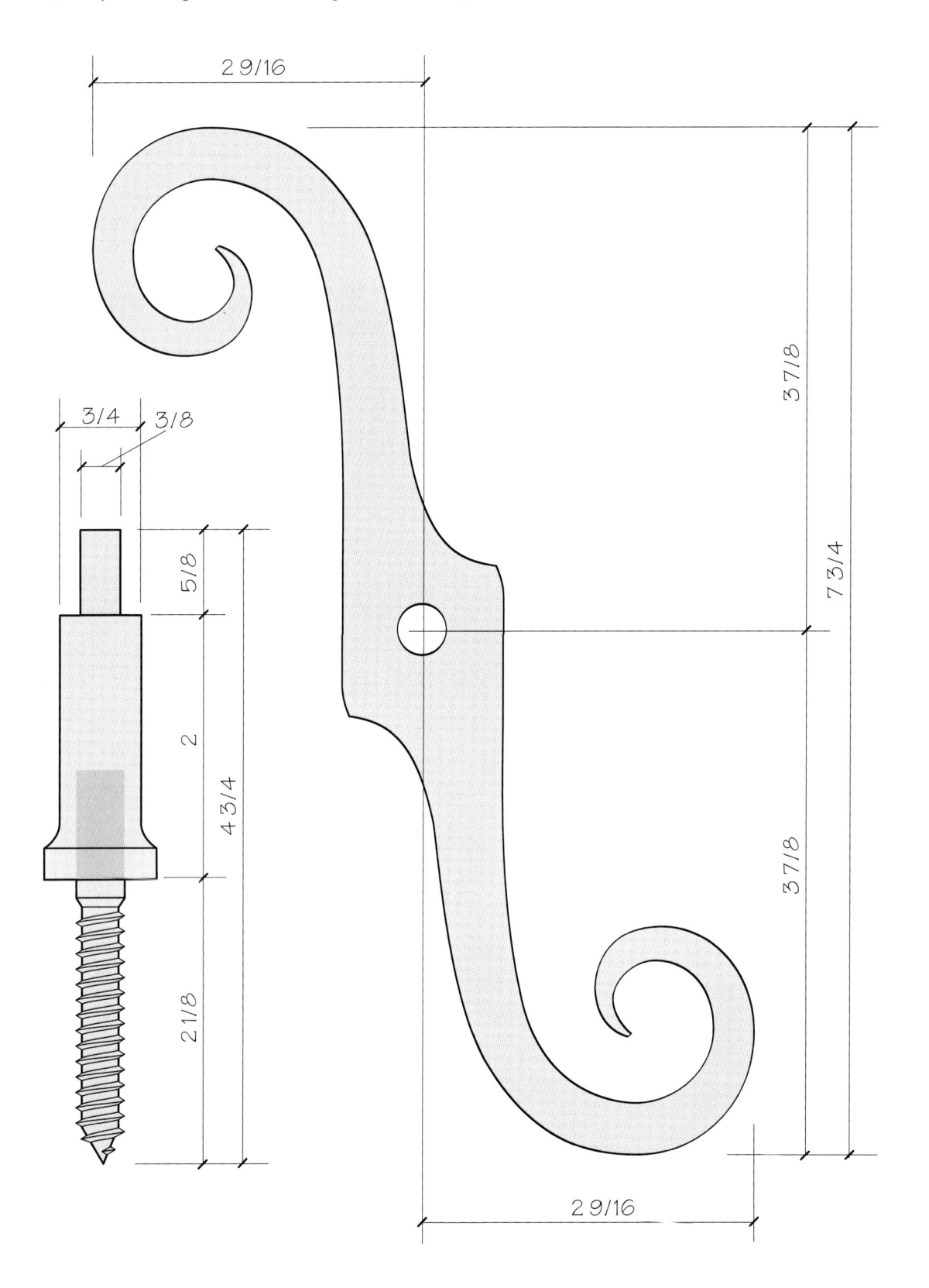

Strap Hinges -not to scale

These hinges represent two examples of flush mount strap hinges. The first one is split and opened, then grooved for a woven effect. The second one features a repousse apple and leaves, forge welded to the strap. **168|2105, 69|851**

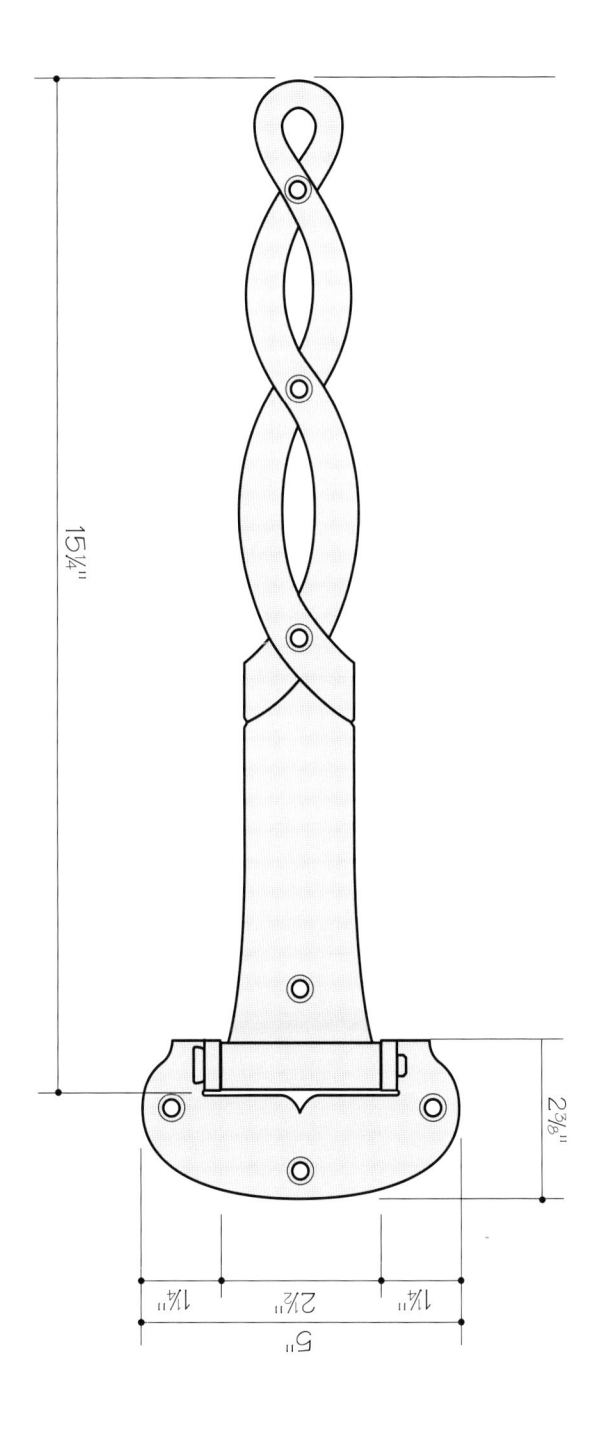

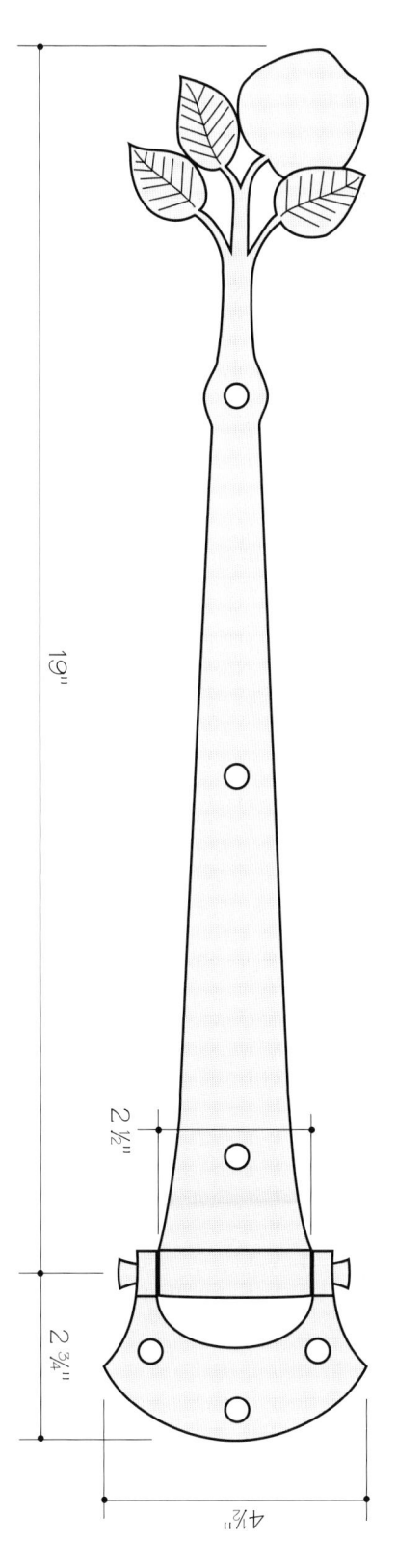

Traditional Door Latch - full scale

This small door latch is representative of a style made in the mid to late 19th century. They featured a knob and cam-lock in conjunction with a more traditional drop bar, and were commonly found in log and timber frame houses. **83|1033**

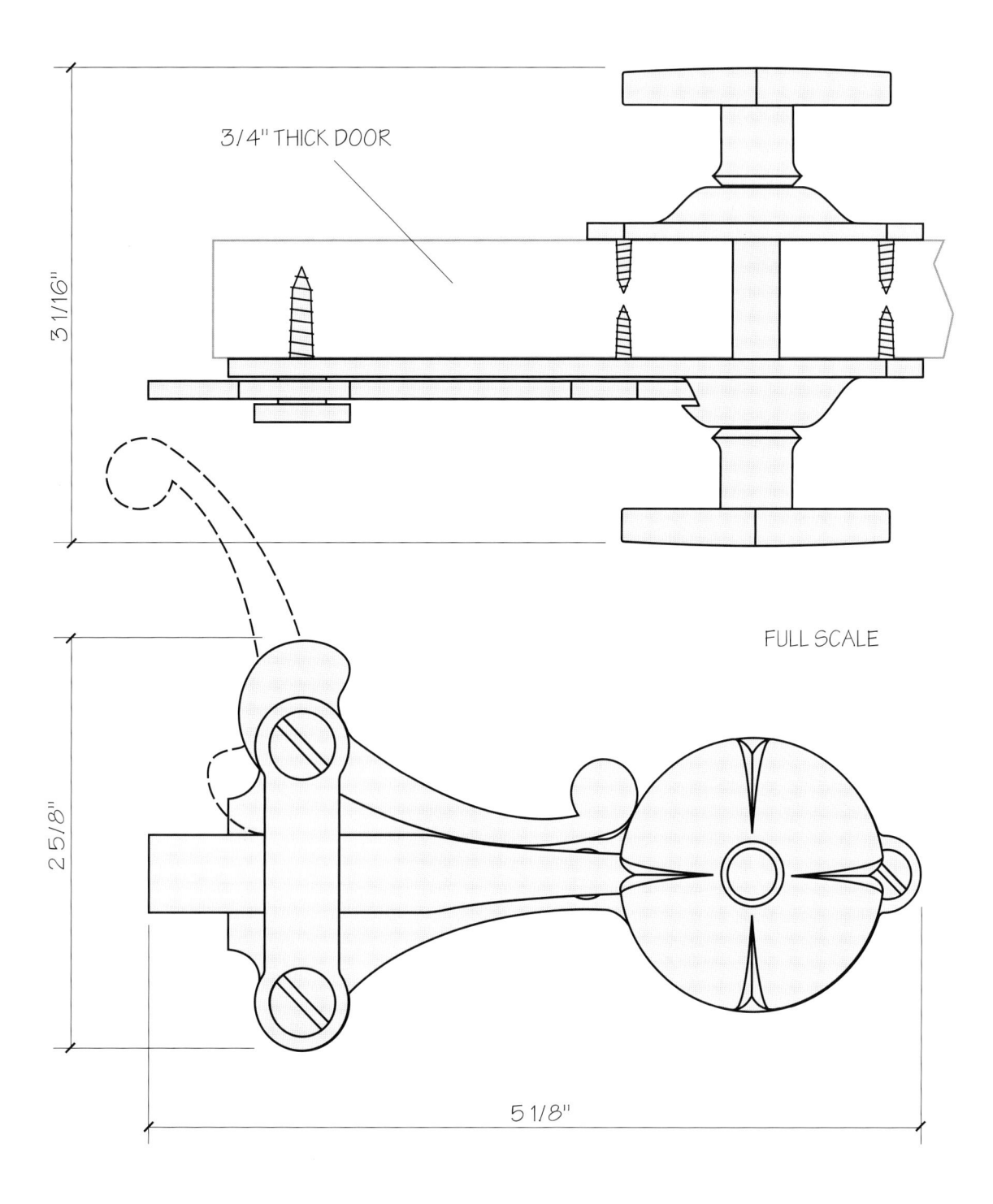

3/4" THICK DOOR

3 1/16"

FULL SCALE

2 5/8"

5 1/8"

85

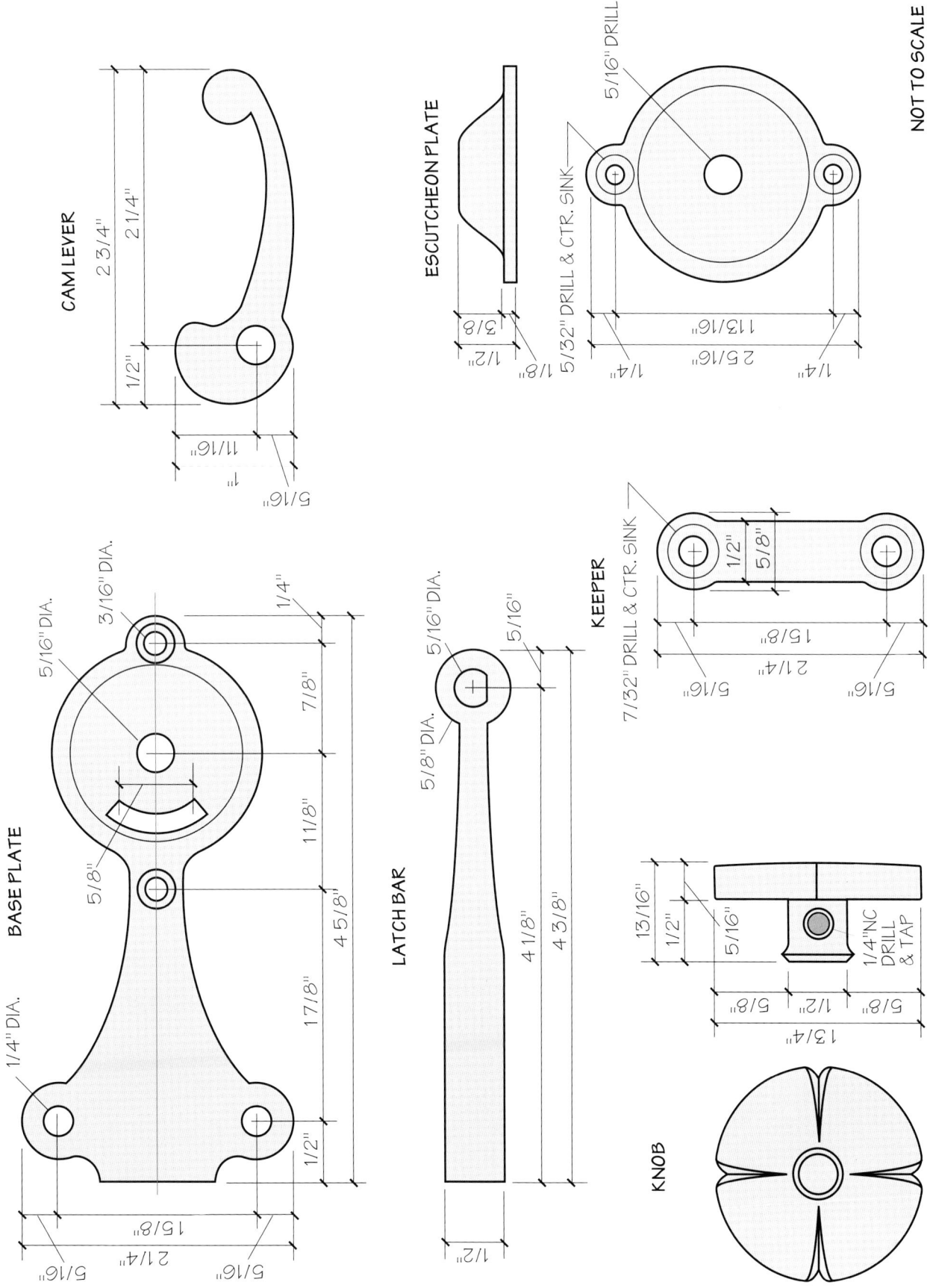

4 Interior Ironwork

Candle Holder #1 - ¾ scale

This hinged candle holder can be arranged into a variety of configurations including square, diamond, and zig-zag. Add more holders for pentagon, hexagon, and other configurations. The ⅜" x ¾" stock must be slot punched, split and drawn out before bending to the final shape. **158|1984**

Candle Holder #2 -not to scale

Designed for 2" square candles, this holder features stems hot cut from the base material. It is made from ¼" thick stock, but can also be made from 5/16" or 3/8" for a bolder appearance. **160|2011**

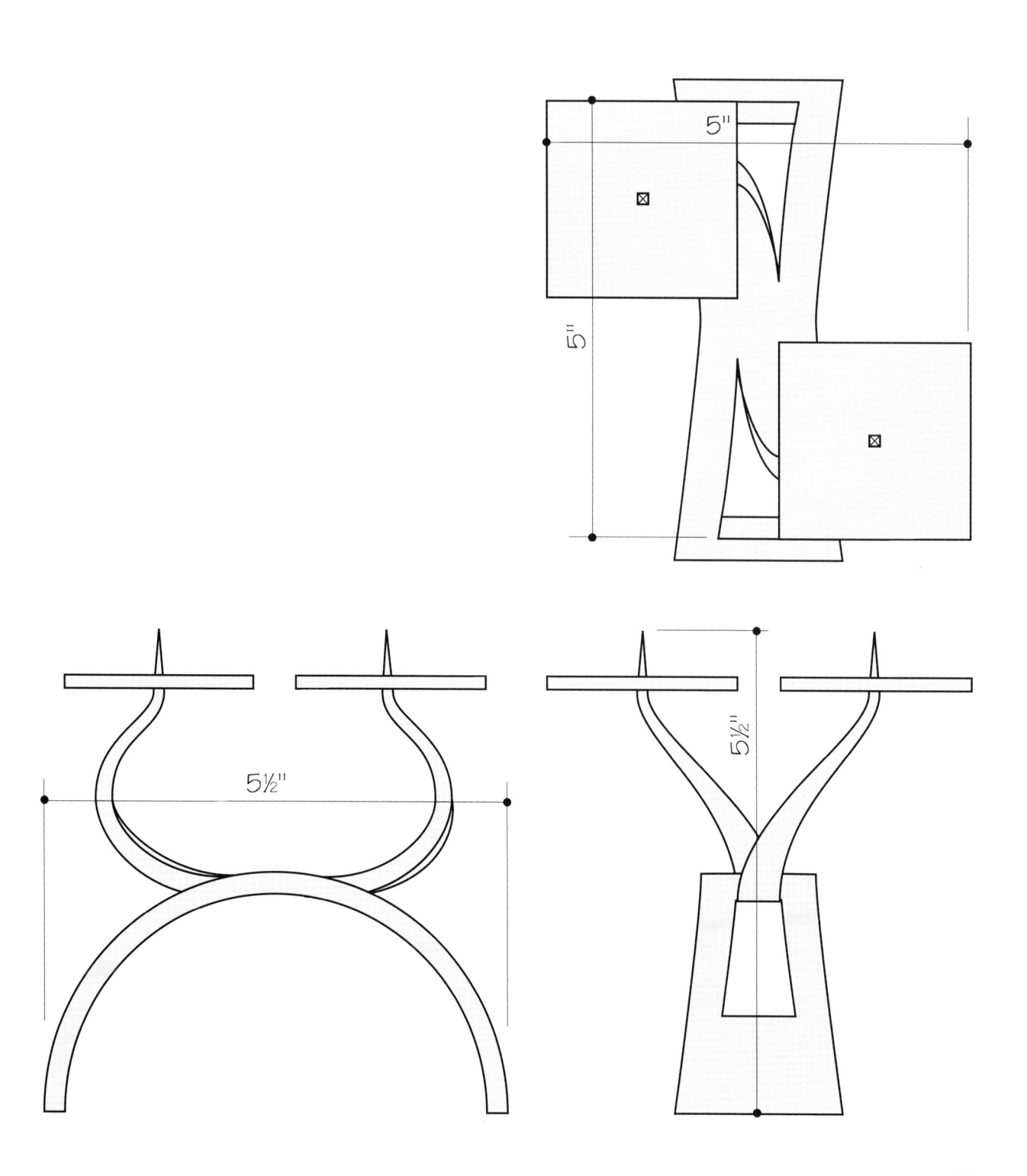

Chandelier -not to scale

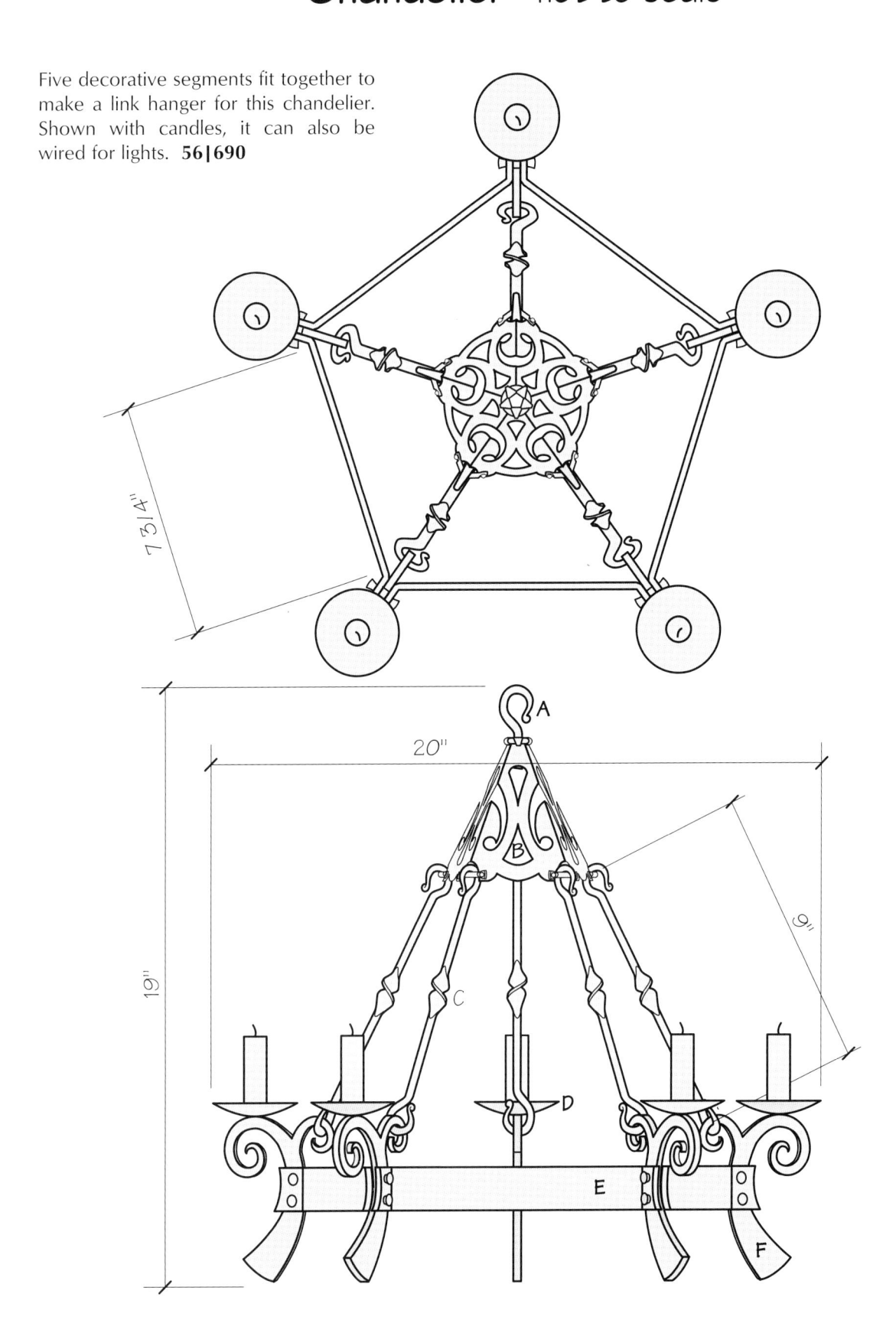

Five decorative segments fit together to make a link hanger for this chandelier. Shown with candles, it can also be wired for lights. **56|690**

7 3/4"

20"

9"

19"

A
B
C
D
E
F

PART F

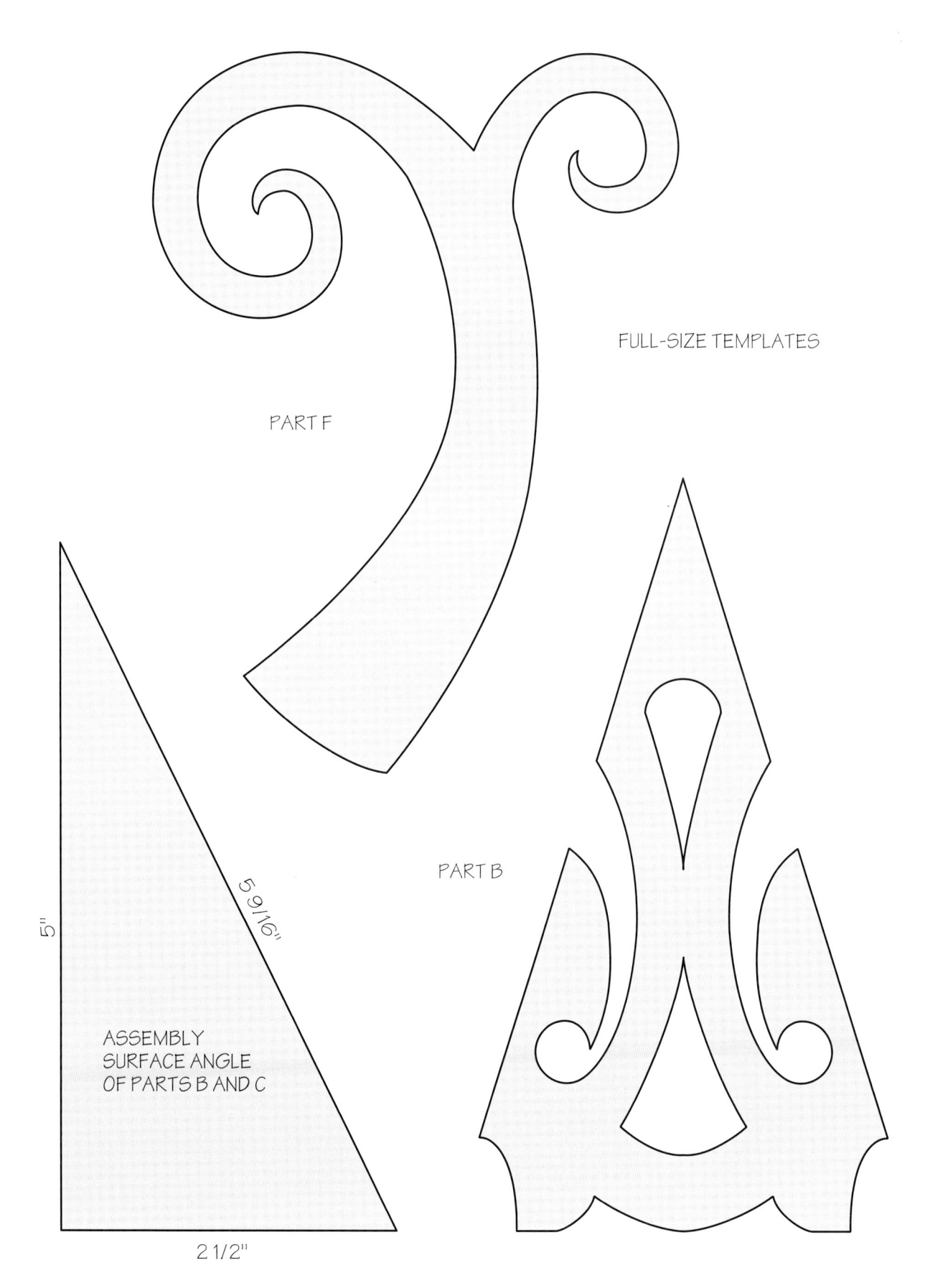

FULL-SIZE TEMPLATES

5"

5 9/16"

ASSEMBLY
SURFACE ANGLE
OF PARTS B AND C

2 1/2"

PART B

Coat Rack -not to scale

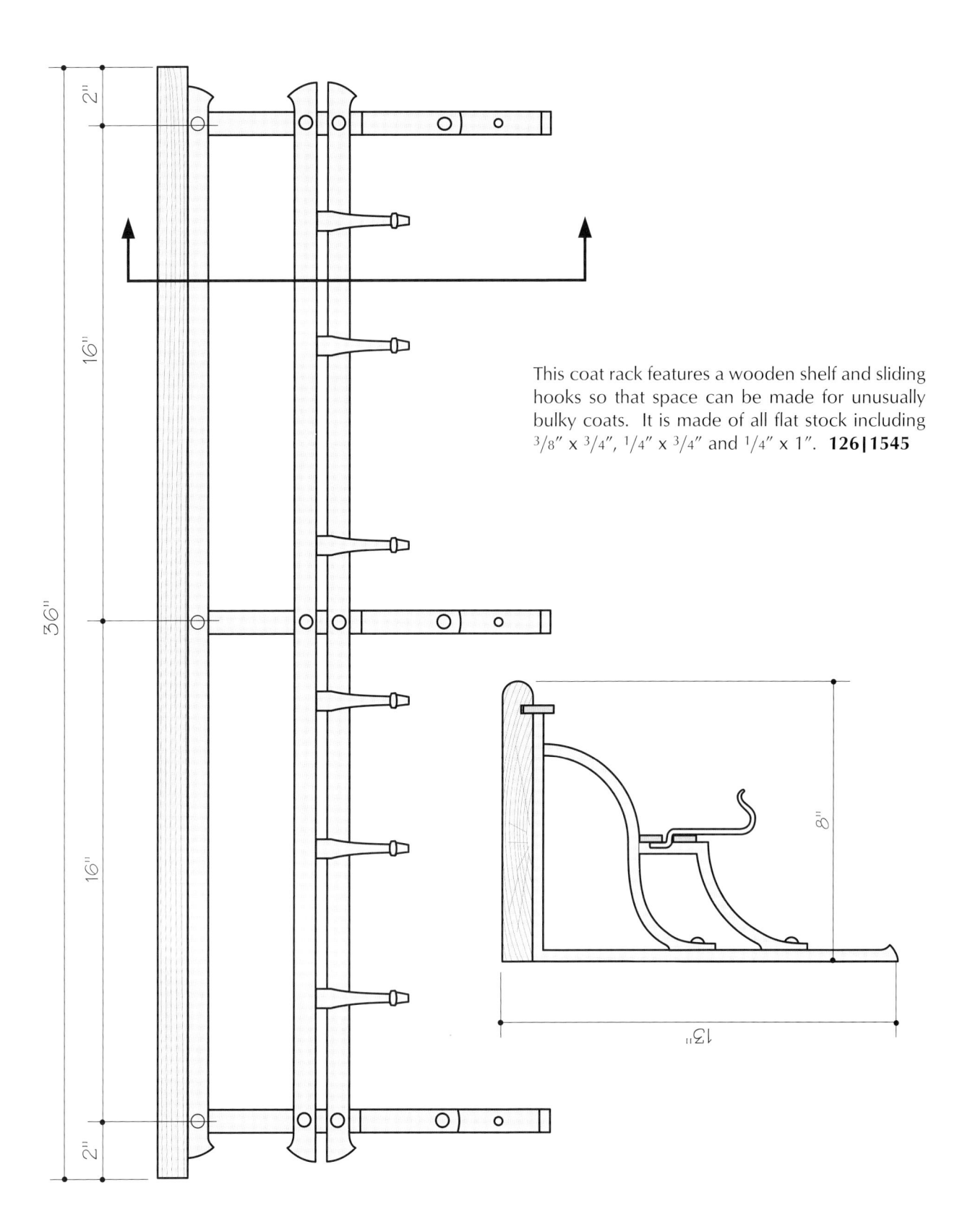

This coat rack features a wooden shelf and sliding hooks so that space can be made for unusually bulky coats. It is made of all flat stock including $3/8'' \times 3/4''$, $1/4'' \times 3/4''$ and $1/4'' \times 1''$. **126|1545**

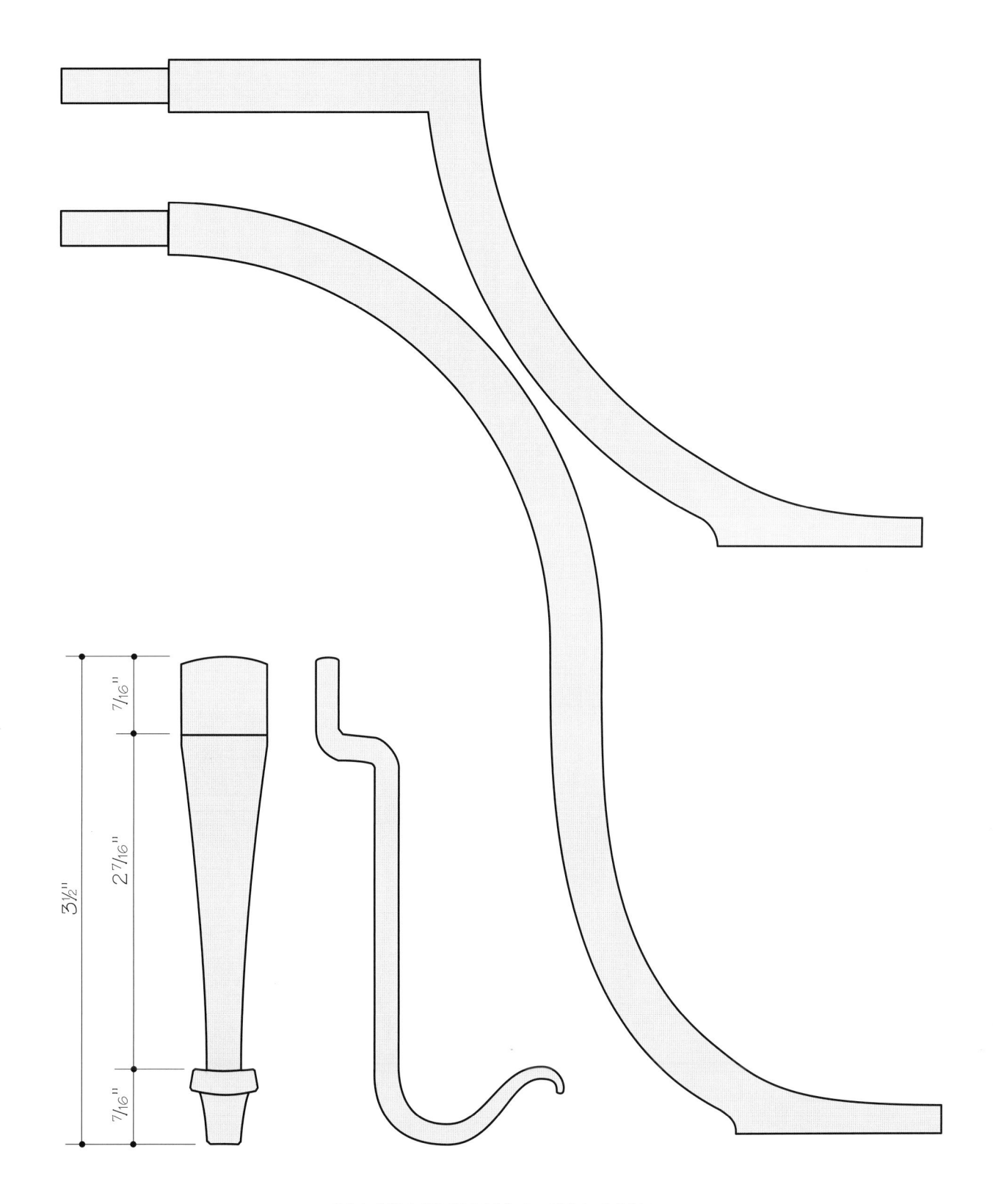

COAT RACK DETAILS - FULL SCALE

93

Curio Shelves -half scale

These tiered shelves an be arranged in any order and slide along two horizontal bars to adjust spacing. The wooden shelves are screwed to the brackets. **165|2078**

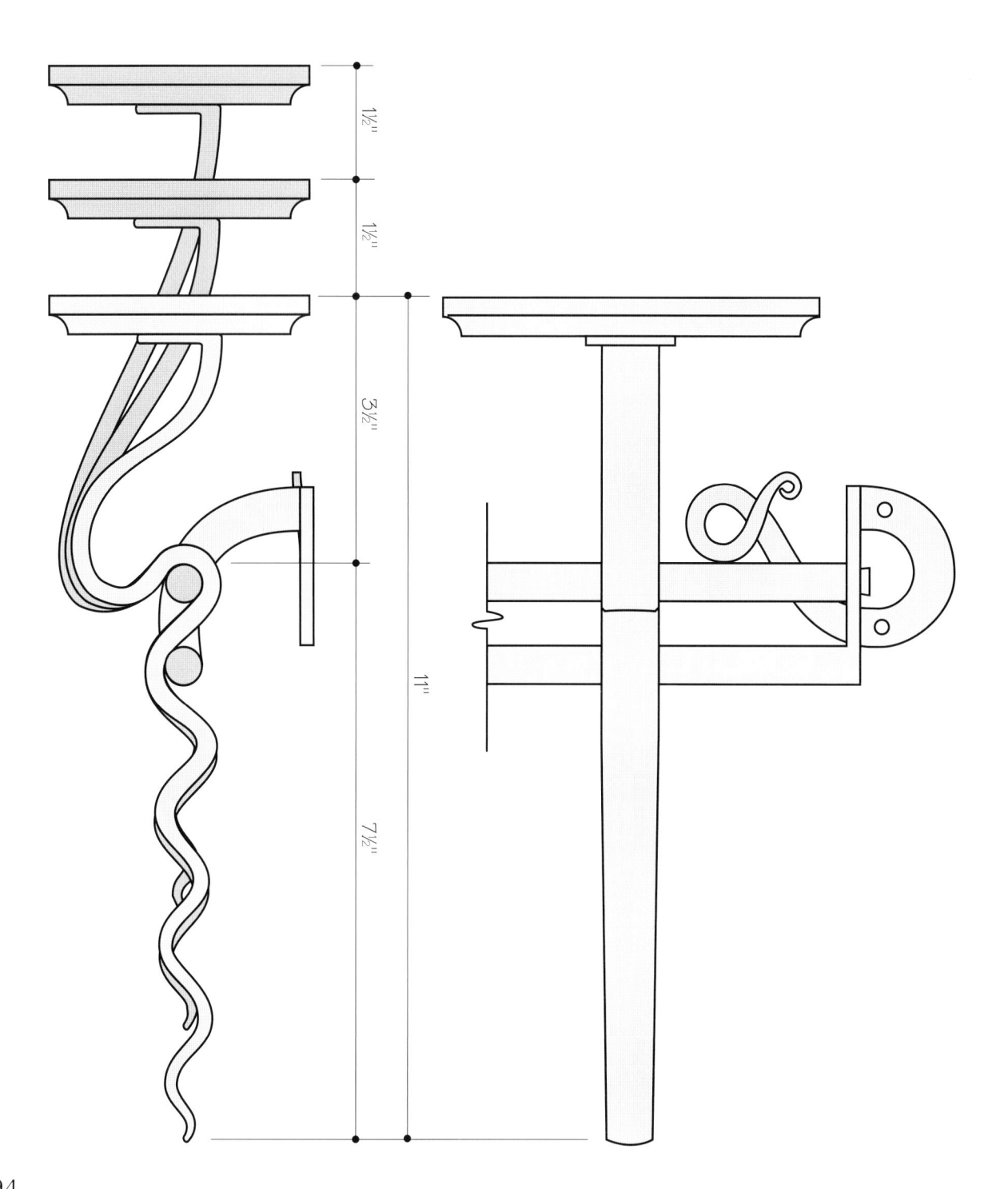

Floor Lamp #1 - ⅛ scale

Sections of forged pipe make up the post for this lamp. The pipe is fullered and drawn out into a cup-like shape at one end, then shouldered and drawn down to a size that will fit inside the previous section. **62|768**

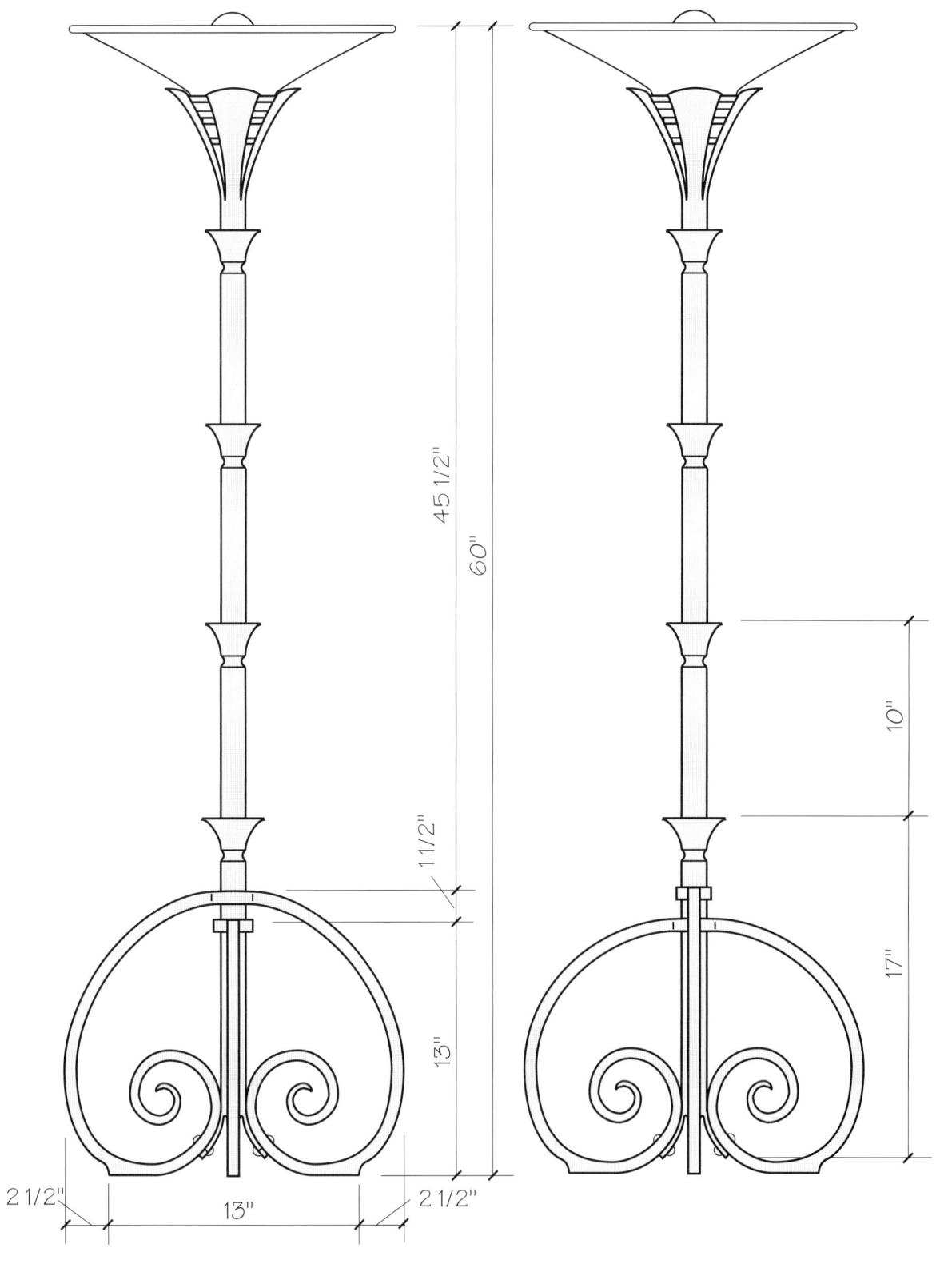

95

Floor Lamp #2 - 1/8 scale

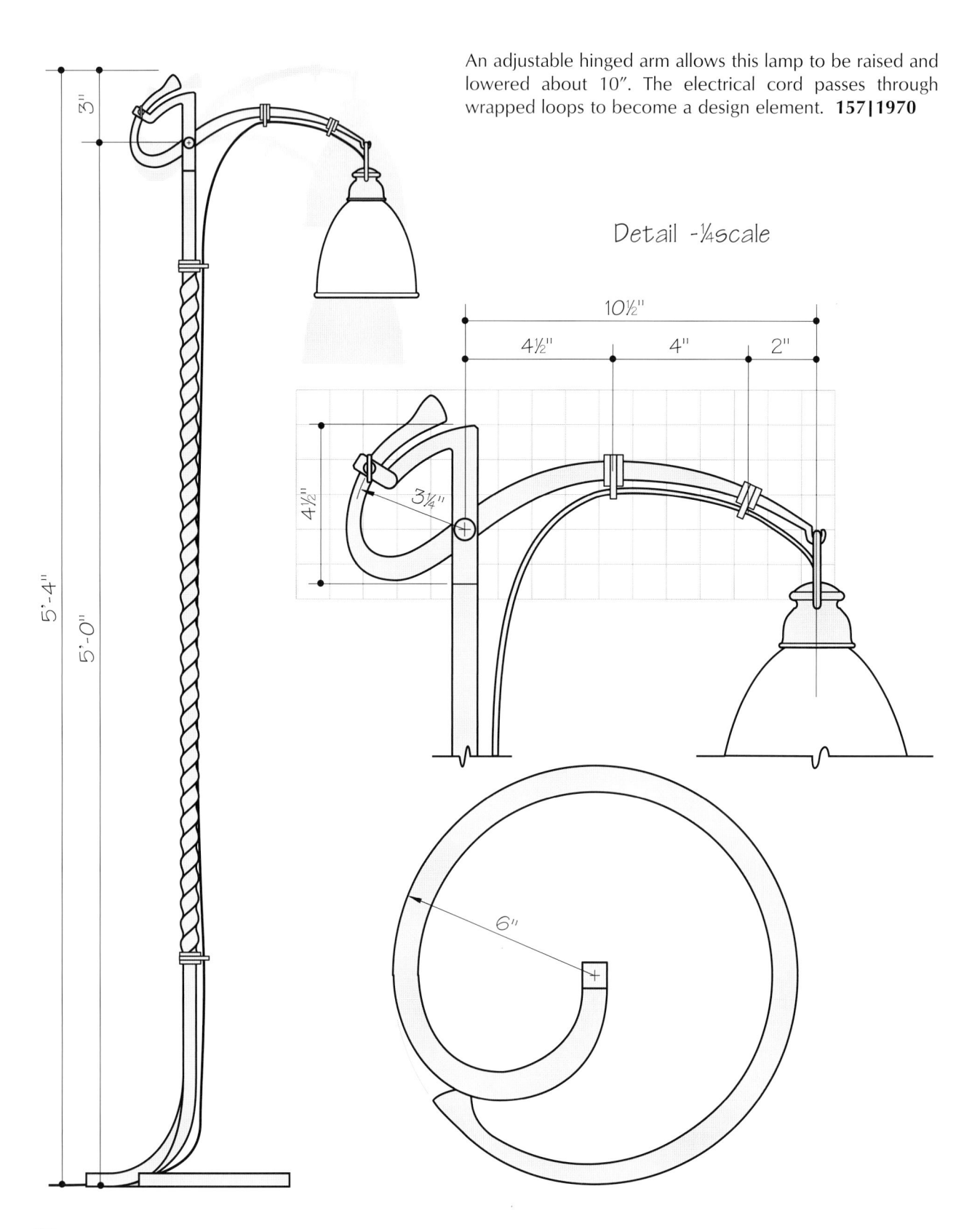

An adjustable hinged arm allows this lamp to be raised and lowered about 10". The electrical cord passes through wrapped loops to become a design element. **157|1970**

Detail - 1/4 scale

3"
5'-4"
5'-0"
10½"
4½"
4"
2"
4½"
3¼"
6"

Floor Register – half scale

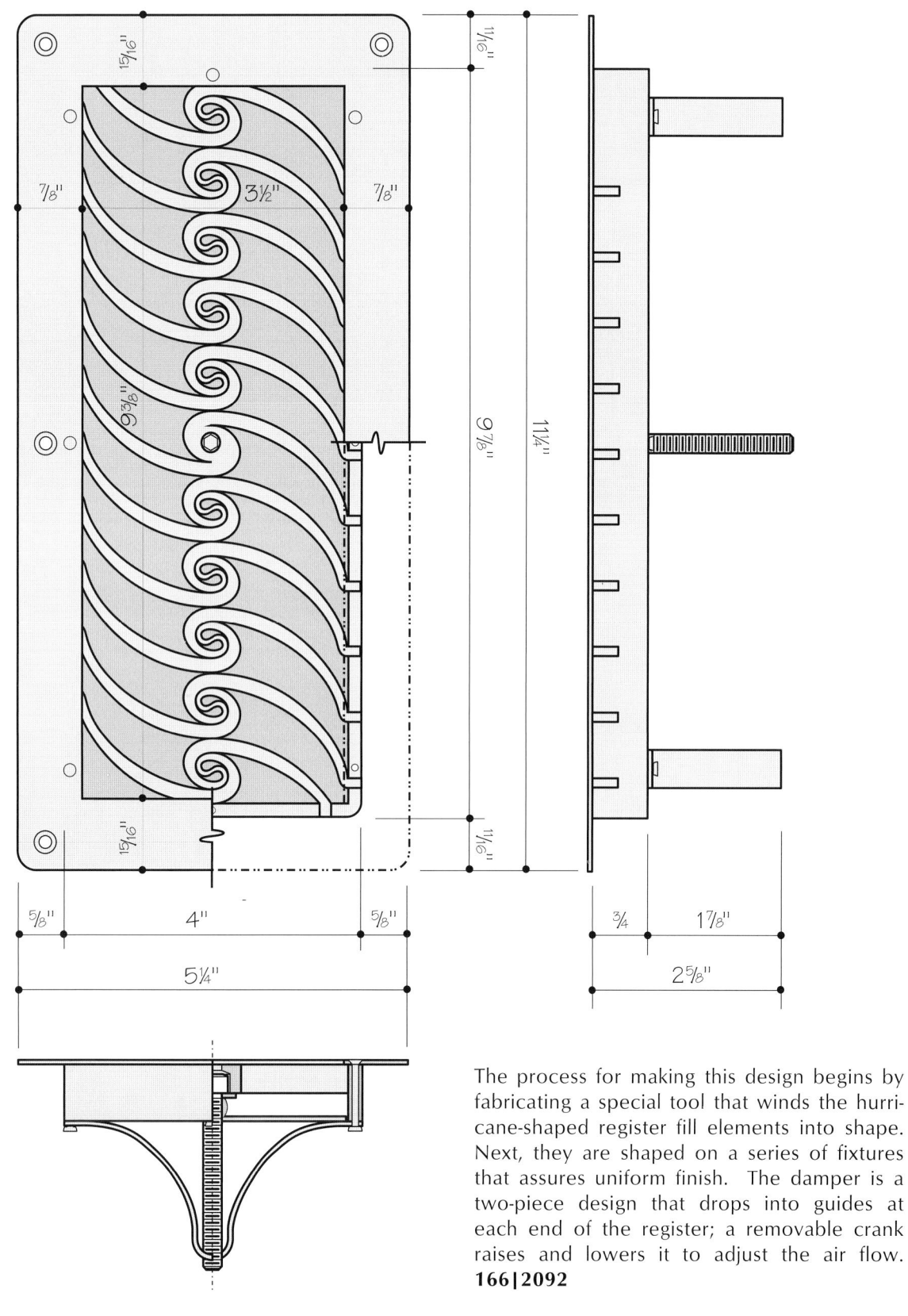

The process for making this design begins by fabricating a special tool that winds the hurricane-shaped register fill elements into shape. Next, they are shaped on a series of fixtures that assures uniform finish. The damper is a two-piece design that drops into guides at each end of the register; a removable crank raises and lowers it to adjust the air flow.
166|2092

Floor Register, cont.

98

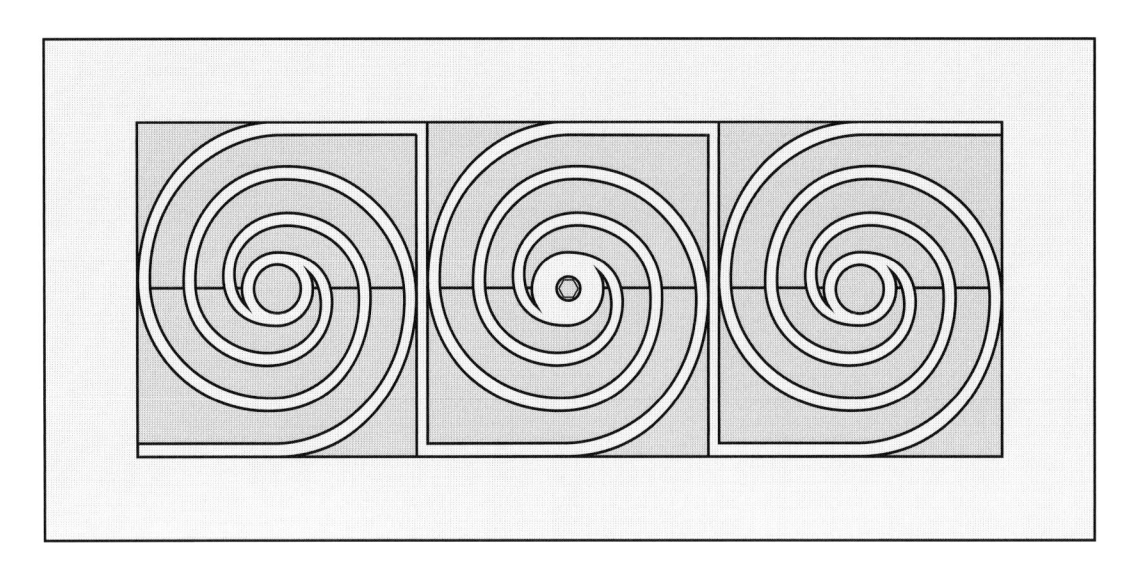

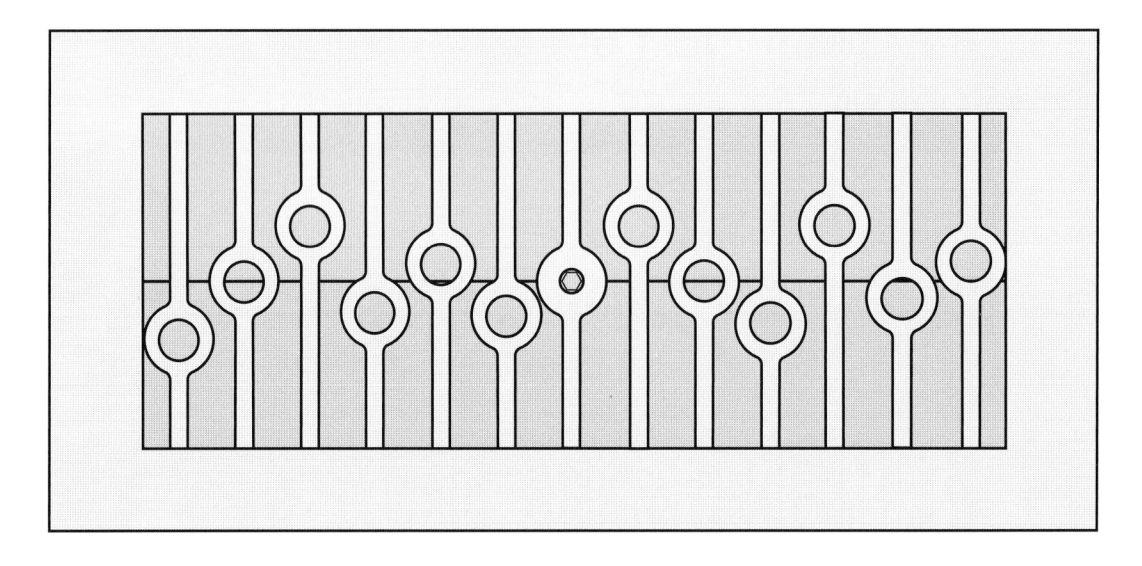

Grill #1 -not to scale

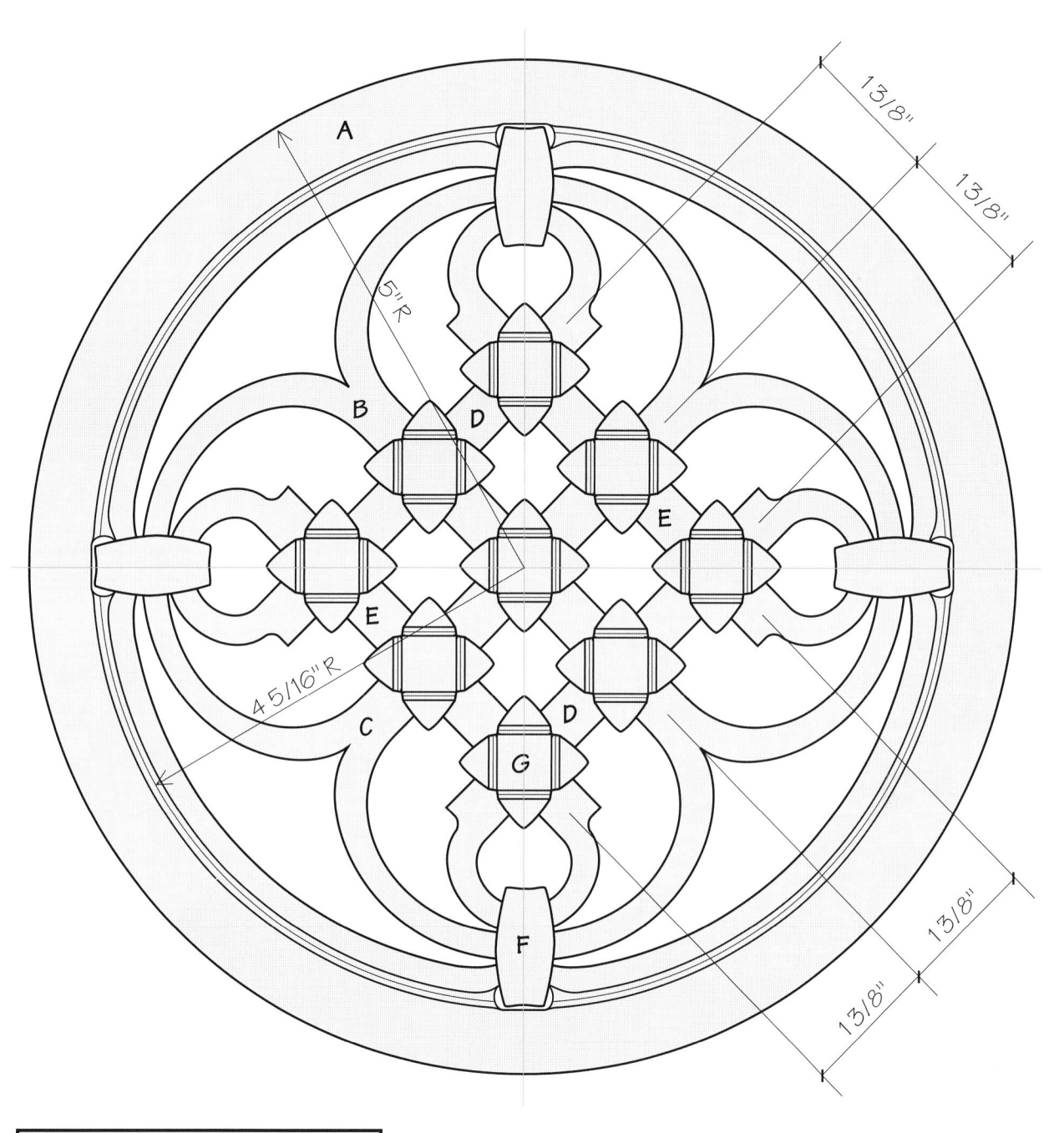

Dimensions shown: 1 3/8", 1 3/8", 5"R, 4 5/16"R, 1 3/8", 1 3/8"

Labels: A, B, C, D, E, F, G

MATERIALS	
A	1/4" x 1" FLAT
B	1/4" x 1/2" & 1/4" x 3/4" FLAT
C	1/4" x 1/2" & 1/4" x 3/4" FLAT
D	1/4" x 1/2" FLAT
E	1/4" x 1/2" FLAT
F	1/4" x 1/2" FLAT
G	3/8" x 3/4" FLAT

The rosettes for this project start with square chunks of flat stock that are saddled and forge welded to the bars below them. The corners are then drawn out and the stock grooved to finish. The whole assembly is fit together in a woven fashion before being collared to a flat ring.
43|531

Grill #1, cont.

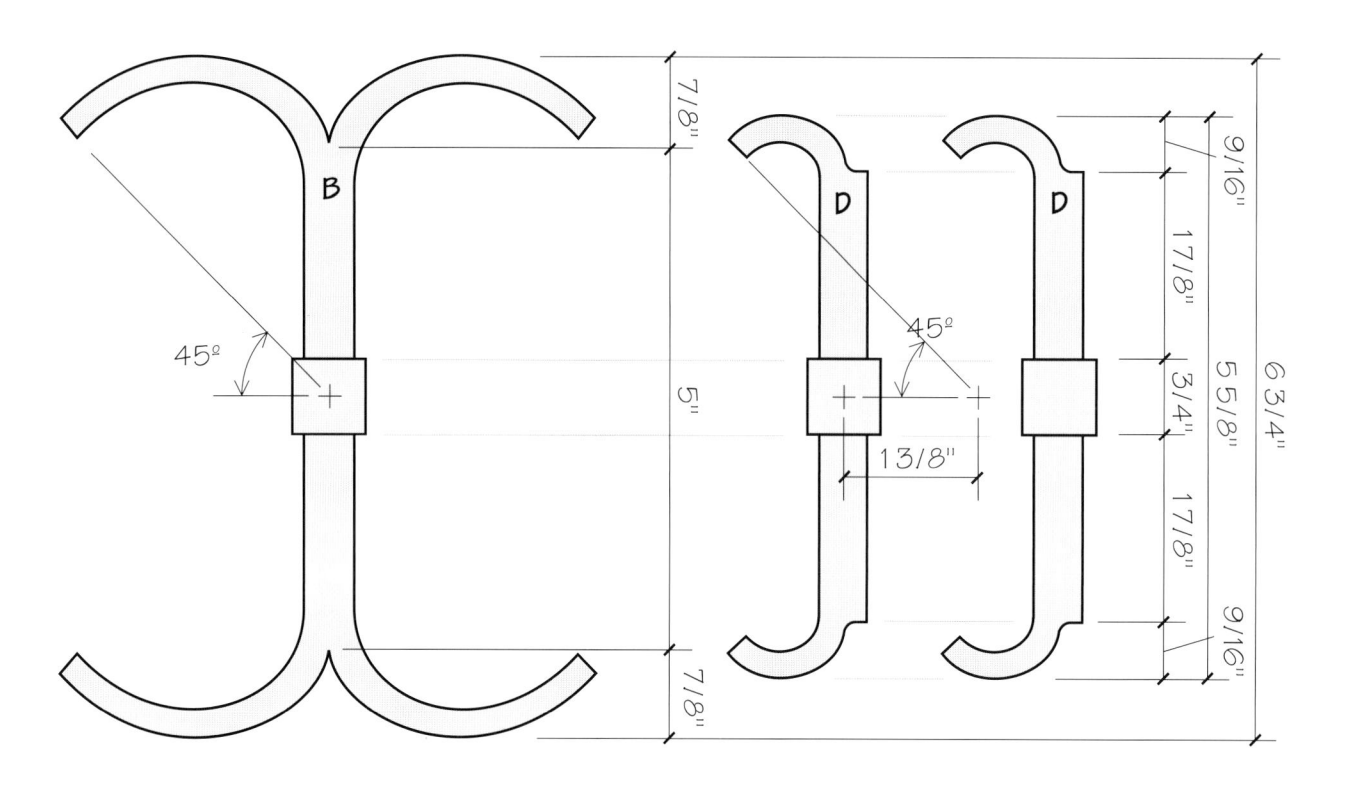

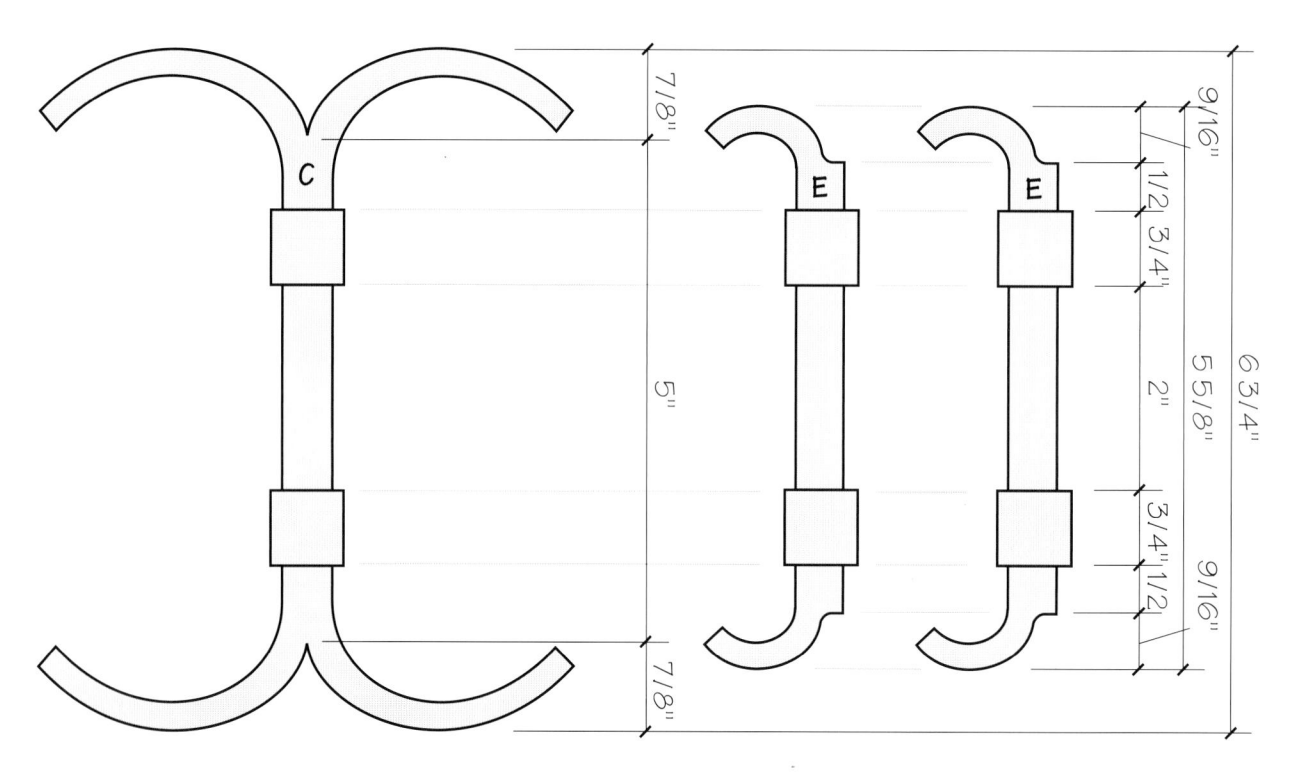

GRILL #1 INTERIOR ELEMENTS

Grill #2 -not to scale

The complexity of this grill is deceiving because it's made from only two elements. These elements—repeated four times—comprise both the frame and the interior of the grill. They are assembled with collars and rivets to create a new design that is more complex than the core elements alone. **87|1075**

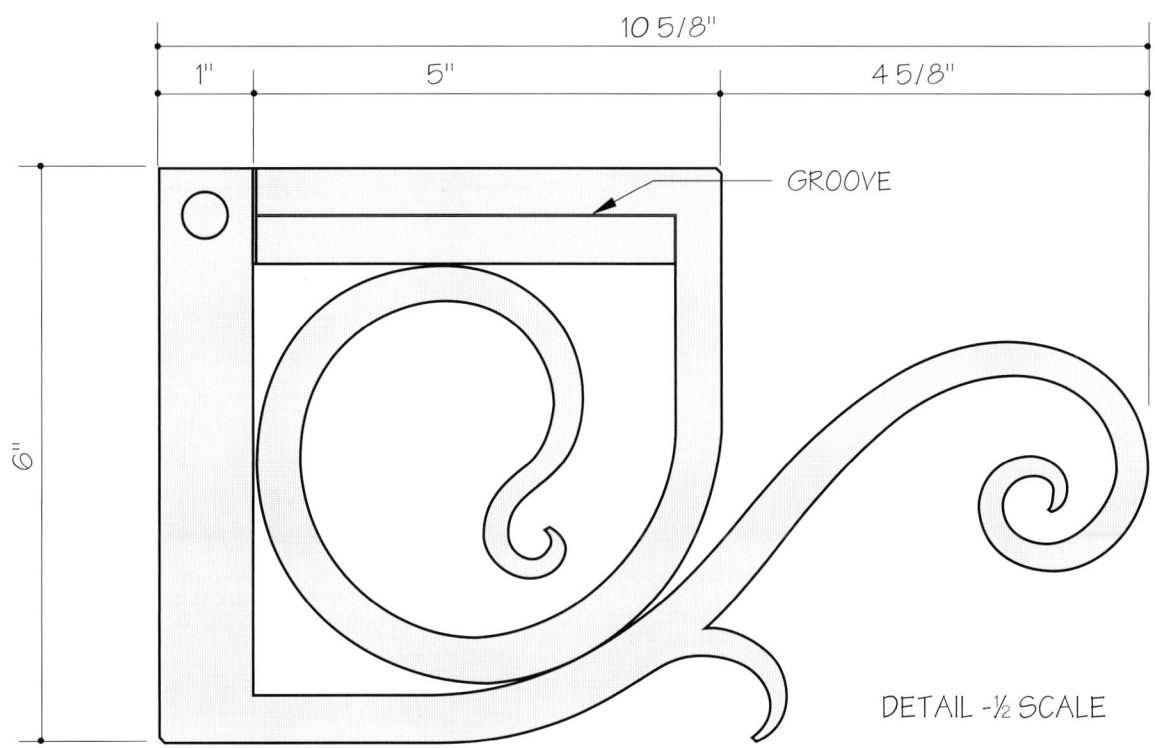

GROOVE

DETAIL -½ SCALE

101

Handrail Bracket -half scale

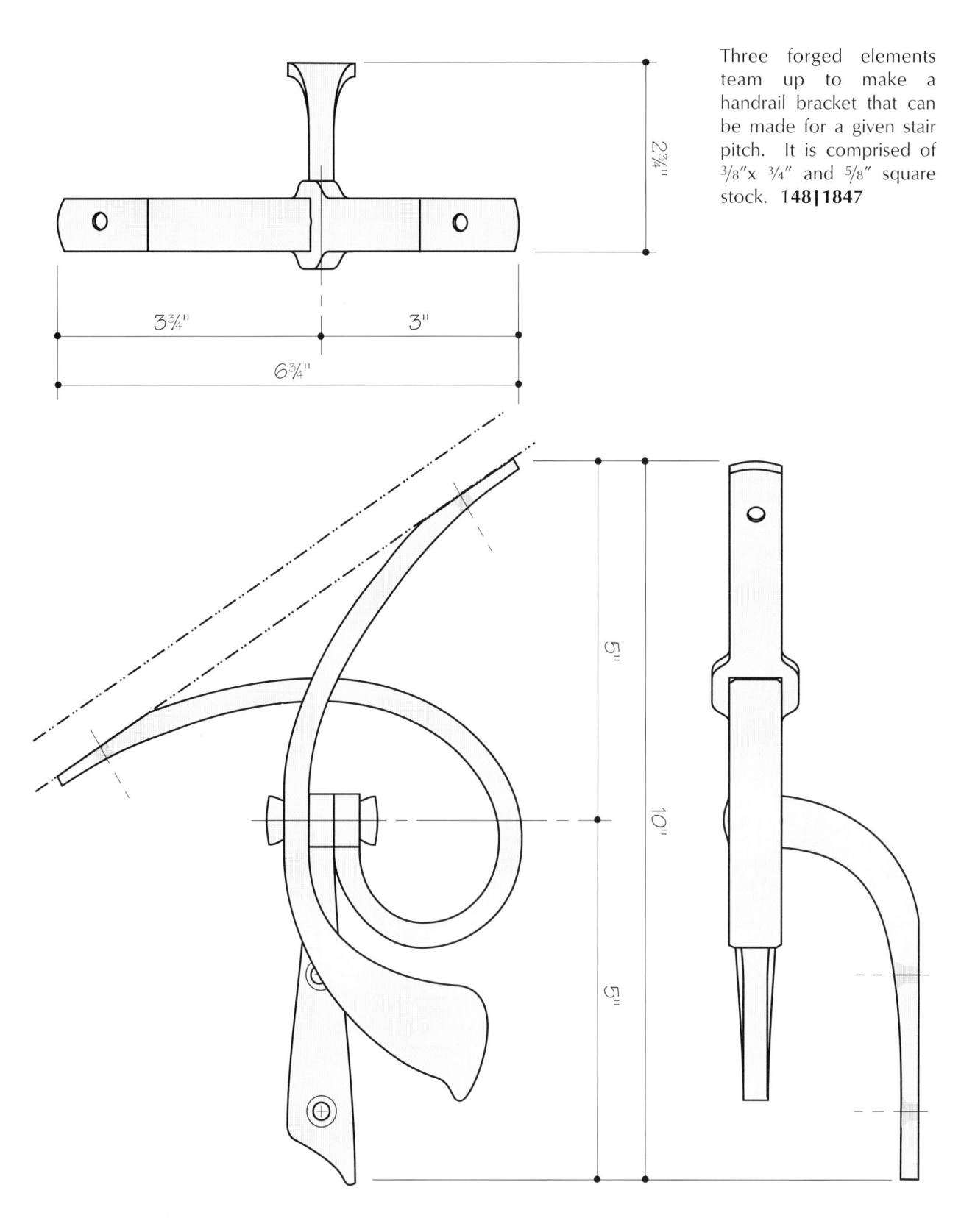

Three forged elements team up to make a handrail bracket that can be made for a given stair pitch. It is comprised of 3/8"x 3/4" and 5/8" square stock. **148|1847**

2¾"

3¾"   3"

6¾"

5"

10"

5"

Headboard #1 -not to scale

Unusual joinery combined with flat and round elements make this item unique. The vertical elements are made from slotted and drifted round stock, forge welded to tapered flat stock. **45|557**

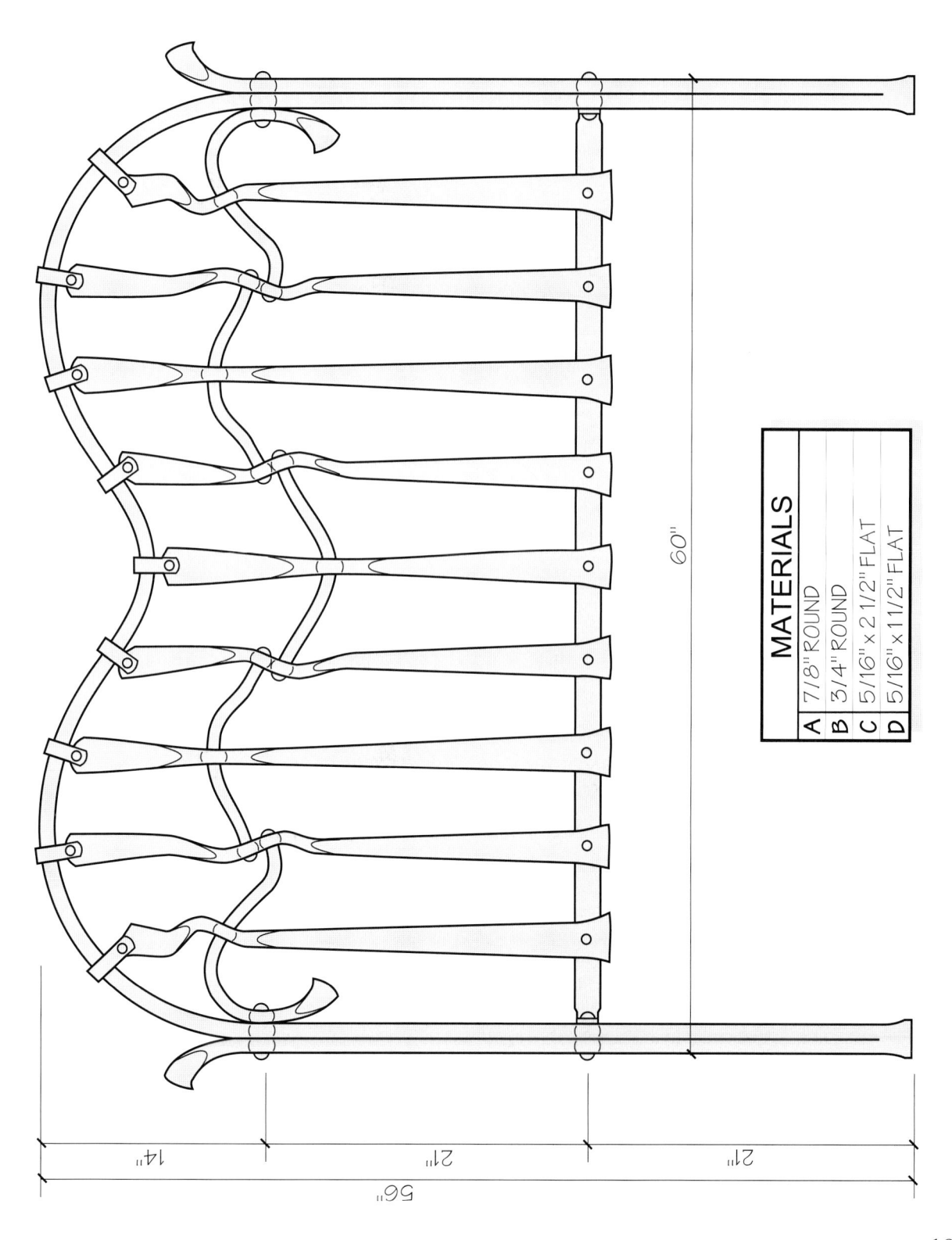

MATERIALS	
A	7/8" ROUND
B	3/4" ROUND
C	5/16" x 2 1/2" FLAT
D	5/16" x 1 1/2" FLAT

Headboard #2 - ⅛ scale

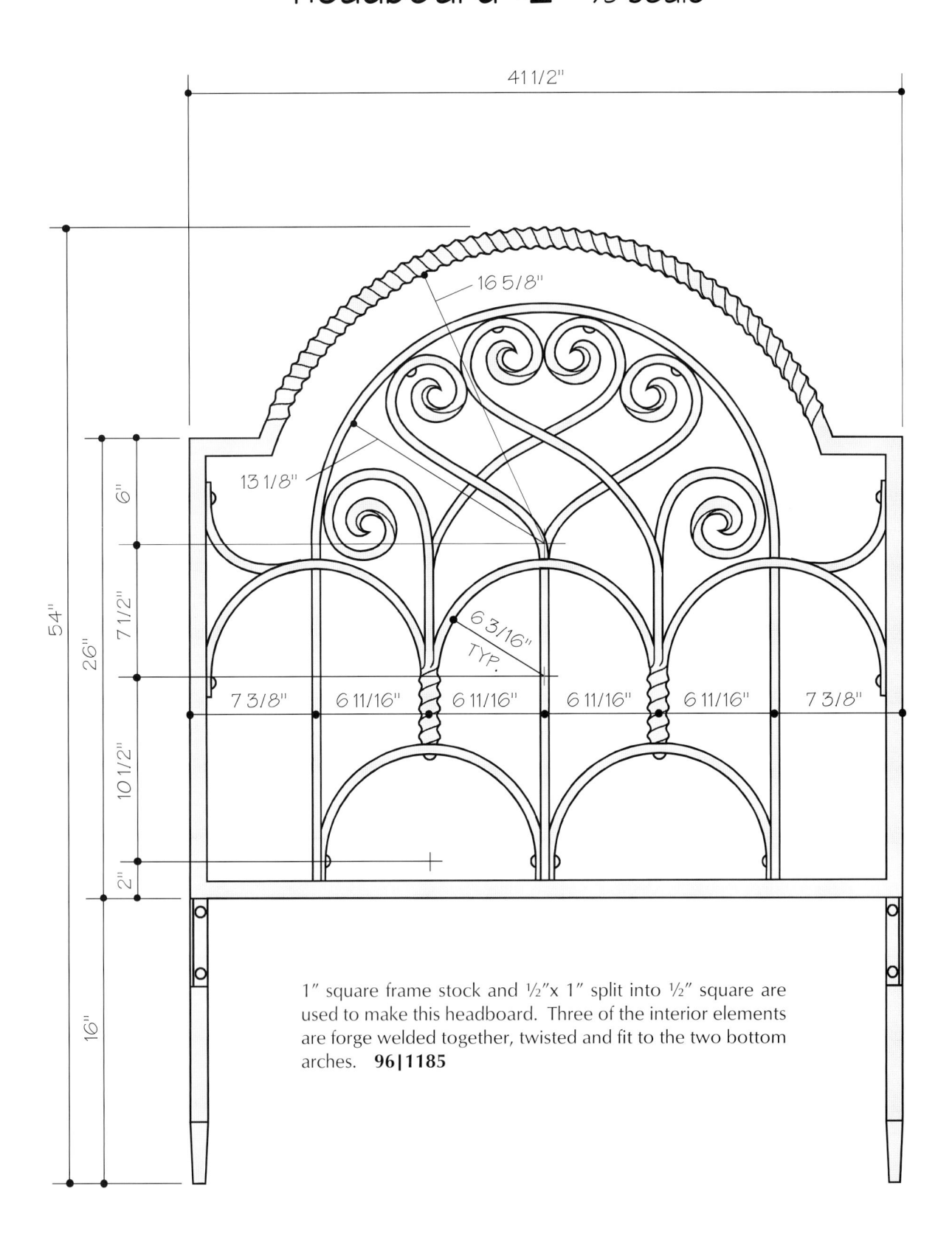

41 1/2"

16 5/8"

13 1/8"

6"

54"

26"

7 1/2"

6 3/16" TYP.

7 3/8" | 6 11/16" | 6 11/16" | 6 11/16" | 6 11/16" | 7 3/8"

10 1/2"

2"

16"

1" square frame stock and ½"x 1" split into ½" square are used to make this headboard. Three of the interior elements are forge welded together, twisted and fit to the two bottom arches. **96|1185**

Headboard #3 – ⅛ scale

This headboard can be stretched from queen to king with the addition of one more arched segment. The leaves are forged flat, folded and reopened; the collars are made from round stock bundled flat and forge welded on edge. **137|1701**

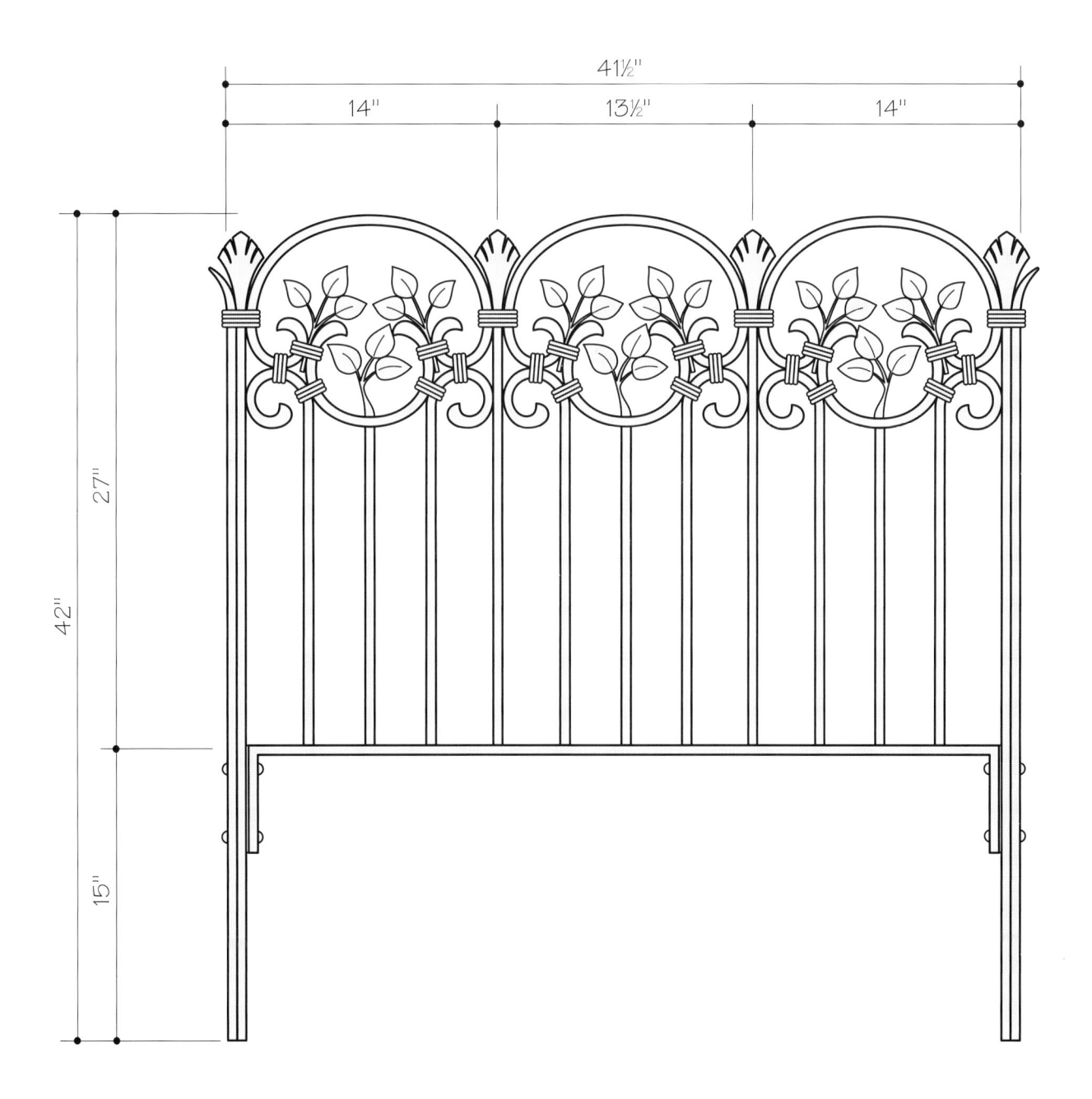

Keepsake Box -not to scale

The front, back and top of this box are fullered to create deep vertical grooves. End pieces are attach to the front and back with mortise and tenon construction, and the hinges are split from the parent stock. **74|919**

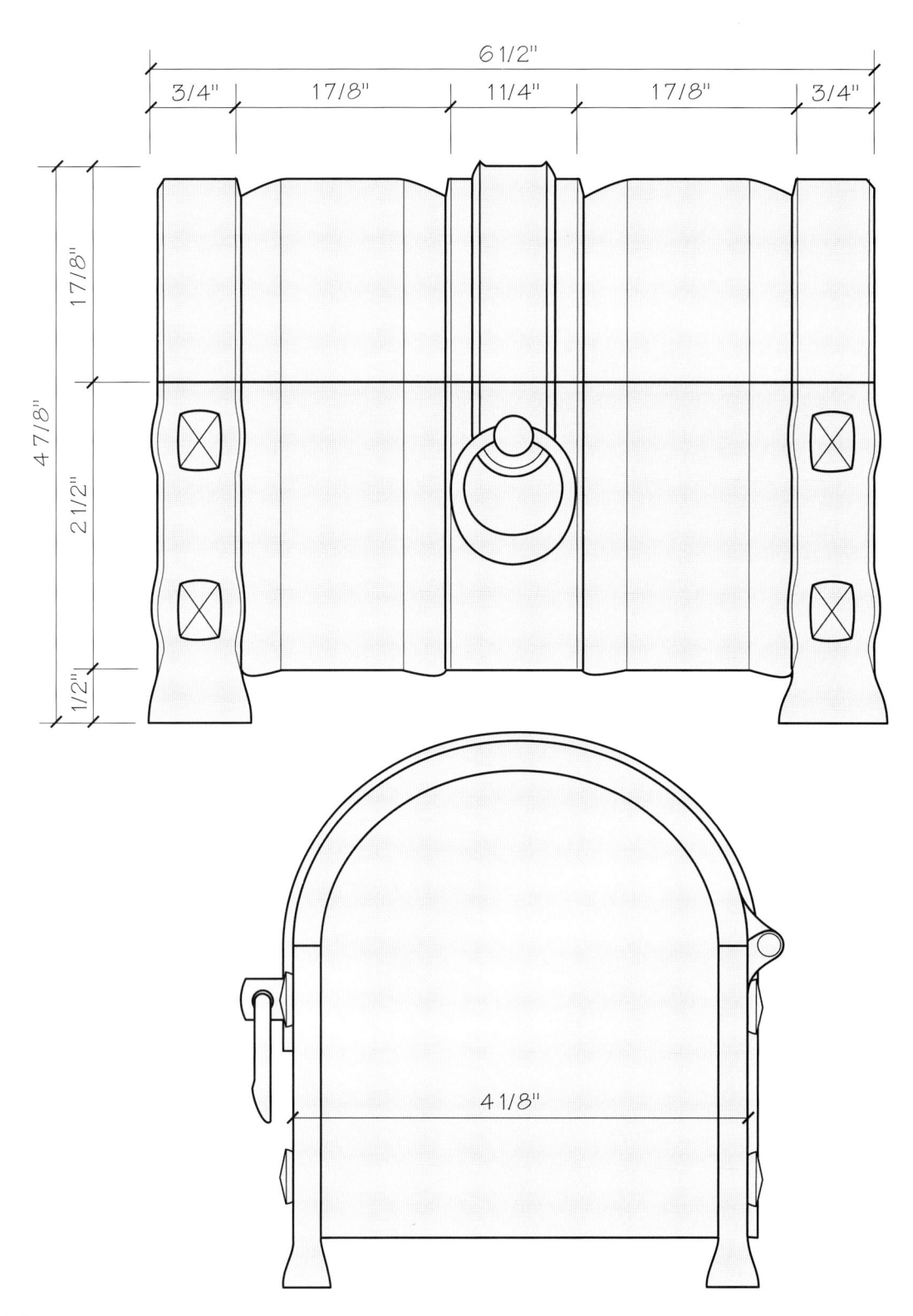

Lamp Base -half scale

Materials for this lamp include 1" square, 1"x 3" bar or plate, ½"x 1" flat and ¼" schedule 40 pipe. Electrical components (not shown) are available at most hardware stores. **142|1765**

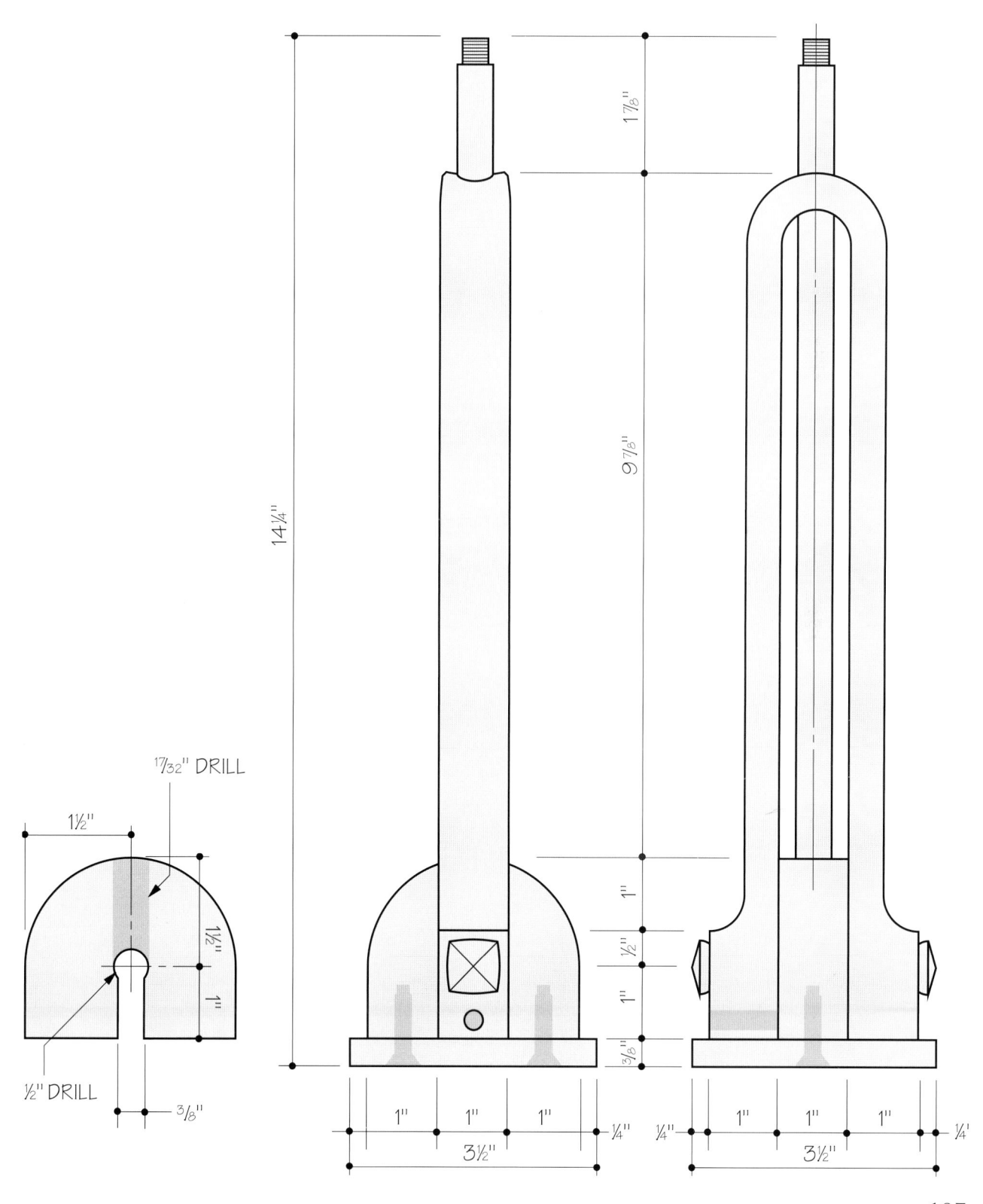

Lamp Shade -not to scale

The frame for this shade must be curved and tapered to conform to a cone shape. In order to accomplish this, the flat stock that makes up the frame rails are bent on edge or "the hard way" before bending to the required radius. Apply a special tea-stained velum shade material to finish. **143|1779**

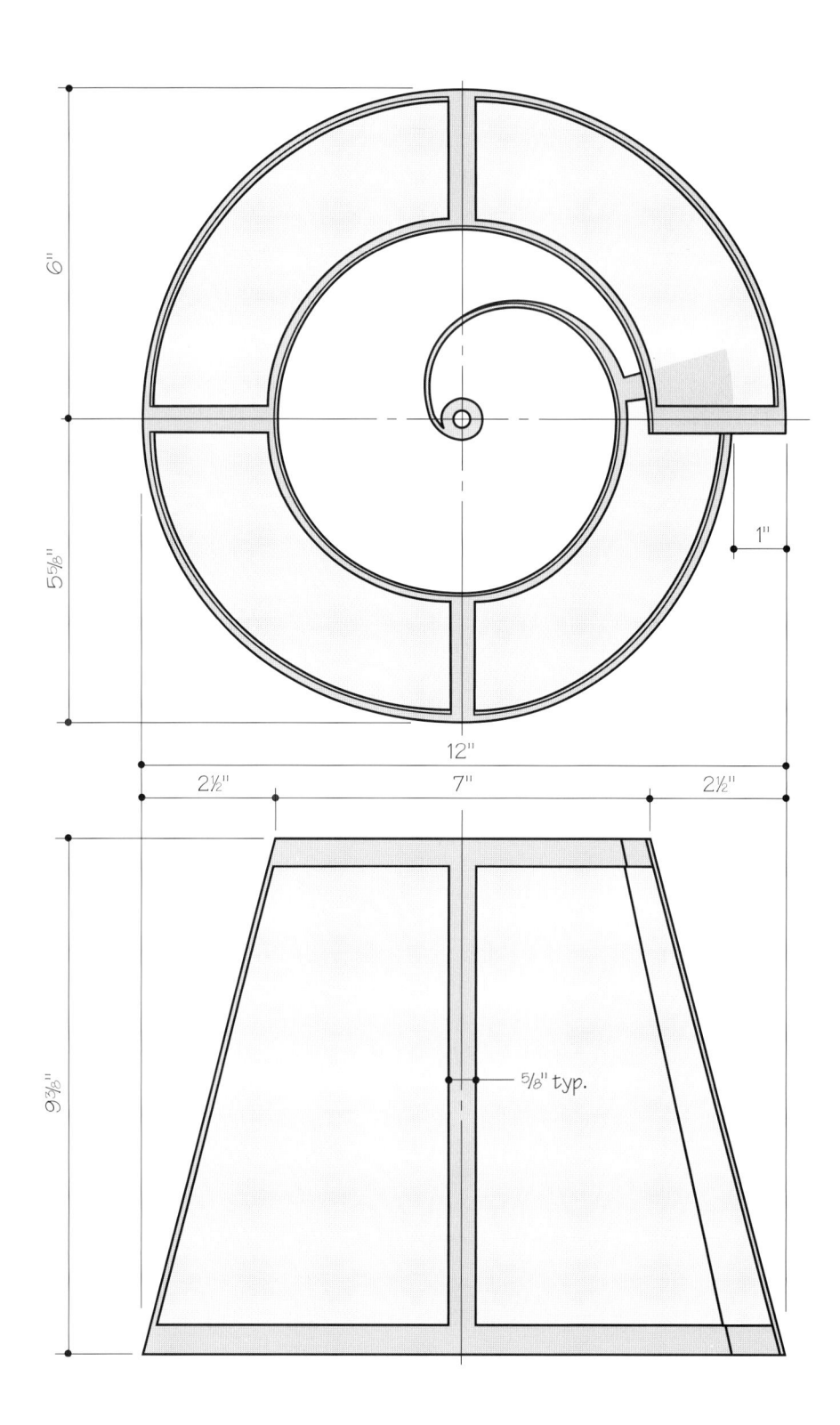

Mahogany Pod -full scale

The fruit of the mahogany tree consists of a woody capsule (or "pod") which contains long-winged seeds clustered to form a ball-like shape in the middle of the fruit. When the five parts of the outer shell are nailed to the woody interior near the end opposite the stem, the fruit opens up into a beautiful flower-like shape as it dries. Recreated in iron, it makes a striking ornament by itself, or for a variety of projects.

156|1955

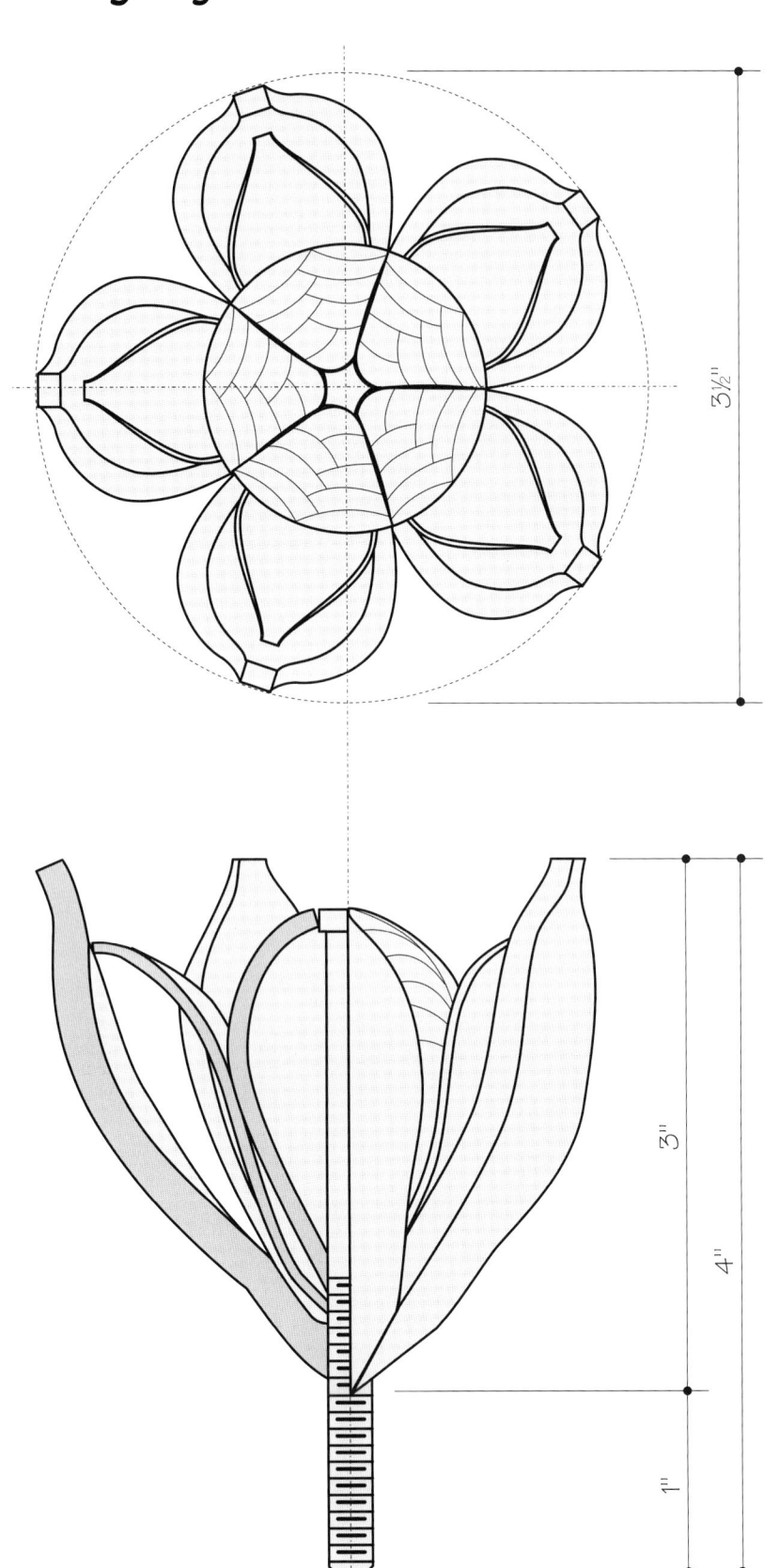

Pedestal -not to scale

Use this pedestal to display artwork, a vase and flowers, potted plant or whatever you desire. The design allows for flexible proportions, and the 1" stock shown here can be substituted with ¾" for a lighter look. The design theme centers around using an intermediate element other than the legs to support the top. **145|1810**

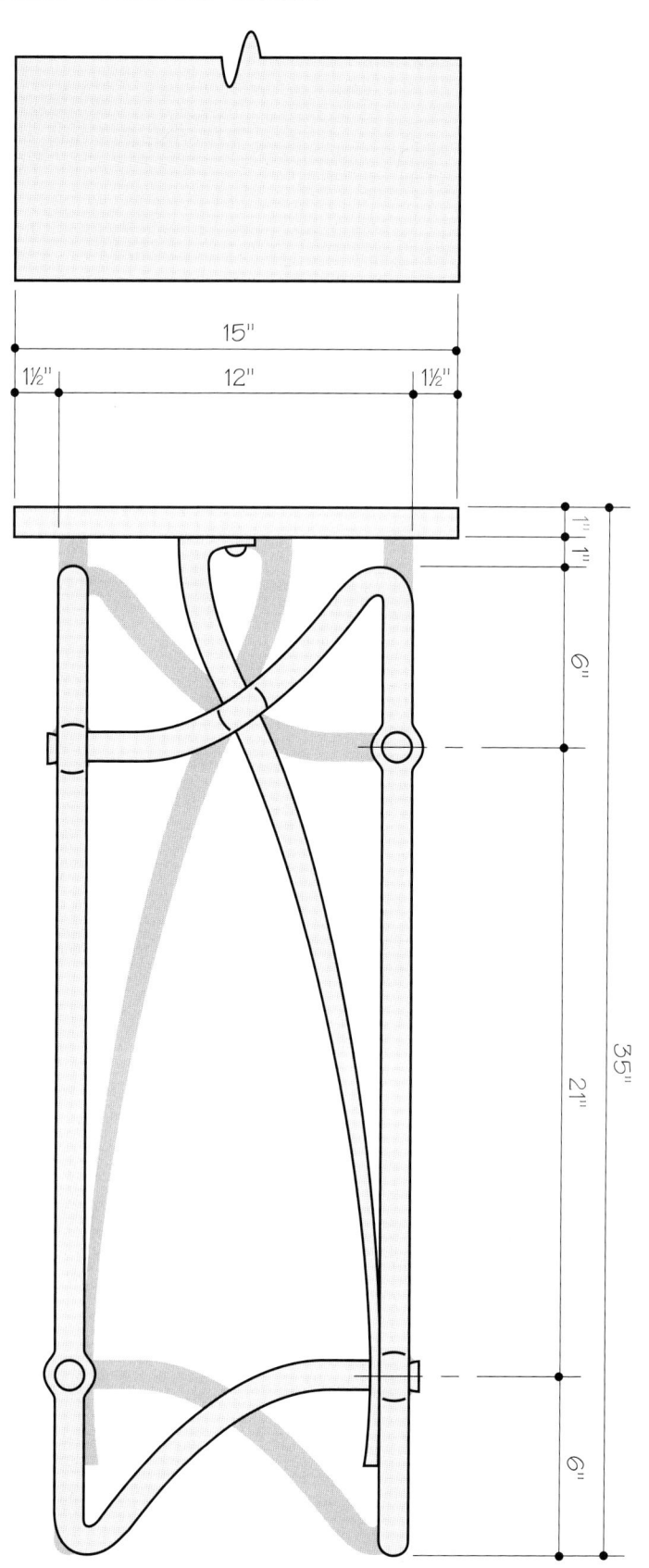

Pot Rack -not to scale

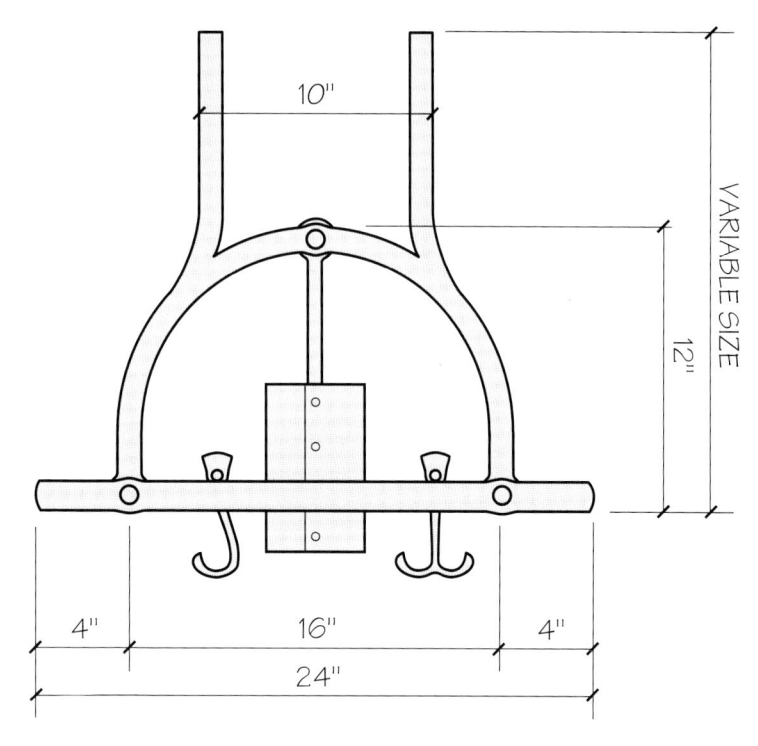

This pot rack is ceiling mounted so that it may hang over an island or similar work surface. The adjustable hook/bar system makes it possible to hang a large variety of pots and pans. Two lamps hang from the horizontal rail.
80|989

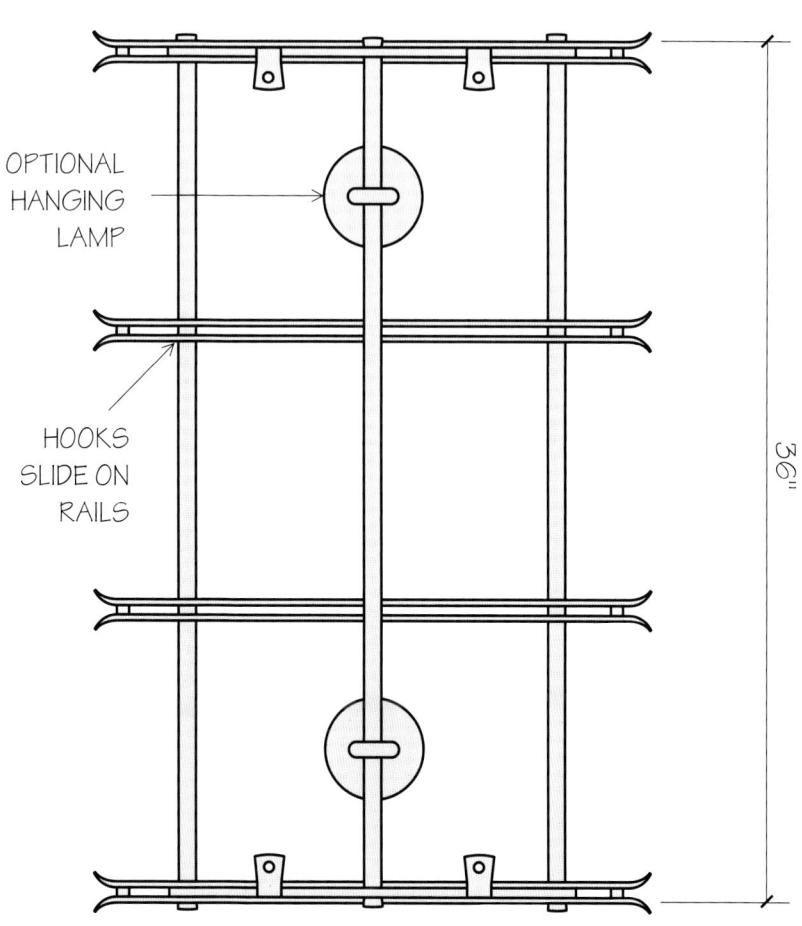

OPTIONAL HANGING LAMP

HOOKS SLIDE ON RAILS

Privacy Screen - 1/12 scale

Use 5/8" square stock for the frame and 5/16" x 5/8" for the scrolls. All horizontal and vertical frame joints are mortise and tenon. Top and bottom 1/4" round rods hold drapery between them. **118|1447**

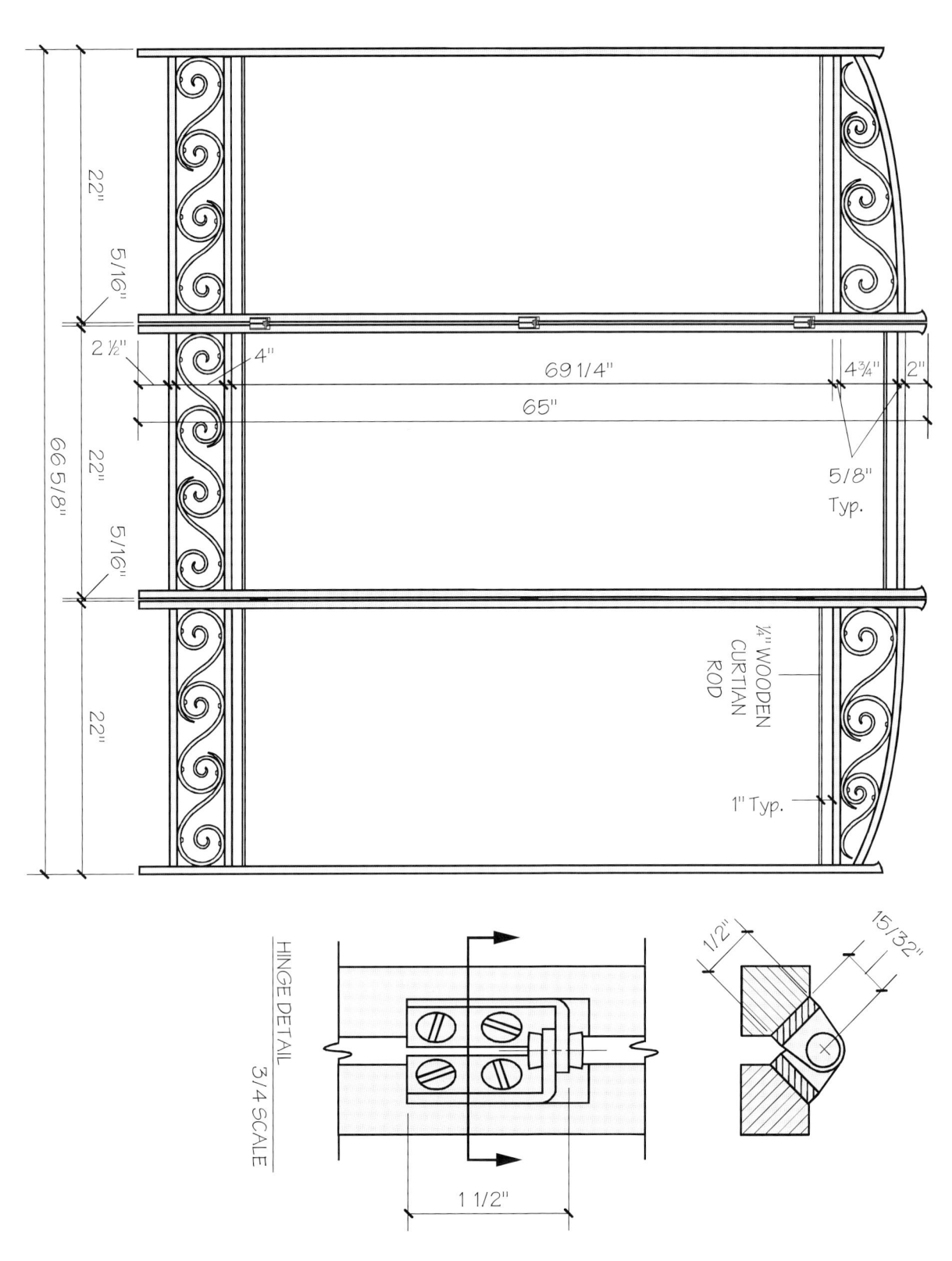

HINGE DETAIL 3/4 SCALE

Scale - ½ scale

Although not extremely accurate, this little scale is a very attractive piece to display. The ¼" thick main upright is flanked by two ⅛" outer pieces. Sandwiched at the base is a ½" thick block; the whole assembly is fastened to a ¼" thick base. The 16ga. sheet metal trays are supported by a ⅛" thick hanger and beam. **78|963**

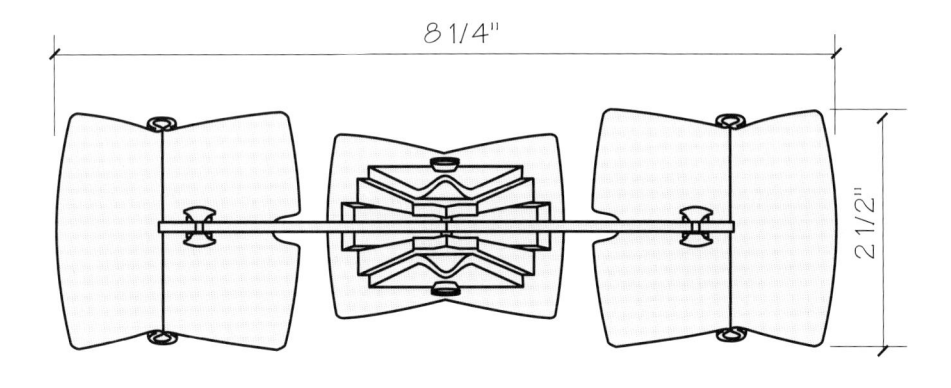

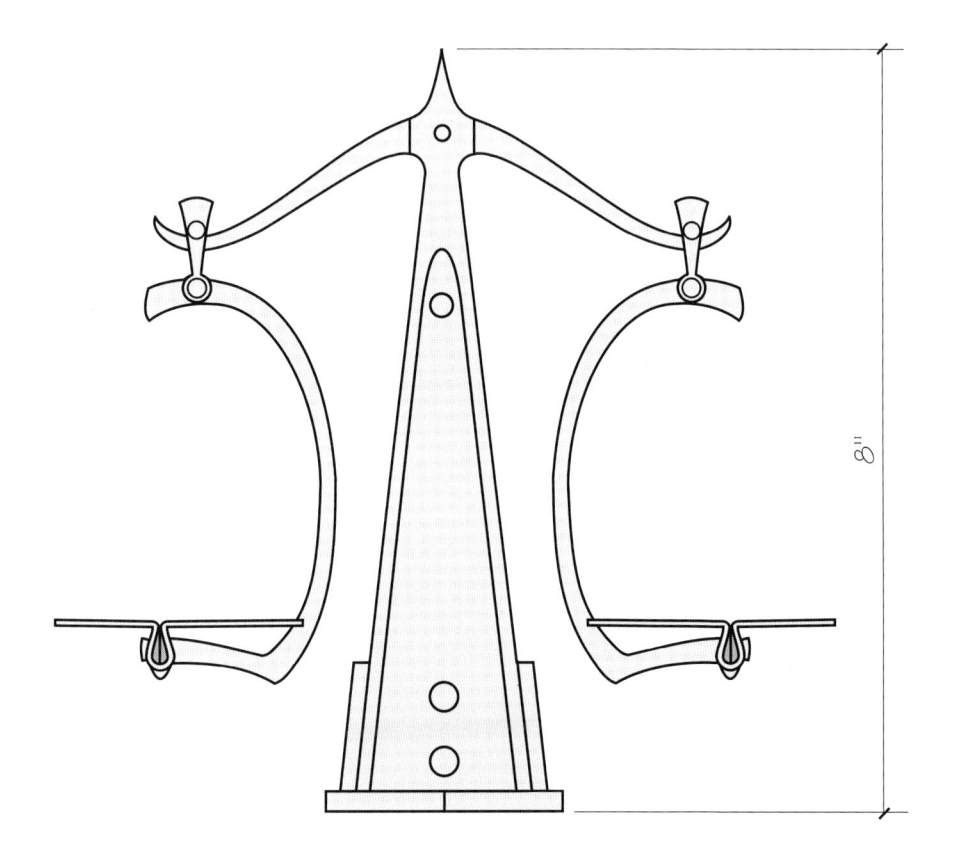

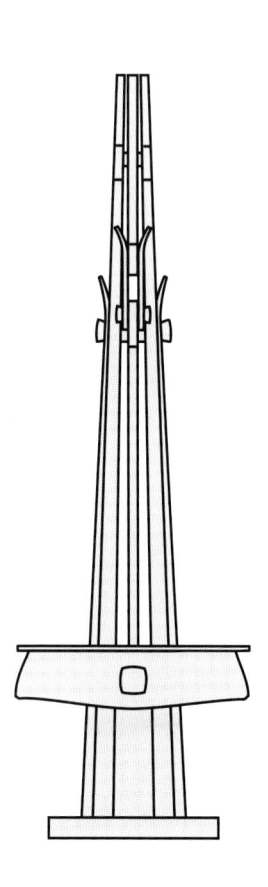

Spiral Stairs – not to scale

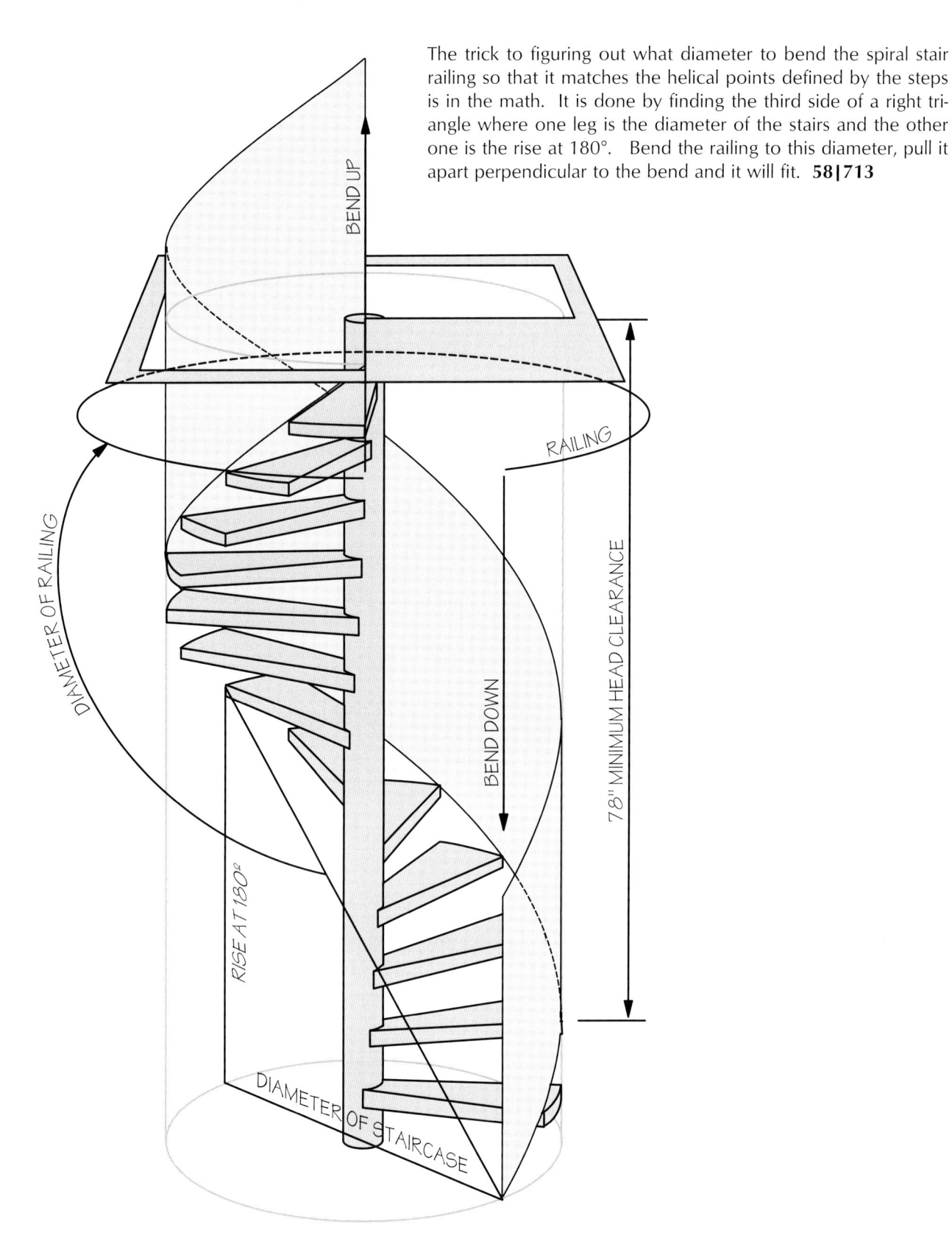

The trick to figuring out what diameter to bend the spiral stair railing so that it matches the helical points defined by the steps is in the math. It is done by finding the third side of a right triangle where one leg is the diameter of the stairs and the other one is the rise at 180°. Bend the railing to this diameter, pull it apart perpendicular to the bend and it will fit. **58|713**

Table and Stools – 1/12 scale

The basis for this design is the laminated top in which two of the steel spacers sandwiched between wood also serve as a mounting bar for the legs. Other unusual features include the joinery between the legs, and the forged tie-rod nuts. **100|1231**

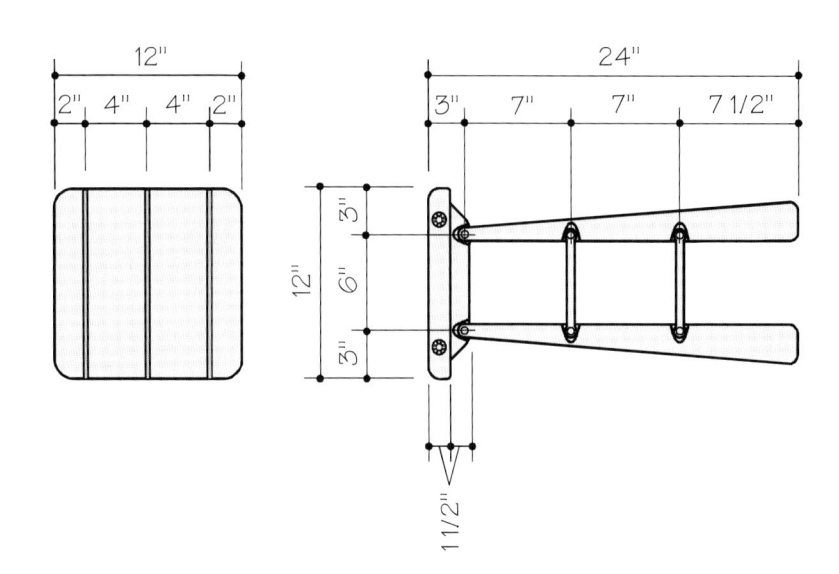

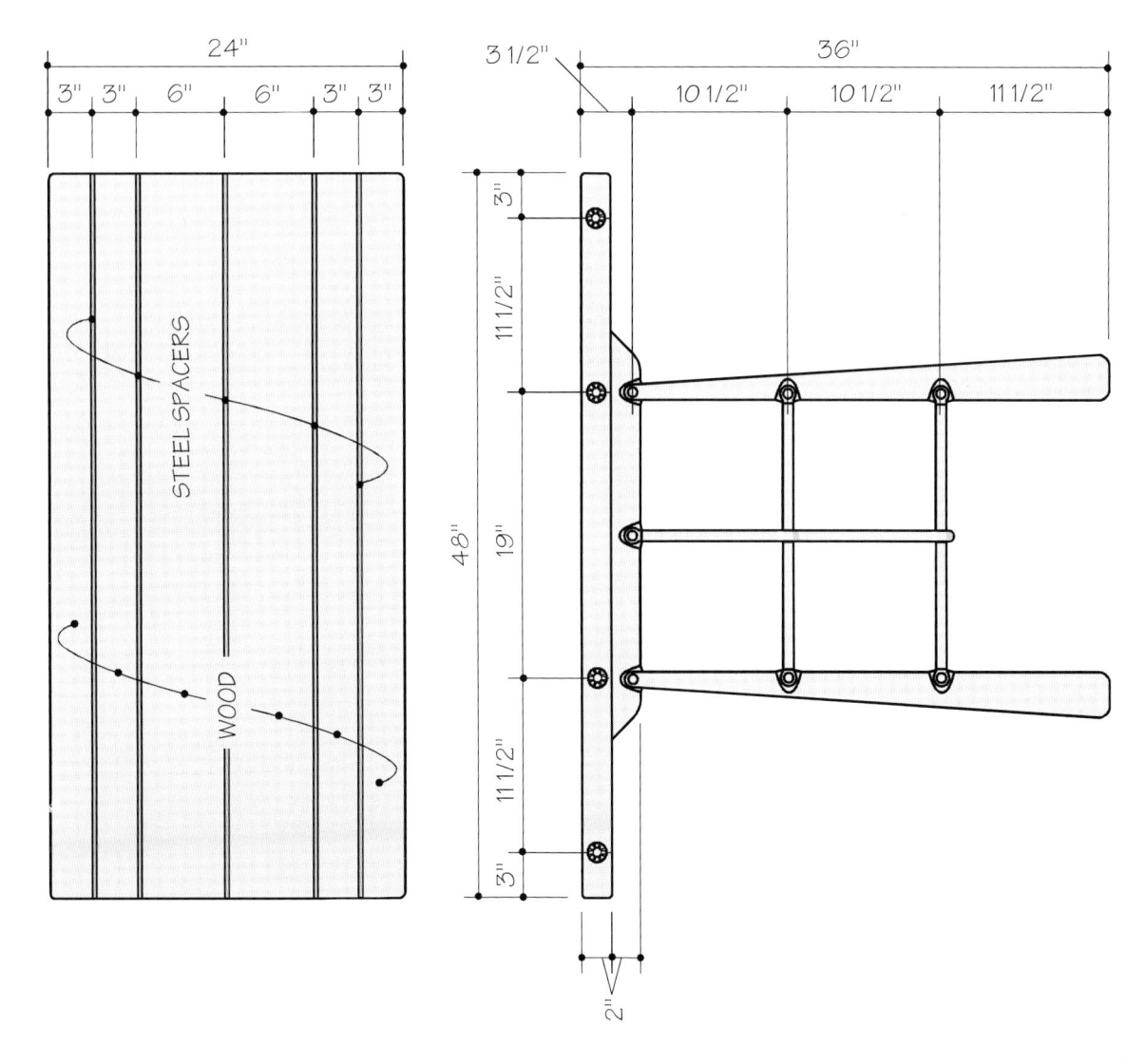

Tissue Stand -not to scale

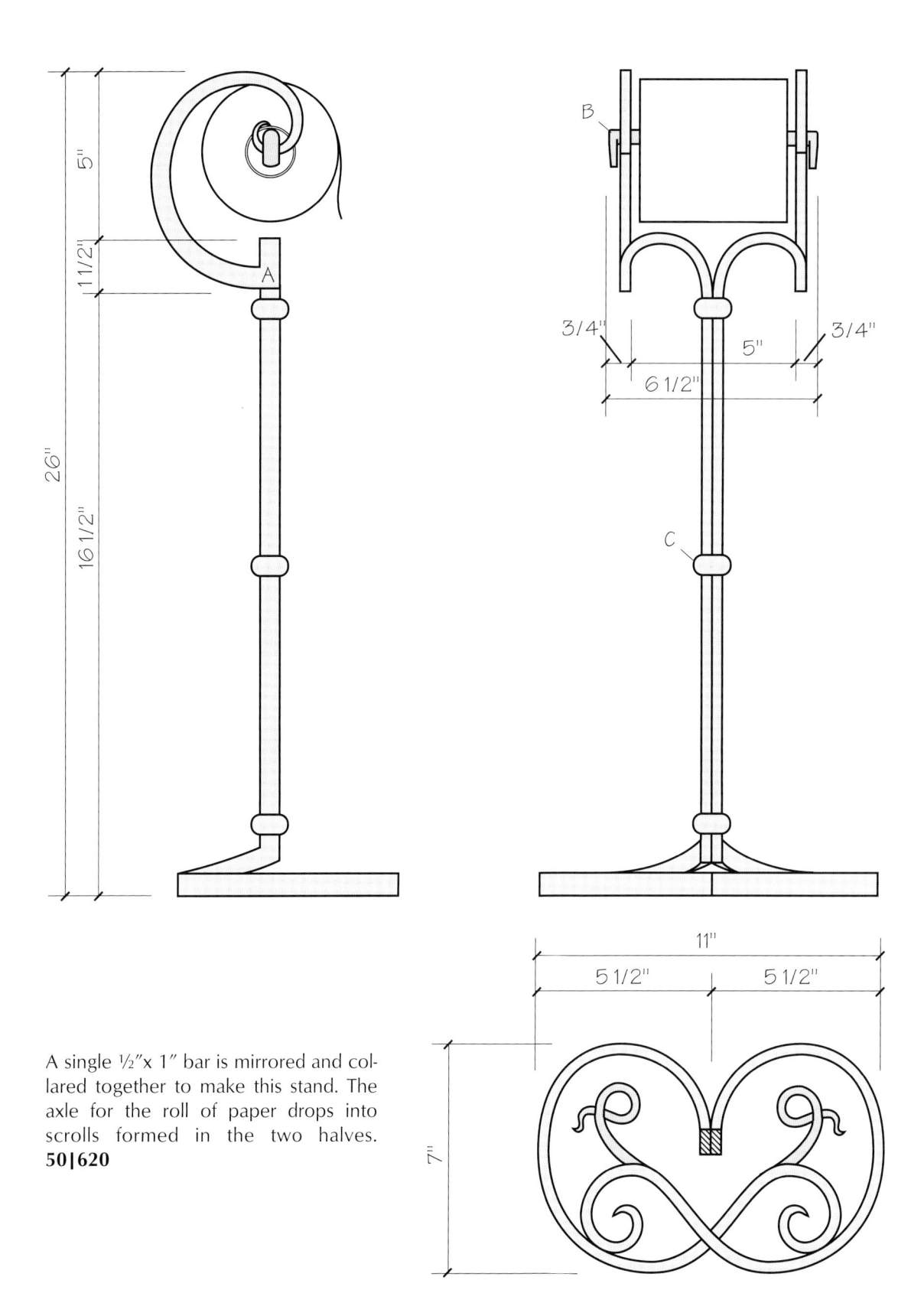

A single ½"x 1" bar is mirrored and collared together to make this stand. The axle for the roll of paper drops into scrolls formed in the two halves.
50|620

Vessel -3/4 scale

Cut the pattern for this vessel out of 1/8" plate before grooving hot at the corners. Heat along the grooves and bend into the final shape. The handle is sandwiched between the connecting joint and occupies both the inner and outer space. **30|369**

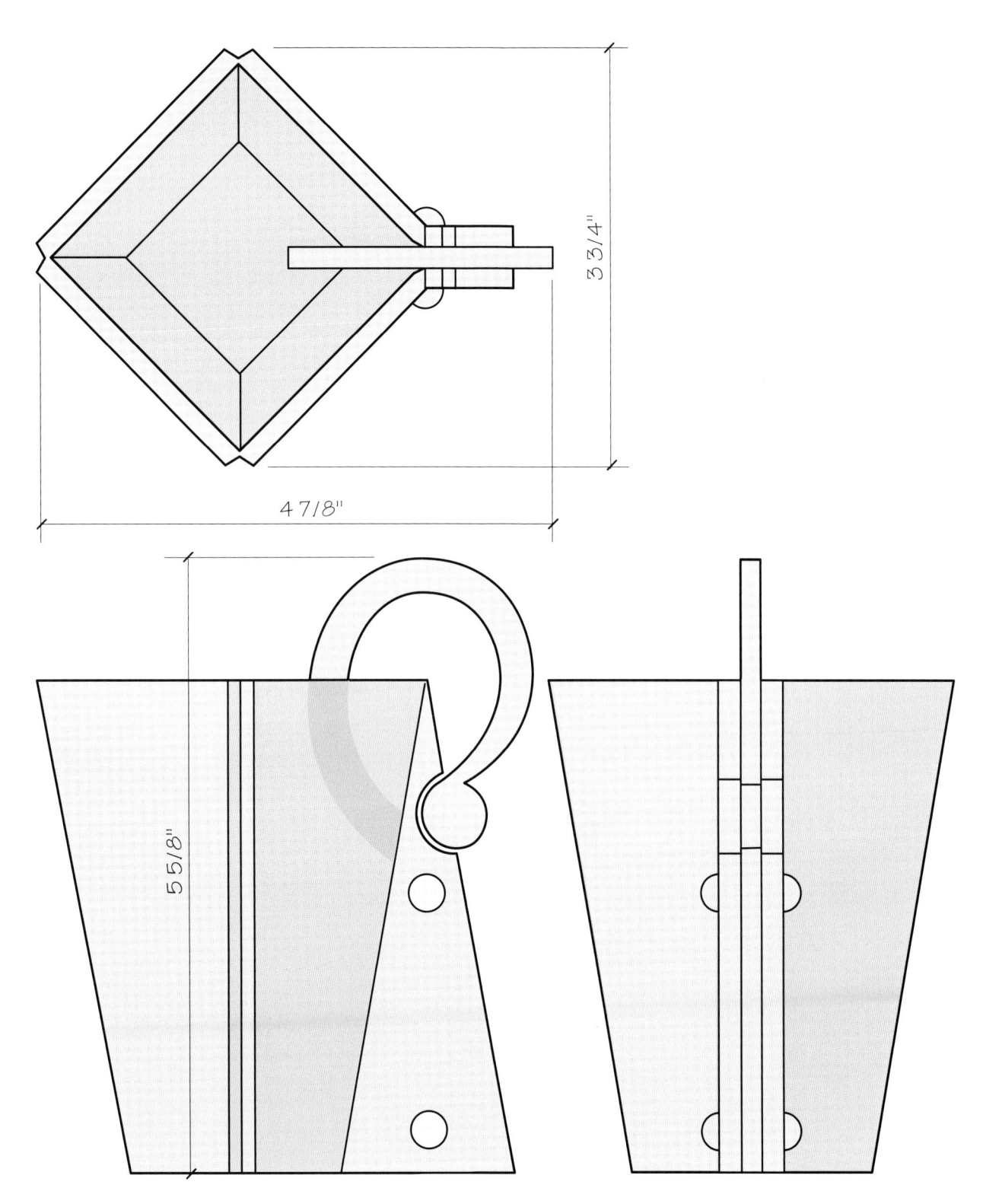

Vessel, cont.

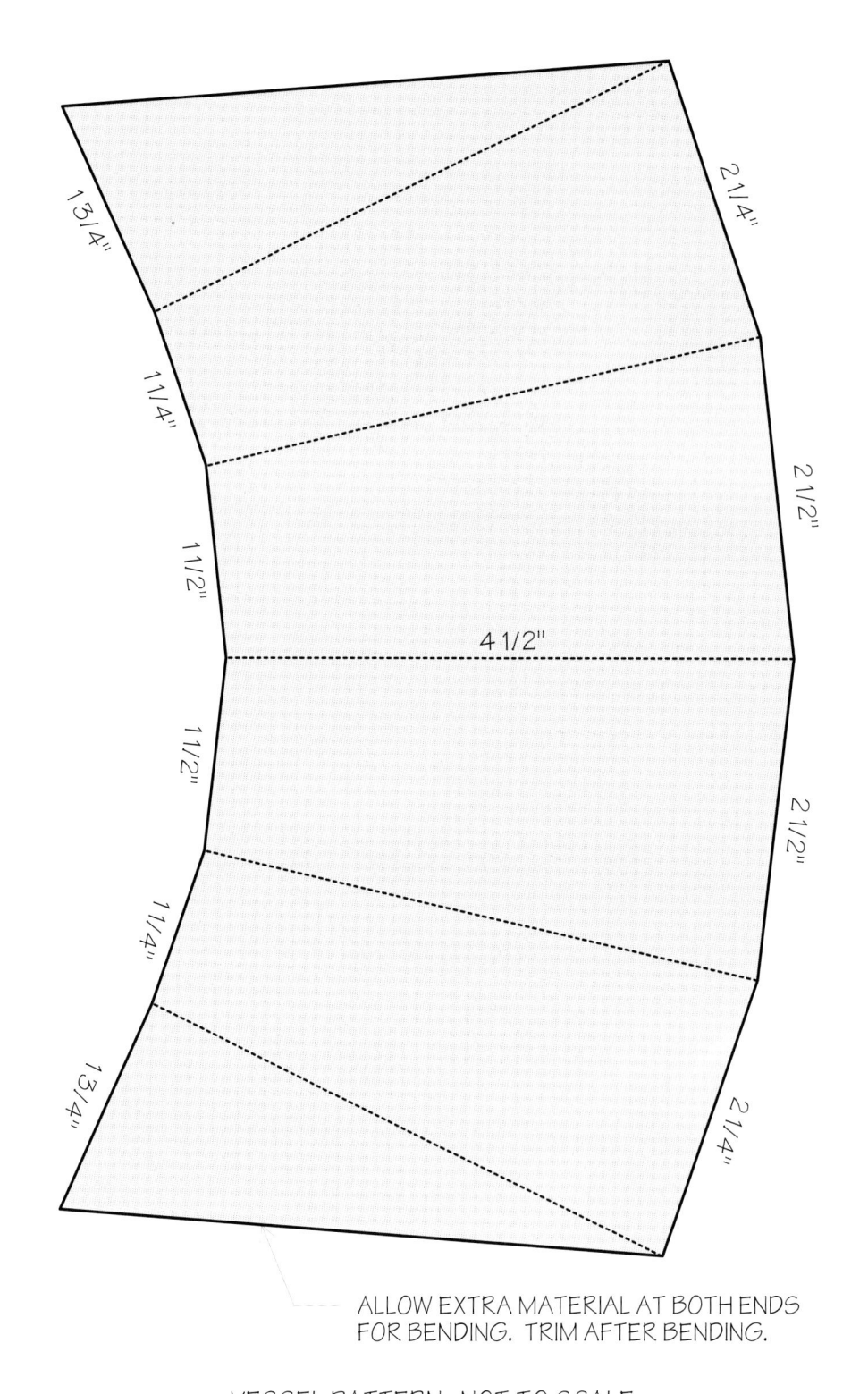

1 3/4"

2 1/4"

1 1/4"

2 1/2"

1 1/2"

4 1/2"

1 1/2"

2 1/2"

1 1/4"

1 3/4"

2 1/4"

ALLOW EXTRA MATERIAL AT BOTH ENDS FOR BENDING. TRIM AFTER BENDING.

VESSEL PATTERN - NOT TO SCALE

Wine Rack - 3/8 scale

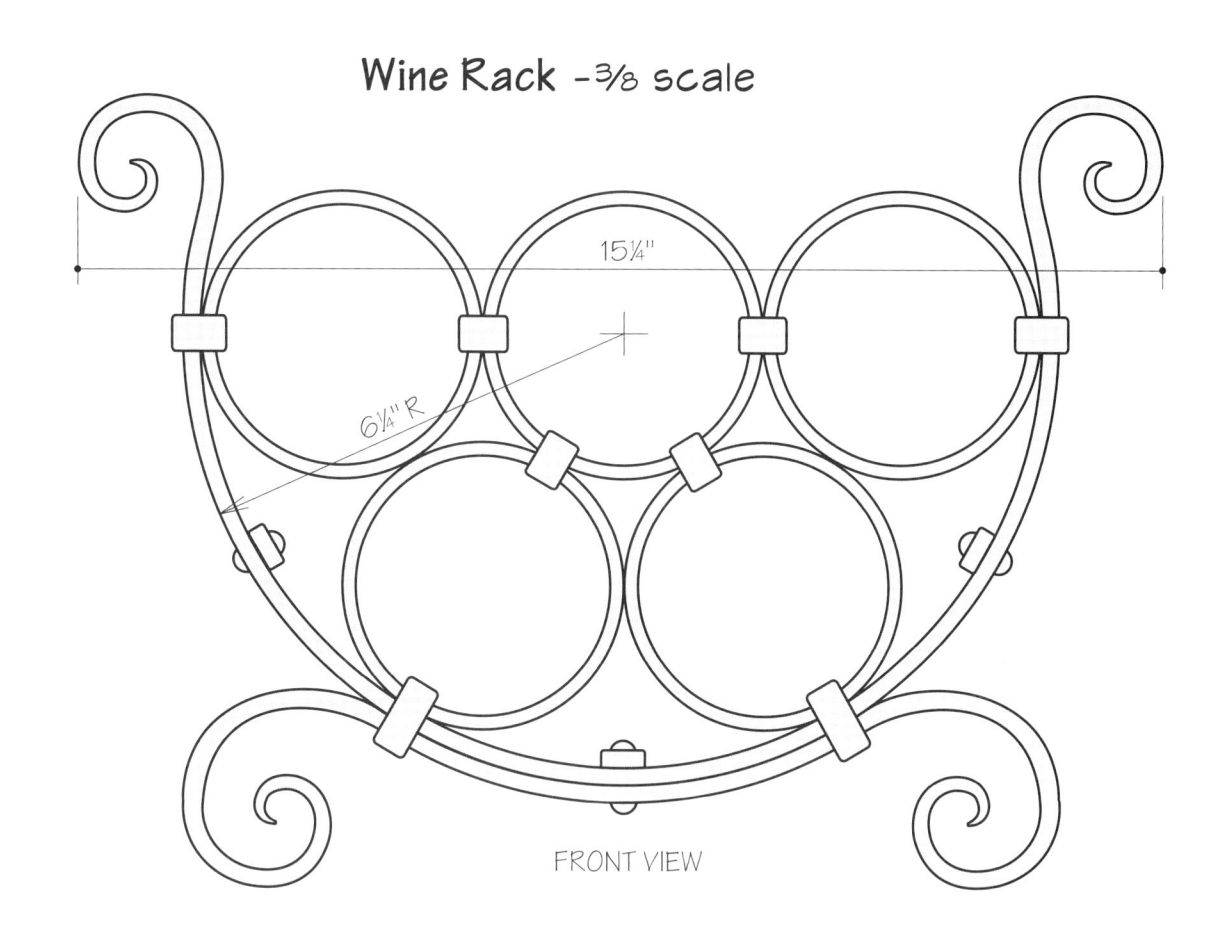

15¼"

6¼" R

FRONT VIEW

Use collared and riveted ¼"x ½" stock to make this countertop wine rack. The round bottle holders can be sliced from 3½" pipe or formed and welded from flat stock. **124|1525**

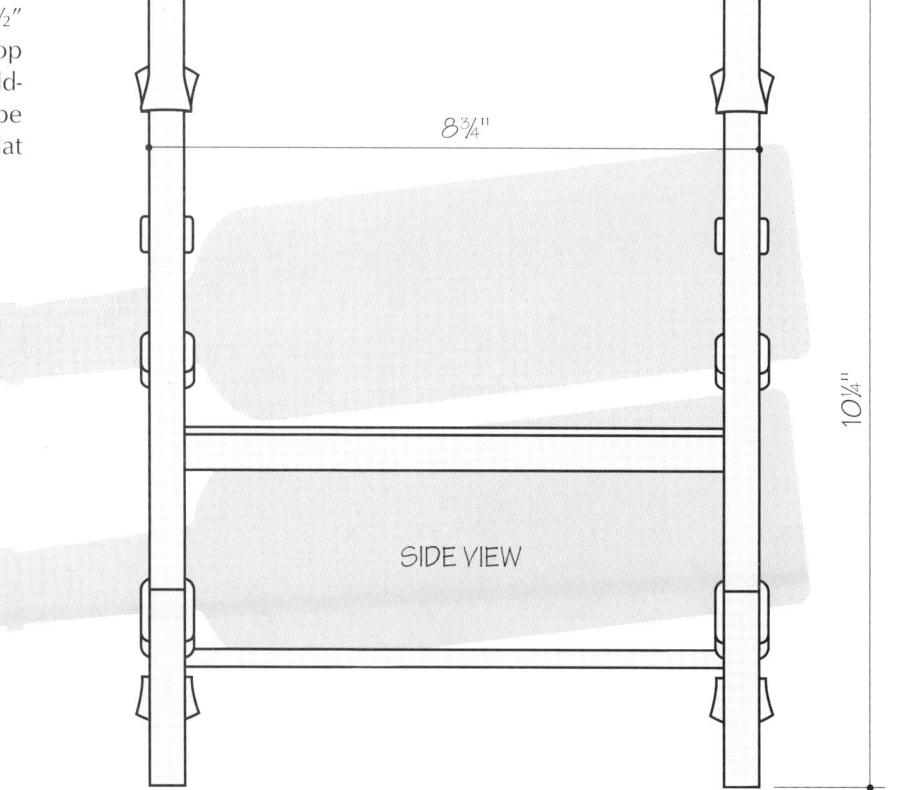

8¾"

10¼"

SIDE VIEW

4 Fireplace Accessories

Andiron -not to scale

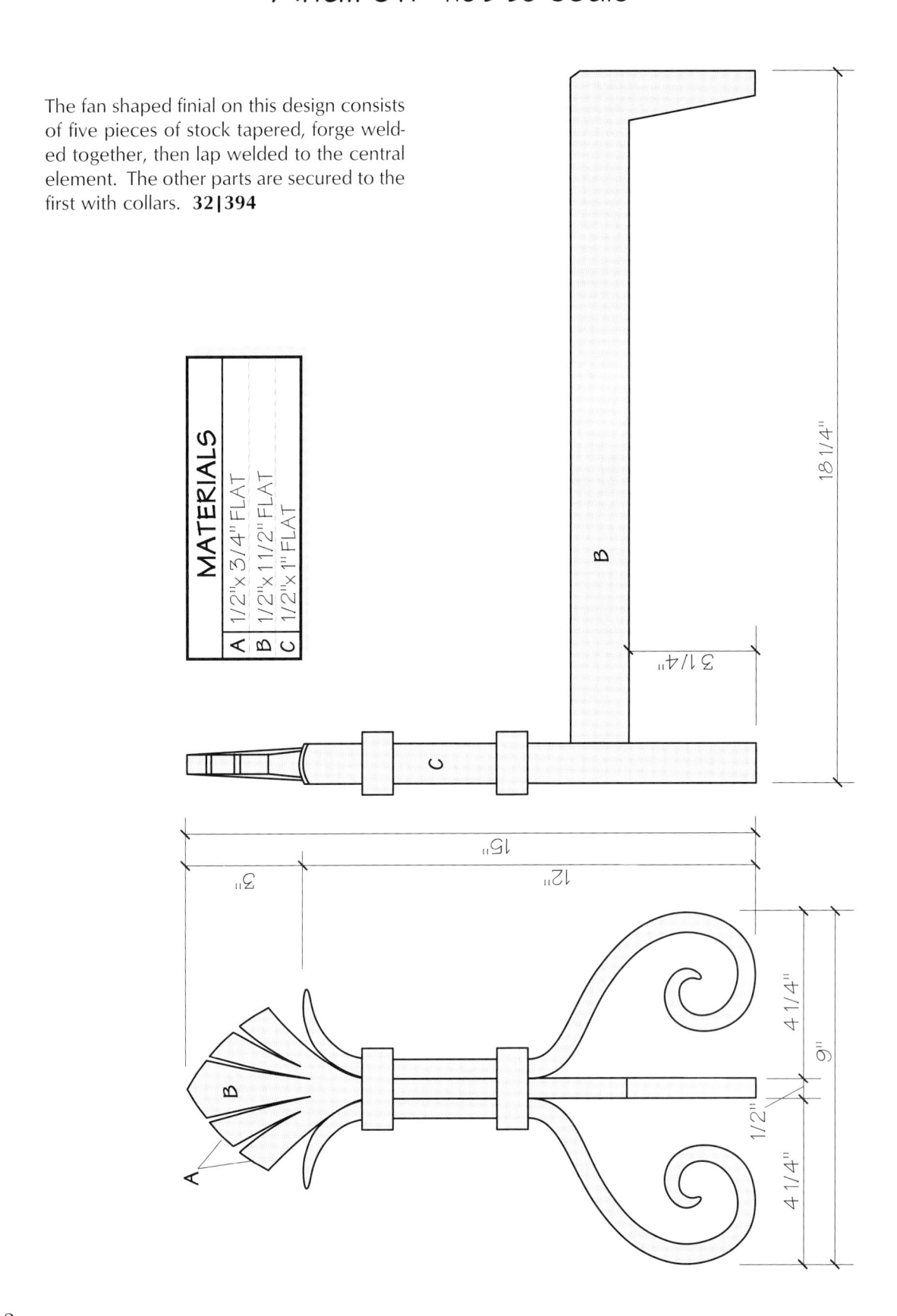

The fan shaped finial on this design consists of five pieces of stock tapered, forge welded together, then lap welded to the central element. The other parts are secured to the first with collars. **32|394**

MATERIALS	
A	1/2" x 3/4" FLAT
B	1/2" x 1 1/2" FLAT
C	1/2" x 1" FLAT

122

Fireback/Grate -not to scale

Firebacks provide radiant heat in a room when placed behind the fire in a fireplace. This one also includes a fire grate with interchangeable bars that can be replaced when they sag or deteriorate over time. **63|779**

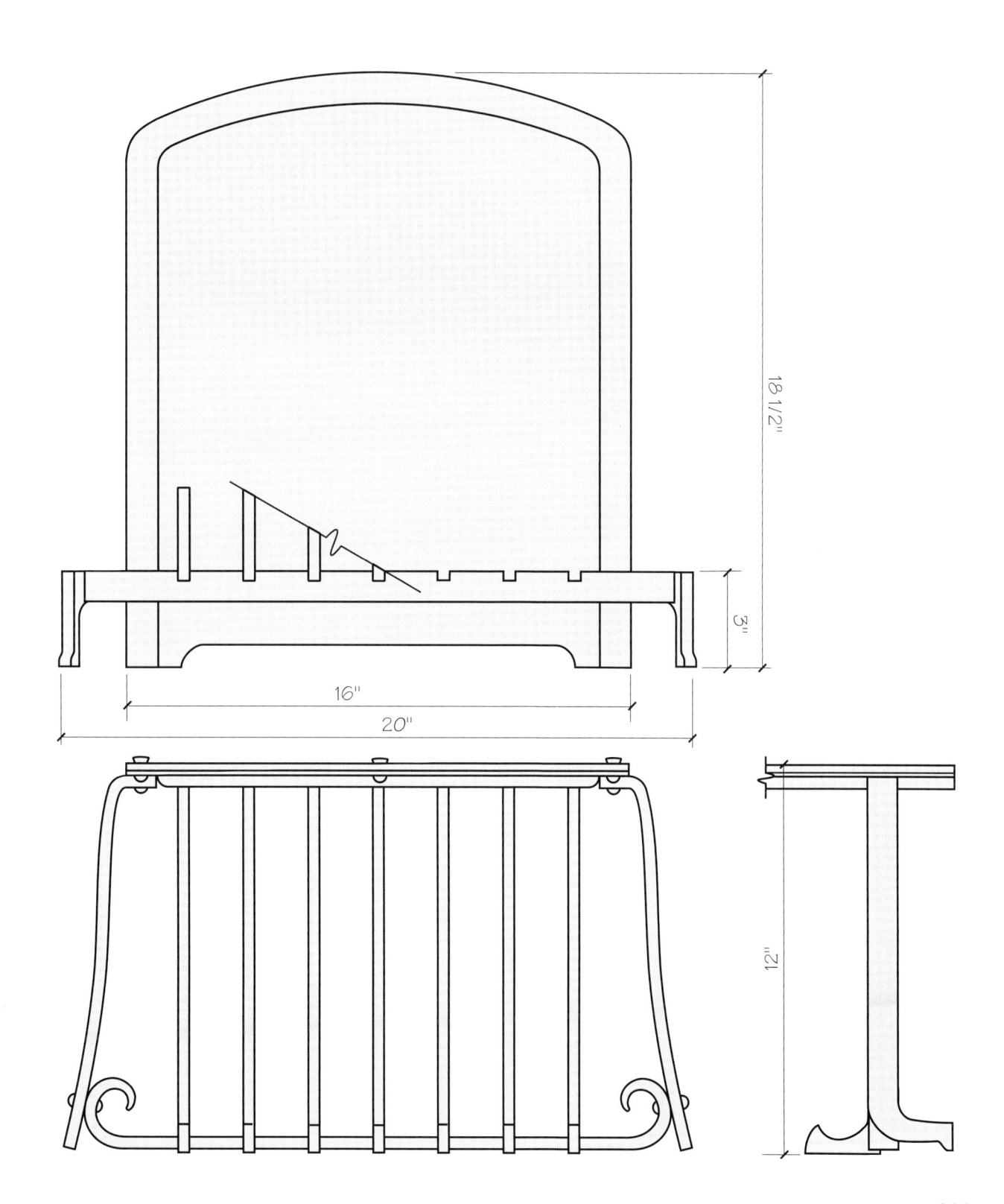

18 1/2"
3"
16"
20"
12"

Fireback/Grate, cont.

7 - 3/8" x 1" HOLES EQUALLY SPACED

1"
1 1/4"
3/4"

1" 13/16" 12 3/8" 13/16" 1"

11 5/8"

3"

3/8" x 3/8" NOTCH. SEE ABOVE FOR SPACING

18 3/4"

2"
11 3/4"
3"

5/8" x 5/8" NOTCH

124

Fireplace Crane - ¼ scale

Unlike some fireplace cranes that are mortared in place, this one has a gate style hinge that permits removal. The decorative bracket is held in place with tenons. **52|645**

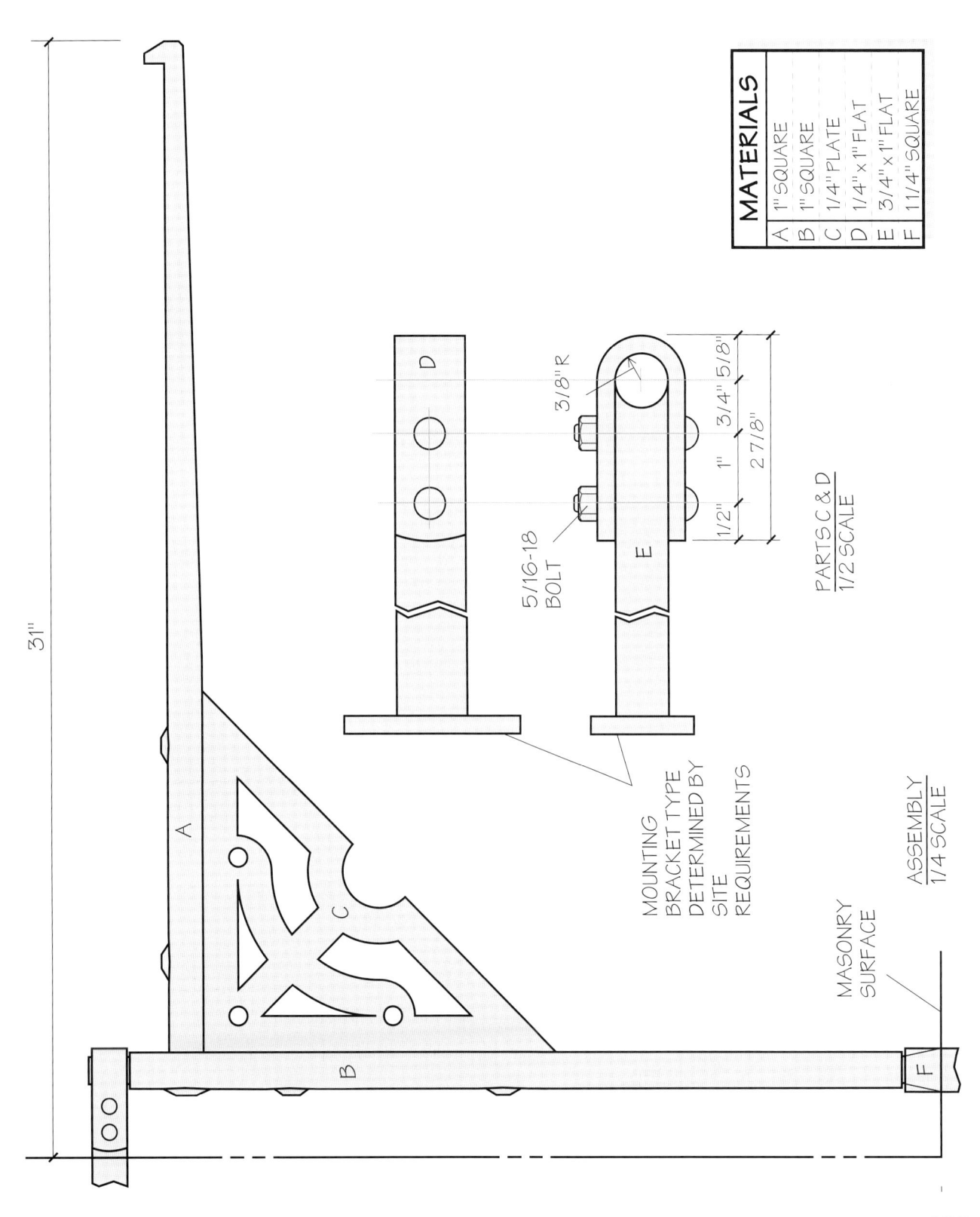

	MATERIALS
A	1" SQUARE
B	1" SQUARE
C	1/4" PLATE
D	1/4" x 1" FLAT
E	3/4" x 1" FLAT
F	1 1/4" SQUARE

PARTS C & D
1/2 SCALE

5/16-18 BOLT

3/8" R

3/4" 5/8"
2 7/8"
1"
1/2"

MOUNTING BRACKET TYPE DETERMINED BY SITE REQUIREMENTS

MASONRY SURFACE

ASSEMBLY
1/4 SCALE

31"

125

Fireplace Doors #1 -not to scale

Fireplace doors are much like miniature gates, only smaller and lighter.   This one mimics its larger counterpart in its hinges, but makes use of unique design opportunities in the handles and center motif. **67|826**

NOT TO SCALE. DIMENSIONS WILL VARY ACCORDING TO FIREPLACE OPENING SIZE & PROPORTIONS

DOOR

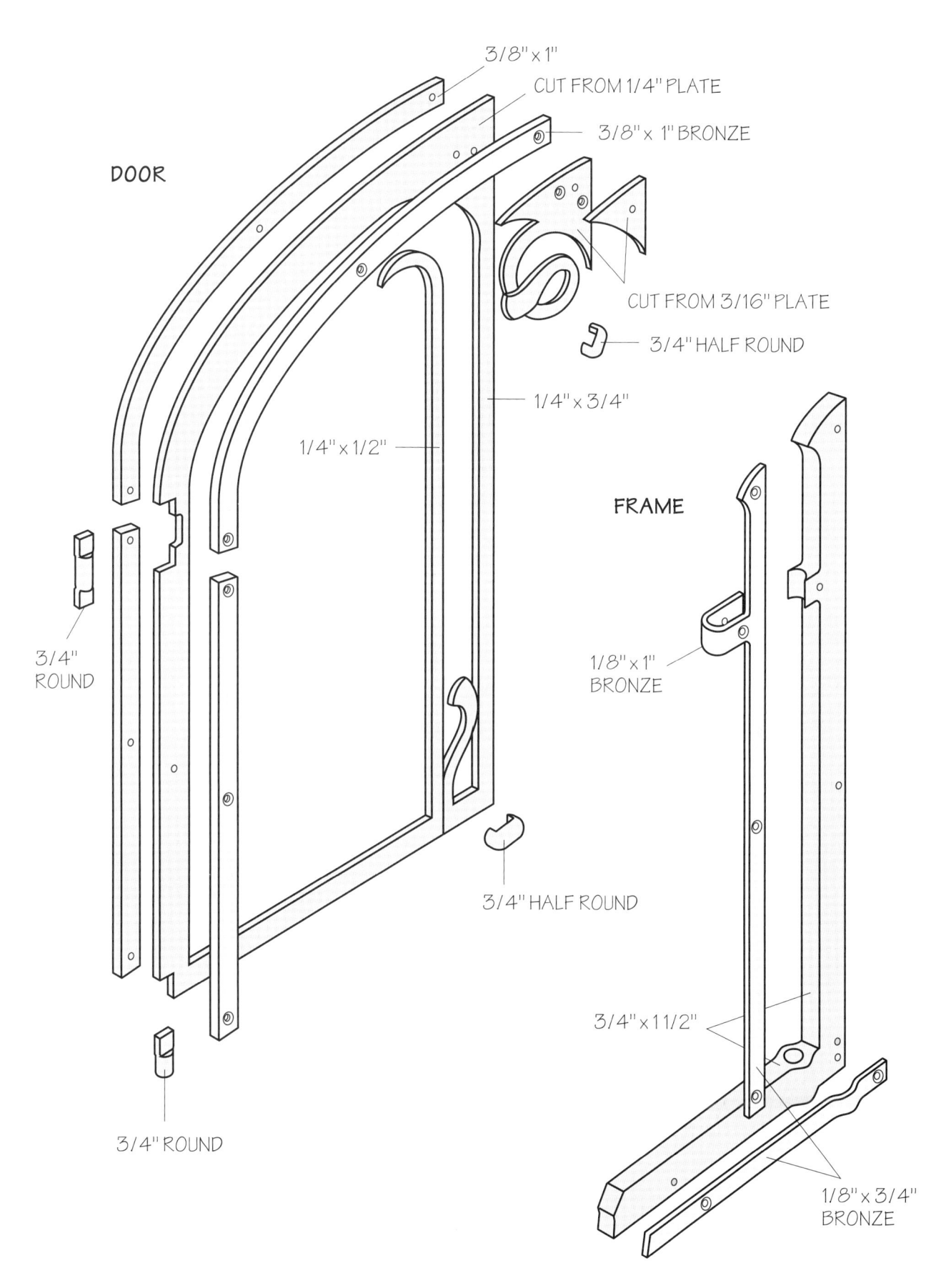

3/8" x 1"
CUT FROM 1/4" PLATE
3/8" x 1" BRONZE
CUT FROM 3/16" PLATE
3/4" HALF ROUND
1/4" x 3/4"
1/4" x 1/2"

FRAME

3/4" ROUND
1/8" x 1" BRONZE
3/4" HALF ROUND
3/4" x 1 1/2"
3/4" ROUND
1/8" x 3/4" BRONZE

127

Fireplace Doors #2 -not to scale

If you have enough space along your hearth, fireplace "sliders" make ideal fireplace doors. Unlike hinged or bi-fold doors, they never get in the way and always operate smoothly. In this case the hanger is part of the design.

120|1471

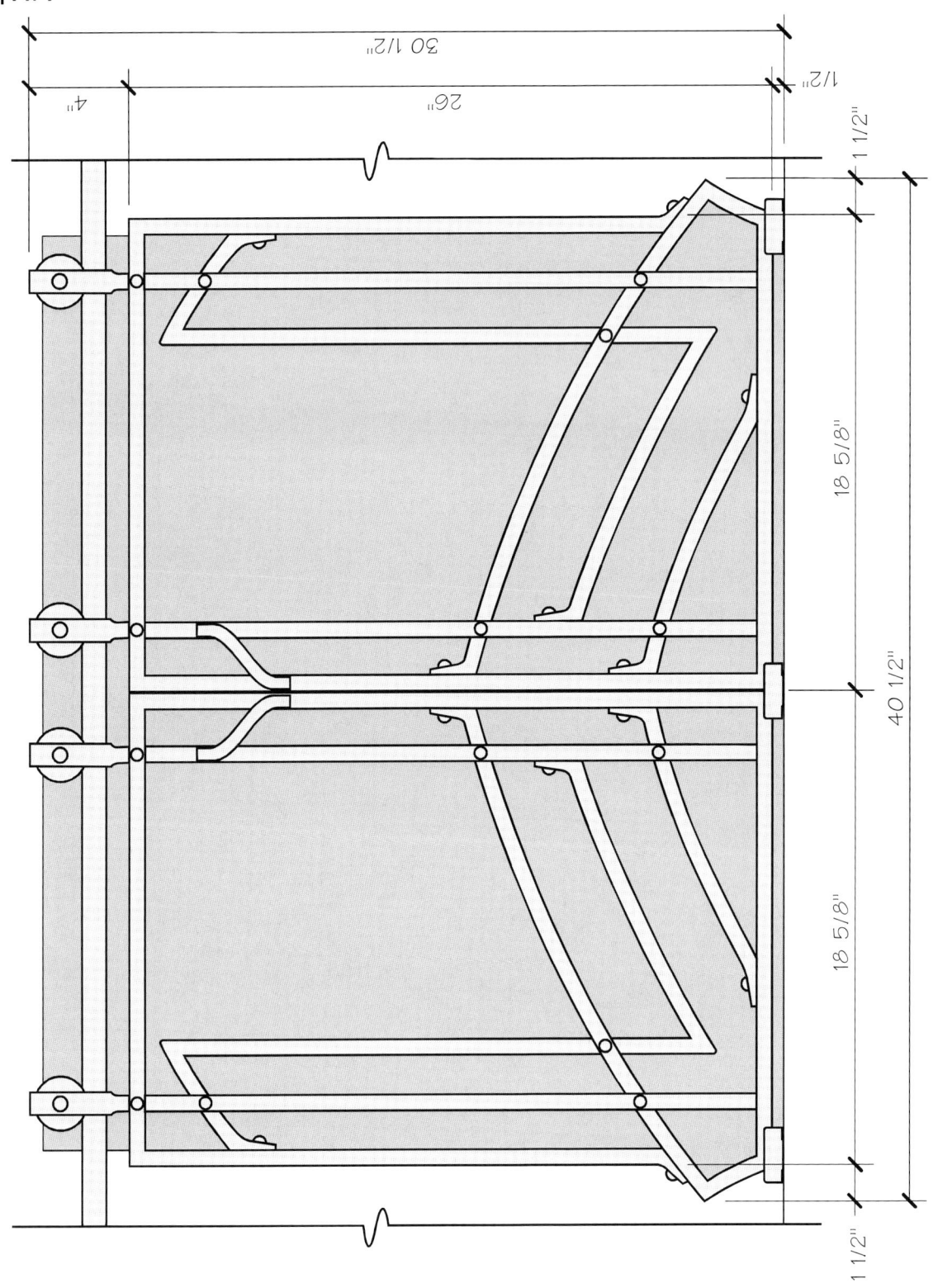

Fireplace Screen #1 - ⅛ scale

The wings on this free-standing screen swing in to support it, and also adjust to variations in the width of the fireplace opening. It is made from 3/8" square stock with rigid screen held in place by a frame screwed to the back side of all three sections. **90|1114**

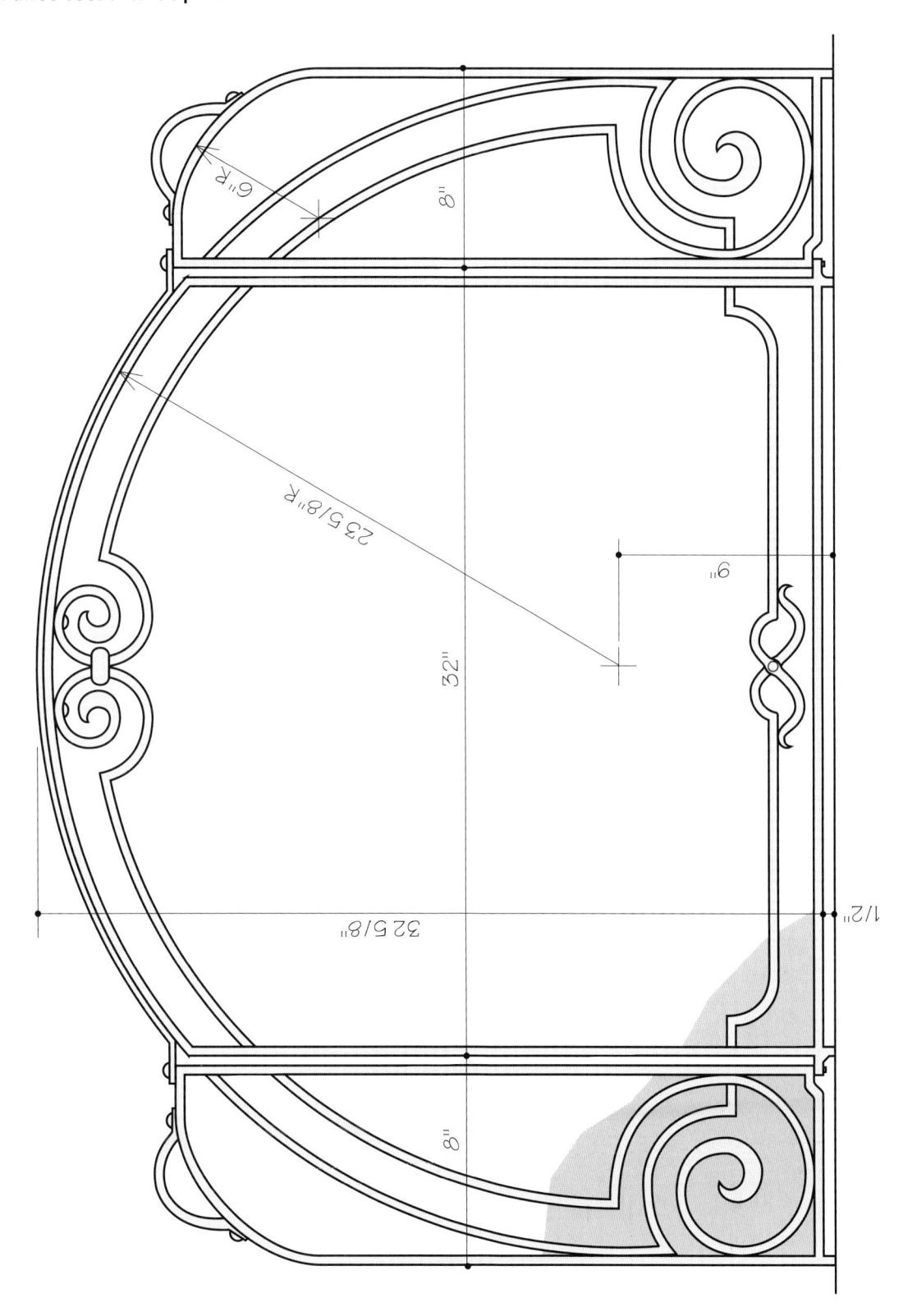

Fireplace Screen #2 -not to scale

Placing logs on a fire with a free standing screen necessitates having to move it out of the way each time. This one is cradled at the bottom and swings out from the top to the limit of chains hooked on each side. Logs are place on the fire through this opening without having to move the screen. Just unhook the chains to remove it completely. **130|1599**

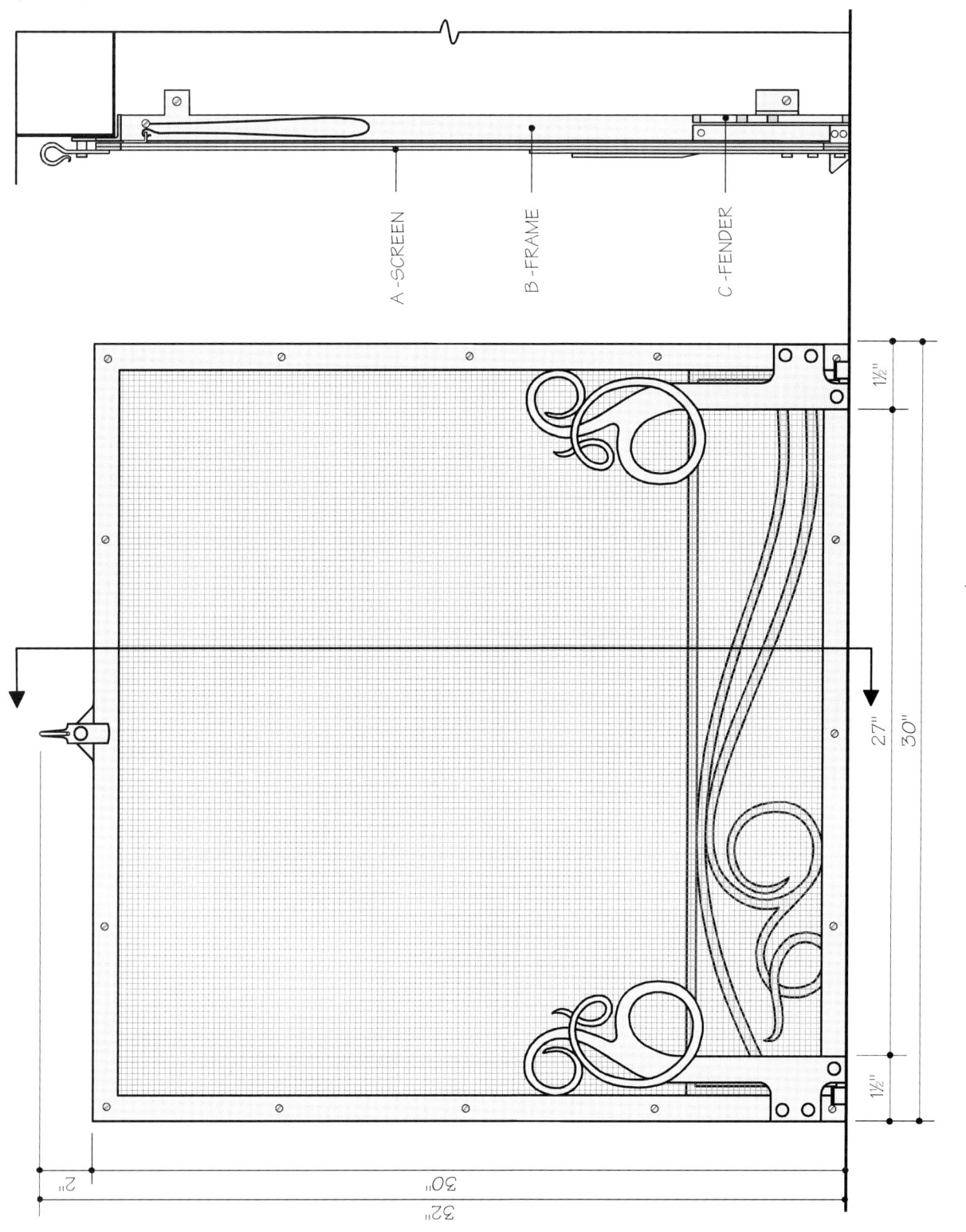

130

½"

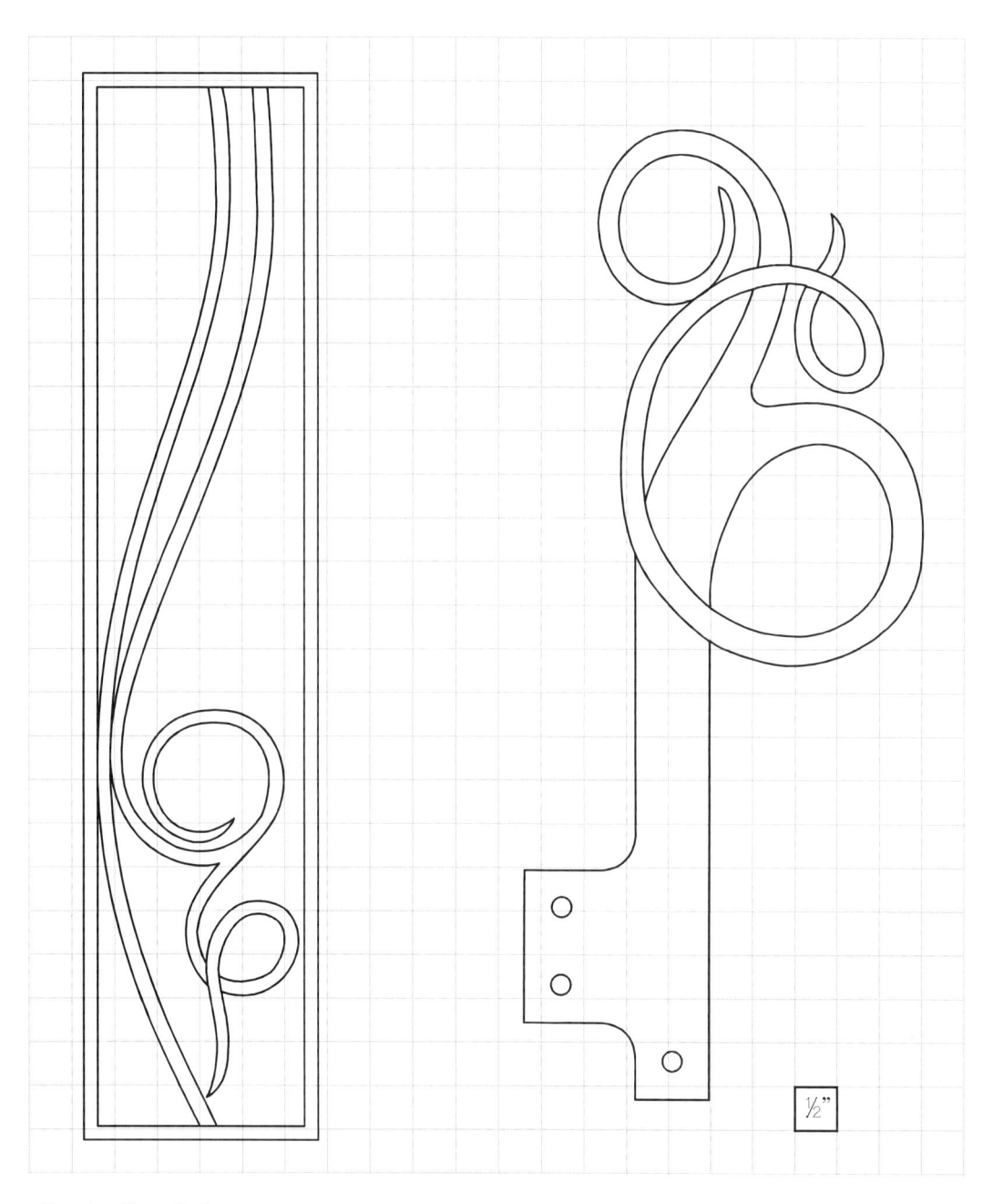

Fender Detail -fits inside screen

Scroll work Detail

Fireplace Tools #1 -not to scale

Split, saw or forge weld 3/8"x 3/4" stock to 3/4" square to make these split handle fireplace tools. A finial is held in place with a collar to complete the handle. Slot and drift a hole and draw out the 3/4" square to make a shank for the broom and poker. **32|395**

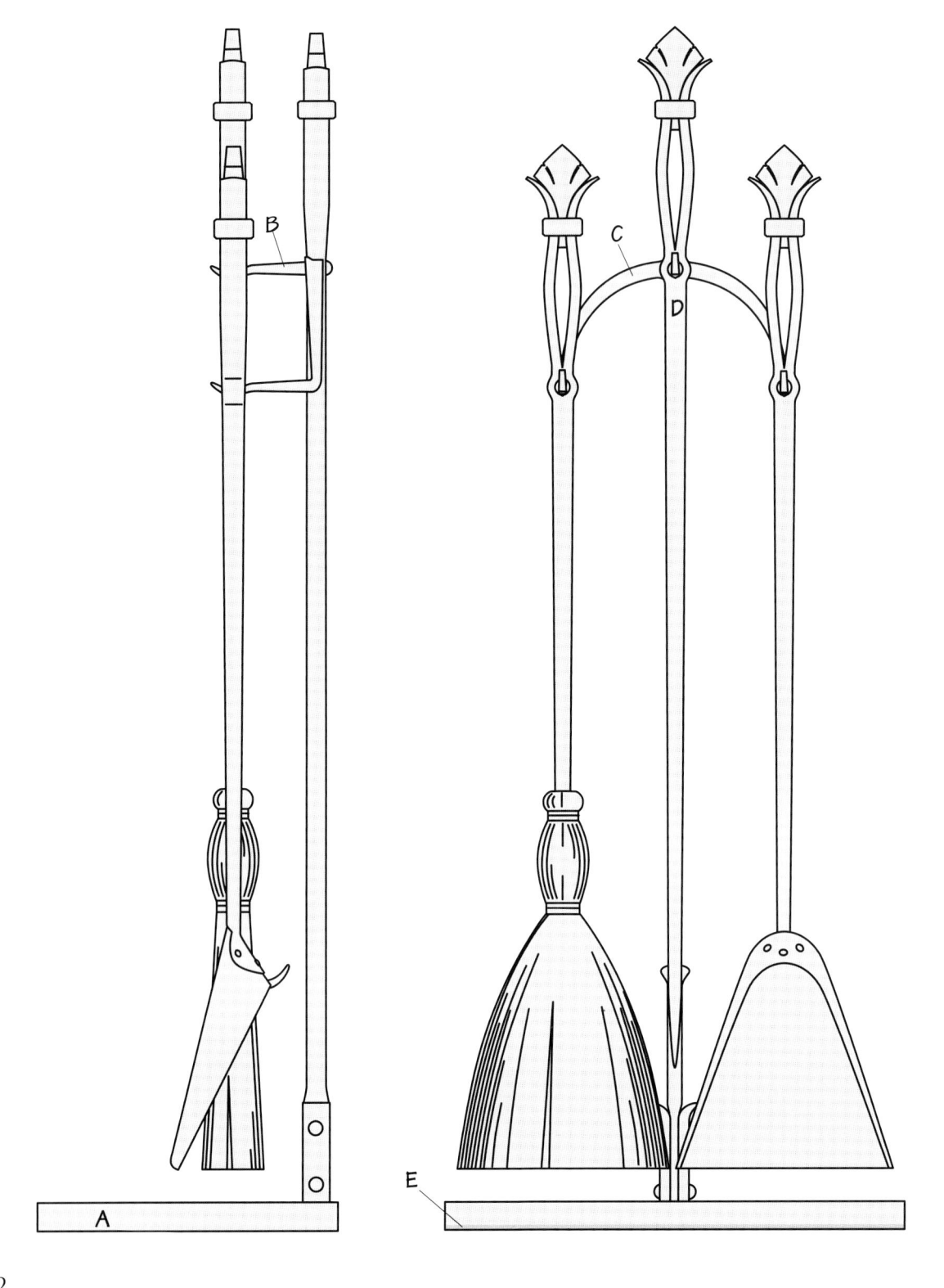

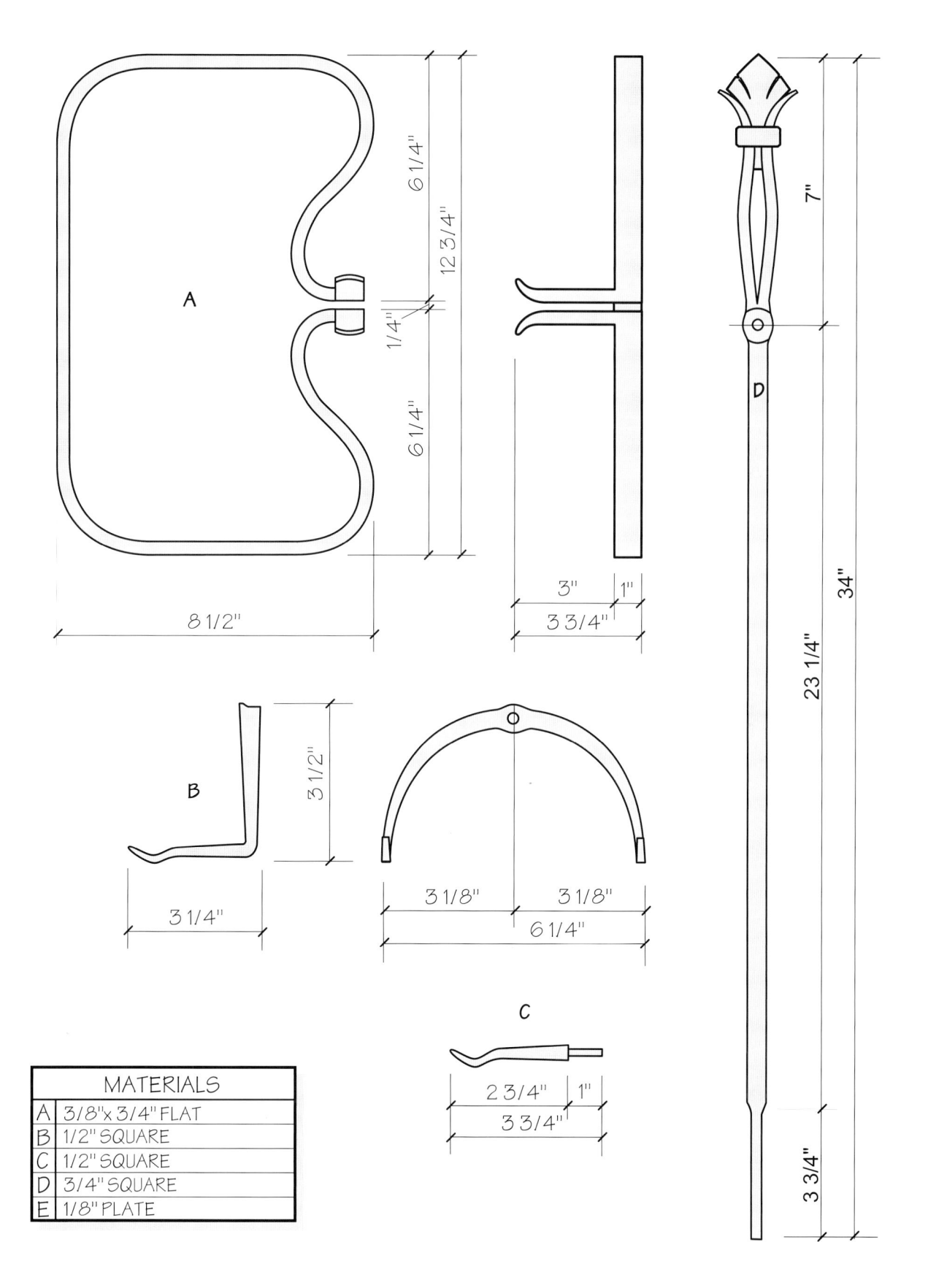

MATERIALS	
A	3/8"x 3/4" FLAT
B	1/2" SQUARE
C	1/2" SQUARE
D	3/4" SQUARE
E	1/8" PLATE

Fireplace Tools #2 -not to scale

Three piece construction makes these tools unique. The handle is forged from flat stock and wrapped around a mandrill before being riveted to the tool shank. Splitting the shovel blade into two segments actually makes it easier to form. **46|571**

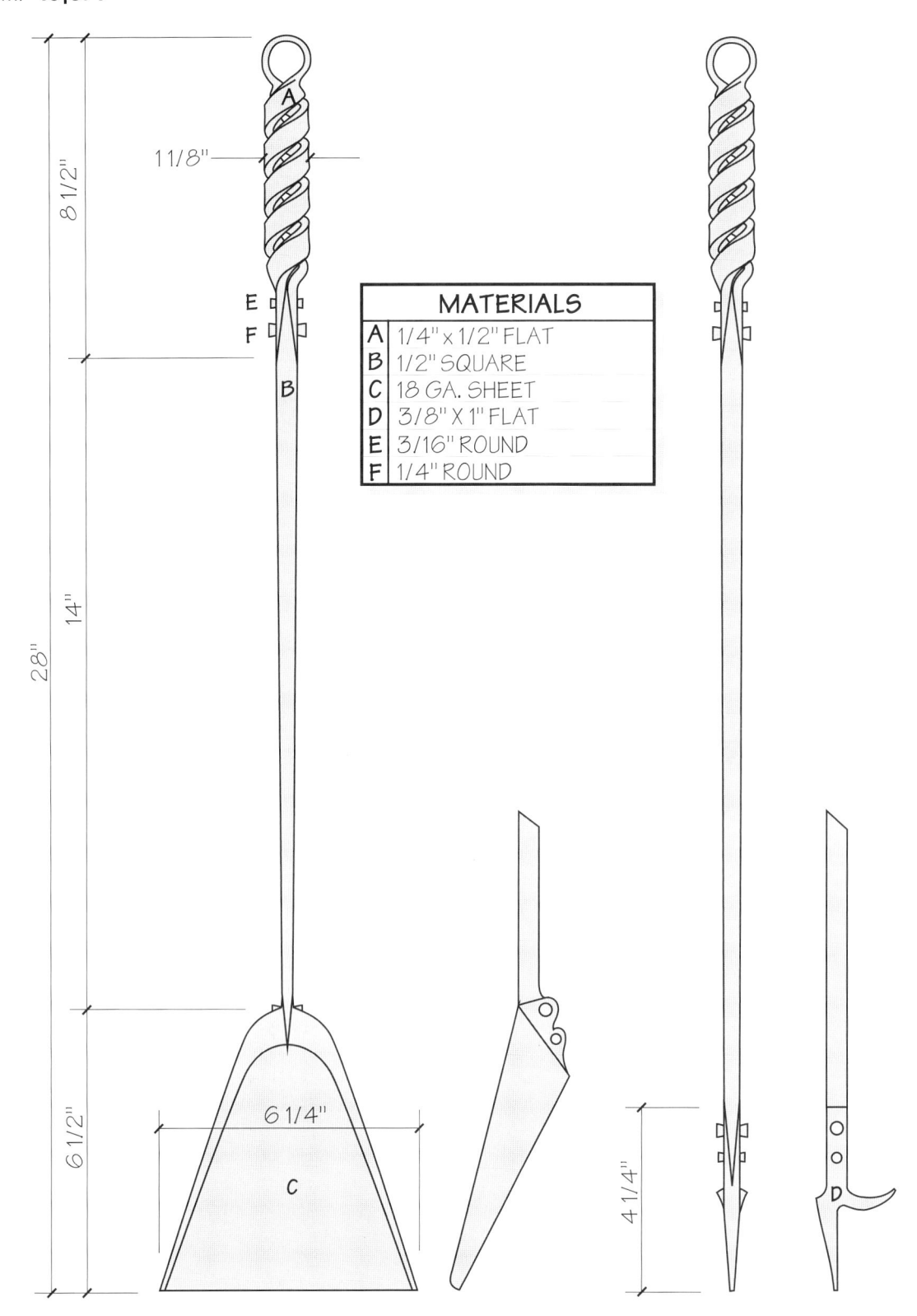

MATERIALS	
A	1/4" x 1/2" FLAT
B	1/2" SQUARE
C	18 GA. SHEET
D	3/8" x 1" FLAT
E	3/16" ROUND
F	1/4" ROUND

Wood Rack - ¼ scale

The flat stock joinery used for this log rack combines folding and joining with a "T" shaped collar on the end of the stock. Tenons on the ends of round stock join the two halves together. **125|1533**

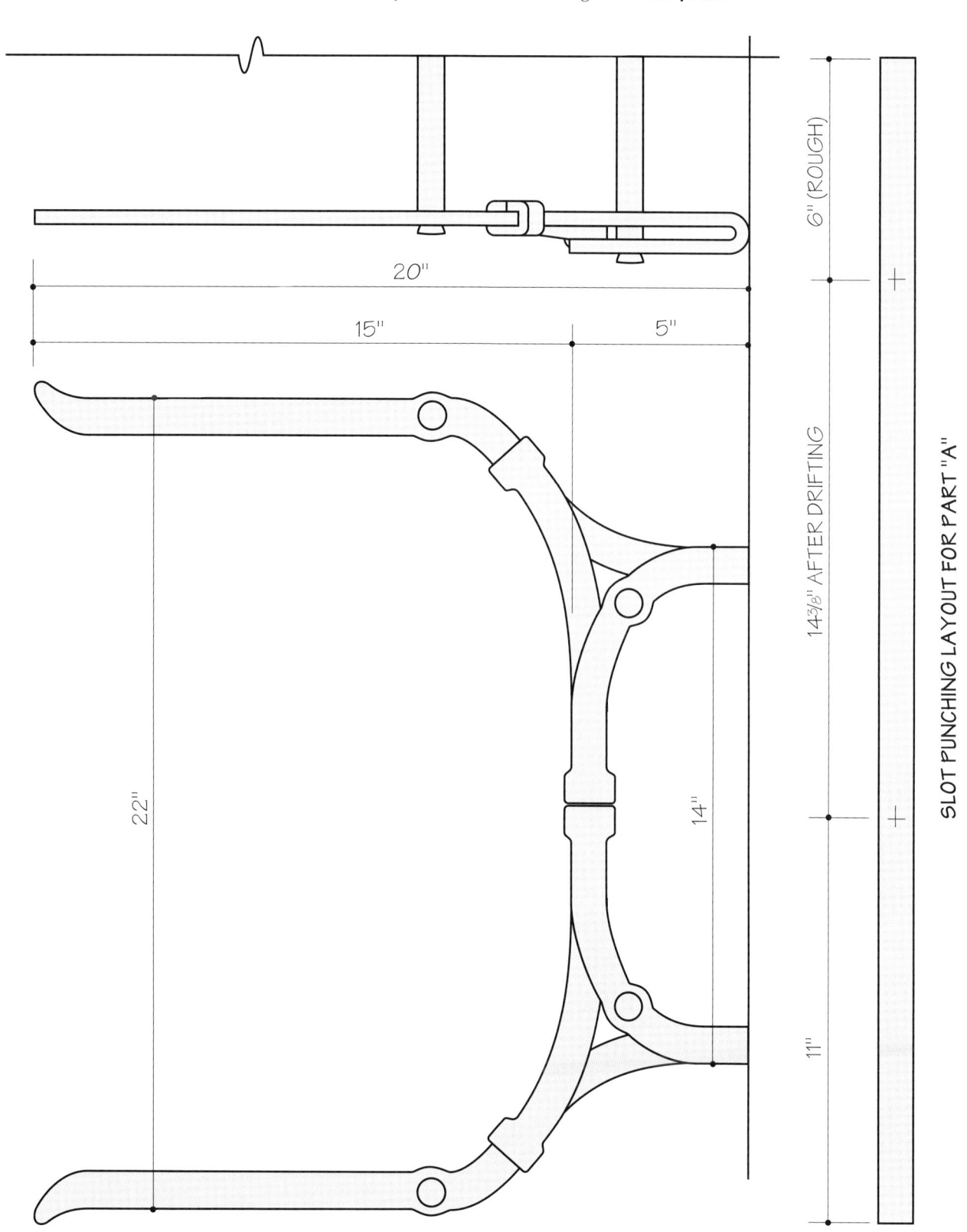

20"

15" 5"

22"

6" (ROUGH)

14 3/8" AFTER DRIFTING

14"

11"

SLOT PUNCHING LAYOUT FOR PART "A"

6 Exterior Ironwork

Patio Bench -not to scale

The base for this bench is substantial enough to outlast many wooden tops. A power hammer is needed to draw out the legs using 2" square stock. They are split and formed, then riveted to angle iron rails that support the top.
150|1875

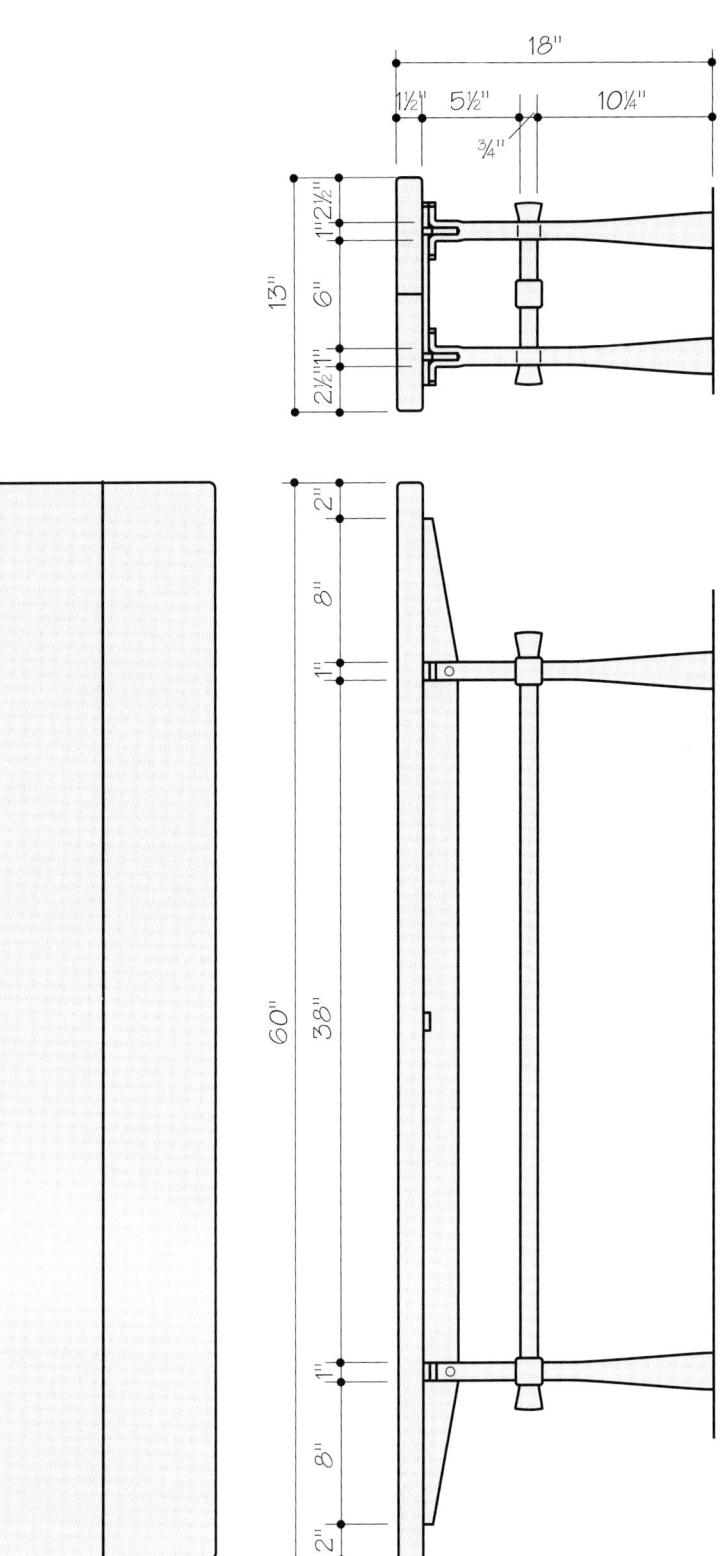

Boot Scraper –not to scale

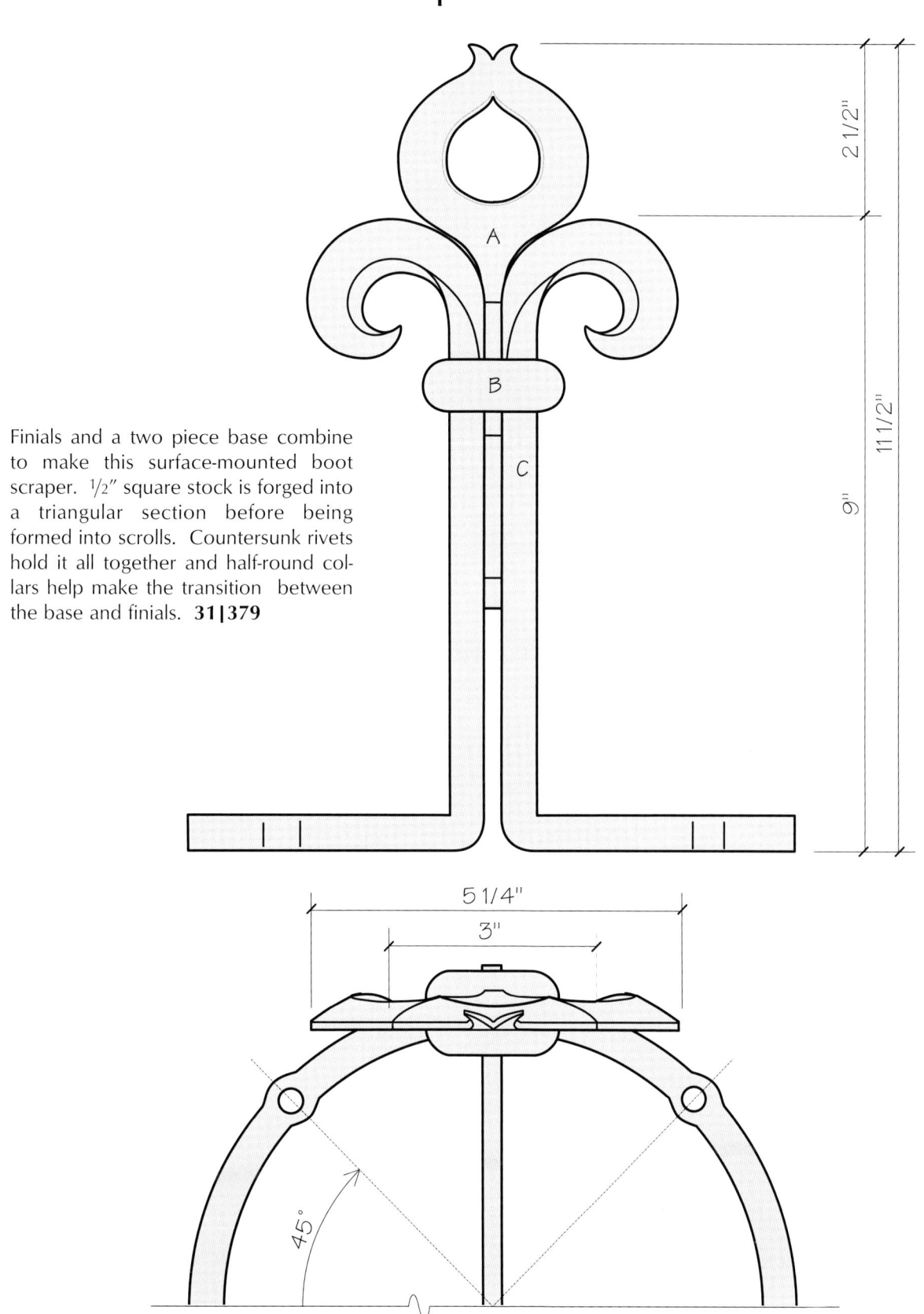

Finials and a two piece base combine to make this surface-mounted boot scraper. 1/2" square stock is forged into a triangular section before being formed into scrolls. Countersunk rivets hold it all together and half-round collars help make the transition between the base and finials. **31|379**

139

Boot Scraper, cont.

BOOT SCRAPER - FRONT VIEW

D

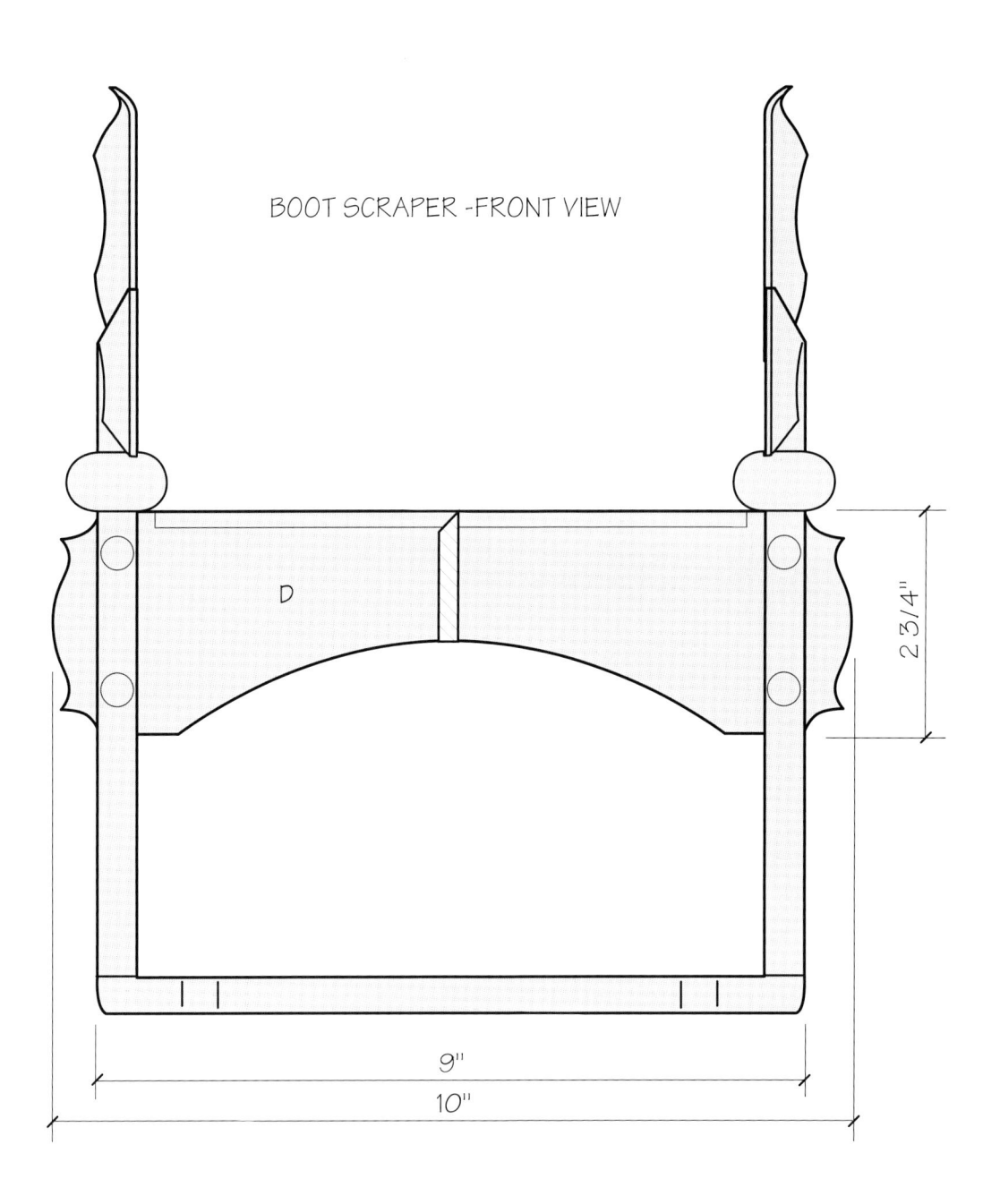

2 3/4"

9"
10"

MATERIALS	
A	1/2" x 3/4" FLAT
B	3/4" HALF-ROUND
C	1/2" SQUARE
D	1/4" FLAT
E	1/4" RIVETS

Bracket #1 - ½ scale

This bracket is a traditional design using forged components and "rolled" mounting holes for screws or nails. The branched scrolls are forge welded to the main brace, and all the parts are joined with rivets and collars. **168|2121**

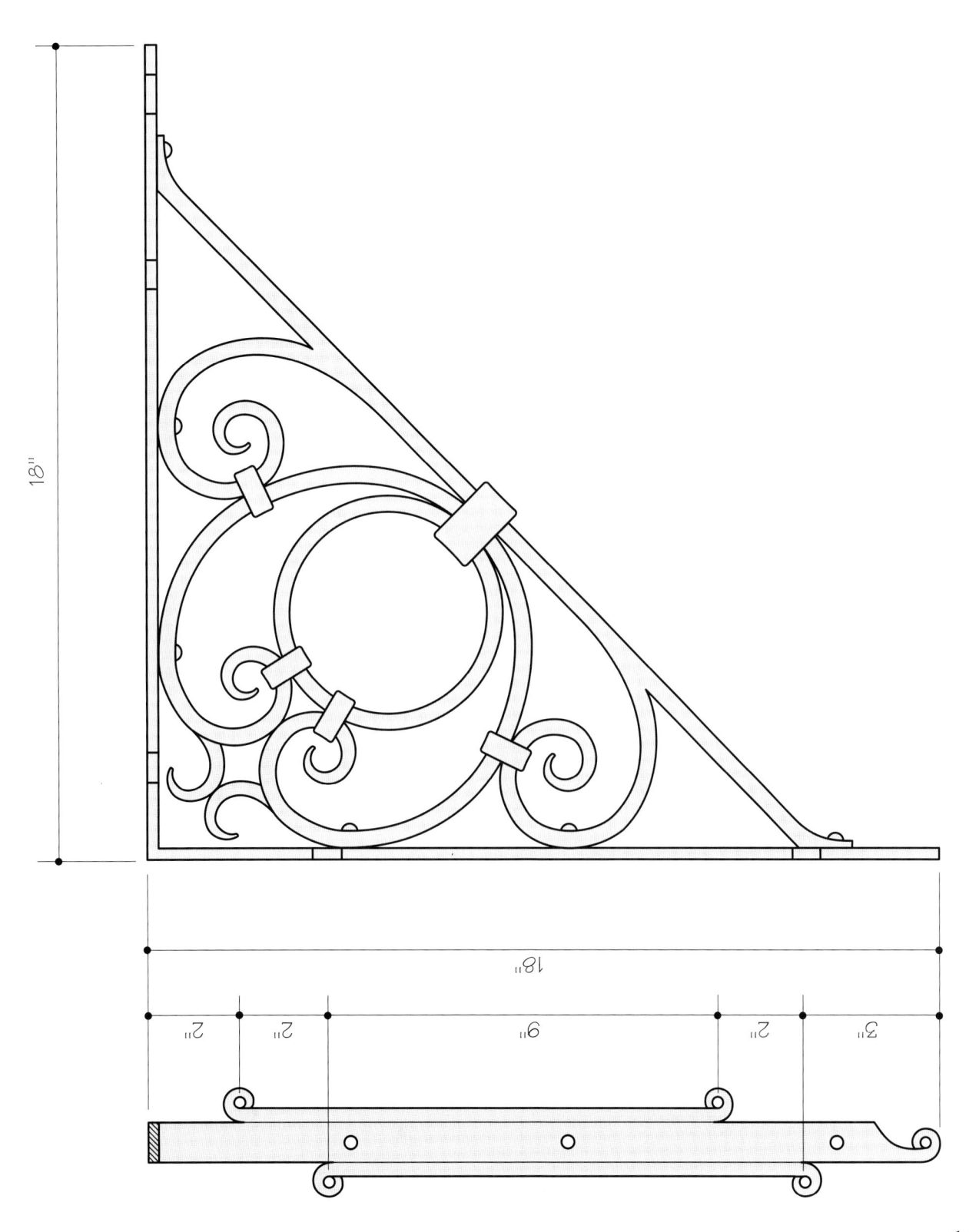

Bracket #2 - ½ scale

Bracket #2 is made entirely from ⅝" square stock (an additional flat stock outer border can be added if needed). Drifted holes on curved parts are tapered wider on the inside when the stock is flat, then become straight once the stock is bent. Multiple brackets can be joined in symmetrical patterns to make additional configurations.
168|2125

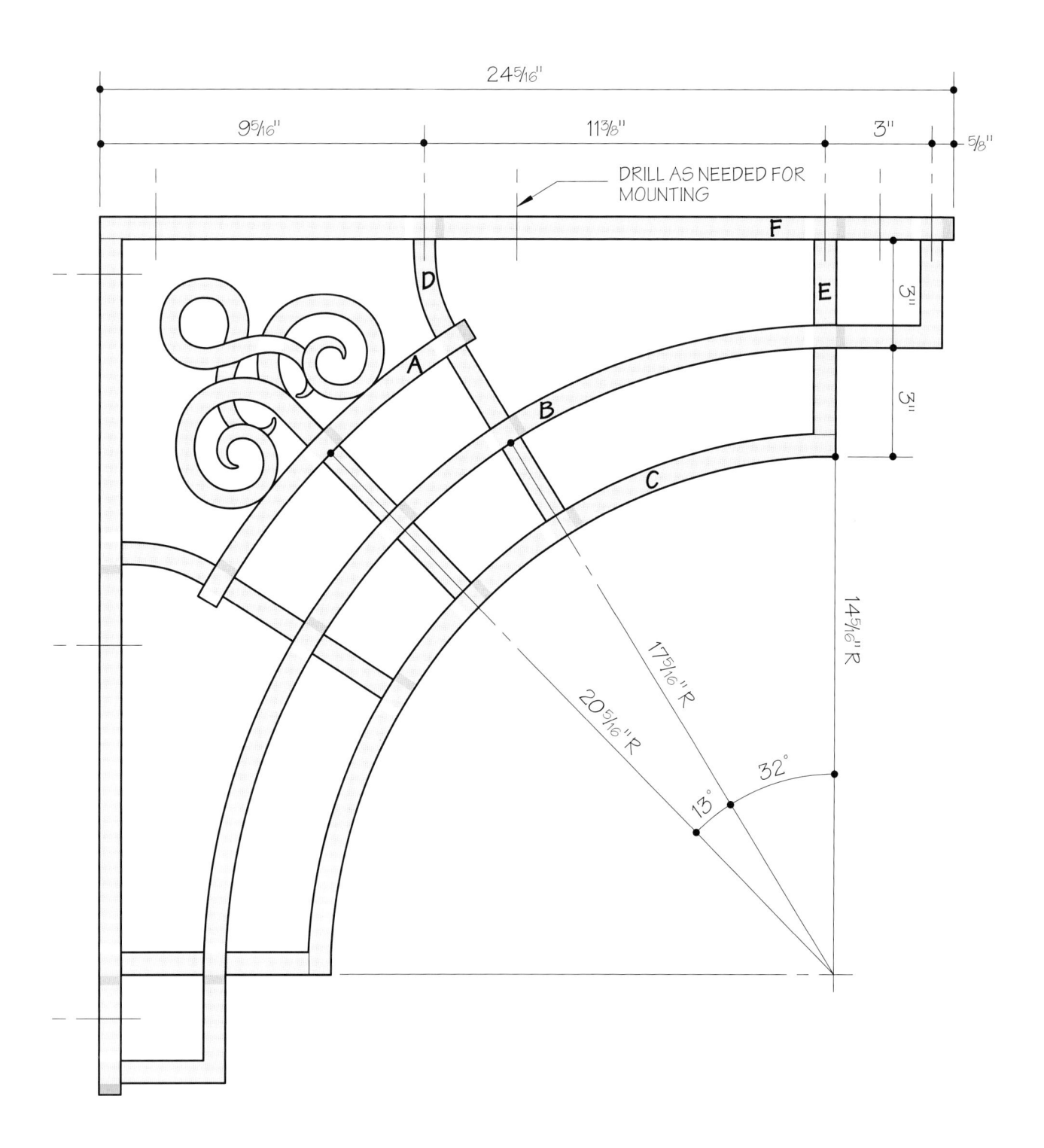

Cresset - not to scale

Intended for use around a patio or deck, This wood burning heater provides light and a place to warm your hands on cool fall or early spring days. It incorporates a sandstone base that is drilled for ½" round legs. **132|1625**

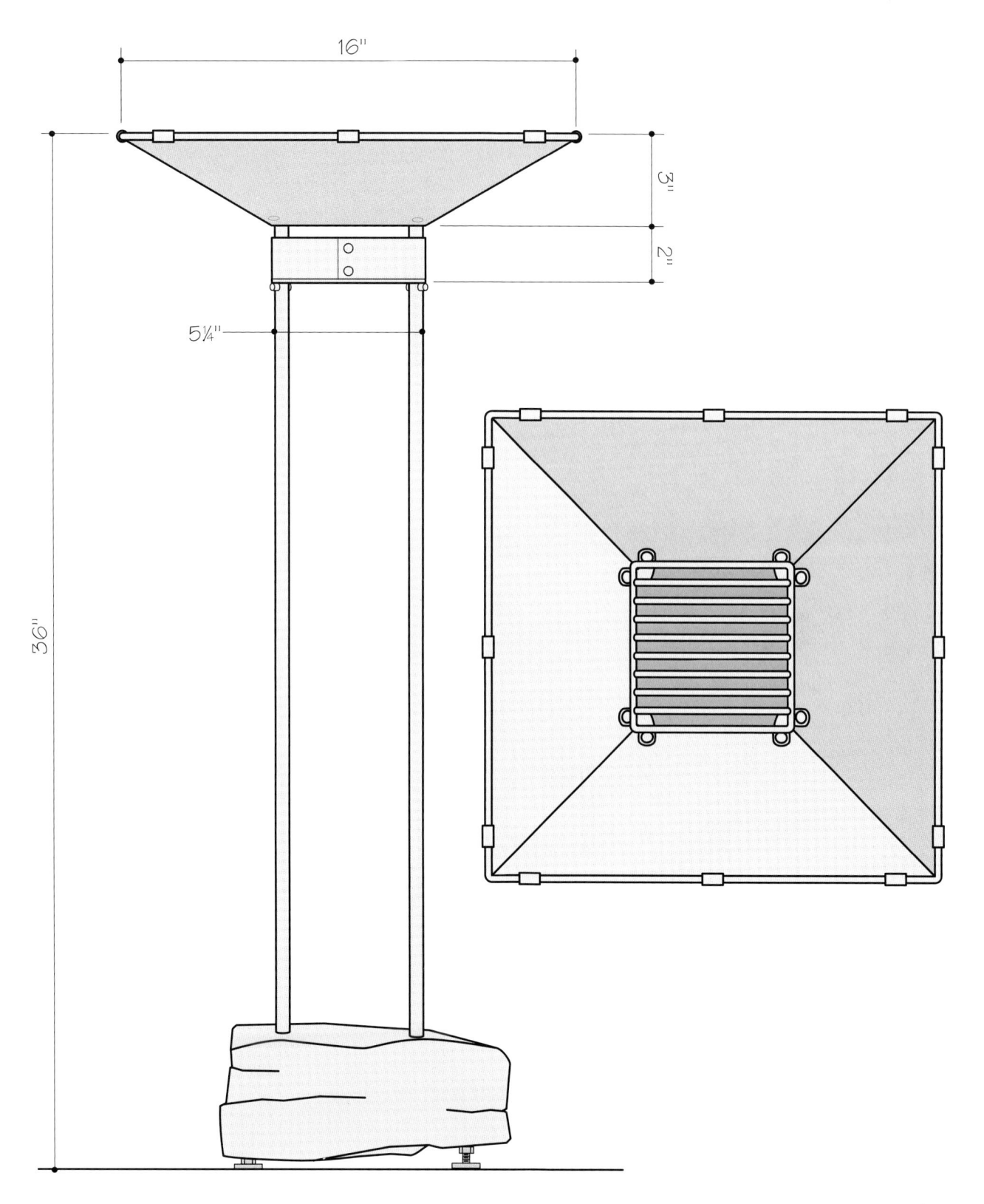

143

Flag Holder - ½ scale

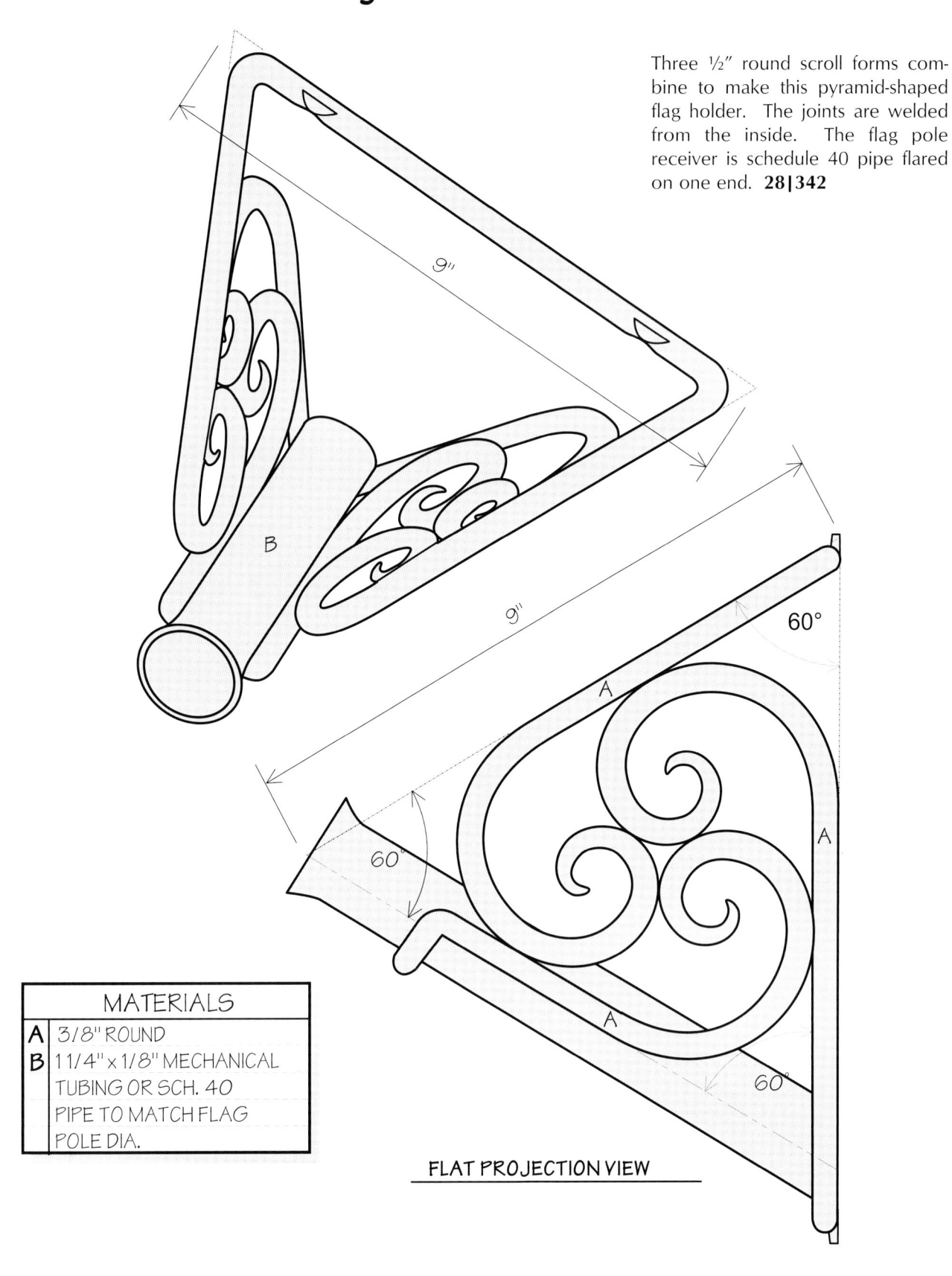

Three ½" round scroll forms combine to make this pyramid-shaped flag holder. The joints are welded from the inside. The flag pole receiver is schedule 40 pipe flared on one end. **28|342**

9"

9"

60°

60°

60°

A

A

A

B

FLAT PROJECTION VIEW

MATERIALS	
A	3/8" ROUND
B	1 1/4" x 1/8" MECHANICAL TUBING OR SCH. 40 PIPE TO MATCH FLAG POLE DIA.

144

Flat Bar Floral Elements - full scale

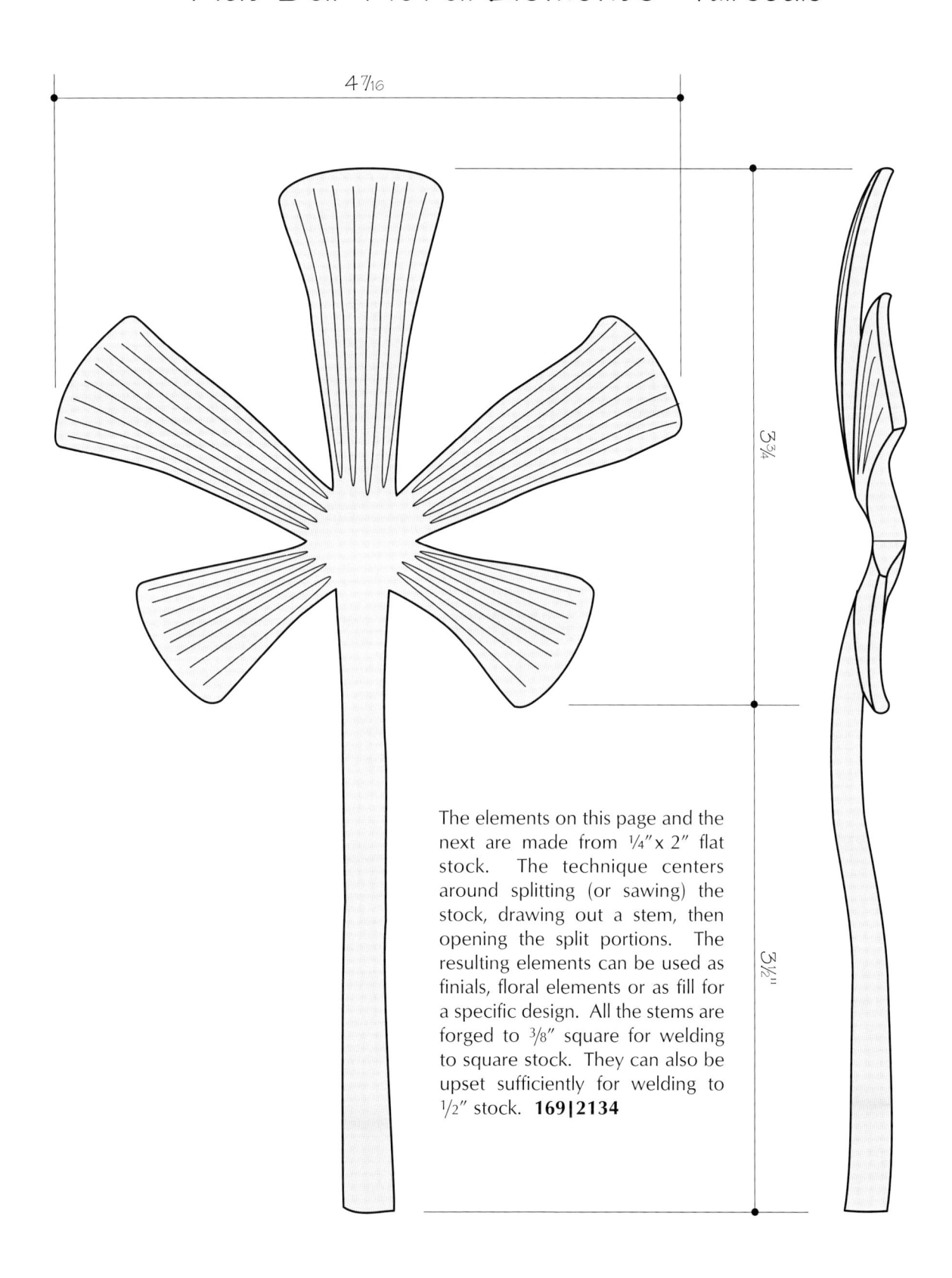

4 7/16

3 3/4

3 1/2"

The elements on this page and the next are made from ¼"x 2" flat stock. The technique centers around splitting (or sawing) the stock, drawing out a stem, then opening the split portions. The resulting elements can be used as finials, floral elements or as fill for a specific design. All the stems are forged to ⅜" square for welding to square stock. They can also be upset sufficiently for welding to ½" stock. **169|2134**

Flat Bar Floral Elements, cont.

5¾"

6½"

2"

5½"

146

Historic Marker - ⅛ scale

The foundation for this relatively light item must be substantial enough to keep it plumb through climactic changes. The verticals are 1″ square stock split and scrolled to support an informational plaque. **111|1363**

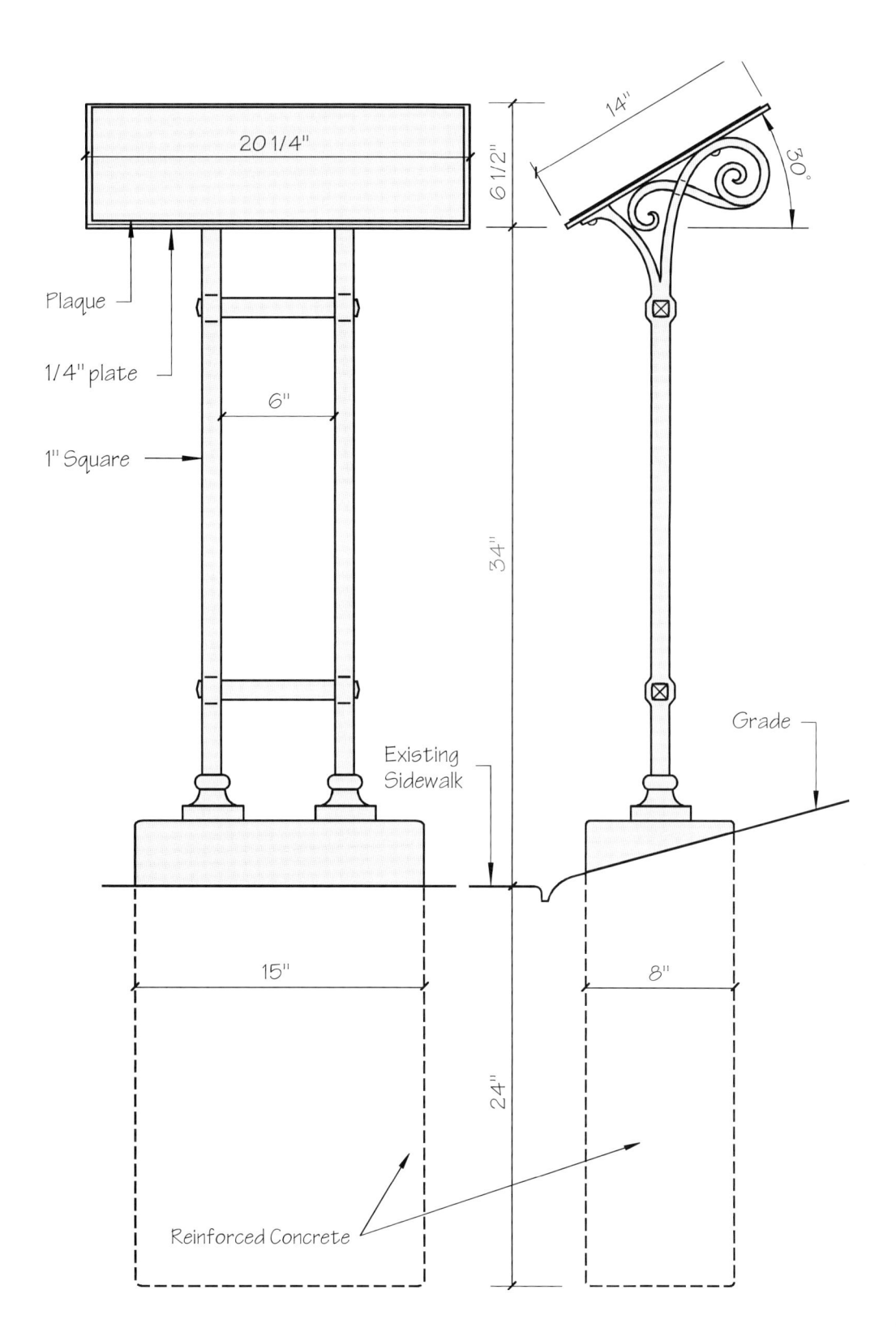

House Number Sign - 1/8 scale

The most interesting parts of this sign are the forged numbers. They are sawn or split and drawn from flat stock, then shaped as needed. The posts are pointed so they can be pushed into a lawn, and temporarily pulled out for trimming or mowing. **37|457**

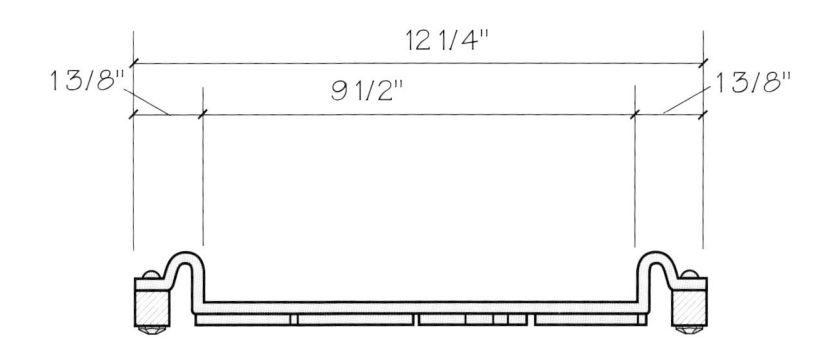

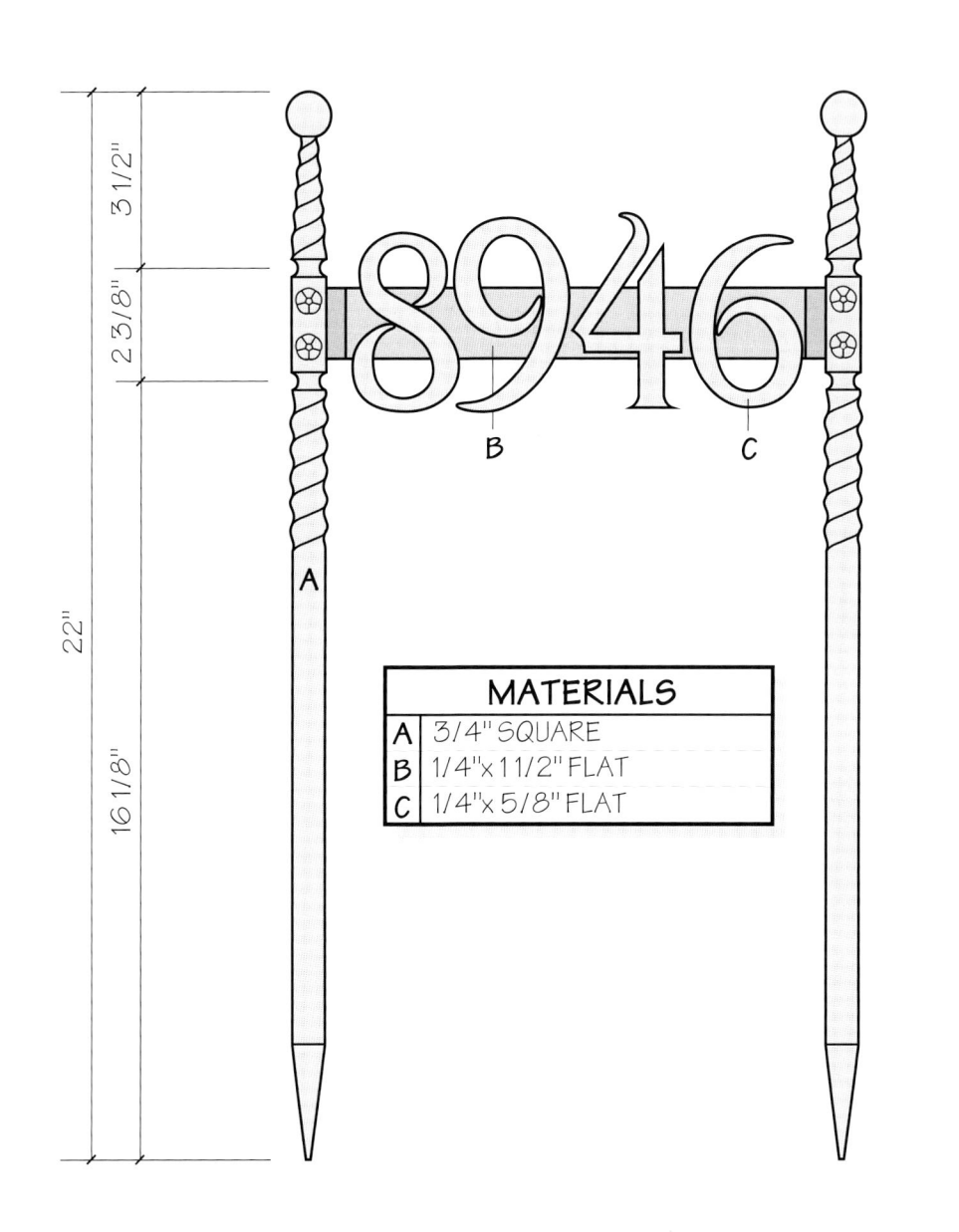

MATERIALS	
A	3/4" SQUARE
B	1/4" x 1 1/2" FLAT
C	1/4" x 5/8" FLAT

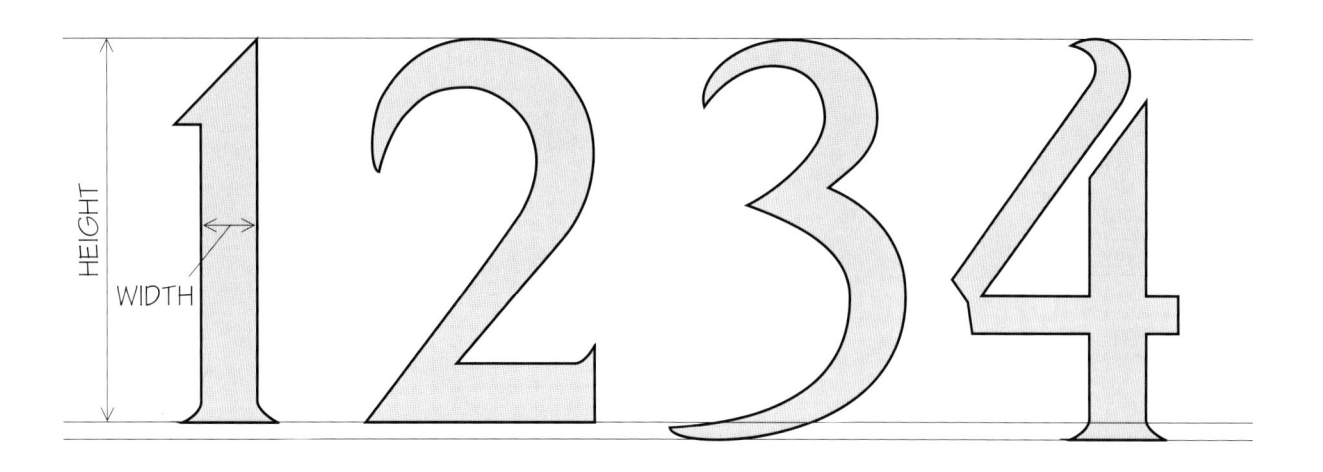

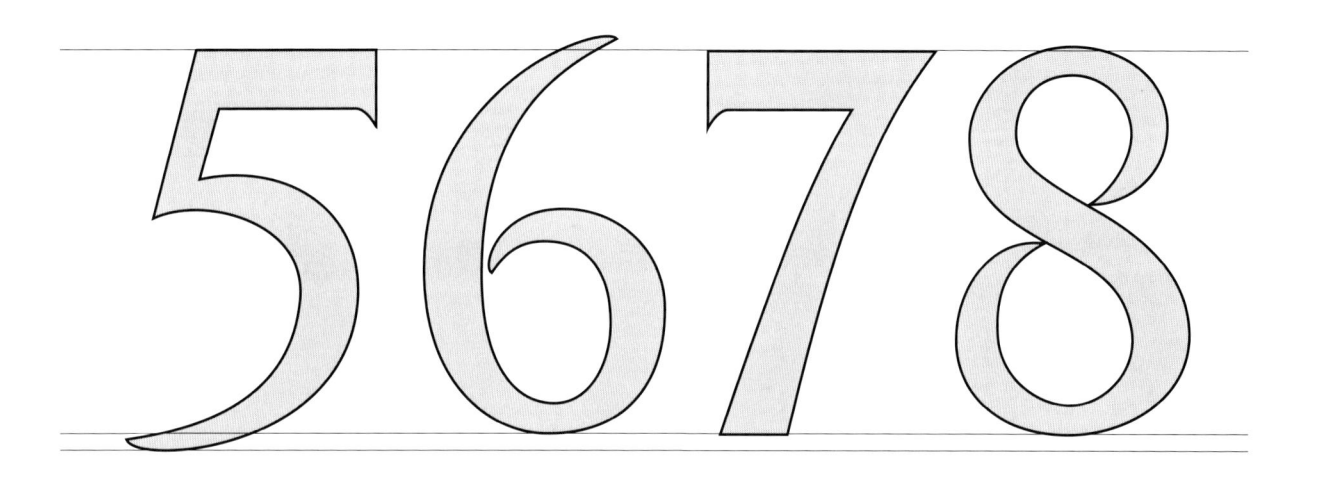

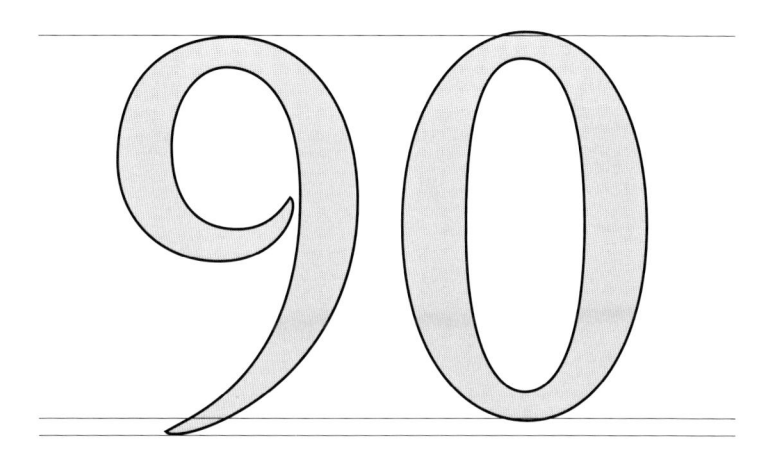

Enlarge the characters on this page the percentage indicated for given stock width & height.

Width*	Height	%/Original
5/16"	2"	100%
5/8"	4"	200%
3/4"	4 7/8"	243%
1"	6 1/2"	325%

Notes: 1. Characters based on Italian Garamond typeface. 2. Use 25% wider stock per given height for bold characters.

*Thickest part of each character.

Lamp and Bracket - ⅛ scale

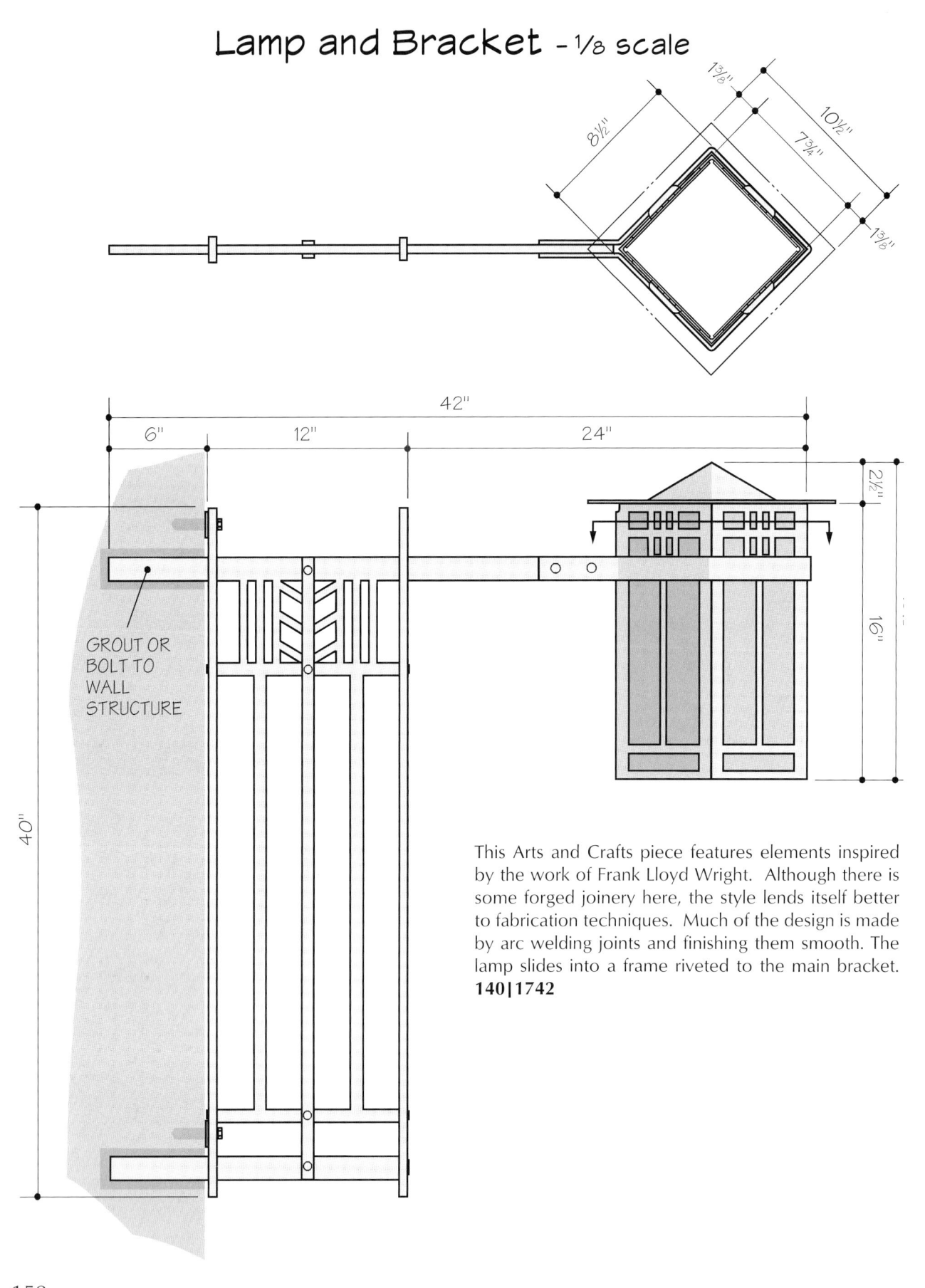

GROUT OR BOLT TO WALL STRUCTURE

This Arts and Crafts piece features elements inspired by the work of Frank Lloyd Wright. Although there is some forged joinery here, the style lends itself better to fabrication techniques. Much of the design is made by arc welding joints and finishing them smooth. The lamp slides into a frame riveted to the main bracket.
140|1742

Clam Shell Wall Sconce - not to scale

The idea for these two designs center around easy access for cleaning the interior glass. A wall mounted vertical member supports hinges that provide access. The top is held by the upper portion of the vertical member.

147 | 1844

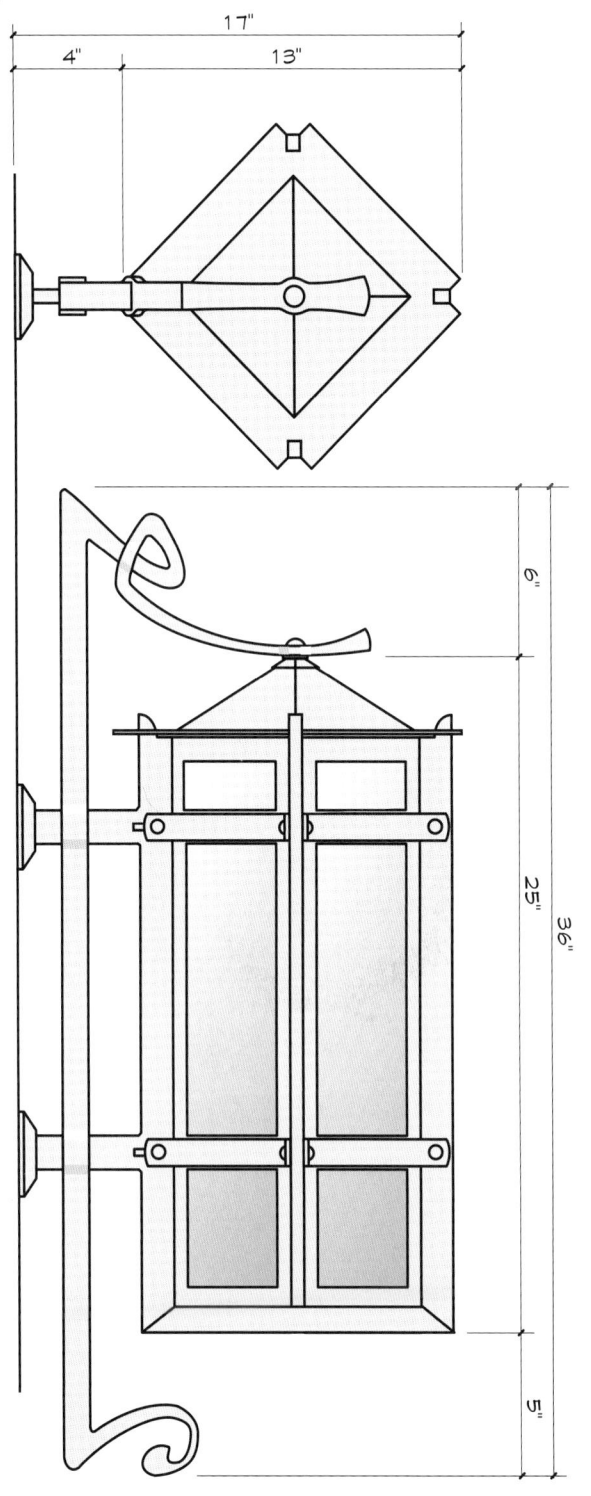

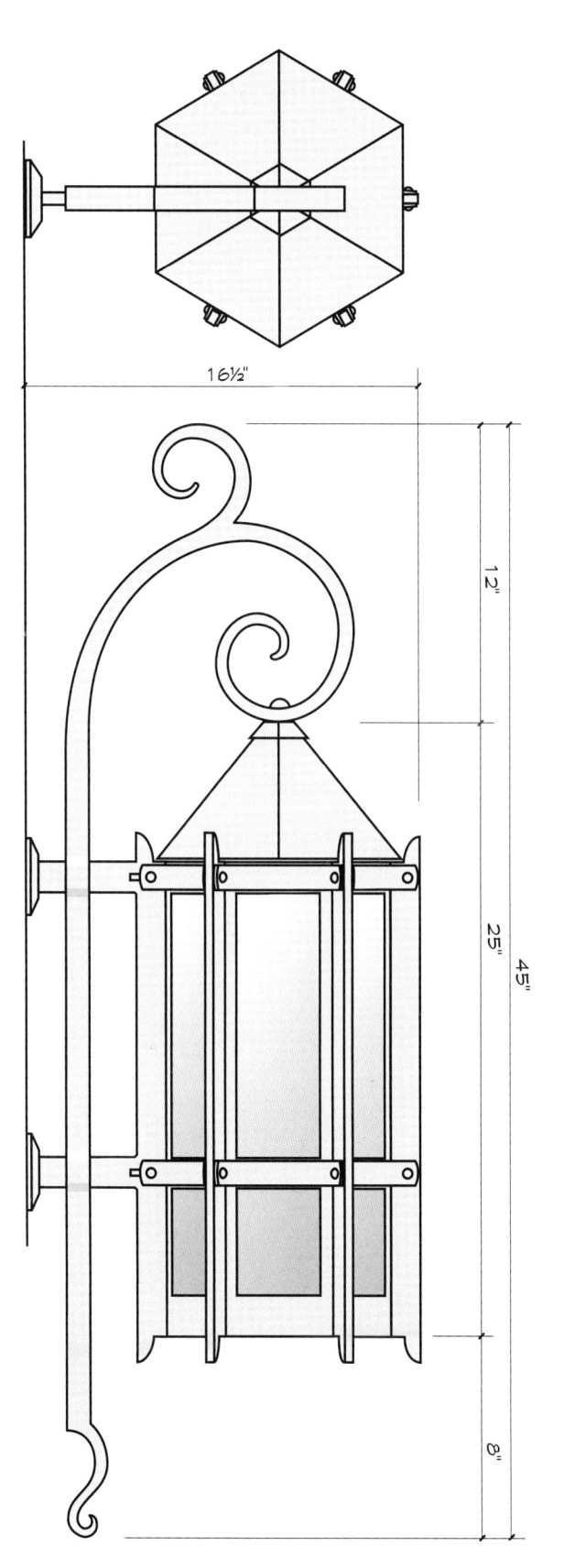

Mailbox -2/3 scale

A 9" x 12" envelope will fit flat in this mail box. It is meant to be mounted near a door in an alcove or under a porch to protect the mail from the weather. Change the scale or proportions accordingly for different size boxes. The sheet metal box is held in place with forged flat stock straps. **86|1063**

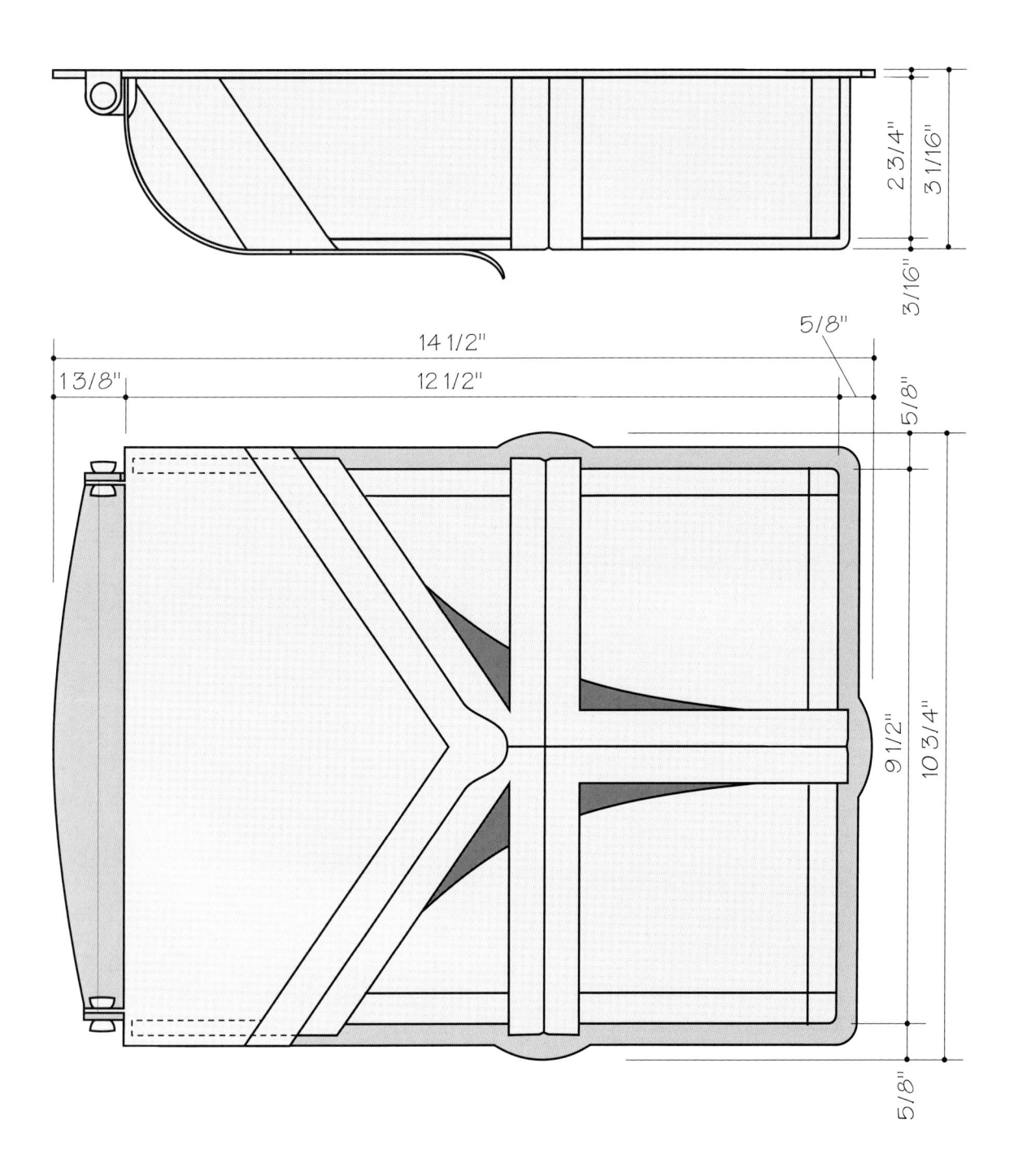

3/8 SCALE (ENLARGE 266% FOR FULL SIZE)

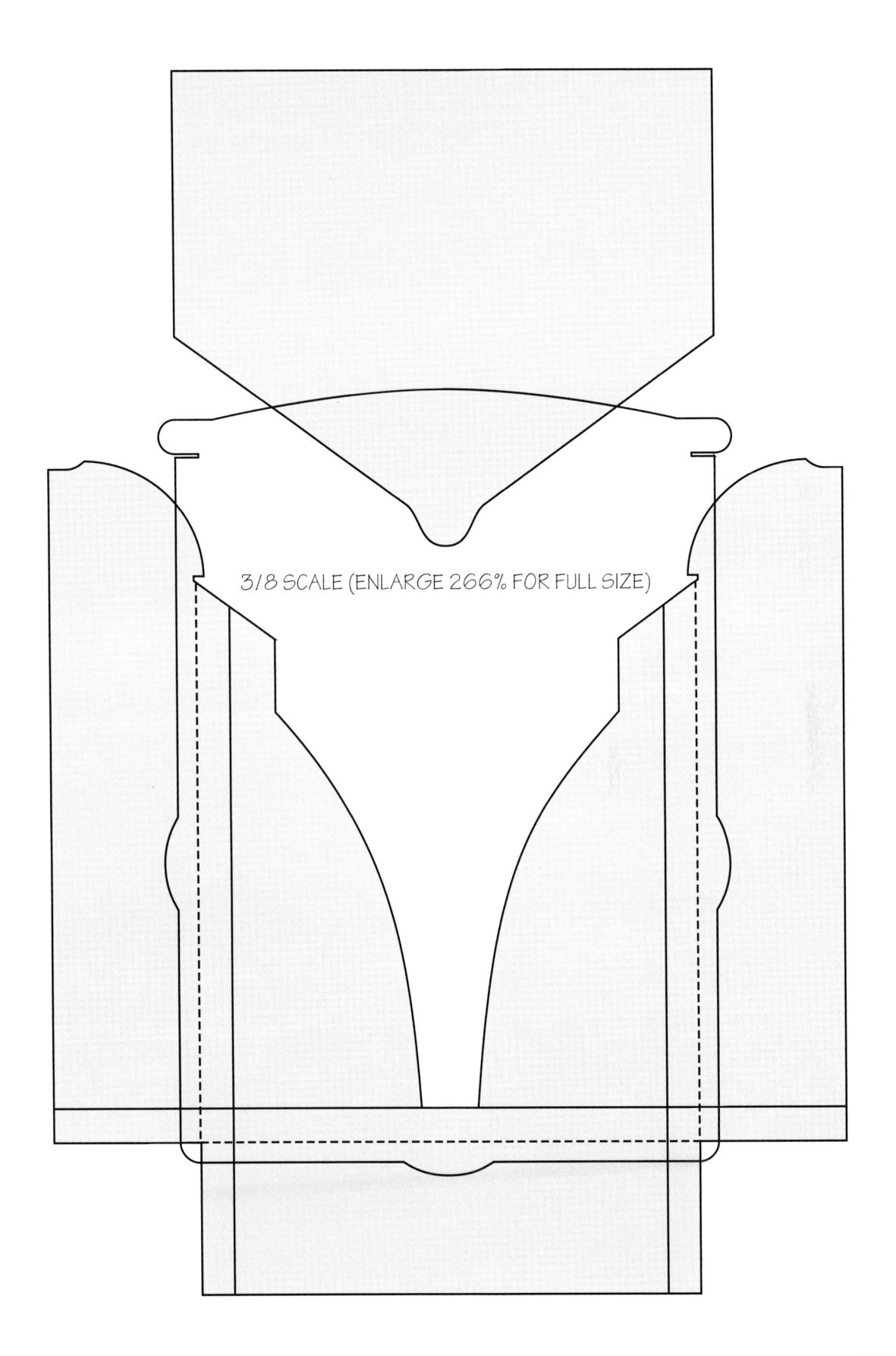

Ornamental Bell #1 - ½ scale

A single piece of ¼" plate is cut out and punched to receive a ring and a clapper, then formed into a 4" diameter bell. The clapper starts as 1" round, drawn down to ¼" round on each end. **103|1269**

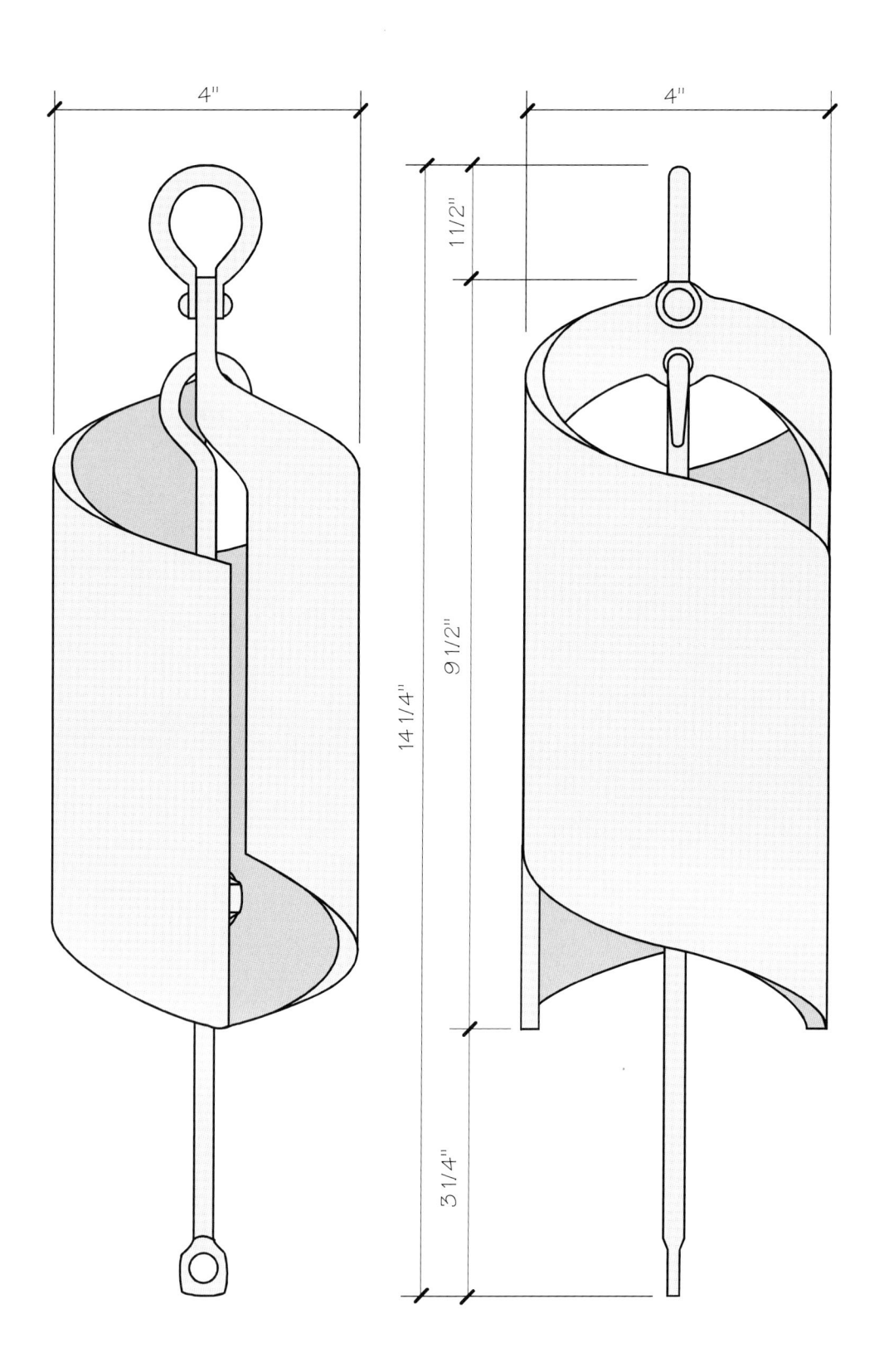

154

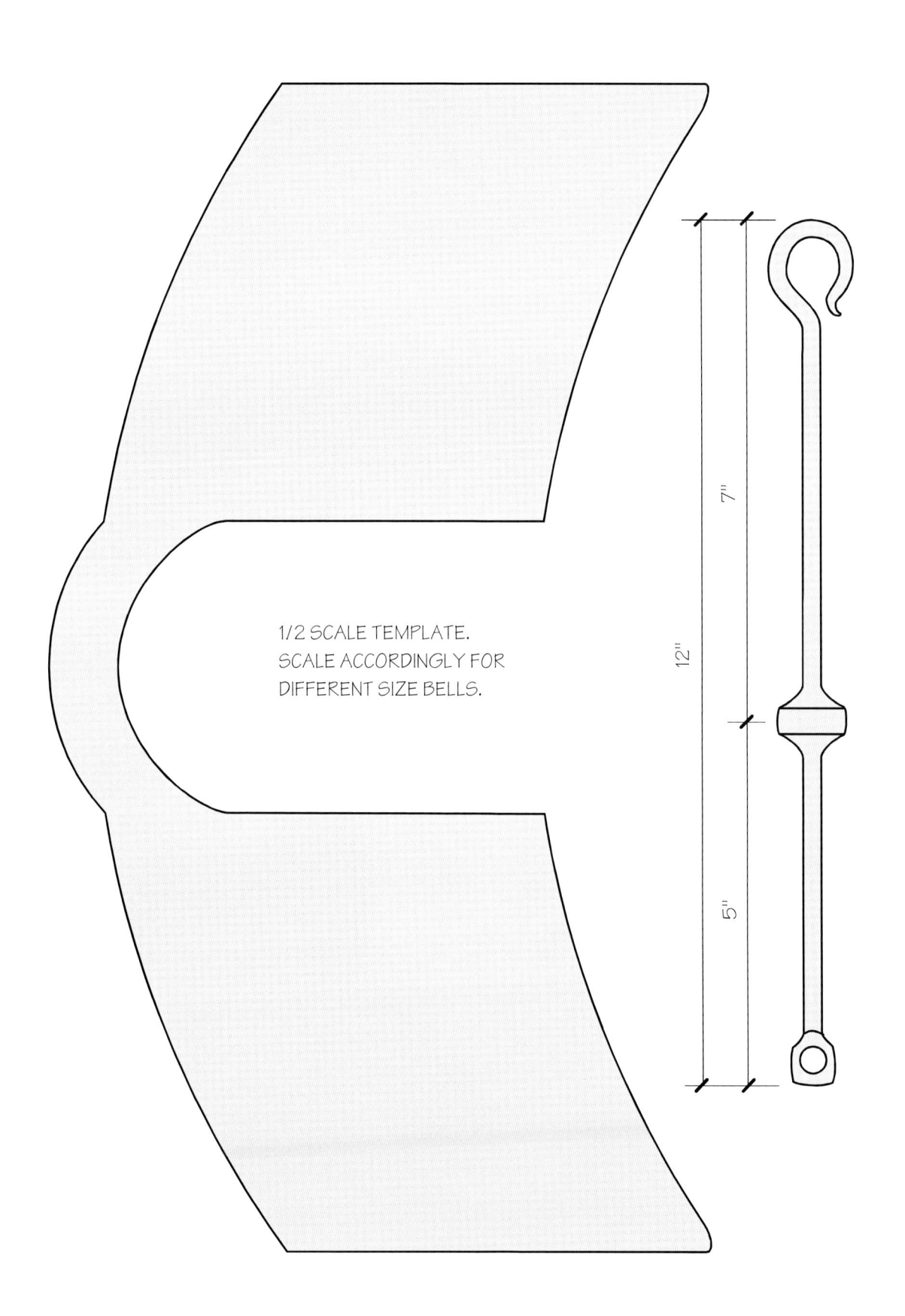

1/2 SCALE TEMPLATE.
SCALE ACCORDINGLY FOR
DIFFERENT SIZE BELLS.

7"

12"

5"

155

Ornamental Bell #2 -2/3 scale

This bell is rough flame cut from either schedule 40 or schedule 80 6" pipe. ⅝" round stock connects the two halves together. The clapper is 1" round, drawn down to ¼" round on each end. **71|875**

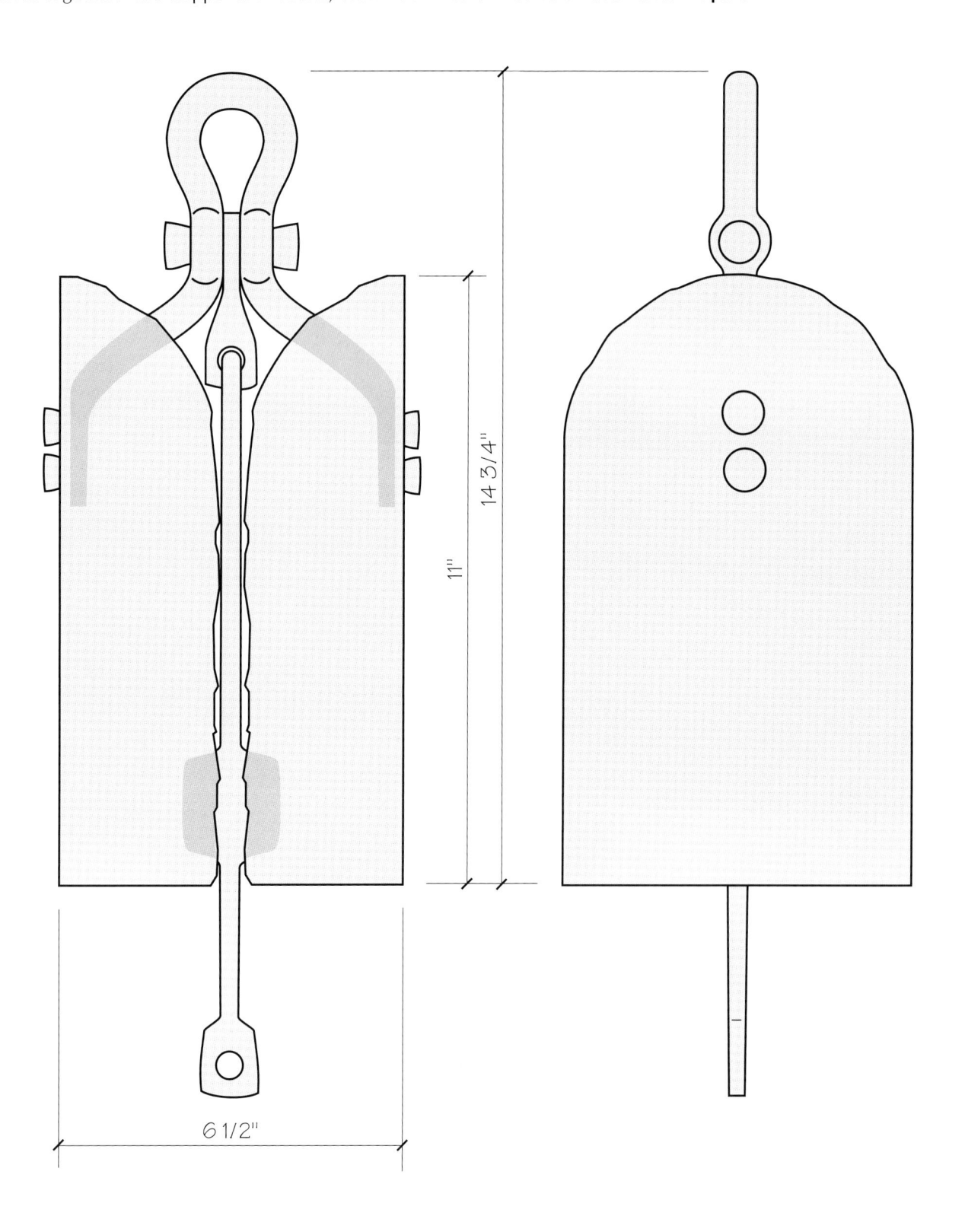

Flower Pot Bracket - ¼ scale

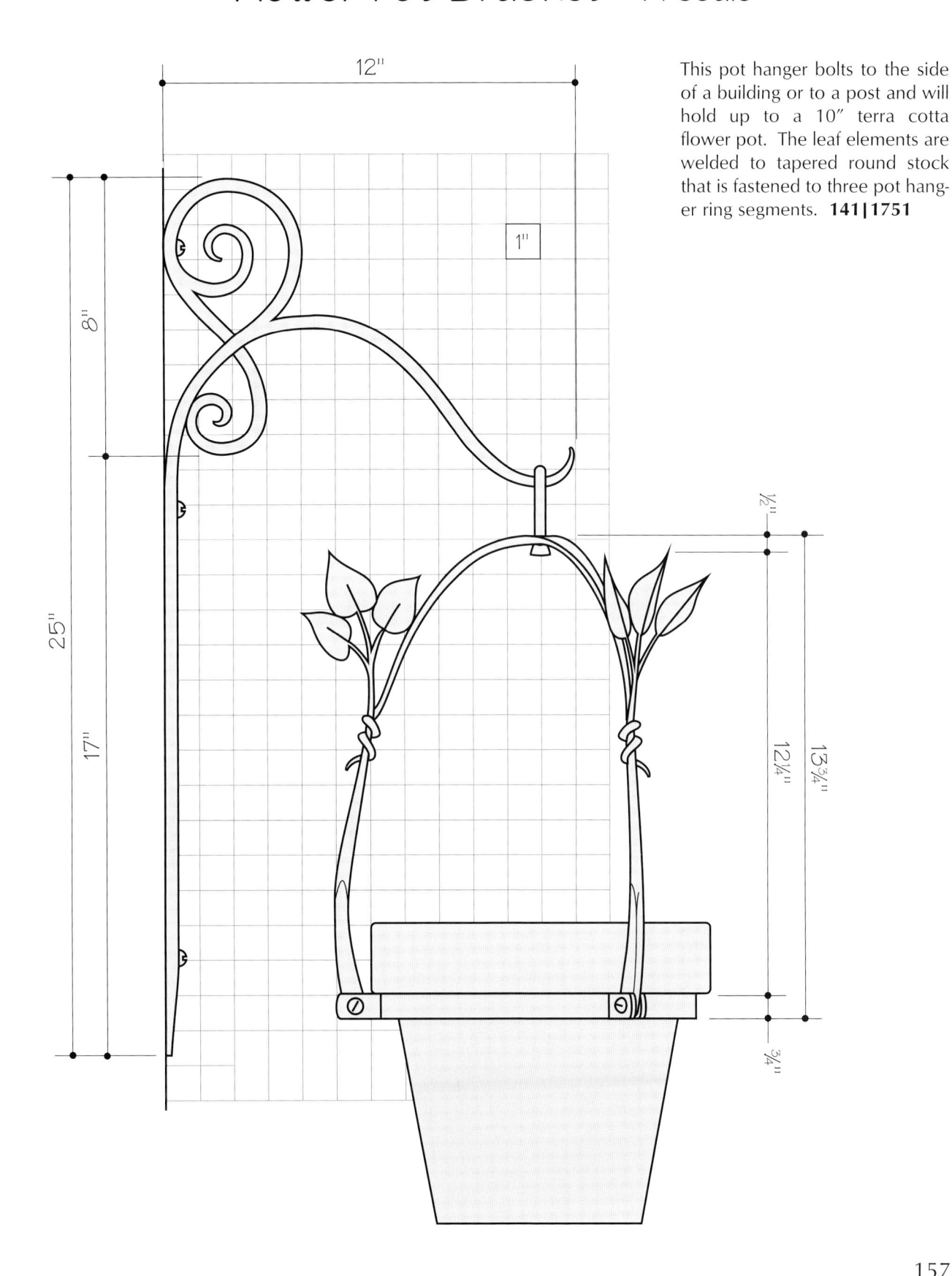

This pot hanger bolts to the side of a building or to a post and will hold up to a 10" terra cotta flower pot. The leaf elements are welded to tapered round stock that is fastened to three pot hanger ring segments. **141|1751**

Sign Frame - not to scale

The lettered portion of this sign is sand blasted and painted wood. Frame elements are made from ½"x 1" bar stock, held together by rivets. All the leaves have tapered stems gas welded to each other. **27|329**

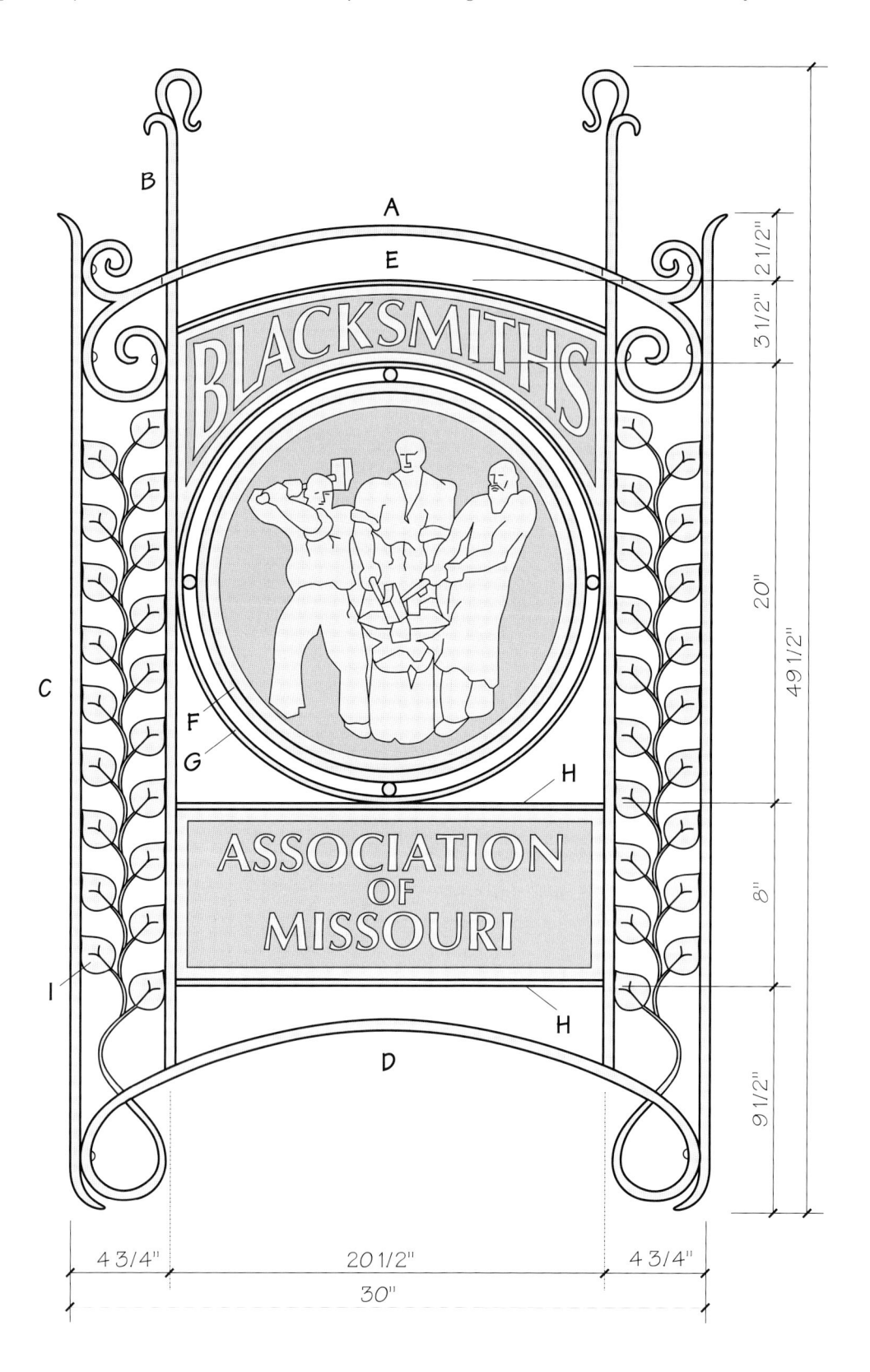

159

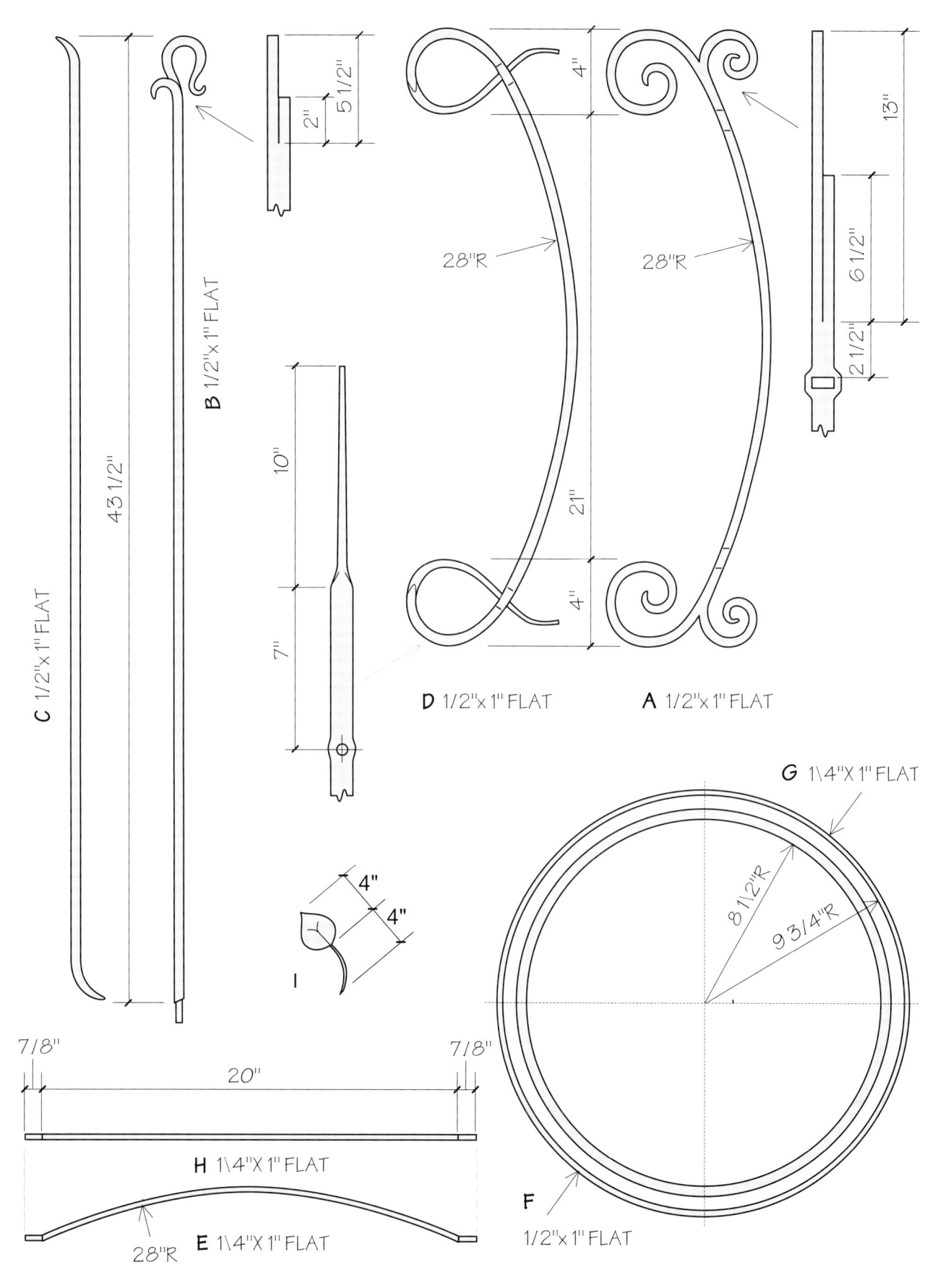

Sign Bracket - ⅛ scale

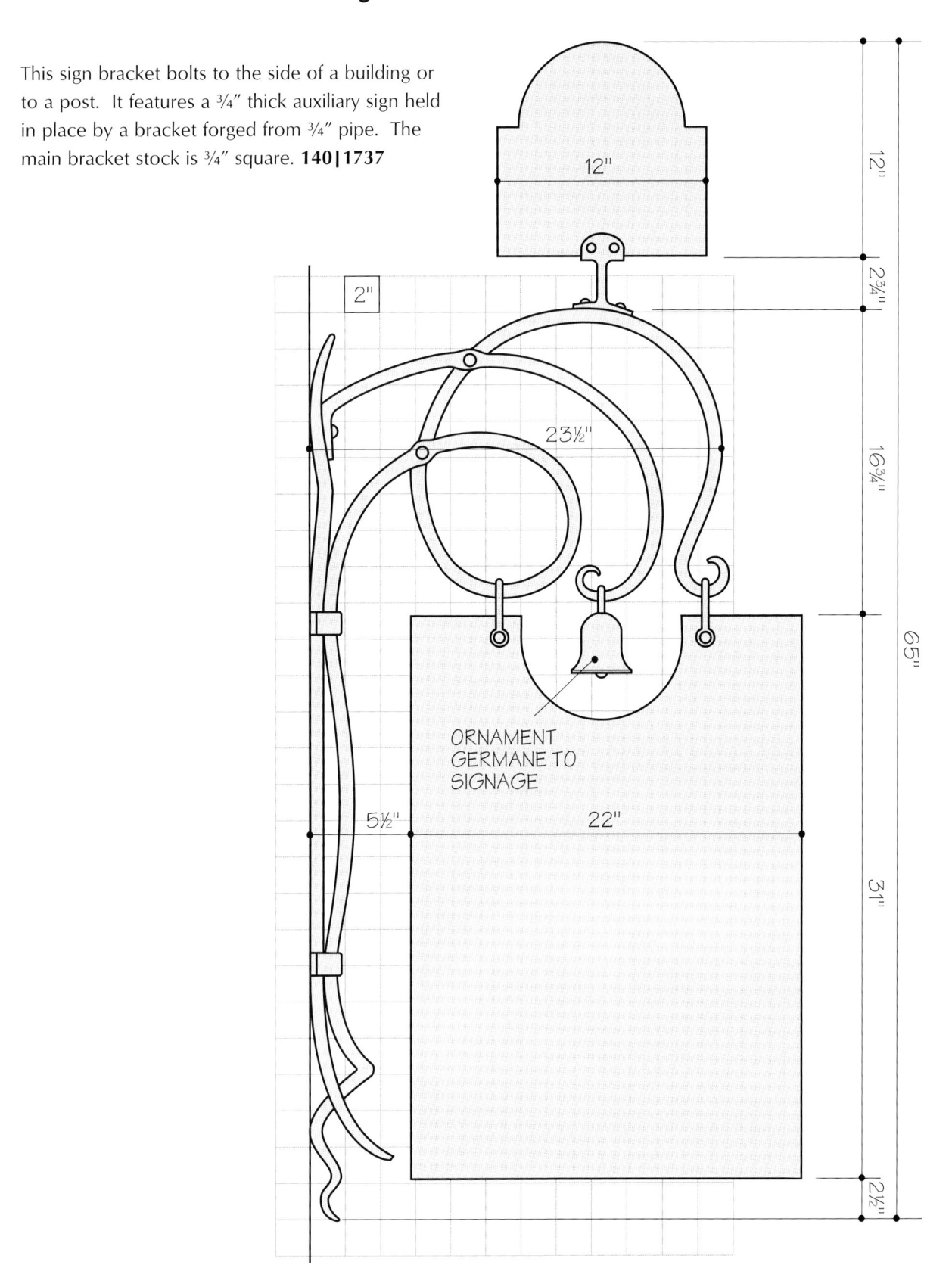

This sign bracket bolts to the side of a building or to a post. It features a ¾" thick auxiliary sign held in place by a bracket forged from ¾" pipe. The main bracket stock is ¾" square. **140|1737**

12"

2"

23½"

ORNAMENT GERMANE TO SIGNAGE

5½" 22"

12"

2¾"

16¾"

65"

31"

2½"

Sundials - not to scale

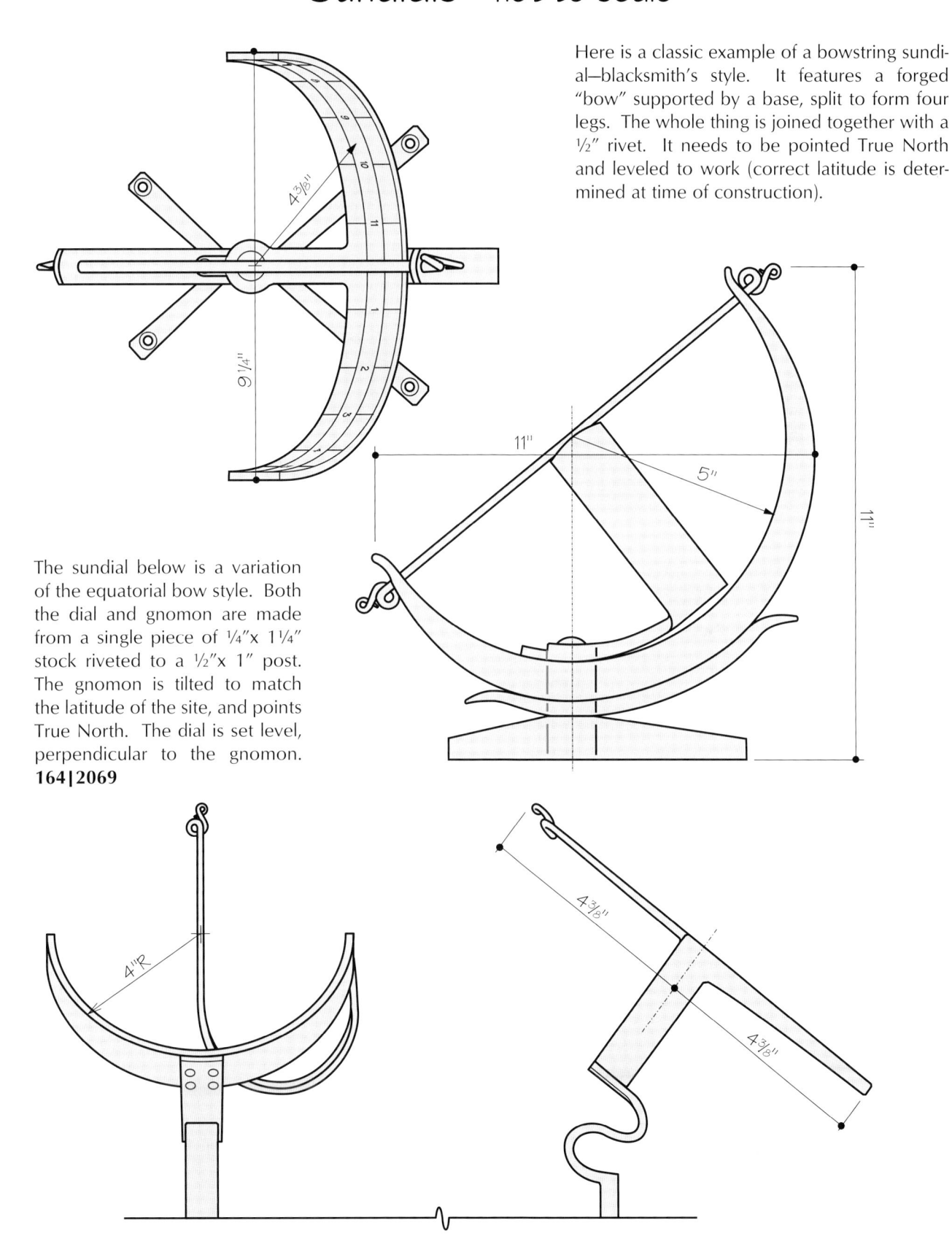

Here is a classic example of a bowstring sundial—blacksmith's style. It features a forged "bow" supported by a base, split to form four legs. The whole thing is joined together with a ½" rivet. It needs to be pointed True North and leveled to work (correct latitude is determined at time of construction).

The sundial below is a variation of the equatorial bow style. Both the dial and gnomon are made from a single piece of ¼"x 1¼" stock riveted to a ½"x 1" post. The gnomon is tilted to match the latitude of the site, and points True North. The dial is set level, perpendicular to the gnomon.
164|2069

Weathervane - not to scale

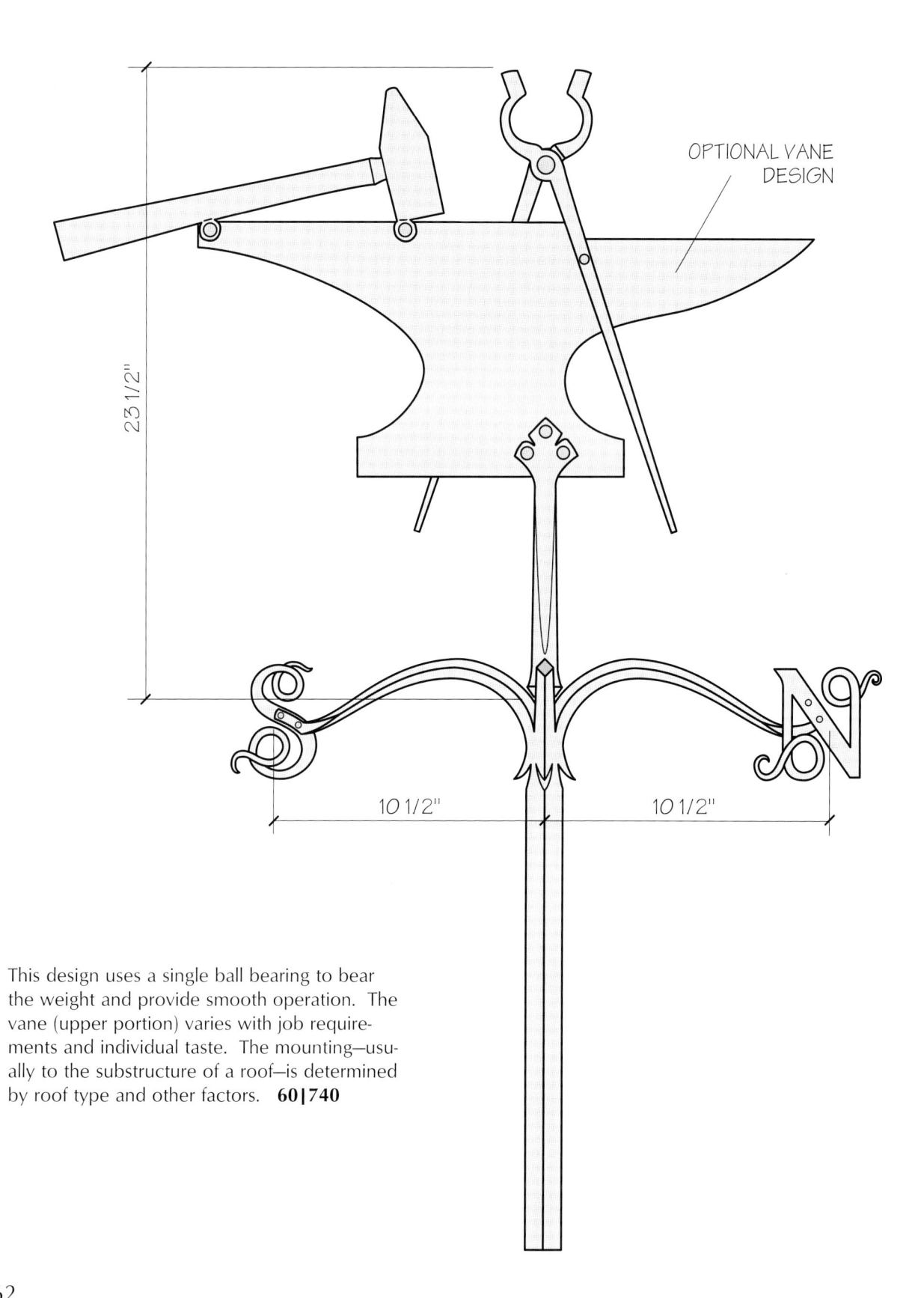

OPTIONAL VANE DESIGN

23 1/2"

10 1/2"   10 1/2"

This design uses a single ball bearing to bear the weight and provide smooth operation. The vane (upper portion) varies with job requirements and individual taste. The mounting—usually to the substructure of a roof—is determined by roof type and other factors. **60|740**

162

LETTERS
1/2 SCALE

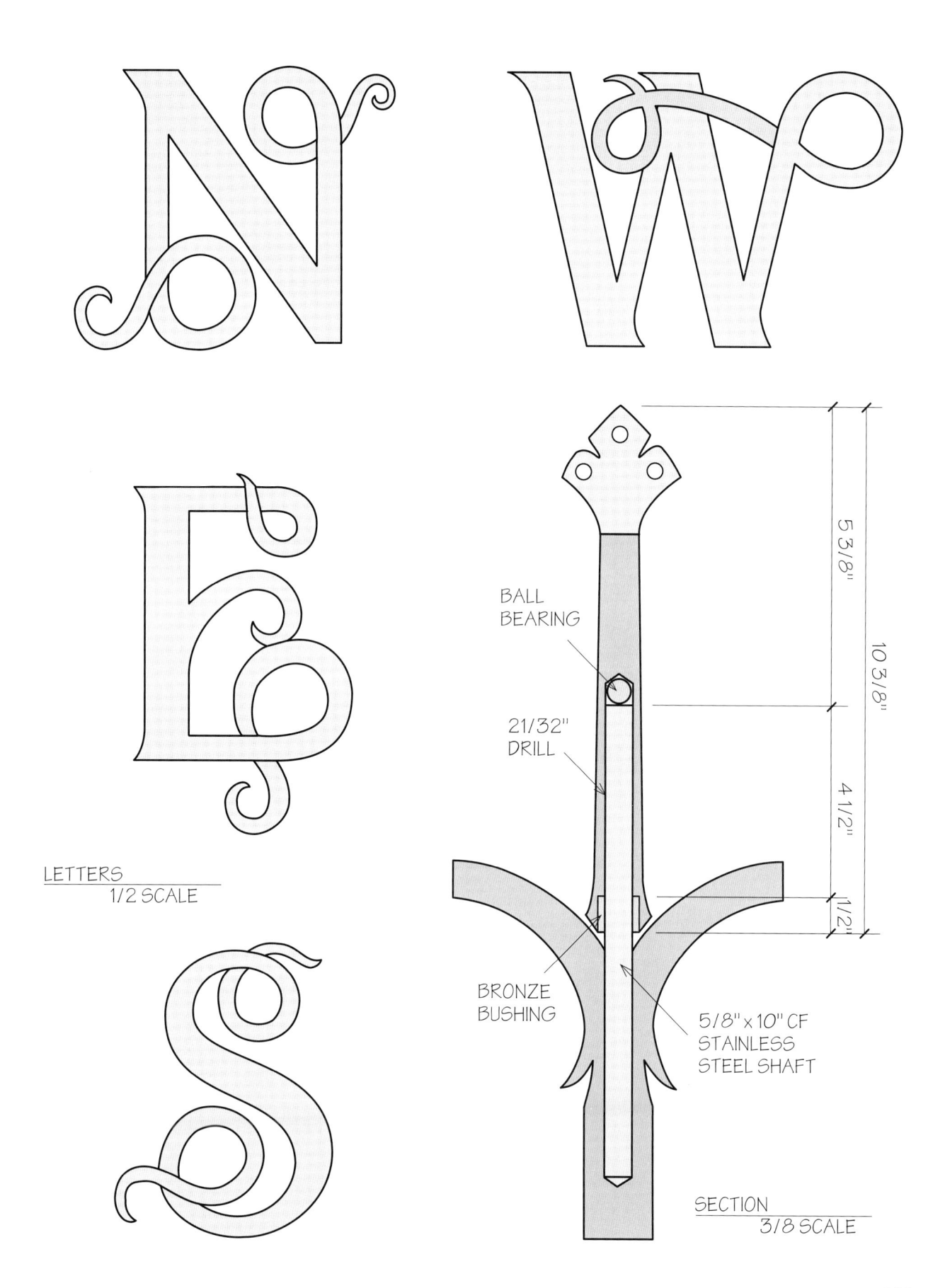

BALL BEARING

21/32" DRILL

5 3/8"

10 3/8"

4 1/2"

1/2"

BRONZE BUSHING

5/8" x 10" CF STAINLESS STEEL SHAFT

SECTION
3/8 SCALE

163

Window Grill - not to scale

Although designed as a window grill, this piece can also be modified for use as a small gate. The main body is 3/4" square and the horizontals are 5/8" x 1" stock.
108|1327

24 3/4"

24"

62"

19"

19"

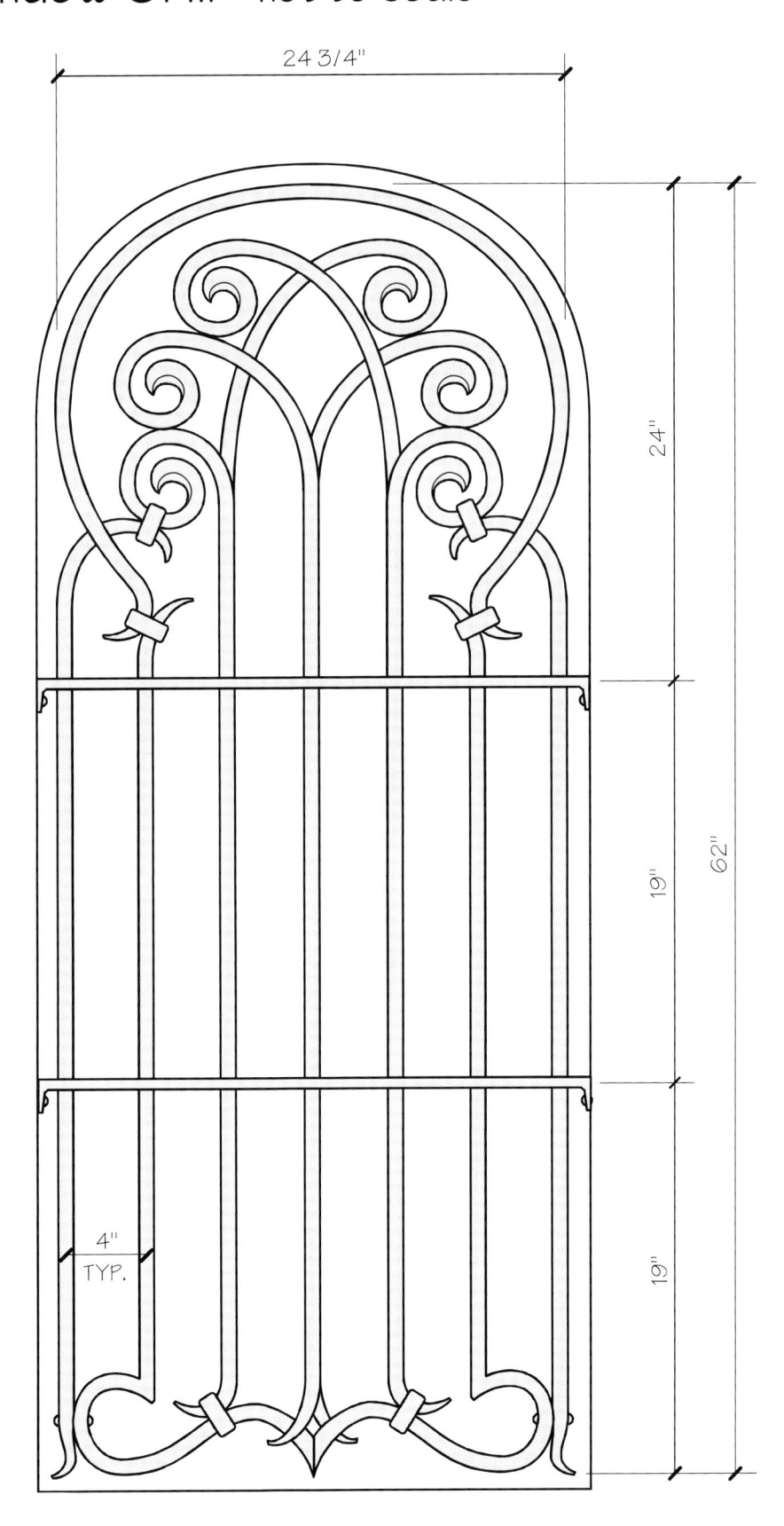

4" TYP.

7 Gates and Railings

Back Bar Hinge - ¾ scale

Back bar hinges are made for large gates and typically bear the load at the foot of the hinged back bar. A keeper near the top of the bar facilitates removing the gate. This hinge features a ball bearing in the bottom hinge socket for smoother operation. **24|290**

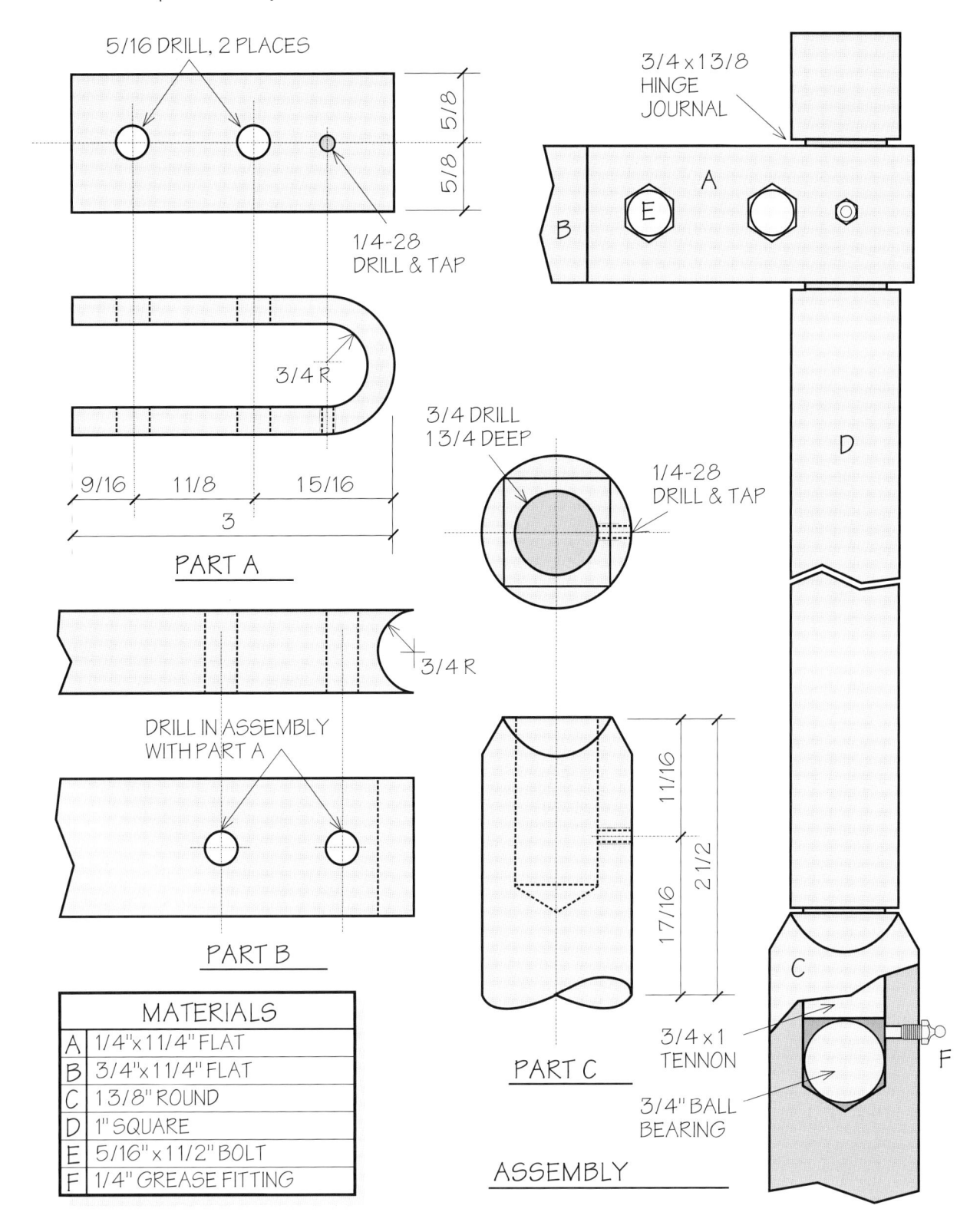

PART A
- 5/16 DRILL, 2 PLACES
- 1/4-28 DRILL & TAP
- 5/8, 5/8, 5/8
- 9/16, 1 1/8, 15/16
- 3
- 3/4 R

PART B
- 3/4 R
- DRILL IN ASSEMBLY WITH PART A

PART C
- 3/4 DRILL 1 3/4 DEEP
- 1/4-28 DRILL & TAP
- 11/16
- 17/16
- 2 1/2

ASSEMBLY
- 3/4 x 1 3/8 HINGE JOURNAL
- A, B, E, D, C
- 3/4 x 1 TENNON
- 3/4" BALL BEARING
- F

MATERIALS

A	1/4" x 1 1/4" FLAT
B	3/4" x 1 1/4" FLAT
C	1 3/8" ROUND
D	1" SQUARE
E	5/16" x 1 1/2" BOLT
F	1/4" GREASE FITTING

Cane Bolt - ½ scale

Cane bolts secure doors and gates at the grade or floor level. This one uses the lock bar of a gate frame, twisted 90°, as a guide for the bolt and handle. A keeper secures the bolt near the bottom of the gate. **25|291**

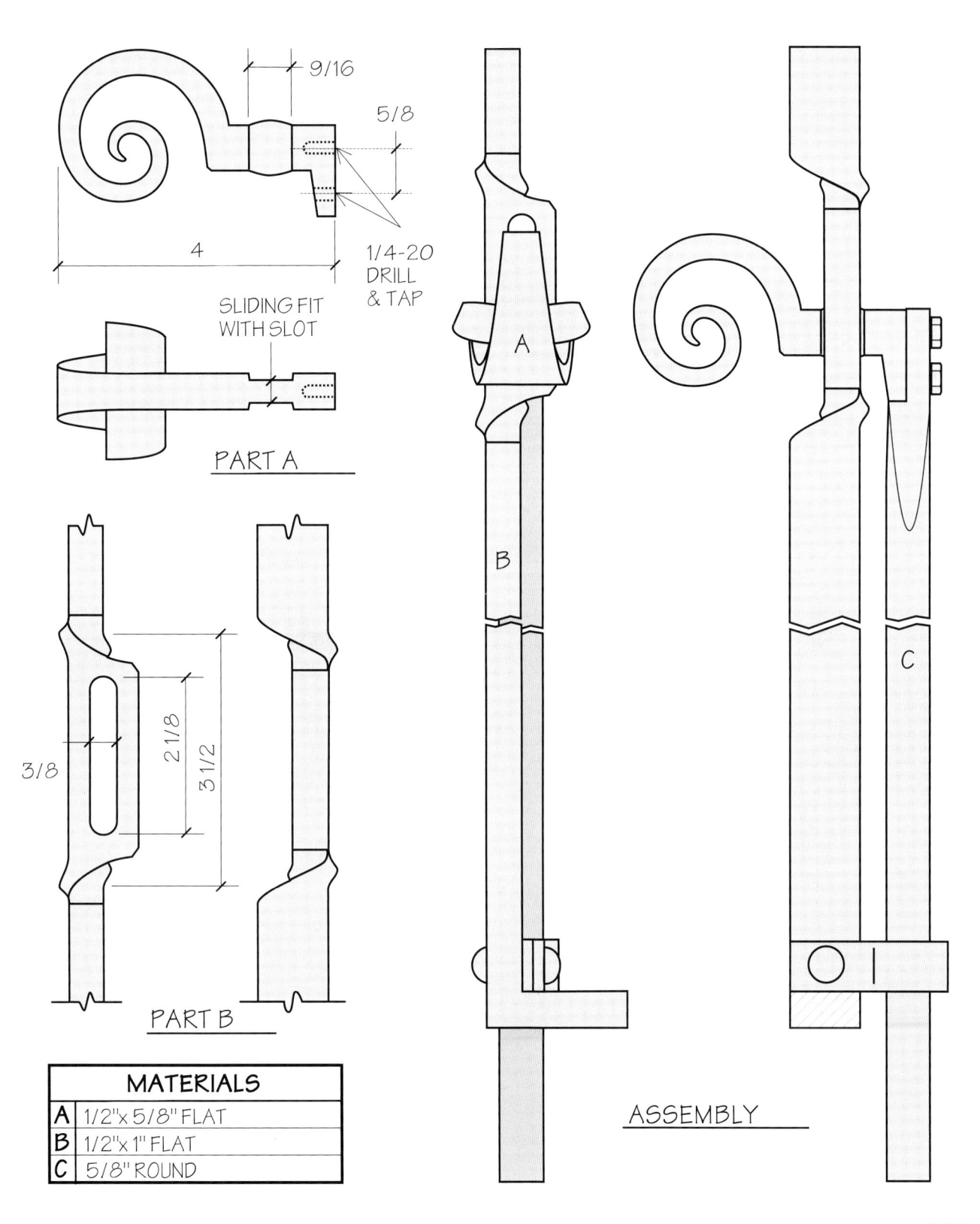

PART A

PART B

ASSEMBLY

MATERIALS	
A	1/2" x 5/8" FLAT
B	1/2" x 1" FLAT
C	5/8" ROUND

Post and Handrail - ⅛ scale

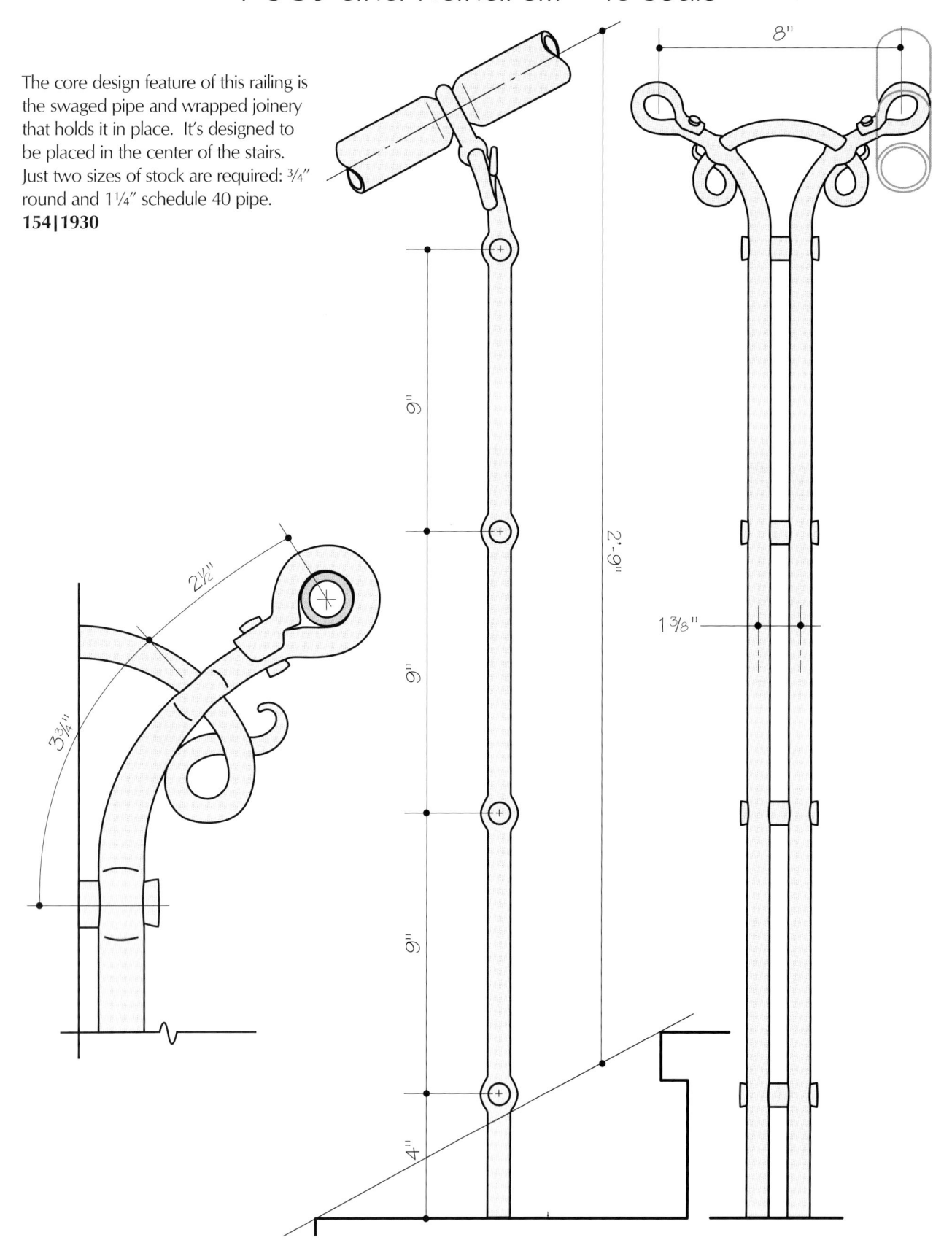

The core design feature of this railing is the swaged pipe and wrapped joinery that holds it in place. It's designed to be placed in the center of the stairs. Just two sizes of stock are required: ¾" round and 1¼" schedule 40 pipe.

154|1930

Post and Railing #1 - not to scale

With just one hole per baluster, this railing features an intricate woven top line. The only joints are the wrapped end around each baluster and a tenon or weld at the bottom of the baluster. **53|653**

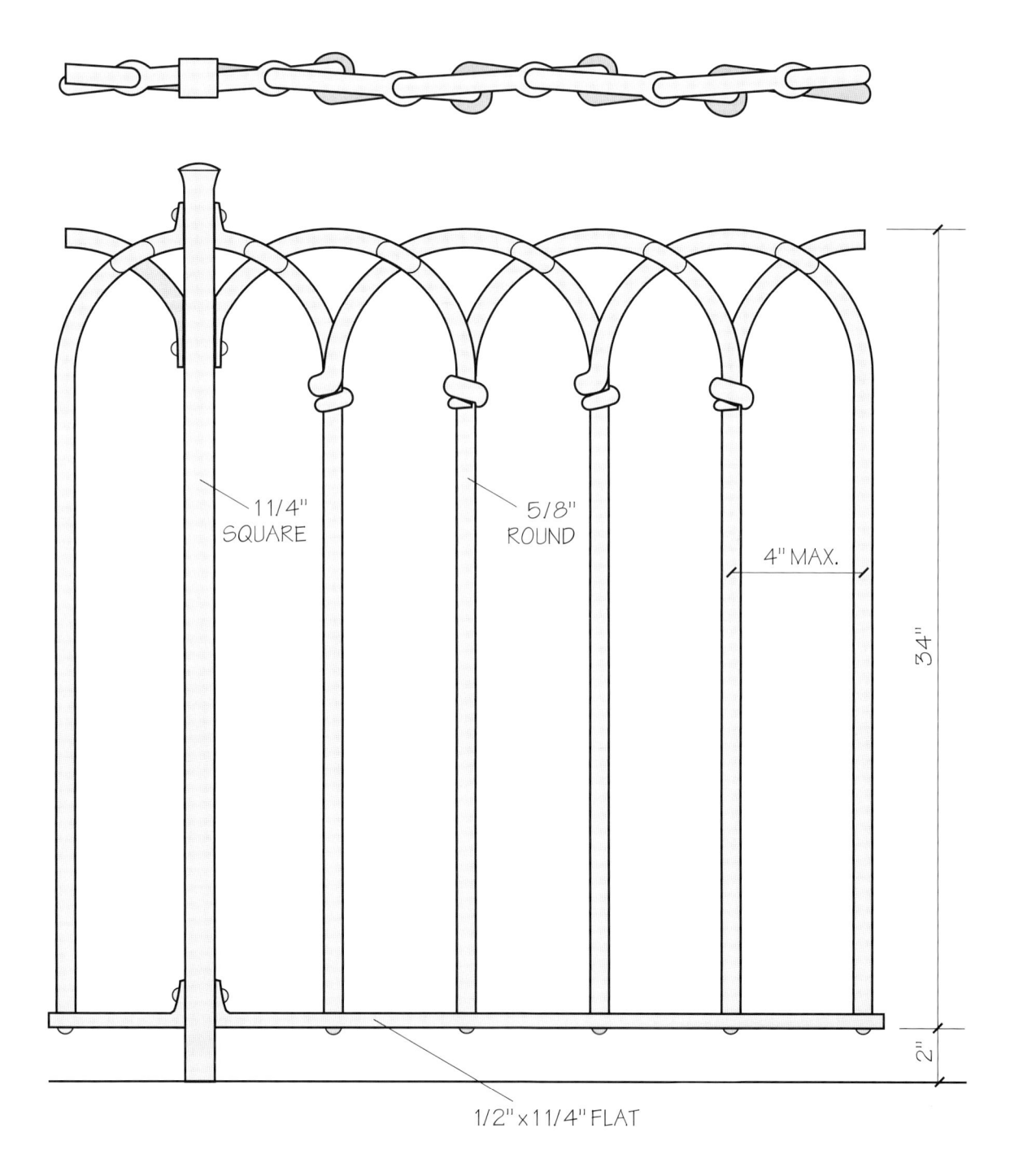

1 1/4" SQUARE

5/8" ROUND

4" MAX.

34"

2"

1/2" x 1 1/4" FLAT

169

Post and Railing #2 - not to scale

Structural shapes are fabricated to make the profile of this post. The railing has three horizontals, with the middle one floating between the posts. This a good example of how forged and fabricated work can be used together.
35|431

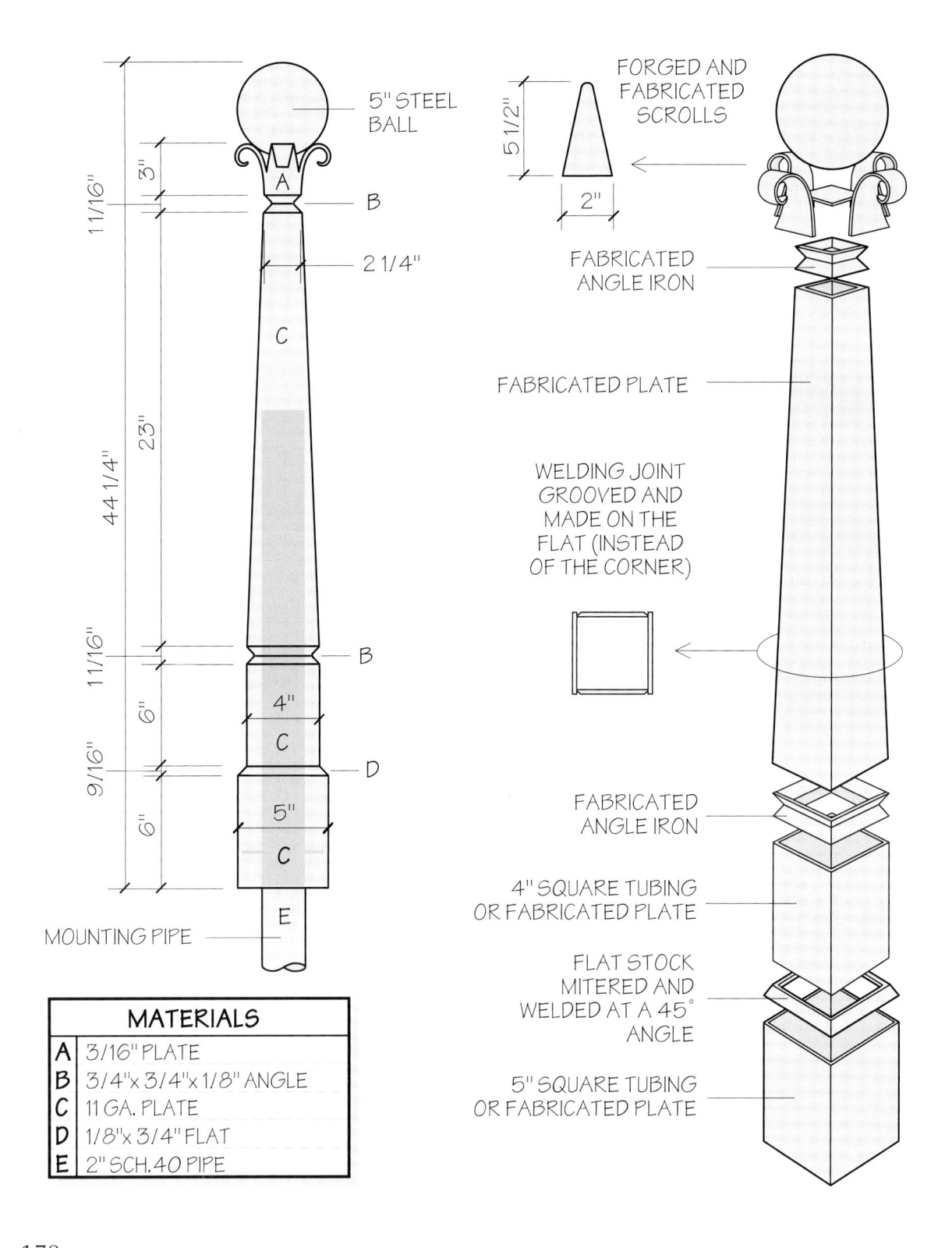

5" STEEL BALL

5 1/2"
2"
FORGED AND FABRICATED SCROLLS

11/16"
3"
44 1/4"
23"
2 1/4"
A
B
C

FABRICATED ANGLE IRON

FABRICATED PLATE

WELDING JOINT GROOVED AND MADE ON THE FLAT (INSTEAD OF THE CORNER)

11/16"
9/16"
6"
6"
4"
5"
B
C
D
C
E

FABRICATED ANGLE IRON

4" SQUARE TUBING OR FABRICATED PLATE

FLAT STOCK MITERED AND WELDED AT A 45° ANGLE

5" SQUARE TUBING OR FABRICATED PLATE

MOUNTING PIPE

MATERIALS	
A	3/16" PLATE
B	3/4"x 3/4"x 1/8" ANGLE
C	11 GA. PLATE
D	1/8"x 3/4" FLAT
E	2" SCH. 40 PIPE

170

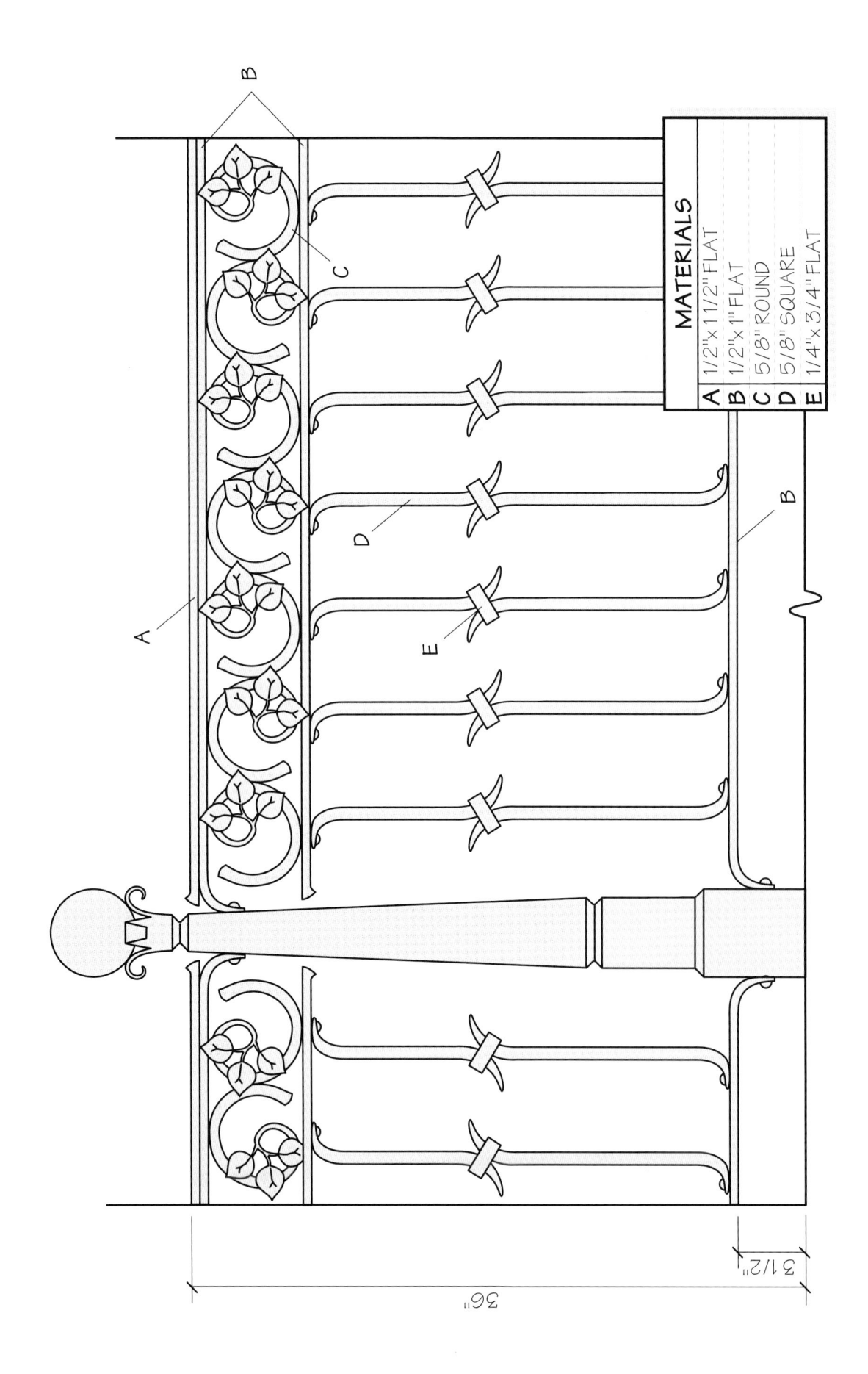

MATERIALS	
A	1/2" x 1 1/2" FLAT
B	1/2" x 1" FLAT
C	5/8" ROUND
D	5/8" SQUARE
E	1/4" x 3/4" FLAT

36"

3 1/2"

171

Post and Railing #3 - not to scale

Wood and steel combine to make this post and railing intended for use on a limited access balcony or porch roof. (The railing height won't conform to building codes in most areas). The finials are cut from 1/8" stock and formed hot into a three-dimensional profile. Finishing all one color blends the wood and steel into a harmonious design.
81|1002

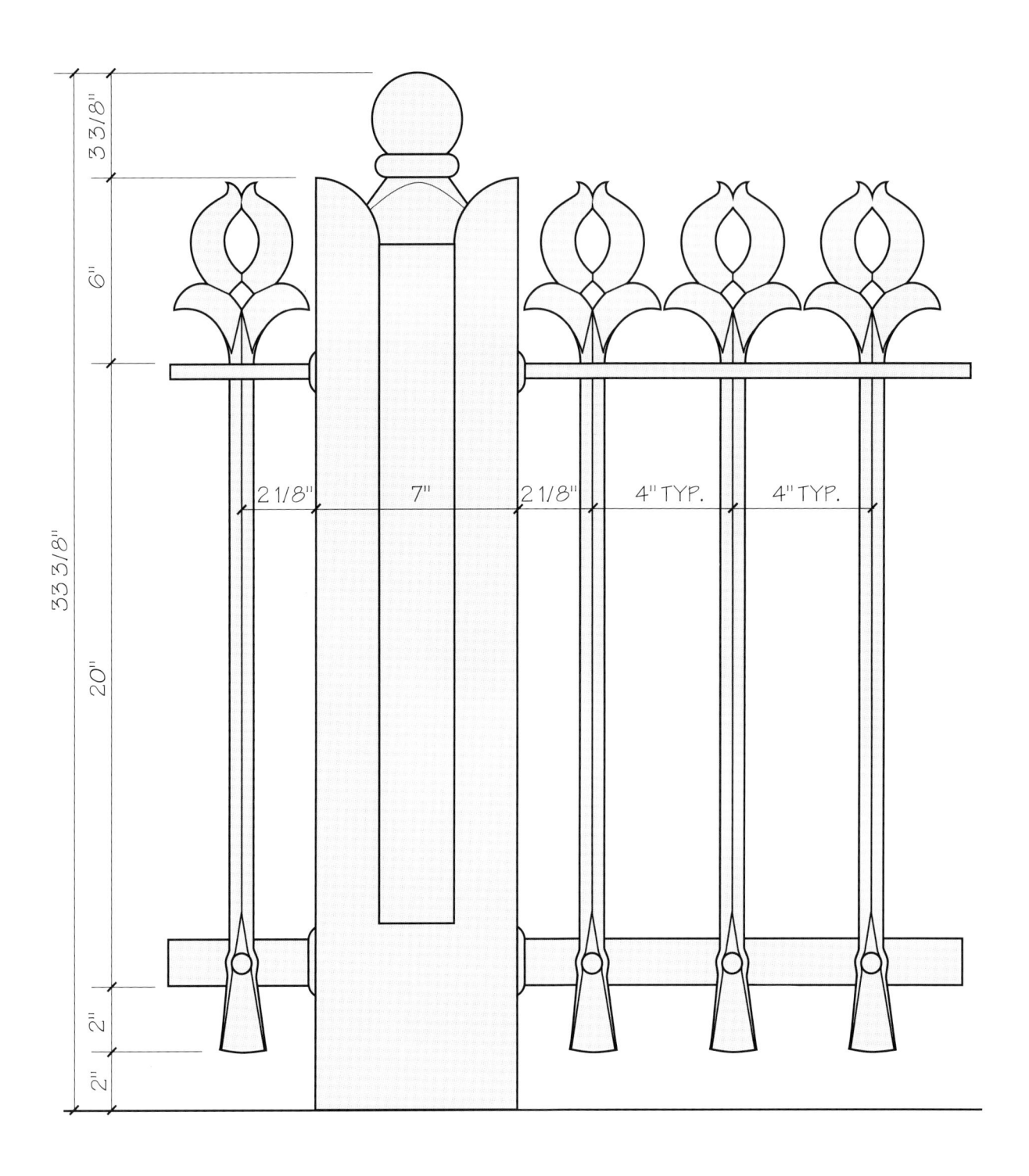

Railing Panel #1 - not to scale

Four similar elements, each turned 90°, make the panels in this railing. Top and bottom flat stock horizontals are added to tie it all together. **91|1129**

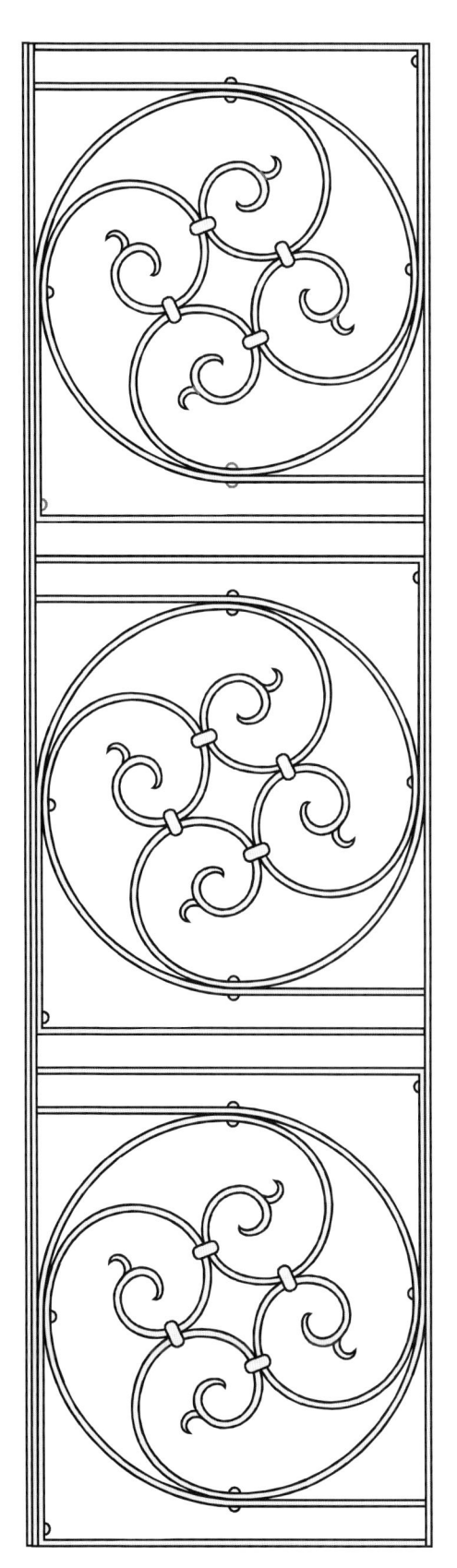

Railing Panel #2 - not to scale

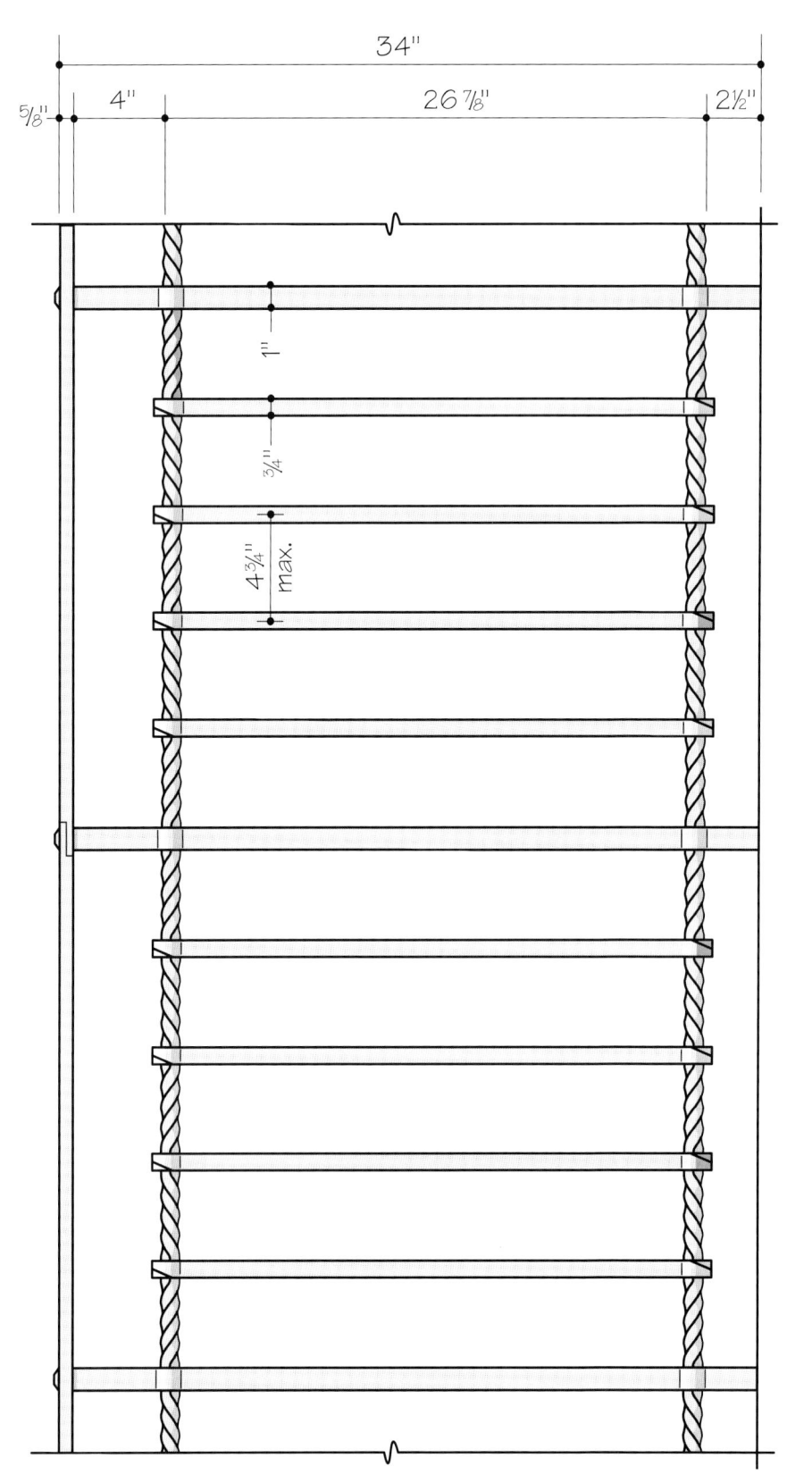

The panels in this railing are held in place by slot punched holes in the posts. The baluster joinery features "wrapped collars" split from the end of the stock. **133|1639**

Spring Latch - ½ scale

Designed for small gates, the handles for this latch straddle the frame of the gate. The latch extends through the frame and engages a latch plate on a post or door frame. Flat stock (part B) acts as a leaf spring to keep the latch engaged. **38|470**

MATERIALS	
A	3/8"x 3/4" FLAT
B	3/16"x 1" FLAT
C	1/2" SQUARE

Dimensions: 1 1/4", 1 7/8", 3 1/8", 1 3/4", 1 1/8", 1 3/4", 3 1/4", 1", 4", 8 1/4", 12", 3"

17/64" DRILL & CTR. SINK, TWO PLACES

Trellis Gate - ⅛ scale

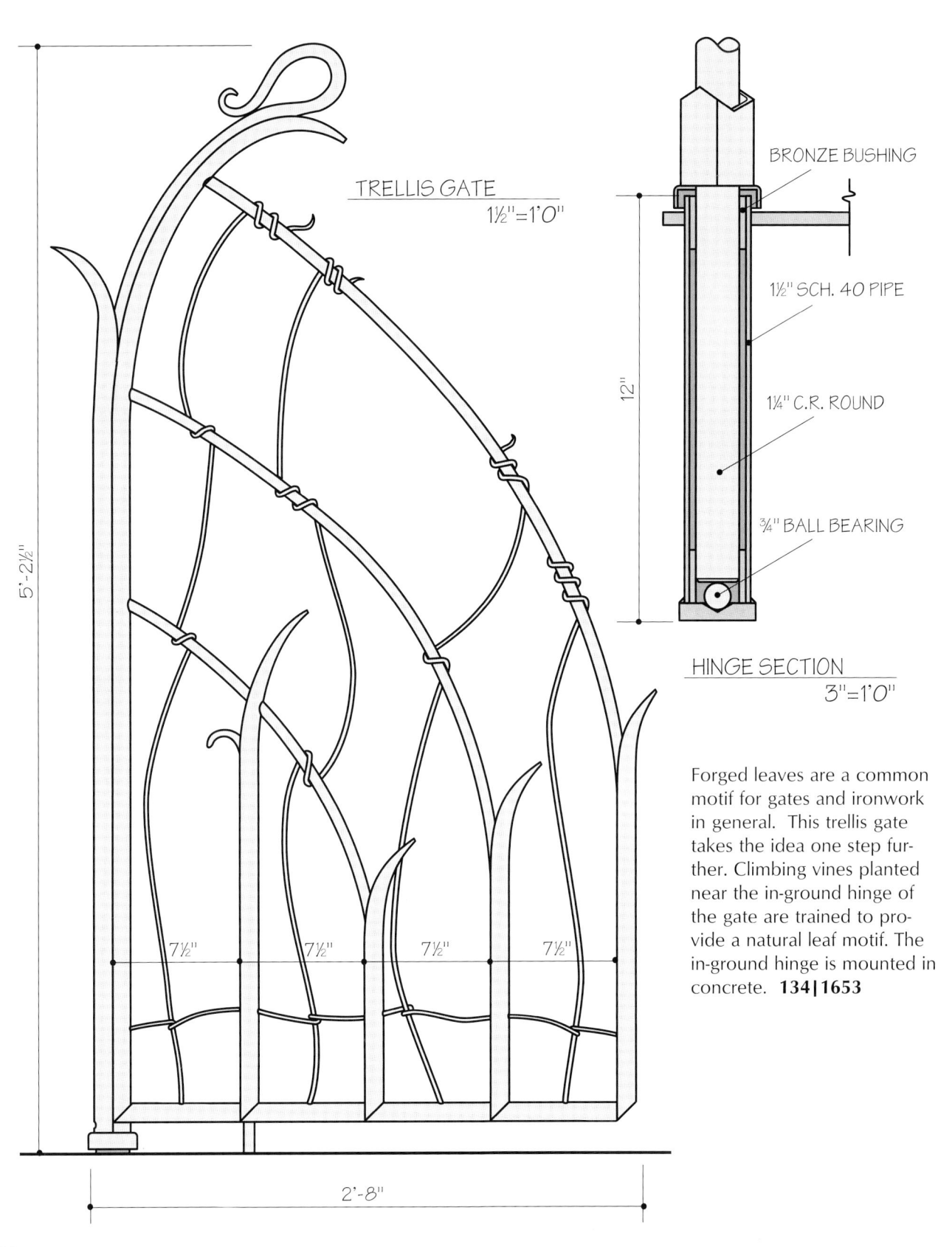

TRELLIS GATE
1½"=1'0"

HINGE SECTION
3"=1'0"

- BRONZE BUSHING
- 1½" SCH. 40 PIPE
- 1¼" C.R. ROUND
- ¾" BALL BEARING

5'-2½"

7½" 7½" 7½" 7½"

2'-8"

12"

Forged leaves are a common motif for gates and ironwork in general. This trellis gate takes the idea one step further. Climbing vines planted near the in-ground hinge of the gate are trained to provide a natural leaf motif. The in-ground hinge is mounted in concrete. **134|1653**

Walkway Gate - 1/16 scale

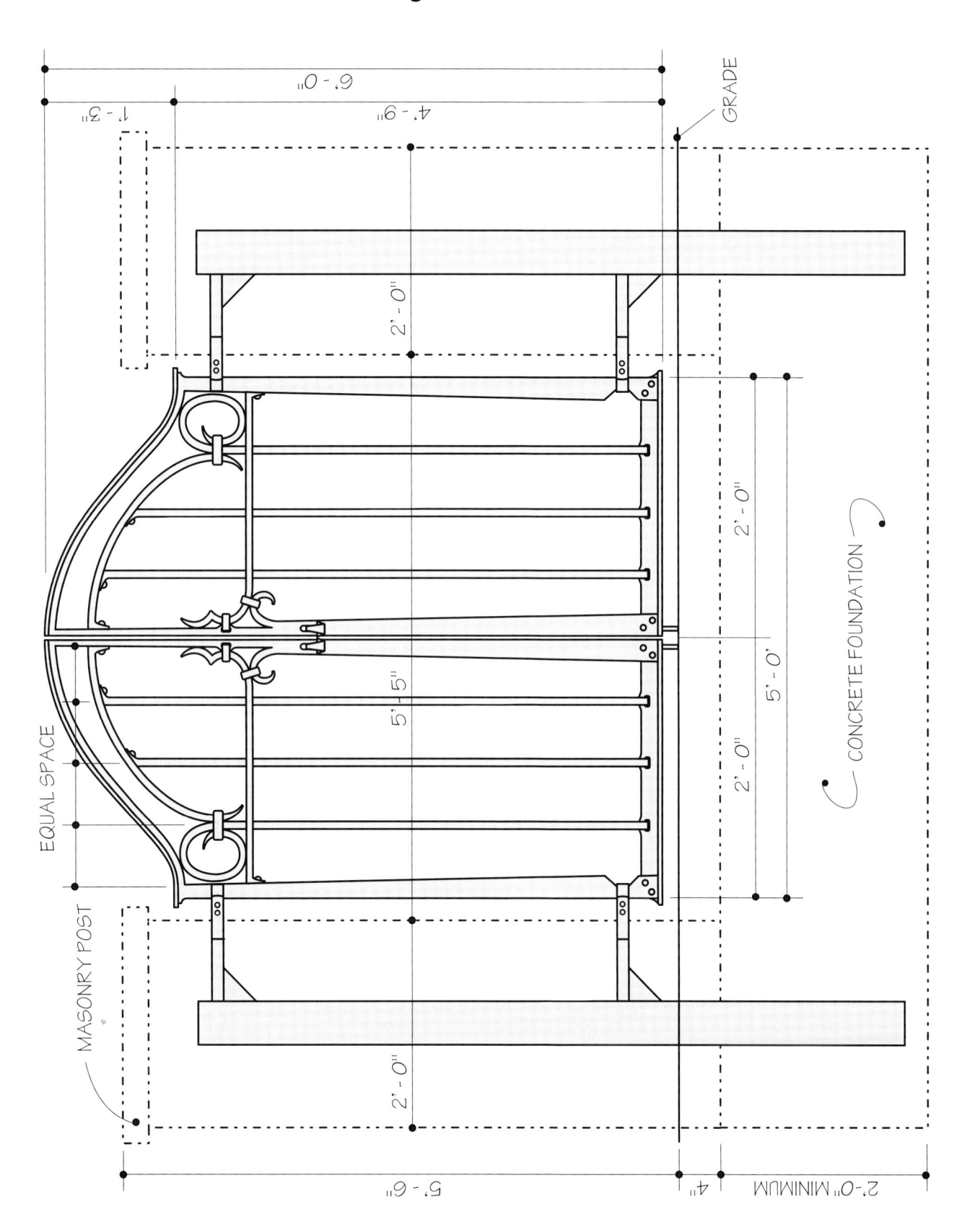

Walkway Gate, cont.

A concrete footing is poured prior to setting this gate. Steel posts, already welded to the hinge receivers are set on the footing, and concrete poured around them. Masonry posts are then constructed with the steel posts at their core. Hinges with a machined collar that bears the weight (shown below) are welded into the back bar of the gate. They bolt to receivers welded to the steel posts. **89|1099**

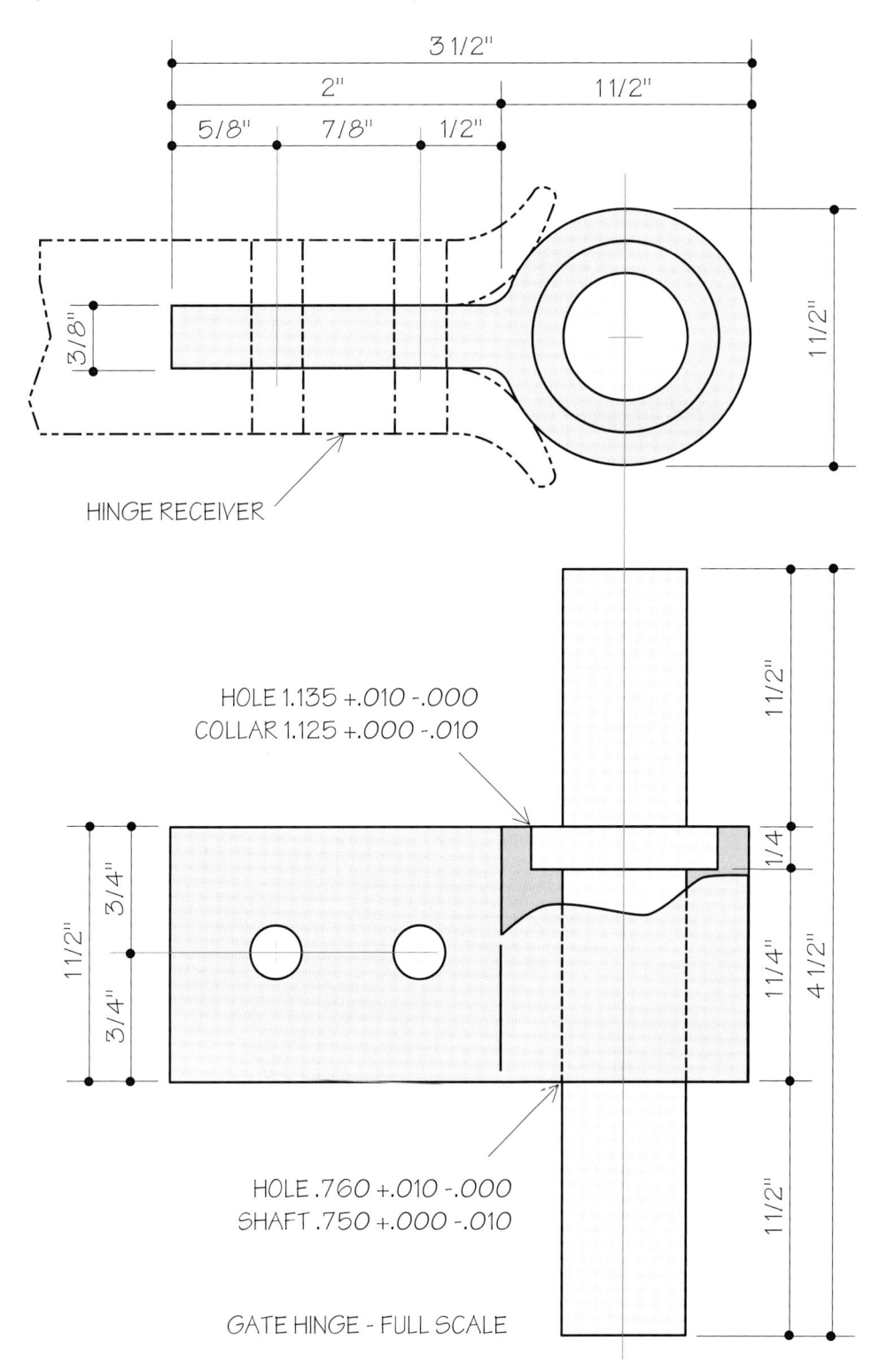

HINGE RECEIVER

HOLE 1.135 +.010 -.000
COLLAR 1.125 +.000 -.010

HOLE .760 +.010 -.000
SHAFT .750 +.000 -.010

GATE HINGE - FULL SCALE

For more information about the *Blacksmith's Journal* visit

www.blacksmithsjournal.com